Business Plan, Business Reality

Starting and Managing Your Own Business in Canada

James R. Skinner

Fourth Edition

Toronto

Vice-President, Editorial Director: Gary Bennett
Sponsoring Editor: Kathleen McGill
Acquisitions Editor: Deana Sigut
Marketing Manager: Leigh-Anne Graham
Developmental Editor: Toni Chahley
Supervising Developmental Editor: Madhu Ranadive
Project Manager: Richard di Santo
Manufacturing Coordinator: Karen Bradley
Production Editor: Tania Andrabi, Cenveo® Publisher Services
Copy Editor: Sally Glover
Proofreader: Susan Bindernagel
Compositor: Cenveo Publisher Services
Permissions Project Manager: Joanne Tang
Photo Permissions Research: Cordes Hoffman, Q2A/Bill Smith
Text Permissions Research: Khalid Shaskshir, Electronic Publishing Services Inc., NYC
Art Director: Zena Denchik
Cover Designer: Suzanne Behnke
Cover Image: Fotolia

For permission to reproduce copyrighted material, the publisher gratefully acknowledges the copyright holders listed throughout the book, which are considered an extension of this copyright page. All photos provided by James Skinner.

9   18

Library and Archives Canada Cataloguing in Publication
Skinner, James R. (James Ross), 1950-, author

    Business plan, business reality : starting and managing your own business in Canada / James R. Skinner. – Fourth edition.

Includes bibliographical references and index.
ISBN 978-0-13-337026-3 (pbk.)

    1. New business enterprises–Canada–Textbooks. 2. Self-employed– Canada–Textbooks. 3. Small business–Canada–Management–Textbooks. I. Title.

HD62.7.S55 2014   658.1'1410971   C2013-907066-4

ISBN: 978-0-13-337026-3

Brief Contents

Contents

Preface

WHY THIS BOOK?

At colleges and universities across Canada there is a flourishing interest in entrepreneurship. The reasons for this include:

- **The E-Revolution** Tablets, smartphones, the cloud, robotics, and a host of other technologies have changed how we communicate, navigate, purchase, persuade, research, and run many other aspects of our lives. And each of these changes has produced a myriad of opportunities to make money. How to make that money is what today's student wants to learn.
- **The Contract Worker Economy** The days of big companies providing lifetime jobs and indexed pensions are history. Business support functions are increasingly outsourced and short-term employment contracts are common. Graduating students need to see themselves as self-employed, as their own brands, responsible for developing and selling their own skills and services; they need to see themselves as entrepreneurs.
- **The Growth in Entrepreneurship Research** In years past, the teaching of entrepreneurship was based, at best, on poorly supported theories. But over the past three decades, scientists around the world have been creating new methodologies, testing hypotheses, and building a body of data about entrepreneurs and the economies in which they work. Today, we have increasingly reliable information to help graduates reduce the risk of being in business for themselves.
- **The Rise of Social Entrepreneurship** The set of tools that entrepreneurs use to make profit (marketing research, promotion, management, financial planning, etc.) are today's tools of social change. Non-profit organizations and co-operative enterprises are operated with "business plans" in increasingly competitive markets, and basic entrepreneurial knowledge is expected from entrants to these fields.
- **The Demand for Entrepreneurship in the Arts** Canadian post-secondary institutions have a proud history of producing highly skilled graduates in music, creative writing, visual arts, film-making, and so on. Unfortunately, many of these graduates ended up in careers outside their chosen fields; not because their artistic skills were lacking, but because they did not know how to turn those skills into money. Now, however, there is a trend to see entrepreneurship as a necessary part of any arts curriculum.
- **The Refocusing of Business Schools** Business-related programs are arguably the country's largest post-secondary field of study. No longer training centres for large employers, business schools are Canada's innovators in entrepreneurial education, hubs for business communities, and incubators for small firms.

There is an obvious need for a concise, adaptable textbook—a book about planning, starting, and managing a small business or some form of self-employment. This text is designed for post-secondary-level courses and workshops. It can also be used by anyone who wants a "do-it-yourself" plan for self-employment (actors, animal wranglers, bodyguards, bush pilots, choreographers, computer geeks, decorators, fashion designers, landscapers, private investigators, researchers, singers, sound mixers, video editors, writers . . .) as well as those who will start more traditional small businesses (clothing stores, consulting firms, machine shops, paralegal offices, photography studios, publishing companies, restaurants . . .). The list is endless.

Part 1 of the text is organized the way a simple business plan is organized. Chapters 1–5 correspond to the five sections of the basic start-up business plan. **Part 2** of the text is about alternatives in the business plan—different ways of getting into business. And **Part 3** covers the long-term management of the business as well as more theoretical issues in entrepreneurship. Some courses or individuals will use only the first five chapters, some will use all of them, and others will use various selections of chapters. (See the Course Application Chart below.)

The style of this text is intended to:

- **Show students where to get help.** You don't have to know everything there is to know about business to make money. The emphasis is on getting professional help for the hard stuff. *Get Help* items recommend sources of assistance.
- **Provide practical examples.** Many real-life examples are used in the body of the text and each chapter includes a realistic mini-case where students can solve particular issues **(new for this edition)**. As well, *Ask Yourself* prompts, throughout the text, encourage readers to think of examples and issues from their own lives.
- **Use learning time efficiently.** A series of *Memory Check* (true/false) questions are sprinkled throughout the text as an easy way of checking whether the reader is absorbing the information. Encountering a question where the reader doesn't know the answer means either taking a break or skipping back a few pages and re-reading. Also, simple *Head Start* exercises provide an easy, painless way to create key components of the business plan. Alternatively, these exercises may be used by the instructor as short assignments.

WHO SHOULD USE THIS BOOK?

This text can be used by:

- **Business students,** typically in undergraduate diploma and degree programs that usually include one or two required courses in entrepreneurship.
- **Non–business students,** including a huge array of arts, technology, and applied science programs that may lead to some form of self-employment for the graduate.
- **Start-up entrepreneurs,** often in continuing education classes, short courses, and workshops leading directly to self-employment or small business ownership.

The Course Application Chart below shows typical chapter selections for different levels of courses.

COURSE APPLICATION CHART

Program Type	Chapters (Typical)	Example Course Titles
• Practical non-credit start-up workshops	1–5	– Writing a Business Plan – Developing a Business Plan
• 2–3-year business diploma (as introductory course) • 2–4-year non-business degree or diploma • 3-year business diploma • 3–4-year non-business degree or diploma (as advanced course) • 4-year business degree (as introductory course)	1–8 or 1–8 & 12	– Planning a New Business – Introduction to Entrepreneurship – Starting a Small Business – Introduction to Business Ownership – Independent Business – Small Business Ownership – Organizing a New Business
• 3-year business diploma (as advanced course) • 4-year business degree (as advanced course)	1–11 or 1–10 & 12 or 1–12	– Small Business and Entrepreneurship – New-Venture Development – Small Business Management – Managing Business Growth – Small, Medium Enterprise Management – Building an Independent Business – Entrepreneurship and Management – Strategic Entrepreneurship – Advanced Entrepreneurship

WHAT'S NEW TO THE FOURTH EDITION?

As of result of reviews by, consultations with, and volunteered advice from professors, students, and entrepreneurs, the following changes have been made to this edition:

- Chapters have been reorganized to put the broader, more theoretical discussion of business plans at the end of the book. Chapter 12 includes a comprehensive example business plan that is now more easily accessible as a running example for other chapters.
- New mini cases have been added at the end of chapters to give students more opportunity for applying knowledge. Longer supplementary cases are still available to instructors as hand-out material.
- More e-business and technology examples have been used in an attempt to reflect the changing economy.
- More extensive use has been made of diagrams to show the business plan as an ongoing process.
- Learning objectives at the start of chapters have been condensed to fewer outcomes that will more closely reflect course outlines.
- Profiles of entrepreneurs have been changed or updated (as Business Reality boxes) to better capture the interest of students.

WHAT DO INSTRUCTORS GET?

The following instructor supplements are available for downloading from a password-protected section of Pearson Canada's online catalogue. Navigate to your book's catalogue page to view a list of those supplements that are available. See your local sales representative for details and access.

- **Instructor's Manual (ISBN: 978-0-13-354262-2).** Includes a number of valuable resources, including discussion questions to accompany the CBC Dragon's Den Videos, a guide to the supplements that accompany this book, course applications, templates for financial statements, and best practices for teaching entrepreneurship. The Instructor's Manual also includes a copy of the workbook from text in Microsoft Word format. This electronic version of the workbook contains references to examples and lessons in the textbook and links to helpful web resources for each of the questions and activities. Finally, the Instructor's Manual also includes a series of 24 short case studies that are available to illustrate specific concepts from the text. For business programs, these use examples from a wide selection of industries. For a number of non-business programs, the cases have been customized and are available as a package specifically for internet management, film and TV, photography, paralegal, electrical technology, hospitality, golf, immigration consulting, spa and cosmetics management, and other programs.
- **Test Item File (ISBN: 978-0-13-377253-1).** The test item file includes over 200 questions, including multiple choice, true/false, fill-in-the-blank, short answer, and essay questions for each chapter of the text. This supplement also includes a comprehensive final exam, which can also be used as a comprehensive challenge test. Correct answers for objective test questions are provided as well as suggested marking schemes for short answer and essay questions and for business plan submissions.
- **PowerPoint® Presentations (ISBN: 978-0-13-354264-6).** Lesson topics are provided as PowerPoint slides for each of the chapters.
- **CBC Dragon's Den Videos (ISBN: 978-0-13-354258-5).** This textbook is also accompanied by a DVD containing **CBC Dragon's Den** segments. These segments are accompanied by discussion questions, which are found in the Instructor's Manual.
- **CourseSmart for Instructors.** CourseSmart goes beyond traditional expectations—providing instant, online access to the textbooks and course materials you need at a lower cost for students. And even as students save money, you can save time and hassle with a digital eTextbook that allows you to search for the most relevant

content at the very moment you need it. Whether it's evaluating textbooks or creating lecture notes to help students with difficult concepts, CourseSmart can make life a little easier.

- **CourseSmart for Students.** CourseSmart goes beyond traditional expectations—providing instant, online access to the textbooks and course materials you need at an average savings of 60 percent. With instant access from any computer and the ability to search your text, you'll find the content you need quickly, no matter where you are. And with online tools like highlighting and note-taking, you can save time and study efficiently.

- **Pearson Custom Library.** For enrollments of at least 25 students, you can create your own textbook by choosing the chapters that best suit your own course needs. To begin building your custom text, visit www.pearsoncustomlibrary.com. You may also work with a dedicated Pearson Custom editor to create your ideal text—publishing your own original content or mixing and matching Pearson content. Contact your local Pearson Representative to get started.

Chapter 1

The Business Model: What Is the Concept for My Business?

Deciding to go into business for yourself is a single decision. But *how* you're going to get into business involves lots of interrelated decisions that need to be made in a logical order. For this, you need a business plan. This first chapter covers the first section of the business plan. This is where the entrepreneur explains the overall concept for the new business. The chapter will answer the following questions:

- What Does It Mean to Be "in Business"?
- What Is My Business Idea?
- Do I Need a Partner?
- What Will My Business Mean Legally?
- How Do I Get Started?

Learning Objectives

On completion of this chapter, you should be able to:

1 Discuss the definition and role of "small business."

2 Assess your own potential as an entrepreneur.

3 Identify at least four advantages and/or disadvantages of an entrepreneurial lifestyle.

4 Define a new business in terms of what it will sell and to whom.

5 Differentiate between "location" and "site."

6 Compare at least three legal forms of business.

7 Prepare the Concept and Summary portions of a business plan.

WHAT DOES IT MEAN TO BE "IN BUSINESS"?

A **business model** is the pattern of activities that a company uses to make profit. For example, you could be in the car rental business, renting out cars to drivers who pay by the day and who are responsible for buying their own gas. Or, you could require that customers pay an annual membership fee and members pay by the hour, with gas and insurance included in the rate. In both cases you're in the car rental business, but these are different business models. A fast-food take-out restaurant is a different business model from a full-service sit-down restaurant. And chances are, the business model you will be using has already been proven successful by someone else, so be prepared to copy successful business concepts from others.

Being in business, however, is more than just copying the successful pattern of a specific business. It also means applying proven principles of business from a wide variety of firms. So, like most textbooks, this one uses examples from a wide variety of companies.

business model The pattern of activities a company uses to make profit.

For many students, this is a problem, because they only want to read about a single successful model from a single industry. For example, if you are studying aviation management, you want to see examples of airlines. If you are thinking about starting a restaurant, you really only want restaurant examples; you don't want to read about a sound equipment rental firm or jewellery store. But this prejudice comes from failing to recognize a simple truth: Business is business. Clearly there are some differences between the business models of independent film producers and of plumbing companies. But they both make money by applying the same principles of business.

Many talented artists and skilled technicians profess little interest in business. They make the critical mistake of believing that financial success will automatically come as the result of their skills or talents. But *ask yourself: How many great artists have died penniless? Know of any third-rate musicians who nevertheless make lots of money?* Skill and talent are only a small part of the route to financial success. The rest is business. Once you see yourself as a businessperson, every time you fill your gas tank, go to the bank, or eat in a restaurant, you'll be learning a little more about how to make money in your own field. You'll truly be in business.

Small Business and Entrepreneurship

small business An independently owned organization that exists to make profit for its owner(s), often measured as having fewer than 500 employees.

This text is about starting a **small business**, and most of us hold a pretty clear picture in our minds of what a small business is. But most of us are wrong; at least according to the experts. *Ask yourself: How many employees can a business have and still be considered small?* There is no standard definition of *business size*. However, many of the academics and researchers who study these matters tend to define a *small business* as an independent company having fewer than 500 employees, sometimes more.[1] Now that's a lot bigger than most of us picture small businesses to be, but there is some logic behind this definition. Strategically, how you plan and run a business of 1 person—or 3 people or 40 people—is not terribly different from the strategy used in firms of up to 500 people.

The lesson here is that organizing and running a business of any size is a complex activity that takes thought and planning. Realistically, over 90 percent of the small businesses in Canada have fewer than five employees.[2] This is a category of businesses that many researchers would call **micro-enterprise**: operations, often family-based firms, which typically have just one or two people.

micro-enterprise A very small business, usually measured as having fewer than five employees.

And what about the one-person business? **Self-employment** is a term used to describe individuals who work on their own, often out of their homes, and often on a contract basis for various companies. Some of these people may not be classified as business "owners," but rather as "contract employees." In fact, **Canada Revenue Agency** (CRA) treats many of these people as employees even when they consider themselves to be in their own business. This raises the question: *What is a business?*

self-employment An entrepreneur working either as a freelancer or as a short-term contract worker—not a permanent employee of any firm, but not technically a business owner (not having employees or any significant business assets).

Generally, a business must have some value of its own, apart from its owner. *Ask yourself: Could I sell the business?* If you're a one-person plumbing company, the answer is probably yes, in that selling the business would mean selling the truck, the tools, the company name, and maybe some contracts. If you're a **freelance** speechwriter, however, the answer is probably no. In this case, the entire existence of the business would depend on you, the owner, without whom there would be nothing to sell.

Canada Revenue Agency A department of the federal government that acts as Canada's tax collector.

freelance An independent service provider, not employed by any one company, and sometimes producing work before it has been sold.

Ask yourself: Does this mean that freelancers who earn their living by selling their personal services are not "in business" and do not need a business plan? It does not! Even though lenders tend not to treat freelancers as businesses, they still have to plan and carry out most of the same business activities as those who have a business that they could sell. Freelancers, to be successful, should still use a business plan.

Although freelancers may not always be considered business owners, they do practise *entrepreneurship*. They risk their time, labour, and money in order to make profit. This is the essence of entrepreneurship. So even though not all **entrepreneurs** are official business owners, certainly all business owners are entrepreneurs. *Ask yourself: Am I clear on the definitions of entrepreneurship, small business, self-employment, freelance?*

Despite the fact that the above terms have precise meanings, they will be used interchangeably in many instances in this text. That's because all entrepreneurs—small business owners, freelancers, and self-employed people—need business plans. And the business plan is what the first part of this text is all about.

This first component of the business plan demonstrates that you have given some thought as to whether you are the right kind of person to start a business. It demonstrates that you have the right training and experience and that you know what you are getting into. It also clearly states the nature of your business, the location, and the legal set-up, describing any partner or investor relationships.

Entrepreneurship is a great equalizer. It has long been a way to overcome barriers against ethnicity, age, and gender. True, some ethnic and cultural groups are more likely to have a tradition of entrepreneurship, but this is usually because of historical discrimination barring them from trades or professions in many parts of the world. In Canada, for some Aboriginal groups who traditionally lacked access to business capital, entrepreneurship has become a route to self-sufficiency. For the young in Canada, entrepreneurship is now highly encouraged, with many government support programs and non-profit organizations available to assist. And the growth in entrepreneurship by women in the past few years has been explosive. Forty-seven percent of Canadian businesses are now at least partly owned by women, who have access to borrowing money equivalent to that of their male counterparts.[3]

The Entrepreneurial Personality

Ask yourself: What kind of personalities do successful entrepreneurs have? Do you think of terms like aggressive, outgoing, intelligent, dedicated, self-motivated, ruthless, single-minded, charismatic, scheming, and so on? This is how many of us picture entrepreneurs. But take a moment and think about some real-life entrepreneurs you may have met, not the ideal entrepreneurs of popular culture. Think of someone who is, perhaps, the owner of the dry cleaner near your home, the owner of the drugstore where you work part-time, or the owner of the garage that fixes your car. These are people who make a living by running their own business; in other words, successful entrepreneurs who, for the most part, are not the perfect heroes of modern mythology. In fact, they tend to be pretty ordinary people: some of them kind, some shy, some lazy—not the movie image of the successful entrepreneur.

Complete the "trait test" in Figure 1.1 before reading any further.

Many small business texts start out with a self-assessment test of some sort, something to see if you're the right kind of person to run your own business. So, what characteristics are these entrepreneurial tests typically looking for?

Most of these tests are looking for the same characteristics that are *popularly believed* to be true of entrepreneurs. They are typically based on some form of research, but for the most part, this research lacks validity. In fact, much of it is "**junk research**"—looking at characteristics of people who are already successful business owners, instead of looking at the traits that entrepreneurs had *before* they became successful business owners. There are a few rigorous studies of the traits that help people to *become* successful entrepreneurs, and the results of these show that *most people have the potential to start and run a business.*[5]

entrepreneur Someone who risks money (or their own time and effort) to make a profit. All business owners, freelancers, and otherwise self-employed people are entrepreneurs.

☑ **Memory Check 1.1**
True or False? Most Canadian businesses have more than five employees.   F   *90%*

☑ **Memory Check 1.2**
True or False? A freelance journalist is generally considered to be a business owner.   F

☑ **Memory Check 1.3**
True or False? A freelance journalist should be working with a business plan.   T

97% of Canadian business are at least owned by women.

junk research Studies that are based on flawed logic or poor application of scientific methods.

Figure 1.1 Trait Test[4]

Score each of the following statements according to how true it is of you. Calculate a total at the bottom.

    0 = never true of you
    1 = occasionally true of you
    2 = usually true of you
    3 = always true of you

I am confident in my ability to influence others.   _____
I work harder than most others I know.   _____
I have a clear picture of my future.   _____
I spend more time attending to responsibilities than most people do.   _____
I have specific long-term goals.   _____
I spend time each week planning my future.   _____
Compared to most people, I take work or school seriously.   _____
I do a thorough job in completing my tasks.   _____
The steps to success are obvious to me.   _____
I believe in my own ability to succeed.   _____
I work more hours per day than the average person.   _____
I see myself as controlling my own destiny.   _____
Compared to others, I am more likely to exercise self-control.   _____
I make the major decisions that affect my life.   _____
I know what I want to achieve.   _____
TOTAL   _____

Self-Analysis Generally, but not universally, successful entrepreneurs tend to be a little more hard-working than the rest of the population; they tend to be more goal-oriented; and they tend to have more confidence in their own ability to influence their futures. These are the characteristics that the self-scored test above is looking for.

Scores	
Above 38	well above average
34–38	above average
26–34	average
22–26	below average
Below 22	well below average

☑ **Memory Check 1.4**
True or False? A "small business," by definition, has fewer than 20 employees.

❓ **Get Help 1.1**
If you are unsure about your own suitability to run a business, arrange an interview with an employment or career counsellor through your community college or check with your local Service Canada office (1-800-OCanada) for any programs near you.

If you didn't get the score you wanted, don't worry about it. Remember, with self-assessment tests like this there are always questions of validity and reliability—if you were to have something different for breakfast tomorrow and were to rewrite the test, you might get a different score. There is little evidence that these tests can actually predict entrepreneurial accomplishment. Besides, the real value in tests like the one above is that they make you ask yourself about yourself. *Ask yourself: Am I the kind of person who can start and run a business?*

There is little doubt that a certain combination of personality, skills, and desire produces the ideal entrepreneur. But some of us have no inclination to run our own business, regardless of our talents in these areas. Circumstances, however, can make people believe that self-employment, though not their first choice, is the only option available to them: the graduate with a diploma but no job prospects, the aging "downsized" middle manager, the new immigrant with no Canadian work history, the mature homemaker who has been out of the workforce for many years and can't find employment. These people are often categorized as "reluctant" entrepreneurs. **Reluctant entrepreneurs** are less likely to be committed to the business and often will abandon the process of starting their own firm as soon as a suitable job becomes available to them.[6]

The question of *desire* to start one's own business is perhaps much more important than ability. This desire is certainly influenced by a person's concept of being "in business." Many consider it a lot more prestigious to be president of a five-person company than to be manager of a 500-employee division of a giant organization. Most entrepreneurs have strong feelings about the importance of business ownership—they really want to do it. *Ask yourself: Do I really want to do it?*

Personal Demands

There is a strong emotional component to entrepreneurship. It is the passion that an owner has about his or her business that provides the tremendous amount of energy required to start a new venture. Right now, you probably spend too much time watching TV. If you go into business for yourself, that won't be a problem. Surveys show that business owners, especially at start-up, may work significantly more hours than the average employed person works. One Canadian study shows that entrepreneurs work about one-third more hours than salaried employees.[7] About a third of entrepreneurs routinely work more than 50 hours per week.[8] This lifestyle is demanding: It's not for the dabbler, the hobbyist, or the part-timer. Furthermore, you have to know what you're doing. This is why *having worked for someone else in the same industry is one of the stronger predictors of new-business success.*[9] Unfortunately, many people go into a business where they have no experience. Lack of experience and not understanding the time demands—these are among the main reasons that the majority of new businesses fail. In fact, two-thirds of new micro-enterprises don't last 5 years[10] and only 20 percent make it to the 10-year mark.[11]

With all that extra work and all the responsibility and risk of running a business, the stress can be significant. Nevertheless, the research is still unclear on whether it's more stressful to be an employee or to be the boss. But if you've got a job, *ask yourself: Of all the people in my life, who gives me the greatest amount of stress?* If your answer is "my boss," you're in the same boat as most employed people. The great irony is that by becoming the boss yourself, in owning the company, you may work as though you were a slave to the business. Despite that, the majority of successful entrepreneurs report that they love the independence. *Ask yourself again: Do I really want to be my own boss? How badly?*

Time & financial demands —→

Family Issues

If you're involved in a committed relationship, the decision to go into business cannot be yours alone. Because of the time and financial demands (even for successful firms, it usually takes a good while to start making money), it is important that you have the total support of your life partner. Without this support, you may find your spouse and the business competing for your attention: One of them will have to lose.

Some couples resolve this by going into business in partnership, an arrangement that has its own set of advantages and disadvantages. When your life partner and your business partner are one and the same, you could end up together 24 hours a day, 7 days a week. This kind of closeness works well for some pairs, but for others, absence makes the heart grow fonder. *Ask yourself: How will starting a business affect my relationship with my life partner, spouse, or fiancé?*

Similar issues arise when you have children. Obviously, when starting a new business, you will have less time to devote to your kids than if you were employed or a stay-at-home parent. Home-based businesses may seem like a solution, but picture yourself on the phone with a demanding customer while a determined three-year-old tries to get your attention. (See "Home-Based Businesses" in Chapter 2.) When the kids are older, however, one of

☑ **Memory Check 1.5**
True or False? A freelance journalist is an entrepreneur. T

❓ **Get Help 1.2**
The Business Development Bank of Canada has an interesting online quiz to help assess your potential as an entrepreneur. Go to www.bdc.ca and click on Advice Centre, then Benchmarking Tools, then Entrepreneurial Potential Self-Assessment.

❓ **Get Help 1.3**
To read about recent Canadian small business success stories, go to http://sbinfocanada.about.com/od/successstories.

☑ **Memory Check 1.6**
True or False? Most of the "entrepreneurial ability" tests are accurate predictors of one's ability to start a business.

☑ **Memory Check 1.7**
True or False? "Junk research" is still of good quality even though it is not recognized by most scientists.

the big advantages of owning your own firm is that it can provide employment for family members. As children mature, the tendency to socialize less and less with parents can be offset by the closeness of working together. *Ask yourself: How will owning my own business affect my relationships with my children?*

Employee vs. Entrepreneur

There is lots of good news about being in business for yourself, including the money. Small businesses that are successful can provide their owners with incomes far above the average for employed people. The statistics don't always reflect this clearly, but still show entrepreneurs as making somewhat more than the average.[12] The statistics, however, can be misleading. When small-business incomes are reported, they tend to include the failing companies (with little or no personal income for the owner) and they do not include the **underground economy** (the billions of dollars in unreported income that is funneled through small companies each year).[13] When working for an employer, there are many factors that limit the employee's income, including what society thinks is fair pay for a particular job and the labour market itself. *Ask yourself: Why would an employer pay any more for help than is necessary?* But when working for yourself, you can take home as much money as the business can produce. The sky's the limit. Every one of Canada's billionaires got that way by owning businesses, not by working for the government or big companies. If becoming wealthy is your goal in life, your single best chance for it is through entrepreneurship.

For a number of years, educators and employers in Canada have been co-operating to help foster **employability skills** in today's graduates. These include skills in

- oral and written communications;
- mathematics;
- time management;
- teamwork; and
- computer literacy.

Certainly, all of the above could be advantageous, not just in employees, but to the small business owner personally. In addition, however, the entrepreneur needs some skills in the following areas:

- *Financial planning.* A huge number of *potentially profitable* firms go bankrupt each year simply because of the entrepreneur's inability to understand and plan *cash flow.*
- *Sales/negotiation.* The entire profit-making process starts with convincing someone to buy your product or service. Profit can also depend on an entrepreneur's ability to make deals with suppliers, regulators, and even employees.
- *People management.* While not necessarily important at start-up, the eventual growth of a business is going to depend on employees, which the entrepreneur will have to recruit, train, and motivate.

These are **entrepreneurial skills**.

To be a successful entrepreneur, however, *you don't have to do it all on your own!* While employees may be judged on their personal skills, entrepreneurs are not. Entrepreneurs are judged solely on their ability to make profit. An entrepreneur who lacks financial skills can rely on an accountant for help in this area. A poor negotiator can partner up with a strong negotiator. It is also possible to start a business by buying a franchise where all of the management systems and training are provided. So, the real skill of the successful entrepreneur becomes the ability to assess himself or herself and seek help in any weak areas. *Ask yourself: What entrepreneurial skills do I have? Which do I need help with?*

underground economy All of the illegally unreported business and consumer transactions conducted for cash or barter on which taxes are not paid.

employability skills The general knowledge and abilities that employers seek in prospective employees. Examples are literacy, numeracy, time management, teamwork, and computer skills.

entrepreneurial skills The knowledge and abilities necessary to make profit in business. These include financial, negotiation, and people skills.

1.1 Prepare a brief résumé of your education and work experience. Then, in three or four short sentences, explain why a career as an entrepreneur would be appropriate for you (1 1/4 page maximum).

WHAT IS MY BUSINESS IDEA?

Causes of Demand

Every change produces a business opportunity, sometimes called a **gap**. The kind of change doesn't matter: political, economic, social, cultural, environmental, technological. . . . A growth in the number of school-aged children means a need for more photographers taking class and graduation pictures. An increase in purchasing via the internet means a need for more webpage designers. More online magazines means a need for more freelance journalists.

Why is now a good time to start a business of the sort you are proposing? This is a natural question from lenders or prospective investors when approached by someone starting a business. The best way to answer this question is by pointing out some sort of change that has given rise to this business opportunity. For example: "There has recently been a big increase in home schooling, so I am starting an online service to sell teaching aids to parents who teach their kids at home." *Ask yourself: What was the change that produced an opportunity for my favourite band? My favourite restaurant?*

gap An unsatisfied need or opportunity in the marketplace, produced by some kind of change that has taken place.

Specialization

The highest-paid medical doctors are the superspecialists—those who treat only a certain organ or fight a particular group of diseases. When something is wrong with your heart, you want only a cardiologist. Even though a family physician may be well enough trained to diagnose and treat you, if it's your heart you probably want to see a cardiologist. If you are accused of tax evasion, the lawyer who handled your will or real estate transaction may be perfectly competent to handle the problem. But you would rather have a specialized tax lawyer, even though you know it will cost you more.

It works pretty much the same for other small businesses: Generally, those that specialize make the most money.[14] This isn't always an easy concept to accept. It might seem that the greater the variety of goods or services you sell, the more opportunity you will have to make money. But that's wrong. An electronics store that specializes in audio equipment does not have the overhead of a store that has to carry TVs, DVDs, cameras, computers, smartphones, burglar alarms, and so on. And the true audiophile shopping for those special speakers wants to buy them (and will willingly pay more) from a specialist.

There is also the issue of efficiency from specialization. If you're a freelance writer who specializes in speech writing, you can generate speeches more quickly and of better quality than the writer who does a magazine article one day, an instruction manual the next, and a promotional pamphlet the day after. Each of these writing styles has a time-consuming learning curve associated with it. Furthermore, you, as the specialist, have the advantage of being perceived as a monopoly: the right one (the only one) to deal with.

⭐ Head Start Exercise

1.2 Make some notes explaining how you will make money by specializing in particular products or services (1/4 page maximum).

For small businesses, it is generally more profitable to specialize in a narrow range of products or services. But there is another way that a business can and should specialize: in

targeting Specializing in a
particular group (or groups) of
potential customers.

the types of customers that it aims to capture. This is called **targeting** and, generally, small businesses that target narrow groups of customers are more profitable than businesses that tend to see themselves as being for everyone.

Targeting

This is often a difficult concept for new business owners to accept, since the narrower the target that a business pursues, the fewer the potential customers that are available.

Let's say you own a CD store and you have never met anyone who didn't like music. So your store could be for "everyone." However, if your store targets a particular age group—say, 18 to 35—there will be fewer potential customers than if you target "everyone." Nevertheless, your business is likely to make more profit by going after this smaller group. And if your business narrows its focus to people in a particular geographic area—say, uptown neighbourhoods—there will be even fewer potential customers, but your business will likely make even more money. And if your business narrows its focus even more—say, to people in a particular economic group—it will likely make even more profit. It may seem strange since each narrowing of the target group leaves fewer potential customers, but it's true! You'll make more profit.

If your store is targeting people who are all the same age, all live in the same area, and all have the same incomes, the same education, the same attitudes, you can be fairly sure they will all listen to basically the same music. A business such as this can carry everything that its customers want without having the big expensive inventory needed to satisfy "everyone." In addition, advertising to this target group will be a lot cheaper than advertising to everyone (because they all live in the same small area). This saves you money, allowing for more profit.

⭐ Head Start Exercise

1.3 Make a list of particular customer groups you could target and note why each might be a good idea (1/4 page maximum).

Location

location The general
geographic area where
a business can be found,
expressed as a neighbourhood
or municipality or even a
region of the country.

site A specific place where
business is conducted,
expressed as a particular block,
address, suite, or part of a
building.

✔️ **Memory Check 1.9**
True or False? Specializing in a
particular product or service is
called "targeting."

Where you locate your business helps define your business concept or model. *Ask yourself: How important is the location to the success of my business?* Is there a difference between **location** and **site**? Where you put the business, in a general sense, is what we mean by location: a certain city, a certain region, or a certain neighbourhood. When we talk about site, we are being much more precise: a particular corner, an exact address, or even a specific part of a building. For example, you may decide to locate your business in downtown Halifax (a neighbourhood) but the site of your business might be the Halifax Shopping Centre, the first store on the right, inside the main doors from Mumford Street (a particular unit.)

For retail and consumer services businesses, site can be a critical factor to the success of the business. These are businesses where the customer comes to you. So, it is necessary to get a site that is accessible to your kind of customer, or even better, already has high traffic of your kind of customer.

For manufacturing or wholesale firms, site tends to be less important, but location is often critical. For example, if you plan on wholesaling precision bearings, it may be important that you are located in Southern Ontario, where most of your customers (machinery manufacturers) and most of your suppliers (metal cutting firms) will be found. But it won't make much difference whether your site is in downtown Hamilton or suburban Mississauga since both have access to local transportation.

For some companies, the site of the business is the owner's car, or a cell phone, or the back part of the basement. These are "home-based" businesses. You are most likely to have a home-based business when you either don't meet the customer face-to-face (e.g., mail-order or online businesses), or when meetings usually take place at the customer's premises (you go to them). The number of home-based full- and part-time businesses is growing rapidly as a result of new technologies and the increased contracting-out of work. In fact, you may be using this text as part of an online course where the instructor is working from his or her home.

The idea of working out of your home may be very appealing to you (work all day in your pyjamas and be able to fix lunch for the kids). However, the decision to work from home should always be based on what you're selling and to whom you're selling it. If your business is booking DJs for small local clubs, working out of your basement is great since your customers (the club owners) may believe that your low overhead will mean lower prices for them. But if you want to be a talent agent for high-priced models and actors, then producers will expect you to have an office in the business or arts district of the city: It's an issue of credibility.

At this point in the business plan, you are making a "working decision" about where to run your business. Later, in Section 2 of the business plan (Chapter 2), you will do a more detailed analysis of your location and site, which may lead you to revisit this decision. In practice, however, most entrepreneurs don't do a detailed analysis first and then open their firms where data shows the greatest likelihood of success. Instead, they open up in the location where they already live, have families, go to school, and know their way around. They are likely to pick sites that they are familiar with or where they have a connection with the landlord. If this is the case for you, you must stay aware of the fact that your choice of location should be influencing your choices of what you are selling and to whom you are selling it.

⭐ Head Start Exercise

1.4 Write a brief description of the location for your proposed business and note one or two advantages of this selection (1/4 page maximum).

Defining the Business

The definition of your business is as statement of *what you're selling* and *to whom you're selling*. Let's say you have training in graphic arts and you worked for a sign manufacturing company. Perhaps, at the same time, there is an *opportunity* in the sign industry based on recent technological changes allowing for inexpensive computer-based design and colour printing. And let's say there is a store for rent on the main street of your hometown and you see it as an opportunity to start a "quick-sign" store. The two specialization questions you must ask yourself are

- What am I selling?
- To whom am I selling?

The easy answer is "*I am selling signs to anybody who wants to buy them.*" Unfortunately, this is also the wrong answer. If Shell Oil wants to buy 11 000 high-tech illuminated signs for its gas stations in Europe and North Africa, your small business obviously cannot supply them. In fact, the business you can afford to set up involves a single graphics computer with one printer that can print only on fibreboard, plastic, or paper surfaces to a maximum size of one square metre (i.e., no large illuminated signs like Shell needs). You are already specialized by the limitations of your company. So what you expect to be selling can now be defined as *small non-illuminated signs*.

✅ Memory Check 1.10
True or False? A new business should try to have as wide a variety of potential customers as possible.

✅ Memory Check 1.11
True or False? For the purposes of the business plan, the terms *location* and *site* are totally interchangeable.

✅ Memory Check 1.12
True or False? Specialization in fewer products or services generally means more profit for a small business.

❓ Get Help 1.4
After you write out the definition of your business as completely as you can, show it to a journalism student, a marketing teacher, or the best writer you know. Ask them to summarize what you've written. Repeat this process several times. Try to remember that you are only getting editing help, and that the actual business concept must be your definition.

A Special Site for a Highly Specialized Retailer

After textile school, Diana Sanderson's love of silk weaving led her into creating scarves, shawls, and other garments that she started selling at craft fairs. Her clientele grew steadily until 1986, when she was able to open a studio on Vancouver's trendy Granville Island.

This site was originally a boiler room but was remodelled into a warm, inviting showcase for Diana and other artists to demonstrate their skills, teach others, and sell their fine creations. Today Diana is recognized around the world as an established silk weaver and clothing designer.

Although Granville Island is geared toward the well-heeled tourist traffic, a large portion of Diana's business comes from her own Vancouver-area clientele. To support the area as an important tourist location, businesses on parts of the island receive rent subsidies. But this is not the case for the Silk Weaving Studio, which is in a more secluded, privately owned section of the island. Diana, however, is able to control her costs by sharing her studio space with several other weavers. Even though Diana is the lessee, decisions about the premises are generally made co-operatively by all the artists. The studio is also used to showcase the work of guest artists working in a variety of fibres. It is open seven days a week and visitors can watch artists at work in the weaving process.

As is more typical of arts-based enterprises than other categories of business, Diana explains that the various artists tend to be "complementary to each other, rather than competitive." Working in different styles, they produce different products but all appeal to the same upscale clientele seeking a less trendy, more classic look in their wardrobes. "One of the most exciting things for me," says Diana, "is when a client comes in wearing something they bought 15 years ago and it still looks great,"

Diana admits to being influenced by the tastes of her clients but would never produce something (and has even turned down requests to do so) just because it's trendy. She feels that the challenge for her is finding the right balance between business and art. For example, the business does not do typical retail promotion, other than her tasteful sign and websites (www.silkweavingstudio.com and sanjosilk.com), where visitors can see the quality and style of Diana's products.

Defining *what you're selling* also helps to define who the potential customers will be. Who is able and likely to buy the type of signs you are selling? Independent gas stations offering tune-up specials, real estate agents needing "for-sale" signs, pizza parlours pushing two-for-one deals, car dealers with finance rate discounts—these are all small retail and service businesses. Logic tells us that small companies such as these are not going to chase halfway across the country to buy signs; they will shop in their own geographic area. So maybe your market now becomes *small retail and service businesses within the town (or neighbourhood) where you are located.*

We are getting closer to a definition of the business. But remember, writing the business plan is really a process of rewriting, and the thing we are going to rewrite the most is the definition of the business. So, defining the business is often a process of *redefining* the business, many times. Therefore, our current definition is only a working definition, and we can expect it to be modified and refined when we look into issues of market research, sales strategy, location, competition, and so on.

⭐ Head Start Exercise

1.5 Take a few minutes right now and write out the first few lines of the plan for your business idea. Briefly indicate what you will be selling and to whom you plan on selling it (1/8 page maximum).

DO I NEED A PARTNER?

The "business opportunities" column of the newspaper lists many people looking for business partners. Typically, these are *people with ideas* looking for *partners with money*. There are few legitimate ads from people with lots of cash but fresh out of ideas. People can and do find partners, but it's usually from less formal sources than newspapers. Relatives, fellow employees, classmates, friends . . . these are the people one is most likely to partner up with in a new business. In many cases, the partnership is formed before the concept for the business is clear and before anyone has asked whether they really need a partner. *Ask yourself: Do I really need a partner? Why?*

There are lots of legitimate reasons for having a partner: sharing the risk, increasing financial resources, personality reasons, reasons of expertise, and so on, but the fact that someone is your cousin or long-time friend is not, by itself, reason enough to include them in the business. You should not form partnerships because of past obligations, but rather for mutual future benefit.

✓ **Memory Check 1.13**
True or False? The definition of a business may change a number of times during the writing of a business plan.

Partner Personalities

You may well need a partner—sometimes more than one. The question then becomes, What personality traits and skills do you want in your partners to complement your own personality and skills? Ideally, your weaknesses will be their strengths and vice versa. Also keep in mind the extraordinary number of hours that you will be working with your partners. At the very least, you want people you will get along with.

Don't forget that starting a new business is an emotional undertaking and your relationship with any partner will be emotionally charged—that means conflict, even fighting. But the purpose of a partnership is to spend your time making profit, not war. Partnership conflict is inevitable and not totally counterproductive. It can often help to look at problems from more than one perspective, but protracted fights among partners are just bad for business. *Ask yourself: Am I likely to fight longer with someone who is just like me, or with someone who is my opposite?*

As with most human conflicts, the battle is likely to be over quickly if one of the partners is dominant. Forget about trying to find a partner with whom you are perfectly evenly matched. Having one of the partners dominate could well be to the advantage of both. And when partners cannot resolve conflict themselves, it is worthwhile to seek the help of a professional mediator.[15] If **mediation** is not successful, partners can then turn to **arbitration** so that the conflict can be settled and they can get on with making some money. Over the past few years there has been tremendous growth in Alternative Dispute Resolution (ADR), and professionally designated mediators (Chartered Mediator—C. Med.) and arbitrators (Chartered Arbitrator—C. Arb.) are easy to find.

❓ **Get Help 1.5**
If you're planning to have your life partner as your business partner, you may want to look at *Partners at Home and at Work*, by Annette O'Shea and Sieglinde Malmberg, published by the Self-Counsel Press. Out of print now, but available in many libraries, it offers techniques for dealing with specific problems of a double-partnership arrangement.

mediation The use of a neutral third party to settle a dispute by assisting the disputing sides to come to a voluntary agreement.

arbitration The use of a neutral third party to settle a dispute by examining the arguments of the disputing parties and then imposing a binding decision on the parties.

Partnership Agreements

We know that it is important to reduce conflict between partners, and one of the most effective ways to do this is with a detailed **partnership agreement**.[16] *Ask yourself: What kinds of issues are likely to be covered in a partnership agreement?*

The basic questions to be answered by a partnership agreement are:

- Who puts in how much of the capital?
- Who gets what portion of any profit?
- Who has authority over which decisions?
- What are the responsibilities of each partner?
- How can disputes among the partners be settled?
- How can the partnership be changed?
- How can the partnership be ended?

partnership agreement
The contract between two or more people who are entering business ownership together.

❓ **Get Help 1.6**
The website of the ADR Institute of Canada (www.amic .org) provides information on Alternative Dispute Resolution. It can help partners find appropriate mediators and arbitrators.

These issues seem pretty simple, but simple issues become enormously complex if they are not clarified at the beginning of the relationship. What if you were to start a partnership with your friend? You agree that the friend will invest 60 percent of the capital to start the business and he will have 60 percent ownership. You will invest 40 percent, but you will have to borrow your initial investment from the friend. The friend will receive both his and your share of the profits until the borrowed amount is paid back. But what if there are no profits? Do you still owe the money to your friend?

Let's say you enter into partnership with two friends of yours who happen to be cousins to each other. At some point, the cousins decide that they would like to bring in a fourth partner, another of their cousins. You don't know the new cousin and are against the idea. What happens now? Can they outvote you? Do you have a veto?

You and a friend each invest $5000 to start a partnership. A few weeks into the business, your friend tells you that he has changed his mind and wants out. You say, "Okay, you're out." The friend says, "Good, now give me back my $5000." You explain that the money has been spent on equipment, but when the business starts to make money you will pay him the $5000. Your friend wants his money immediately and insists that the equipment be sold and that he get his share. You refuse. Who is right?

If the above eventualities are not covered in the partnership agreement, they might have to be settled by a court and involve the expense of lawyers. Better to pay the lawyer less up front to have a proper partnership agreement drafted that all of the partners fully understand. *Ask yourself: What happens to the friendships in the above three examples?*

⭐ Head Start Exercise

1.6   Draft a brief list of provisions you would demand in any partnership contract (1 page maximum).

You can get a do-it-yourself partnership agreement from a business supplies store. However, partnership agreements are an area where paying for some legal advice can be a great investment. This doesn't mean you should be scared away from the idea of partnerships. Many of Canada's most successful businesses were started as partnerships. Just be sure that you "partner up" very carefully.

WHAT WILL MY BUSINESS MEAN LEGALLY?

One of the early decisions to be made in starting up a business is the selection of a legal form. Like other early decisions, you might change this one by the time you complete the business plan, or even at some point after the business is up and running. For the majority of new businesses, the choice of legal form is a simple decision of whether or not to incorporate. Nevertheless, you should know that more than two choices are available and understand the advantages and disadvantages of each.

Sole Proprietorship

This is the simplest, cheapest, and most common form of business. It is a business owned and operated by one person. It doesn't mean that the company has only one employee—it can have any number of employees. It just means that only one person has the inherent right to control the business. If you have a **sole proprietorship**, you and the business are one and the same as far as the law is concerned.

Let's say the owner of a sole proprietorship arts-supply store passes away. The owner no longer exists and, legally, the business no longer exists. Members of the owner's family will inherit the assets (i.e., the property) of the business (the sign, the art supplies, the cash register) just as they will inherit the owner's other personal assets: cash, clothing,

sole proprietorship A legal form of business where only one person owns and has the legal right to operate the company. The sole proprietor has unlimited liability for the company's debts.

broken guitar. The family may decide to keep the business going. But what they are doing in a legal sense is taking the inherited assets (the sign, the supplies, the cash register) and investing them into a brand-new business. The assets of the business are the personal assets of the owner.

And just as the owner *personally* owns the assets of the firm, so does he or she *personally* own the debts of the firm. This is what is meant by the expression **unlimited liability**: There is no limit to how much the owner is personally responsible for the debts of the business. If a sole proprietorship is closed down because it cannot pay its debts, the owner is still responsible for them; the owner must use personal assets to pay the debts.

Each province and territory has its own business registration rules. Generally, registration is required if you are operating a business under any name other than your own exact first and last name. Even then, it is a good idea to register because you may need the registration certificate to get other business documents and it's not expensive. If you do carry on a one-owner business without registering, you will be considered to have a sole proprietorship. If you carry on a business that has more than one owner and fail to otherwise register the business, you will be considered to have a **general partnership**.

General Partnership

The general partnership legal form is similar to sole proprietorship, but it applies to a business that has two or more owners, each of whom has the right to make decisions about the business and each of whom has *unlimited liability*.

This is the single most important issue to be aware of when entering into a general partnership. It means that each partner has 100 percent responsibility for the debts of the business: not just responsibility for their own share, but responsibility for the entire amount of debt. It means that you can personally be liable for any mistakes your partners make as far as the business is concerned. The implication here is that you must be prepared to have considerable trust in your partners and should know as much as possible about their financial circumstances as well as any agreements they might make on behalf of the business.

Despite some of the obvious inherent dangers, a general partnership is inexpensive to register and may offer significant tax advantages at start-up.

Corporation

People talk about the "big corporations," but size has nothing to do with legal form: A one-person company can be a **corporation**. The owners of a corporation are referred to as shareholders. Generally, for small corporations, owning 51 percent (or more) of the shares gives someone the power to decide who will run the company. Also, in most cases the percentage of shares a person owns reflects the percentage of any dividend (profit that the company decides to pay to shareholders) that the person will receive.

The owners of a corporation, however, unlike the above forms, do not personally own the assets of the company. When a business is incorporated, the law recognizes the company as an "*artificial person*," and it is this artificial person who owns the assets.

It is also the artificial person who is responsible for the debts, and this is what we mean by **limited liability**: The owner's responsibility for the debts of the business is limited to however much he or she has invested in the firm—the owner's personal assets are not at risk if the business has failed.

Compared to a sole proprietorship or general partnership, it is considerably more expensive to form a corporation, ranging from several hundred dollars for "do it yourself" to several thousand dollars for having one of the more expensive law firms handle the incorporation.

unlimited liability Total personal responsibility for the debts of a business.

general partnership A business where two or more people own and have the right to manage the company. Each owner in a general partnership has unlimited liability for all the debts of the company.

✔ **Memory Check 1.15**
True or False? In a good business partnership, no one partner should ever be dominant.

✔ **Memory Check 1.16**
True or False? The decision of an arbitrator must be adhered to by the disputing parties.

corporation A legal form of business that exists separately from its owners (shareholders), who have limited liability for the company's debts.

limited liability A situation where company owners do not have personal responsibility for the debts of their company.

❓ **Get Help 1.7**
Check with your provincial business registrations office for the cost of registering a sole proprietorship or general partnership.

Other Legal Forms

limited partnership A legal form of business with some partners (at least one) having unlimited liability and some having limited liability.

The vast majority of new small enterprises are registered as one of the above three forms. There are, however, other forms you should know about. The three most common of these are limited partnership, limited liability partnership, and co-operative.

Limited partnership is a form rarely used by new small businesses and it can be more expensive to set up than a corporation. It requires one or more limited partners who will have limited liability (just like investors in a corporation) but will have the same tax advantages as general partners. Unlike corporate shareholders, however, limited partners may not participate in the management of the company. In this form, there must be at least one general partner (there can be any number) who will have unlimited liability.

limited liability partnership A legal form of business available to professional firms that provides partial liability protection to the partners.

Limited liability partnership (LLP) is an increasingly popular form that applies to firms in self-governed professions (like lawyers and accountants). Be careful about confusing LLPs (as they are usually designated) with the limited partnership form. These kinds of firms are not permitted to incorporate, but the LLP form allows limited liability for the partners, provided that they carry insurance at sufficient levels to meet potential liabilities. The LLP protects you from being liable for the mistakes or wrongdoing of your partners in the firm only, not against liability for your own mistakes or wrongdoing. LLP is not available in all Canadian jurisdictions at the time of writing, but most have it at least under consideration.

worker co-operative A legal form of business where the employees (at least a majority of them) are the owners of the company. Each owner has one equal vote in selecting management and directing the company.

Worker co-operatives exist largely to provide employment for their members. The employees of the company are the shareholders and they have the limited liability protection of corporations. Unlike corporations, however, where the number of shares owned can mean the number of votes in running the company, in co-operatives each member (owner) gets only one vote, regardless of how many shares he or she owns. In this sense, co-operatives are governed democratically. This form of business has been used successfully in artisan-based, food production, and forestry companies, and it could be applied to many emerging industries. For example, an information technology-based firm owned by a group of talented programmers could work as a co-operative.

The decision of legal form is usually influenced by

- initial cost
- liability
- tax considerations
- the image the entrepreneur wishes to project
- the number of investors and their financial circumstances

Choosing a legal form is one of the more complex planning decisions and often requires the advice of a lawyer, an accountant, or a marketing adviser. Nevertheless, a preliminary decision on legal form should be made in the early parts of the business plan. The Canada Business Network website (www.canadabusiness.ca) is a good place for information on legal forms. This site is referred to frequently throughout the text. Be cautious of U.S. sites in this area (their rules are a little different). If you have any doubts before deciding on a legal form, call a lawyer's office and start by asking how much they will charge you for an initial consultation.

> ✔ **Memory Check 1.17**
> True or False? In a sole proprietorship, the owner of the business has unlimited liability for company debts.

⭐ Head Start Exercise

1.7 Choose a legal form for your business and make up a list of reasons explaining why this is the most appropriate form for you (1/2 page maximum).

A History of Partnerships

In Canada, coffee is a hot topic. And no one knows this better than Vida Radovanovic, owner of The Canadian Barista & Coffee Academy. Vida is the sole owner of the company and plans to keep it that way, although, at different times, she has been involved with three different partners.

Vida's first coffee business was started when she was a freelance writer working with another writer on a guide to coffee houses in Toronto. In doing their research, the pair saw that there was no trade magazine for the Canadian coffee industry, which had to rely on several U.S. publications. Once the pair had their magazine up and running, they expanded the business by producing a major conference and trade show: The Canadian Coffee and Tea Expo. Then, a new partner was brought on board with the three owners all having equal shares in the magazine and the expo.

But the partnership was not a success, so Vida and the newest partner bought out the third. Unfortunately, the new two-member partnership also failed. So Vida bought out her remaining partner, operated on her own for a while, and then sold a half interest in both ventures to another new partner, who already had other publishing interests. This final partnership was eventually dissolved, with Vida taking full ownership of the expo and the partner owning the magazine. Vida eventually sold her rights to the expo but stayed within the coffee industry by starting the Canadian Barista and Coffee Academy. Here, she provides training to existing and would-be coffee house owners as well as to baristas, the espresso machine *chefs* of the coffee industry. The Academy is located on Toronto's busy downtown Esplanade and has its own coffee shop, the Academy Café.

After years of partnerships, some good, some bad, Vida is now the only owner of her small corporation. When asked if she would ever go into another partnership, Vida indicated that she would not rule it out. However, she urged caution for anyone thinking of doing so. "Get a draft partnership agreement down on paper, right from the start. And include details of everything: who puts in how much money, who is responsible for what, what will be the time commitments and remuneration for the partners . . . absolutely everything you can think of. And don't sign the actual agreement until you have had your lawyer look it over."

See the website for The Canadian Barista & Coffee Academy at www.canadianbaristaacademy.com.

HOW DO I GET STARTED?

The Business Plan

Most new businesses are started without the owner ever having written a formal business plan. But then, most new businesses fail within a year or two.

Pretty much every human activity is more likely to have a successful outcome if it is planned. This includes a chess game, an athletic contest, a vacation, asking someone for a date, and so on. The plan isn't always written out, but it does exist. A business, however, is much more complex than a chess game or a party. No reasonable person would attempt to build a house or a vehicle or anything else that complicated without a written plan. So it only makes sense to use a written plan in building a business. Having a written business plan will improve your chances of survival.[17] *Ask yourself: What other reasons might I have for needing a business plan?*

Formal business lenders and investors require written business plans. If you want to borrow money from a bank or sell part of a business to investors (other than your grandparents), you almost always have to have a written business plan. There are many uses and variations in business plans, the details of which are covered in Chapter 12. But for most

☑ Memory Check 1.18
True or False? In a general partnership each of the partners can be held personally responsible for all of the company's debts.

☑ Memory Check 1.19
True or False? In a limited partnership, all of the partners have limited liability.

☑ Memory Check 1.20
True or False? An individual may be the only owner of a corporation.

Memory Check 1.21
True or False? An individual may be the only owner of a general partnership.

start-up businesses, all the necessary components of the basic business plan are covered in Chapters 1–5. Each of these chapters (including this one) covers one of the five components of the basic business plan:

- the business model
- feasibility
- marketing
- operations
- finances

At the end of each of these chapters, there is an outline for that section of the business plan You will have already completed much of this work if you have been using the *Get Started* exercises.

On the principle that it is easier to fix up a bad plan than it is to write a great plan from scratch, start by writing something that is less than perfect—or even fairly bad. Just get something down on paper or into a computer. It can always be fixed up later. Remember, most of the work of writing a business plan is in rewriting. Section 1 of the plan lays the groundwork for Section 2, which must be completed before Section 3, and so on. But as the decisions for each section are made, they sometimes require you to go back and rewrite earlier parts of the plan.

Notice that the outline for Section 1 of the business plan starts with a summary, often called an *executive summary*. If you are using the plan for your own purposes and it is not intended for other readers, then the summary is really not necessary. For readers other than the entrepreneur(s), the summary is a valuable overview of what the plan is about. If you are using one, even though it is at the beginning of the plan, it will be written after the rest of the plan is completed.

Memory Check 1.22
True or False? An executive summary is necessary for all business plans.

If you want to be in business for yourself, the first step must be taken by you, the entrepreneur. You must start writing the business plan. There is little point in hiring a high-priced consultant to write a plan that is not made up of your ideas; you just won't follow it. That doesn't mean you can't get help for the process. Throughout this text there are tips on who and what can help you in preparing the plan. And if writing is just not your strength, there are lots of professional writers willing to proofread for you and fix up your grammar and spelling. But the ideas must be yours, because your real purpose in writing a business plan is not just to end up with the document. Rather, it is the process that's important. By having to prepare each element of the business plan, you are forced to think through all of the critical decisions involved in starting a business in a logical order—an order that will let you see contradictions and areas where your plan does not make sense. Writing it down forces you to make a better plan.

Memory Check 1.23
True or False? Writing a business plan is largely a process of rewriting.

Ask yourself: What will be the most difficult part of writing a business plan? What will be the easiest? The biggest problem with writing a business plan is the same problem encountered in any type of writing: overcoming procrastination. It is amazing how creative people can be in finding critical things to do instead of writing the plan: looking at locations, calling suppliers, shopping the competition—these are the easy parts. But the writing has to be done, so just do it!

Take the first step and start writing.

Answers to Memory Check Questions

1.1 F	1.2 F	1.3 T	1.4 F	1.5 T	1.6 F	1.7 F	1.8 T
1.9 F	1.10 F	1.11 F	1.12 T	1.13 T	1.14 F	1.15 F	1.16 T
1.17 T	1.18 T	1.19 F	1.20 T	1.21 F	1.22 F	1.23 T	

Questions for Discussion

1. Identify a movie or TV show where the main character is a successful entrepreneur. Discuss whether the portrayal of the character is realistic or artificial.
2. "Eventually, everyone in Canada will be in business for themselves." How would such a system work and what evidence is there that we are moving in this direction?
3. Suppose that someone who owns a restaurant asks you to marry him/her. If you accept the proposal, how would your life be different from a life where you were married to a government employee?
4. Debate this proposition: "Canadian colleges and universities are in the business of training employees, not entrepreneurs."
5. Make a list of the major changes (political, social, economic, cultural, technological, etc.) currently under way in our society. Identify at least one entrepreneurial opportunity that each of these changes will create.
6. Identify how you could be highly specialized as a self-employed person in a variety of industries (e.g., golf, music, construction, auto repair, etc.). What are the advantages over being a generalist?
7. Compare the province or territory you are in with the closest U.S. state as potential locations for opening a new small business in an industry such as plastic moulding. Which location has the most advantages? What if the industry were TV animation, specialty chocolate manufacturing, or used computer refurbishing?
8. List a variety of ways that you could be cheated by a business partner. What kinds of provisions could you put in a partnership agreement to prevent your being treated unfairly by a partner?
9. Discuss the advantages and disadvantages of being married to your business partner.
10. Discuss how incorporation (vs. sole proprietorship or partnership) changes the image of a company. When would it be a disadvantage to have a corporate image?

Case for Discussion

Whitney Almeida was tired of hearing "don't do it." She had an idea for a business and everyone she went to for advice was trying to discourage her.

Her mother (homemaker, part-time store clerk): "Yes dear, but perhaps if you were married to someone wealthy, then you could have a business like that. Because let's face it, what you're talking about is really more of a hobby."

Her father (provincial government accountant): "Put in twenty years building a decent pension somewhere. Then you could take early retirement and play around with weird ideas like that."

Her aunt (lawyer, divorced): "These days, a woman has to be able to make a reliable living for herself. You need security. Go back to school, get a professional credential, then you can save money and invest a little of it in risky businesses."

Her uncle (independent plumbing contractor): "It's great to be in business for yourself, but nobody's going to buy what you want to sell."

Her boss (art gallery owner): "Trust me. You don't want all the headaches of trying to run a business. Look at me, I'm barely surviving."

Whitney did not feel convinced by any of them. She had a two-year diploma in graphic arts, had taken a part-time course in photography, and was working full-time in a small art gallery. The previous month, Whitney and her sister had taken a trip to Scotland, where they toured half a dozen ancient castles. Whitney had been particularly fascinated by the many old portraits decorating the castle walls. And on the plane ride home, half asleep, Whitney had envisioned her idea for a business: creating traditional formal portraits that were half painting, half photograph.

It was possible to put photographic emulsion on the same type of canvas that artists use and then print photographs directly onto the canvas. Whitney had used the process in her photography class. It occurred to her that it would also be possible to add paint over top of the picture on the canvas to make it look like an original oil painting, but one that cut out all the painstaking work of the artist. She realized that if she took a picture of someone, she could Photoshop it over any background the customer chose, add a little paint, and it would look like an original oil portrait. She could put it in a fancy frame of the customer's choice, and it would make an ideal gift or ego trophy.

Whitney felt that a shop like the tiny gallery where she worked, in the same upscale shopping district, would be ideal. Once she was established and had examples to show, Whitney could start selling online, with customers emailing in their own pictures. She knew it would be a lot of work to get the business started, but that did not worry her. In fact, she was excited by the prospect.

1. Is Whitney's concept for a business a good one? Why or why not?

2. Why might Whitney's advisors be so negative about her idea? Who else could she go to for advice?

3. Does Whitney seem like the kind of person who could be a successful entrepreneur? Support your answer.

4. Does Whitney have the right background for a business such as this? What else might she need?

5. Create a single sentence that would define Whitney's business: what she is selling, and to whom she is selling it.

6. If Whitney decides to pursue her business idea, what steps should she take next?

Tools for Instructors

A comprehensive package of 24 cases can be found in the Instructor's Manual via the Pearson website. (The cases have also been customized for a variety of specific program areas.)

As well, case discussion questions are available for select CBC *Dragon's Den* segments.

The Business Plan, Section 1:
THE BUSINESS MODEL AND SUMMARY

Summary

Note: The Summary is prepared only after all other portions of the business plan have been completed. Start writing your business plan with the introduction below.

- Using information from Section 1 of the business plan, briefly state what the business will be selling, the sorts of customers it will have, why there is an opportunity for this now, and why the owners are the right people to run this business.
- Using information from Section 2 of the business plan, briefly identify the location and site, the direct competition, and the expected revenue in the first three years.
- Using information from Section 3 of the business plan, briefly explain the firm's image or position in terms of product and price, as well as where the company will fit in the distribution chain.
- Using information from Section 4 of the business plan, briefly outline the capital investment required, the roles the owner(s) will play in the firm, and the roles of any other employees.
- Using information from Section 5 of the business plan, briefly outline the amount and sources of financing and collateral for the business and when the business is expected to start making a profit, as well as how much profit is expected.

Introduction

1. Describe the general nature of the business and identify any important or unusual features.

2. Identify any businesses that use a similar business model to what you propose. Explain how your model might be different.

Products and Services

3. Explain how your business will be specialized in terms of the products and/or services you will offer.

The Customers

4. Explain how your business will be specialized in terms of the customer groups you will be targeting.

The Location

5. Briefly describe the location and site of the business, explaining why these choices are appropriate.

The Opportunity

6. Identify any circumstances or events that have led to a need that your business intends to satisfy. Be clear on why *now* is a good time to start a business such as this.

The Owner(s)

7. Name and give a brief background for each of the owners. Explain why this history is appropriate for running a business such as this one. Attach a résumé for each of the owners as an appendix.

8. Identify any entrepreneurial abilities of the owner(s) and, if there is more than one owner, clarify the "complementary" nature of the relationship. Explain any personal motivation for going into business now.

9. Briefly estimate the minimum amount of money you (and any partners) will have to withdraw from the business each month in order to survive (or how long you can survive without relying on the business for income).

The Legal Organization

10. Identify the legal form of the business and clearly state *who* owns *how much* of the company. Explain your reasons for this legal set-up.

11. If there is more than one owner, explain who will be actively participating in the business and how. If there is a partnership agreement, identify the major provisions and attach a copy of the agreement as an appendix.

Chapter 2

Feasibility: How Do I Know It Will Work?

In Section 1 of the business plan, you defined your business in terms of *what* you will be selling and to *whom* you will be selling it. Section 2 is about checking whether that idea will work. This means answering the following questions:

- How Will I Analyze My Location?
- How Much of My Kind of Business is Out There?
- Who is My Competition?
- How Much Business Will My Firm Get?
- How Can I Protect The New Business?

Learning Objectives

On completion of this chapter, you should be able to:

1. Explain three major considerations for choosing a business location.
2. Define market potential.
3. Differentiate between primary and secondary research.
4. Differentiate between direct and indirect competition.
5. Outline six techniques for estimating future sales.
6. Argue the need for small business insurance.
7. Discuss six types of theft prevention.
8. Distinguish among four methods of protecting intellectual property.
9. Prepare the feasibility portion of a business plan.

This second part of the business plan, **feasibility**, is largely about marketing research. *Ask yourself: Do the terms* market research *and* marketing research *mean the same thing?* In the strictest sense, **market research** means assembling information about the group(s) of potential customers that your business is targeting. This includes things like identifying the numbers of potential customers, their characteristics, and how much they spend on your products or services. **Marketing research** is broader in scope. It includes research on the market, but can also include gathering information about the location, competition, pricing, or any other element of the process for getting products or services to customers. So *market* research is only one part of *marketing* research. In a practical sense, however, for new small businesses, these two terms tend to be used interchangeably. This may be because most of the marketing research done for start-up companies tends to be about the potential customers and how much they spend on a product or service. This is the main piece of information that tells us whether a business idea is feasible.

feasibility The likelihood that a concept or plan could work.

market research Gathering and organizing information about groups of potential customers.

marketing research Gathering and organizing information about the process for getting products or services to customers.

Checking that your business concept is feasible is not just for your personal benefit. Lenders or potential investors also want some evidence that the business will succeed before they hand over any cash. But *ask yourself: What if it starts to look as though my business idea is not going to work?* Then that means you should go back to Section 1 of the business plan and start modifying either *what* you will sell or to *whom* you will sell, until you have a clear business idea that you can demonstrate is feasible.

HOW WILL I ANALYZE MY LOCATION?

For most businesses, the feasibility of the company depends to some extent on where it is located. Of course, just how critical the location is depends on what you're selling and to whom you're selling. The main considerations for location are usually closeness to customers, transportation, suppliers, and various services.

Generally, but not always, the rule is to be as close as possible to your potential customers, regardless of whether they will be coming to you or you will be going to them.[1] But if you are starting some form of online business (where you deliver your service via the internet), the actual physical location of your office may not matter at all. You will be as close to your customers as their own computers.

If you are locating to be close to customers, at a very minimum you must be able to demonstrate that there are sufficient numbers of potential customers in your area to support the business. There is no point in starting a wedding photography studio in a retirement community of 500 households. There is no point in being an investment consultant in a low-income community where no one has money to invest.

Some businesses depend on providing quick delivery to customers. If you are selling to a national or international market, this could require being close to the airport. But if you open a custom T-shirt store where most of your customers will be lower-income high-school students (with no cars), your transportation issue becomes the availability of public transit—so that your customers can come to you.

In most businesses the suppliers come to you, so you don't really care where they are located as long as they deliver on time. But let's say you're a fashion designer who contracts out the making of your sample garments. In that case, you may have to be close to your supplier because of the frequent checking and adjustments that the samples will need. (For manufacturing businesses, being close to your sources of supply is often the number one priority.)

Banks, libraries, hospitals, swimming pools, courthouses, or universities are all services that your business may need to be close to. For example, you might start a highly specialized technology-based firm where you need to consult with top experts in your field. Proximity to a university where these experts likely work as researchers could be a competitive advantage.[2]

To help gather data about your business location, Statistics Canada has excellent mapping tools that can provide information by electoral districts, postal codes, or political or geographical divisions. In fact, becoming familiar with the StatCan mapping tools can even help you define your target customer area. For example, you may know that you are targeting consumers in North West Calgary, but find that it is easier, for research purposes, to define your area by municipal electoral district: Calgary, Ward 2. Remember that reference librarians are usually adept at using the StatCan mapping tools.

Site Issues

If your customers will be coming to you, then the site becomes a critical issue. The main considerations relating to site are traffic, visibility, parking, and neighbouring businesses.

Ask yourself: What kind of traffic do I need for my business? Traffic can be either automobile or pedestrian. If you are selling a frequently purchased product to a broad consumer market, then the trick is to find a site where lots of potential buyers[3] will be walking or

Get Help 2.1
Call the chamber of commerce where you plan on locating. They will likely be able to advise you on the population base as well as the makeup of industry in the area. Many municipalities have a business development office that can supply similar information.

— Closeness to the customers
Transportation
— Suppliers
Various services .

Get Help 2.2
Counting traffic can be labour-intensive, so get help from friends and family. If more sophisticated help is required, you may want to contact a business teacher or marketing student to help you design a traffic study.

driving by—lots of traffic. This is especially true for businesses like convenience stores and restaurants (retail and consumer service firms). If your customers are more likely to make a special trip to your place of business, then traffic is less of an issue. This would be the case if you have a roofing supplies warehouse or a hypnotherapy clinic.

In analyzing your traffic, the question you want to answer is: "How many potential customers pass by my place of business during times when they are likely to buy?" Even if thousands pass by your music store on the way to work at 7:00 a.m., it doesn't do you much good. People are more likely to buy on the way home from work, at lunchtime, on Saturdays, or at other obvious shopping times.

Information about who will come by and when they will come can be easy to get if you are leasing space in a major mall (the mall owners will likely have the information already). But for just about any place else, it means going out and doing some kind of measurement. This could involve renting an automobile traffic counter (easily available). Or it could mean getting a clipboard and lawn chair, sitting at the site, and counting how often the type of person you're looking for comes by, and at what times. If you can compare the traffic at your proposed site to the traffic at a similar business that you know to be successful, you have a strong argument for the success of your business.

Will passersby be able to identify your place of business for what it is? Will the sign be noticeable and readable from the stream of traffic? Can delivery people identify the address? Will the entrance be obvious? These questions are all concerns of <u>visibility</u>. A good lesson here comes from the experts. The key consideration for a U.S. sign company franchisor, in selecting its own sites, is the amount of traffic to which its sign will be visible.[4]

Visibility includes the ability to see into your place of business. If you rely on high traffic volume to provide your customers, you still have to get them out of the traffic and into your business. That's where your store window comes in. Potential customers have to be able to see what you've got before they will come in. And that's not just for retail businesses.

The need for customers to see in can be important even for dental clinics or restaurants or accounting offices. New customers are more likely to come in if they can see inside.

Ask yourself: What parking problems bother you the most? The first question around parking is: "Is there enough of it?" Imagine you are planning to open an insta-print business in a small strip mall. If you go and look at the premises at 10:00 on a Monday morning, the parking may appear more than ample. But on Friday evening around 5:30, when everyone is picking up their baked goods and dry cleaning, your customers may have no place to park. So the real question is: "Is there enough parking for peak times?"

The parking must also be accessible. This means that the entrance <u>will be wide enough</u>, that there will be <u>room to turn around</u>, and that medians or islands will <u>not obstruct traffic</u> from the <u>opposite side of the road</u>. Don't lease a place with <u>parking problems</u> thinking that you can get them fixed later—it's just too difficult and time-consuming for the owner of a new firm to deal with landlords and City Hall on this kind of issue.

If parking is not available on the premises, what arrangements are there for customer parking? Will customers have to use on-street metered parking? Will you have a deal with a local lot that lets your customers park for free and charges the fee to you? How will this be administered? These issues have to be worked out in advance and explained in the business plan.

An advantageous site is one right next to a **complementary business**: a company that chases the same customers you chase, but sells them something different. For example, if you are opening a store that specializes in bar supplies and mixers, you couldn't do better than being next to a busy liquor store. A discount shoe store could benefit from being next to a discount clothing store. Of course, whether you put your new tattoo parlour next to a Harley-Davidson dealer or next to a high-priced beauty salon depends on the market segment you are pursuing.

☑ **Memory Check 2.1**
True or False? It is always important to have a location close to your customers.

☑ **Memory Check 2.2**
True or False? Traffic analysis is very important for retail businesses.

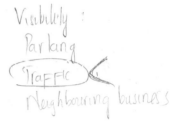
Visibility :
Parking
Traffic
Neighbouring business

❓ **Get Help 2.3**
Check with the clerk's office at City Hall to find out about municipal parking permits and restrictions.

complementary business A company that sells products or services different from yours, but to the same potential customers.

And what if the neighbouring businesses happen to be in competition with you? *Ask yourself: Do you want to be close to your competitors or as far away as possible?* The answer, like just about everything else in the business plan, depends on what you're selling and to whom you're selling it. If you are selling something like office supplies to people who won't compare prices and quality before they buy (they just want convenience), then you don't want to be anywhere near your competitors. Otherwise, you'll just be splitting the available business with the competitors.

On the other hand, if your customers are likely to shop around before they buy, then make it easy for them by being as close to the competition as possible. If you are opening a designer footwear store, make sure you are right beside other expensive shoe stores. If you are selling high-end photographic equipment, do it next door to other camera stores. When the customers are going to shop anyway, situate your business where they will go shopping. The challenge then becomes to specialize in ways that will make you slightly different from your competitors. (This is what you'll do in the marketing section of the business plan.)

Get Help 2.4
The U.S. government offers a website with many resources for setting up a home-based business: http://business.usa.gov./.

⭐ Head Start Exercise

2.1   Identify the site of your proposed business and note one or two advantages of this selection (1/4 page maximum).

Home-Based Businesses

Memory Check 2.3
True or False? Traffic analysis is very important for businesses that are industrial services.

Get Help 2.5
Check with your municipal planning department to see what other types of businesses are permitted in the area around your site.

As discussed in Chapter 1, home-based businesses include those where you do all your work at home as well as those where you might operate out of your car or truck and do the work at the customers' premises, probably only doing your office work at home. Before opting for a home business instead of one with its own commercial space, there are several things to consider:

- *Company Image.* The image of a home-based business might be ideal if you're selling window repair to lower-income homeowners in your own neighbourhood. You will look like someone who can work "quick and cheap," an image that will appeal to your customers. However, if you are an architectural stress consultant, selling your services to municipal engineering departments, you may not be taken seriously if you don't have an office in commercial space to give you that professional image.

- *Zoning Restrictions.* Most cities have zoning regulations that restrict types and locations of home-based businesses. And there are good reasons for this. For example, setting up a welding shop in your garage could present noise and safety hazards for your neighbours. In some cases, you can apply for a variance to be excepted from existing restrictions, but generally, you will never be allowed to conduct a business that could interfere with your neighbour's enjoyment of their homes. As well, many condominiums have their own restrictions on what residents may use their space for. Make sure you check with your local city hall or condominium corporation before setting up.

- *Insurance.* Don't assume that just because your house or apartment is insured that your business equipment, materials, or visitors are automatically covered. Most insurance companies have low-cost policies or policy extensions to cover small home business operations.

- *Family Issues.* For some entrepreneurs, working at home is difficult because of interruptions and distractions from family members. As well, it can be restrictive for family members to give up space or make other accommodations for a home business. Small children, especially, cannot understand the concept of "work time." If Daddy's at home and they want his attention, they have ways of getting it.

If you use part of your home for business purposes, some of your rent (or mortgage interest), maintenance, insurance, and utilities costs become a business expense. There are some restrictions and limitations for these expenses on your tax return. Keeping soft drinks in the fridge for work time does *not* mean that you can use the depreciation on your refrigerator as a business expense. Your accountant can help you identify legitimate expenses for your home business.

Most of the issues around working from home are *double-edged swords*. The advantage of not having to travel to the office also means the disadvantage of never being away from the office. The advantage of being home for the kids means the disadvantage of the kids being able to interrupt you at work. The advantage of saving money on a site could mean the disadvantage of an unprofessional image for your firm. If you decide to work from home, in your business plan, you must be able to explain the decision in terms of why it is best for the business, best for the customers, and not just for your personal convenience.

Leasing the Premises

For a new company, unless your business is home-based, it is usually not a good idea to buy the business premises, even if you can afford it. Owning the place can be confining for a new business. If you own, there is too much of a tendency to plan your business around the limitations of the premises, rather than the needs of your customers. If you lease, however, you are more willing to move, or make demands of the landlord, to meet changes in the market.

Besides, property management is a whole other business from what you plan on doing. Stick to what you will specialize in and let someone else (the landlord) specialize in property management.

When it comes to leases, everything is negotiable. But the landlord is in the business of negotiating leases (you'll only do it once every few years), and so you are at a disadvantage. You can improve the odds, however, by knowing your prices before you start negotiating. Shop around and ask lots of questions.

The issues to be negotiated in a lease can include:

- *Basic rent.* There is usually a going market value of **basic rent** for retail space within a particular neighbourhood, expressed as a certain number of dollars per square foot per year. (The figure is usually based on the average sales per square foot of retailers in the area.) This is the minimum rent you will pay, but usually there are additional charges on top of the basic rent. For a new business, you can always try to negotiate a break on the basic rent—sometimes even a rent-free period to help the business get going.

- *Percentage of sales.* Many landlords will want a percentage of your retail sales on top of the basic rent so they can share in the success of the business. This is a major negotiating point, since the more they share in your profits, the more they should be willing to risk in terms of lowering the basic rent or providing a rent-free period.

- *Maintenance and other expenses.* Aside from utilities you will have to pay directly, your property may have other expenses associated with it, such as your share of garbage pickup or snow removal, or gardening. You want to make sure you are not responsible for these expenses while the landlord retains total control over the amount to be spent and the choice of contractors. These issues, too, are negotiable.

- *Length of lease.* The more the success of your business depends on the particular site, the longer you want the lease to run. The length of the lease can also be important if you plan to eventually bring in other investors or maybe sell the whole business. The more doubtful you are about the site, however, the shorter the term you want to commit to, since you can always negotiate an extension.

- *Lease renewal.* If your business is successful, you want to be able to extend or renew your lease, but not under conditions where the landlord can change the terms to take the

Get Help 2.6
Check the Canada Revenue Agency website at www.cra-arc.gc.ca and search for work-space-in-the-home expenses to find out what expenses are allowable for a home-based company.

Get Help 2.7
Before arranging a lease, you may want to look at *Negotiate Your Commercial Lease* by Dale R. Willerton, published by the Self-Counsel Press.

basic rent The minimum rent charged by a landlord for commercial space, on top of which may be charged a percentage of sales, maintenance fees, and other expenses.

Get Help 2.8
Find a real estate agent in your location but be honest about whether you are only doing background shopping, so you won't use too much of their time. Most agents will be happy to let you browse through the multiple listings and give you an idea of the kind of terms you can negotiate. Alternatively, check the online multiple listing service at www.icx.ca, where you can perform industrial and commercial property searches by geographic area.

☑ **Memory Check 2.4**
True or False? For most kinds of business, it is better to buy rather than lease the property where the business is situated.

leasehold improvements
Modifications to the structure or decor of a commercial property that will remain the property of the landlord, even though they may have been paid for by the lessee.

lion's share of your profits. So you want to have some pre-set conditions that you will be able to renew—maybe not at the same rent, but at some amount indexed to your improved sales and profits. In addition, you would like to negotiate a clause that allows you to terminate the lease if there is some substantial change in the conditions of the property, such as the closing of a road or the loss of pedestrian traffic.

■ *Leasehold improvements*. The landlord will argue that any **leasehold improvements**—renovations, modifications, new fixtures, and so on—are to the benefit of your business and should be paid by you. If you can demonstrate, however, that any of your changes will increase the value of the property and would also benefit any future tenants, you may be able to convince the landlord to share in these costs.

There will be other issues in the lease, including the landlord's requirement for you to carry insurance on your business. (The landlord's own insurance on the property may require this.) Most issues, however, will be negotiable to some extent.

⭐ Head Start Exercise

2.2 Find several vacant office, retail, or industrial sites that would suit your business (see Get Help 2.8). Contact the landlords or real estate agents and explain that you are in the process of writing a draft business plan and need rent figures on a site. Ask about terms such as the length of the lease, maintenance, and other expenses. For one site, create a list of the major lease issues and estimate how much each would cost your business on a monthly basis (1 page maximum).

HOW MUCH OF MY KIND OF BUSINESS IS OUT THERE?

Defining Market Potential

Imagine that you are a banker and someone comes to borrow money to start a piano-tuning business for people who live in the village of Parkside. *Ask yourself: What is the first question I would want to ask the borrower?* For most bankers, it would be "How much piano-tuning business is there in Parkside?"

What if a friend asks you to become her partner in a business that will paint new names on boats (what you are selling) for boat dealers in the Big Bay area (whom you are selling to)? Wouldn't you wonder exactly how much Big Bay boat dealers spend on name-painting? Are they spending enough to support a business of two people? Enough for a business that could grow?

market potential How much money a group of potential customers will spend on a particular product or service.

The thing we want to know about here is called **market potential**: how much money a group of potential customers (whom) will spend on a particular product or service (what). Market potential isn't just how much a customer group will buy from your business; it is how much they will buy of the product or service in total, including from all your competition.

If your business concept is to sell children's photographic portraits to wealthy people living in the downtown area, then the market potential would be *how much money all the wealthy people in the downtown area, together, spend on getting pictures taken of their kids*. If you are starting a business selling something to lots of different customer groups, you will want to know the market potential for each of these groups.

☑ **Memory Check 2.5**
True or False? Market research is one part of marketing research.

☑ **Memory Check 2.6**
True or False? Market potential includes your own firm's sales of a product or service, as well as the sales of your competitors for that product or service.

Market potential is usually expressed as an annual dollar value. And sometimes it can be a big value. For example, you might be starting a daycare centre in the small city of Nanaimo, BC. The market potential here (how much the entire population of Nanaimo spends annually on child care) would be about $13 million. Your tiny daycare centre will only earn a tiny portion of that market. But, as you will see, it's still important that you know the entire market potential.

⭐ Head Start Exercise

2.3 Go back to Section 1 of your business plan and look at how you have defined your business. Now, write a single sentence explaining the market potential you should be interested in; in other words: "I must find out how much money (the customer group you are selling to) will spend annually on (the product or service you will sell)." For example: "I must find out how much money all the consumers in Northtown spend each year on having their pets photographed" (1 sentence maximum).

Applying Market Potential

Ask yourself: Why would I want to know the market potential? Knowing how much business is out there is important at start-up because it helps you focus better on to whom you're selling. Later on, when your business is established, it helps you with the long-range planning for your business.

Maybe you'd like to start a company that installs electronic security systems in your hometown. You see your customers as being homeowners, small businesses, and local government offices—three separate customer groups requiring three different estimates of market potential. When you start your research, you may find that all of the small businesses already have security systems (so they won't be spending anything), and the government offices subcontract their security to large firms that also handle the alarm systems. But it may turn out that most of the homeowners don't have systems, although they intend on getting them. If that's the case, why waste your time chasing business in the other two groups? You can specialize in the single customer target. And remember, the more you specialize in a particular target group, the more money you are likely to make profit (as long as the group has enough market potential to support you).

Of course, a decision to narrow your focus like this means going back to Section 1 of the business plan and rewriting the concept.

Knowing the market potential helps you plan the long-range strategy for your business. First, having this estimate of the total amount of business going on in your field, in your target area, helps you predict your sales. (You're going to do that soon.)

It also helps with issues like planning for expansion. If the market potential is growing, either you have to grow or your competitors will.

Ask yourself: Is a bigger market potential better? In some cases, a really large market potential means that this particular customer group will attract competitors that are so much larger and better financed than you are that you will not be able to compete. For example, you may want to start a smartphone repair business aimed at consumers in the northwest area of the city. Your research may show that with the growth of smartphone sales, the repair business in your target area alone is worth millions of dollars. But if a national franchise operation like The Source decides to go after smartphone repair right across the country, this will include your "northwest corner of the city," and their advertising power will be difficult to overcome.

So you may decide to go after a different target: maybe working on contract, repairing company-owned smartphones for manufacturers in your area. Of course, this means going back and rewriting the concept for your business plan.

Marketing Research Methods

As noted in the chapter introduction, finding out the market potential is a type of marketing research. However, marketing research can include a lot of other things. Finding out the annual incomes of your customers, finding out who in the family does the shopping, finding out whether your customers prefer blue packages or red packages—all of these

? Get Help 2.9
If you are having trouble expressing market potential for your kind of business, language might be an issue. In this case, take your textbook and section one of your business plan to a language instructor or language remediation centre for help.

? Get Help 2.10
Trade journals sometimes do research into how many customers it takes to support their particular kinds of businesses. For example, you may find data on how many consumers it takes to support a single dental office or funeral home or decorating business. (An index or journal search engine will cut down on your work.)

✅ **Memory Check 2.7**
True or False? A separate estimate of market potential is required for each different customer group a business is targeting.

❓ **Get Help 2.11**
For Statistics Canada publications, check a major library. You can get an idea of what is available from the StatCan website: www.statcan.gc.ca.

things are forms of marketing research and all of them might be nice to know. But new business owners can rarely afford to spend money, time, or energy on things that are simply "nice to know."

For a new business, the marketing research priorities are to find out how much business is out there (market potential) and how much of that your company is expected to get (sales forecast).

Beware of marketing research consultants who want to do an expensive survey for you that will be all packaged up in a glossy report but gives you only the "nice-to-knows." If you are going to pay anyone to help with marketing research, make sure that they explain what they are charging for and how it helps estimate your market potential as well as your sales forecast.

Ask yourself: How much time and effort should I put into estimating market potential? If you are borrowing money to start your business, the amount of market potential data required by the lender will depend on how much you want to borrow. If it is a small, government-guaranteed loan, the requirements will be modest: merely some evidence that there is an opportunity to make money—information you could gather yourself using a library, a telephone, and the internet.

The greater the loan, however, the greater the amount of market data that will be required by the lender. Really substantial loans are more likely to be approved if they are supported by professional research completed by a third party—and that gets expensive.

Be realistic! There is no point in spending $20 000 on a feasibility study for a business that will cost $10 000 to start. Better just to risk the $10 000 and see if the business works. Trying out the business is itself the feasibility study: If the business fails, it likely wasn't feasible. On the other hand, if you risk your life savings to go into business, it would be reasonable to spend at least a few days analyzing the market potential. And there are lots of ways to go about this on your own. *Ask yourself: How can I go about estimating market potential?*

Information Sources

trade journal A periodical publication about a specific industry or profession

secondary research Using information that has already been gathered and published.

primary research Gathering new information from original sources.

In any kind of research, it is always easier and cheaper to use information that has already been gathered by others; the kind of information you find in government publications, magazines, **trade journals**, business directories, and so on. Much of this information is available online and at no charge. This is called **secondary research**: information that has already been published. **Primary research** is actually having to measure things yourself, which means it's new information from original sources. This is much more expensive and time-consuming, so always go to the "secondary" sources first—and be prepared to spend some time in a library and on the web.

Government Statistics Many government ministries, departments, and agencies (federal, provincial, and municipal) publish information about the production and purchase of all kinds of goods and services by consumers, businesses, governments, and other organizations.

In Canada, the best place to start is usually with Statistics Canada, even if your target customers are not all across the country. Much of the StatCan info is broken down into relatively small geographic areas. In addition to broad census information, StatCan also publishes data on manufacturing and specialized pamphlets with statistics on a variety of industries. It collects financial data on more than 600 categories of small business, which can be accessed through the Industry Canada SME Benchmarking tool at www.ic.gc.ca/eic/site/pp-pp.nsf/eng/Home.

Federal and provincial government ministries publish data on industries and organizations important to the ministry. For example, ministries of agriculture will have extensive information on the operation of dairy farms, and ministries of education will have lots of information on how school boards spend their money.

Municipal governments will also publish information about the population and industries in their communities. For example, your city hall will likely have data on the number and types of manufacturers in the city as well as the number and types of people these industries employ.

Business Publications A huge variety of business directories are published, ranging from the phone company Yellow Pages to detailed corporate directories giving financial and employee details of particular companies. Many publications go out and do primary marketing research on consumer and business expenditures and provide the information in the form of journals and handbooks. For example, *Sales and Marketing Management* magazine and the *National Post*'s *Financial Post* both produce handbooks on consumer buying behaviour.

Trade Associations and Journals Most municipalities have active chambers of commerce, merchant associations, boards of trade, or industrial associations. Their main purpose is to benefit members by encouraging business and economic growth in their communities. For example, if you are thinking of opening a fast-food restaurant in a tourist town, the local chamber of commerce may well have detailed information on how much both tourists and locals spend on fast food (i.e., the market potential), broken down by food category and time of year.

Many industries have associations set up to provide information and services to their member companies. These associations often research the market potential for particular segments that their industries service, and publish the information in the industry's trade journals. Trade journals are magazines written for people involved in specific industries; for example, commercial fishing publications or professional teachers' magazines. The reference section of your library will likely have a directory of associations and an index of periodicals. Most associations have websites, and many trade journals can also be accessed via the internet.

When All Else Fails, Go and Ask (Primary Research) Gathering new information on your own (primary data) is expensive and time-consuming but at times necessary. This usually means administering some kind of questionnaire by face-to-face interview, telephone, email, or mail-in response. Most of us can do the labour associated with this kind of research but may need professional help in two areas: questionnaire design and sample selection.

Ask yourself: How do you get people to tell you how much they (or their companies) spend on a product or service? Wording the questions properly can be tricky. If you can't afford to hire an expert, at the very least, have your questionnaire looked over by as many volunteers as possible. Tips for designing your own questionnaire include:

- *Prepare an introduction.* This can help get the co-operation of the interviewee, especially by promising to keep it short.
- *Keep it short.* These days, many people suffer from survey fatigue, so ask only for the information you most need.
- *Order questions.* Put those questions that interviewees may be reluctant to answer (e.g., questions about income) at the end. Interviewees are more likely to answer them after they have already given information about themselves.
- *Pre-test your questionnaire.* Respondents don't always understand the questions or respond the way you expect. Pre-testing gives you the chance to refine your questions, making them more effective.

Let's say you're thinking of starting a window-washing company that will target retailers in the small city where you live. You will want to find out the market potential for this kind of business, so the question you must answer is: "How much do all of the retailers in my city spend annually on having their windows washed?" It will likely be easy to find out the

Get Help 2.13
For a broad range of government information, start with the Canada Business Network website at www.canadabusiness.ca.

Memory Check 2.8
True or False? You need to know the market potential for planning long-range strategy.

Get Help 2.14
There are thousands of publications with market data, so you may wish to start with a directory of business publications; for example, *Where to Find Business Information*, published by John Wiley & Sons Inc.

Get Help 2.15
The website for the Canadian Chamber of Commerce, www.chamber.ca, offers a directory of its many local organizations.

Memory Check 2.9
True or False? Trade journals are primarily magazines where different kinds of businesses can swap their goods and services with one another.

? Get Help 2.16

Find a professor or senior student of marketing to advise you on questionnaire design and the validity of your sample.

? Get Help 2.17

Creative Research Systems is a U.S. company that provides research software. Its website, www.surveysystem.com/sscalc.htm, offers a free Sample Size Calculator and indicators of how much confidence you can have in your sample.

☑ Memory Check 2.10

True or False? Secondary research usually requires the use of questionnaires and samples of the market.

number of retail stores in the city from secondary sources: City Hall or maybe the Chamber of Commerce. Now you will need to find the average amount that they spend on getting their windows washed, which is unlikely to be available from secondary sources. The questionnaire in Figure 2.1, however, could get you the information you need to estimate the average expenditure of those businesses surveyed. You could then multiply that average by the number of retailers in the city to get a reasonable estimate of how much the whole target market spends on the service—in other words, your market potential.

But *ask yourself: How many businesses would I have to survey for my conclusions about the market to be valid?*

You don't have to survey every member of a market to get an idea about its potential. Obviously, the bigger your sample, the more valid your conclusions about the whole market will be. However, for some populations, surveying only a tiny fraction can yield precise results. Think of the polling that goes on before an election, where there may be millions of potential voters. But sampling only a few hundred people, pollsters may predict the election outcome claiming 95 percent accuracy 19 times out of 20. A professional researcher can generate statistics about the probability of your conclusions being accurate. The calculations involved in this are logical and interesting for many people, but can be daunting for math phobics.

Even if you're working on your own and have no research background, you can still try to make sure that the sample you survey is somehow representative of the entire market. For example, you could ensure that you interview potential customers from all geographic

Figure 2.1 Telephone Questionnaire: Window Cleaning Expenditures

Does your store hire someone to clean the windows?
yes ❑
no ❑

_____

If **Yes:**

Does your service clean:
interior ❑
exterior ❑
both ❑

How often do you get the windows cleaned:
annually ❑
monthly ❑
other _____

Approximately how much do you spend for each cleaning?
$ _____

_____

If **No:**

Who cleans the windows?
Owner ❑
Employee ❑
Landlord ❑

Why do you use this approach?
Cost-saving ❑
Habit/tradition ❑
Bad experience with previous services ❑
Unaware of available services ❑
Other _____

_____

portions of your market. Or you could demonstrate that your interview sample is similar to your entire market on some dimension you have found in secondary sources: the same average number of employees, the same average house size, the same average age, and so on. Also, if you have some understanding of **inferential statistics**, there are now several websites that can help you with your formulae, perform the necessary calculations, and give you an idea of how many subjects you need to interview to get reliable data.

Applying the Data It is easy to gather "facts" from secondary sources or even interviews and questionnaires, but the trick is to look for information that will be relevant to calculating the market potential.

Much of the secondary data for market potential is for large regional and national areas, but new small businesses tend to specialize in small target areas. So some form of extrapolation (making a prediction based on known facts) is usually involved in calculating the market potential.

For example, you may be starting a community newspaper in a town that doesn't have a paper of its own. You may be able to find out the total value of community newspaper sales for the entire country, but the market potential you are interested in is only for the one town. Well, you can easily figure out the population of the whole town and calculate it as a percentage of the whole country's population. Then, multiply that same percentage by the national market potential and it will give you some estimate of the market potential in the town.

In the business plan, you must be able to explain the logic behind any inferences you may make about the market potential, so always try to have someone knowledgeable check over your work. Be sure to look at the example business plan found at the end of Chapter 12 and see how market potential was estimated.

inferential statistics Using data and logical assumptions to draw conclusions about markets or populations.

?️ **Get Help 2.18**
Ask a reference librarian to help you find business or corporate directories and relevant corporate annual reports.

WHO IS MY COMPETITION?

Your business will have competitors—even if you are offering some kind of brand-new service that no one has ever offered before. If your service makes lots of money, you will quickly have lots of competition. Competitors fit into two broad categories: direct and indirect.

Direct Competition

Direct competitors are firms similar to your own in terms of size, location, and the services they offer, and they pursue the same groups of customers that you are trying to get. If you have an auto-glass replacement shop, your direct competitors are the other auto-glass shops in your area. If you sell water-softening systems to homes in the western suburbs, your direct competitors are other small firms that sell water-softening systems in the same area.

Let's say you have a background in public relations and decide to start a conference management business to service major business associations in your city. Most of these associations sponsor an annual conference, and you will contract for the design, promotion, and logistics of these meetings. You would easily be able to identify a number of established small conference management firms that rely precisely on this type of business. These companies would make up your **direct competition**—businesses similar to your own that provide products or services similar to yours and that pursue the same potential customers you are pursuing.

direct competition Businesses similar to your own that provide products or services similar to yours and that pursue the same potential customers you are pursuing.

Indirect Competition

Continuing with our example above, keep in mind that associations are not obligated to use conference management firms to handle their annual meetings. Some of them will turn to large consulting firms, which—although it is not their primary business—will handle conference management, especially for established clients. Other associations will turn to local colleges or universities that handle this kind of business as a sideline to education and are interested in renting out their own facilities for such meetings. Both of these suppliers would form **indirect competition**: companies that are not like your business but that are an alternative way for your potential customers to satisfy their needs.

Indirect competitors are not primarily in the same business as your firm but are a source of supply for your customers. In some cases, customers themselves can be a form of indirect competition. In the conference example, some associations would choose to manage their conferences entirely with their own permanent staff. *Ask yourself: Where else will my customers be able to get the products or services I offer?*

It is important to note that the concept of direct and indirect competitors involves a judgment call and does not represent precise categories. The concept is very useful for helping to focus marketing strategies, but it can involve grey areas. For example, imagine you have a take-out pizza service, but right across the street is a full-menu Italian restaurant that has seating for eat-in customers and it also has a busy take-out counter for pizzas. *Ask yourself: Is this direct or indirect competition?*

✅ Memory Check 2.11
True or False? The majority of people going into business for themselves will require some kind of help in estimating market potential.

✅ Memory Check 2.12
True or False? Your customers themselves may be a form of indirect competition.

Assessing Competitors

In your business plan you must demonstrate that you have at least identified your competitors and, ideally, that you know their sales volume and their strengths and weaknesses. Typically, this information will come from:

- *Experience.* You may have worked for one or more of your competitors or have extensive knowledge about the industry.
- *Primary research.* You may try to interview those who are knowledgeable about the competition, including employees, customers, or suppliers. You may even just observe your competitors (perhaps by unobtrusively hanging around the cash register, trying to keep track of sales).
- *Secondary research.* Published information about individual small businesses is rare; when it does exist, it is most likely to be found in business directories. Your indirect competition might consist of public corporations. These firms produce annual reports, often outlining the volume and sources of their business.

✅ Memory Check 2.13
True or False? The concept of "direct" and "indirect" competition is precise and measurable.

❓ Get Help 2.19
The SME Benchmarking Tool, at www.ic.gc.ca/eic/site/pp-pp.nsf/eng/Home, is Industry Canada's small-business database of financial ratios.

It can be important to note in the business plan any weaknesses you can identify in your future competition, but it is also important not to rely on these weaknesses because they cannot be considered permanent. As soon as you open up and start to take some of their business, competitors can be expected to clean up their act to defend themselves against you.

⭐ Head Start Exercise

2.4 Make a list of your direct and indirect competitors, noting the strengths and weaknesses of each. List sources where you think you may be able to find information about the sales of these competitors (3/4 page maximum).

HOW MUCH BUSINESS WILL MY FIRM GET?

Ask yourself: How much business will my firm get? The answer to this question is your **sales forecast**, a critical component of the business plan. This will show how much money you can reasonably expect your business to generate each year.

The forecast is necessary because so many of your business decisions will be based on how much money is coming in. Other parts of the business plan will determine your costs

sales forecast An estimate of how much money a business will bring in over a given period. Typically, a business plan includes at least three years of annual sales forecasts.

and expenses (the money going out); the difference between these (money in and money out) over the long term will show whether you can make profit. For established companies, sales forecasting is fairly reliable because it is primarily based on their own past sales. But a brand-new business has no past sales. Despite this, sales forecasting must be undertaken, not only for the sake of your own planning, but also to satisfy the requirements of potential lenders or investors. Most business plans will show sales forecasts for a period of at least three years, even though the longer the forecast is, the less accurate it will be. However, the forecasts will be revised once the business is in operation and actual sales data become available.

Ask yourself: What will I base the sales forecast on? Your sales forecast should come from a variety of different sources that will be used to generate several different estimates of the sales you can expect. These different dollar values can be shown as a range of possible sales. For the purposes of your business plan, however, you will still have to identify a single working forecast from the more conservative end of the range. The process of developing your sales forecast will be closely associated with the work to determine market potential and should follow the same principle of using secondary sources first.

In general, the more sources of information you use in preparing your sales forecast, the more accurate your forecast will be.[5] In addition, many sources will give you ideas for developing your own logical techniques to predict your sales. Nevertheless, it would be unlikely that you could use all of the following sources:

- industry statistics
- customer buying intentions
- how long it takes to get new customers
- expert opinion
- how much business the competition gets
- all the business out there
- the amount of business the firm can handle

Industry Statistics

Much of the same library information on specific industries that is used to determine market potential can be used to look at **correlations of sales** within that industry. For example, you may find information showing how many dollars in sales travel agencies produce in total and also how many people are employed in travel agencies in total. This gives you the correlation of how many dollars, on average, are produced per person working in travel agencies. If you were starting a small travel agency and you expect to employ three people (including yourself), you could multiply the industry average dollars per person by your three people as one measure of what you can expect your agency to sell. Also, industry averages of sales to assets can be multiplied by the value of all the things you need to start your business (your business assets). For example, industry averages of sales per square foot of retail space can be multiplied by the size of your prospective store.

correlations of sales Known facts about an industry that can be expressed as a ratio of the industry's sales.

☑ **Memory Check 2.14**
True or False? A direct competitor is anyone selling the same thing that you sell.

Customer Buying Intentions

If you are already doing a questionnaire for market potential, you might as well also find out about intentions to buy. This basically means asking a sample of potential customers whether they would buy if you were to offer them your services at a particular price. Simply multiply the results from your sample by the number of potential customers in your entire segment. Keep in mind that some of your respondents could be lying in their answers, so get help in phrasing your questions to minimize this problem.

☑ **Memory Check 2.15**
True or False? A business plan will usually show sales forecasts for a period of at least three years.

No Research, No Competition, No Problem

Yuxiang Wang is a Doctor of Traditional Chinese Medicine (TCM). After studying and gaining certification in China, Yuxiang practised for 13 years before moving to Canada. She worked in TCM clinics in Toronto's Asian communities for another six years. Finally, she was able to open her own business, as a sole practitioner, in 2005, in a rather surprising location.

Traditional Chinese Medicine differs from Western medicine (which is also practised in China) in that TCM is as much about philosophy as it is about science. TCM is concerned with maintaining balances within the body, equating good health with a harmonious balance among various competing physical and spiritual forces. In this way, it is focused on preventive medicine, rather than dealing with advanced disease processes. This form of medicine has evolved over 2000 years. In Canada, there is some controversy around TCM and other *alternative* or *complementary* forms of medicine in that the treatments are generally not supported by the kind of scientific evidence required for Western medical practices. The main treatment techniques offered by Yuxiang include

- Acupuncture—which is gaining broader acceptance in the West
- Herbal remedies—Yuxiang's store contains hundreds of containers of dried herbs, roots, and other preparations
- Tuina massage—a particular form of massage that concentrates on specific pain sites and acupressure points.

The City of Toronto has several large concentrations of Asian immigrant and Asian-descent populations, and most of the city's TCM clinics are found in these areas. Had Yuxiang located in one of these pockets, she would be facing lots of direct competition. But this is not the case for Herb Fragrance Oriental Healing Centre. Rather, it is located in the Lakeshore West area, only blocks from the Polish consulate in a neighbourhood dominated by Polish and other Eastern European immigrant populations. The choice, Yuxiang admits, was largely one of lifestyle, as the site is only a few minutes' walk from her home.

No formal research was done prior to start-up, but Yuxiang was banking on the growing acceptance of TCM in European and Canadian populations. This would mean a growing market potential, but what that represented in dollars was unknown. The lack of competition and the high volume of pedestrian and auto traffic were also factors in the choice of the site. For indirect competition, there are several drugstores, pharmacies, and a health food store in the area.

So far, the gamble seems to be paying off. Most of Yuxiang's income comes from referrals (existing patients, other health care professionals) and former patients who travel some distance. Nevertheless, a growing portion of Yuxiang's business comes from walk-in clients.

Despite the risk of the location, Yuxiang's approach to her start-up was extremely cautious, with her main concerns being controlling costs (her husband provided the labour for the leasehold improvements) and securing comprehensive insurance.

How Long It Takes to Get New Customers

If you are starting a business where you will have to go out and sell your service, at first you will spend more time acquiring new customers than you will spend servicing existing customers. (As the business matures, this ratio will change.) But if you know how many hours of selling or how many calls it takes to generate a single new customer, you can estimate your sales based on your selling hours available. Depending on your experience in the industry, you may already have a reasonable estimate of how many hours of calling on customers it takes to produce each sale. Alternatively, you may want to find this out by starting your business on a very small scale and selling your service to a limited number of customers. This is actually the process of **test marketing**. For a new business, of course, this can be done only in fields that do not require major investment for materials, site, or equipment.

test marketing Trying to sell your product or service to a limited number of customers and carefully measuring factors like customer feedback and how long it takes to make a sale.

2.5 If you will be making sales calls, estimate, based on your experience, how many hours of your work it will take to get a new customer. If you lack experience, make a list of sources where you might get this information (1/4 page maximum).

The question of how long it takes to get new customers also concerns the growth of your business, and will be used to modify your other estimates of sales. This is because most of the other estimates assume that your business will be operating at full speed, like an established firm. But it takes more work to get a new customer than to serve an existing one—and at the beginning all your customers will be new. This factor must be considered (and discussed in your business plan) when estimating your sales.

Expert Opinion

This method means interviewing several people who have expertise in your particular industry. These experts could include retirees, former employers, competitors, teachers, or people in the same business as you but in geographic areas away from your market area. In its simplest form, this method means first telling each expert about your business, then asking how much business (in dollars) they think you will be able to achieve. You are really just asking for their "best guess" given their limited knowledge of your business. The idea is to then average these expert guesses as an estimate of your forecast. You may find that the more expertise your experts have, the more reluctant they will be to give you a particular sales number. If this is the case, ask them for a reasonable range. Then, for your calculations, just pick the midpoint in the range. If you can get their "best guess" in writing, be sure to quote them in the business plan. Don't forget to include your own expert opinion (provided that you have sufficient knowledge and experience in the field).

⭐ Head Start Exercise

2.6 Make up a list of individuals whom you consider to have the best expertise available in the kind of business you plan on opening (1/4 page maximum).

How Much Business the Competition Gets

This is another form of correlation analysis—it's like looking at the industry statistics, but instead you are looking at individual direct competitors: businesses similar to your own that are going after the same kinds of customers. The idea is to estimate the sales of a specific competitor (by observation, interview, personal experience, or, in some cases, published financial information) and compare this to some other factor about the firm, such as traffic volume, amount of advertising, number of salespeople, and so on.

For example, you might be opening a translation service for a particular group of new immigrants in your city. You estimate the sales of your existing competitor (you had a summer job with them) at $400 000. You also know that they run daily ads in the business personals column of the ethnic newspaper and that all of their new business comes from that source. You decide you also will run a daily ad in the same column. Obviously, that does not mean you will have sales of $400 000—you will be splitting the market with the competitor, and some of their sales comes from repeat business, which you won't have at first—but it is another indicator of how much business you can do.

All the Business Out There

The market potential—all the business in your market area—can itself provide an estimate of sales when the competition is taken into consideration. For example, if you and three competitors are chasing the same business, with a market potential of $400 000, you might expect that each competitor (yourself included) would be entitled to a share of one-fourth, or a sales forecast of $100 000. The newer the product/service and the newer the market, the more valid this kind of estimate will be. In other words, if all the competitors are just starting up, like you, then this is a legitimate estimate. However, if you are competing against firms that have been around for 20 years, it won't mean much.

The Amount of Business the Firm Can Handle

Let's say you want to start a business maintaining swimming pools for condominium buildings in the east end of the city. You know it will take you half a day, once a week for each pool, to keep them fully maintained. That means that the highest number of pools you could service (assuming you were to work six days a week) would be 12. If your average year-long maintenance contract was priced at about $6000, the highest possible sales forecast you could have would be $12 \times \$6000 = \$72\,000$.

It would be extremely unusual for a brand-new business to be operating at 100 percent capacity right from the start, but it is possible in a market where demand far exceeds supply. Nevertheless, this number—the most business you could handle (100 percent of your capacity)—helps keep other estimates of your sales forecast in perspective. Furthermore, for some industries like hotels, manufacturers, and restaurants, the average operating level (what percentage of capacity) can be found by digging through the industry statistics.

Level of Detail

The sample business plan at the end of Chapter 12 shows estimates for market potential as well as a sales forecast for a fast-food business. Figure 2.2 is an example of a professionally written sales forecast from a business plan for a machine shop. Note how it uses multiple methods to produce conservative estimates and gives the source for each. *Ask yourself: Will I really need to prepare a sales forecast that is this detailed?*

Whether your sales forecast has to be as detailed as the one shown in Figure 2.2 depends on how much risk you are taking. If you plan on borrowing $50 000 to start your business, the answer is a clear yes. If you want to risk $300 on a part-time venture, the answer is "forget it—too much work." But even then, you will need some kind of indicators of how much money will come into your business; otherwise, you can't do any kind of financial planning.

Memory Check 2.19
True or False? 100 percent of your business capacity is the upper limit of your sales forecast.

You may not yet know some of the information involved in preparing the sales forecast—exactly how many people will be working in the business, how many dollars in assets the business will have, how many square feet of space your business will use, and so on. Nevertheless, this does not let you get out of forecasting. You can and must prepare some type of sales forecast at this point, even without all the available information. But don't panic! Right now, your sales forecast is only a draft. So, for information you can't yet know, or decisions you haven't yet made, just use your best guess. When you get to the end of the business plan and have all the missing information, you can come back and redo the sales forecast—maybe several times—because writing a business plan is really rewriting a business plan. (You already know that!)

A word of caution: Throughout this text you are advised to "Get Help" from a variety of professors, as well as from textbooks written by professors. But ask any professor for advice on a particular business decision and the answer is usually a variation on "you need more information before the decision can be made." This is because academics tend to think in terms of perfect data, which can lead to perfect decisions. But real-life entrepreneurs don't work with perfect data. Entrepreneurs must strike a balance between reducing risk and the cost of getting more information. You are trying to get reasonable indicators of

Figure 2.2 Sales Forecast | Machine Shop

1.	Personal first year estimate of contracted sales agent	= $	420 000
2.	Average annual sales per machine shop production employee ($192,871)[1] × 3 production employees in this company	=	578 613
3.	Average annual sales per machine shop employee (all types) ($152,863)[2] × 4 employees in total for this business	=	611 452
4.	Average personal estimate of shop owner, shop machinist, and two retired machinists	=	586 000
5.	Average machine shop sales per dollar of equity ($3.10)[3] × estimated value of owners' equity for this company ($141,998)	=	440 194
6.	Estimate of 100 percent capacity, if all machines were running full-time, ($988,000)[4] × average industry operating level of 80 percent	=	788 400
7.	Market potential (as previously defined)	=	$26 000 000

Method 1 is disproportionately low since it represents the estimate of the sales agent who has offered to work only half-time (on a straight commission of 10 percent) and promises to provide contracts at least in this $420 000 range in the first year. However, the owner would also be selling part-time and his contribution is not included here. Method 2 does not include the part-time production contribution of the owner. Method 3 does not include the part-time sales agent. Method 6 is included only to demonstrate the sales of the business operating at industry capacity levels, and Method 7 shows the entire value of the market. Leaving these last two out of the calculation, the mean average forecast is $527 000.

However, we will use an even more conservative forecast of $450,000 for the second year and allow for a 10 percent increase for the third year. Allowing a full six months to build up to the second-year sales rate, starting from zero sales, would mean a first-year forecast of ($450 000 × 75%) = $338 000, which is still below the sales agent's personal guarantee.

SALES FORECAST

Year 1	$338 000
Year 2	$450 000
Year 3	$496 000

1. Statistics Canada, Principal Statistics for Manufacturing Industries by North American Industry Classification System (NAICS # 33271), From Annual Survey of Manufactures and Logging—2103, 2007.
2. Ibid.
3. Industry Canada/Statistics Canada, Small Business Profiles, Machine Shops (NAICS #3327) 2006.
4. Assumes 50 production hours per week and shop contracts of $380 per hour.

how much business is out there and how much business you can get. You need just enough information to satisfy yourself and your lenders or investors—even though in some cases this will not be enough for the academics.

⭐ Head Start Exercise

2.7 Quickly go back over the sources of information for the sales forecast in Figure 2.2 and note which ones will likely help you in predicting your sales. Think of some other methods you could use. Briefly outline how you will go about preparing your sales forecast (1/3 page maximum).

HOW CAN I PROTECT THE BUSINESS?

As you well know by now, all entrepreneurs are taking a risk. At the very least, when working for yourself, you risk your time and effort. But when you or your business owns assets, these also are at risk from a variety of dangers, which you would like to be protected against. There is no such thing, however, as 100 percent protection against risk. The trick is to understand the risk and then try to reduce it in an economical way. Reducing risk, of course, is also an important issue for lenders or investors who wish to clearly see in the business plan how their capital will be protected.

Small Business Insurance

According to the Canadian Federation of Independent Business, the vast majority of small business owners worry about the high cost of insurance.[6] New entrepreneurs often try to avoid insurance as an unnecessary expense. But as soon as your business or you personally have any significant assets, you must consider the protection of insurance.

? Get Help 2.21
Search the internet using the keywords "small business insurance" to find brokers who will provide quotes online for the coverage and type of insurance you want.

It's possible to get just about any kind of insurance imaginable—at a price. But the types you choose will depend on the nature of your business. For example, as a literary agent you would likely want errors and omissions insurance to protect against the possibility of a problematic contract. As a workplace massage therapist for computer users, you would want malpractice insurance in case a client becomes injured. As a bookstore owner, you would be particularly concerned about fire insurance.

If you started an engineering firm to monitor office air quality, your people would constantly be going in and out of other people's businesses. In such a case, you would use a fidelity bond to protect customers against any illegal actions of someone you might hire. If you were in the office renovation business, you might use surety or performance bonds to protect your customers in case you were unable to complete the work within the contracted time.

As an entertainer with your own band, you would consider disability insurance in case you were to get severe arthritis, leaving you unable to play your instrument. You might also have life insurance on other members of the band, acting as each other's beneficiaries (this is often done among business partners).

Almost everyone in business these days needs automobile insurance. This should include enough vehicle liability coverage to make it unnecessary for anyone to sue the business over and above any insurance settlement. In addition, general liability coverage is common (in case someone gets hurt at your place of business, or you are responsible for some form of injury or loss). And, for those working from home, many insurance companies offer home office packages that are in addition to regular house/apartment insurance. *Ask yourself: What will my insurance priorities be?*

Business Owner Policy (BOP) A package of insurance policies specific to the needs of a particular kind of small firm.

Many insurance companies offer packages of insurance for small business, often called **Business Owner Policies (BOP)**, that cover the most common risks for specific kinds of small firms. For example, there might one BOP for electrical contractors that would include coverage for the contractor's tools and equipment in transit, while another BOP for food shops would cover food spoilage from refrigeration breakdown. Figure 2.3 provides an example BOP for a hair salon.

insurance broker An independent intermediary who sells insurance policies on behalf of a variety of large insurance companies.

Insurance is usually purchased through a broker. The independent **insurance broker** represents a variety of large insurance companies that the broker can "shop" on your behalf for the policy that best suits your needs and budget. *Ask yourself: What's the best way to get a good insurance broker?*

There is always search engines, which make it easy to find someone in your neighbourhood—but do you really know the kind of person you'll be dealing with? Business texts often recommend finding an insurance provider by referral from someone you trust: a friend, lawyer, accountant—although it isn't always comfortable if you have to go back and tell your friend that you decided against his or her insurance broker.

Figure 2.3 BOP for Hair Salon or Spa

Insurance Type	Description	Example Risk
General Liability	Covers against injury or property damage that others may have suffered on your premises or from something they bought from you.	Someone trips on a doormat in your salon and has to be hospitalized for their injuries, suing you for their loss of income.
Professional Liability	Also known as errors and omissions insurance or malpractice insurance, protects you against a claim that you did not act in a competent professional manner, which resulted in loss to a client.	You accidentally nick a client with your scissors and the cut becomes infected, leaving the client with a permanent scar. The client sues.
Business Property	Covers the building and its structure as well as inventory and other property.	A portion of your building's roof falls in, damaging the interior of the salon.
Sewer and Drain	Covers loss of business and personal property caused by drain back-up.	The drains in the salon's basement back up, destroying all the hair products stored there and leaving a horrible smell in the rest of the salon.
Computer and Data	Protects computers used in the business and their data.	A virus invades your computer and wipes out all of your client and appointment information.
Signs	Covers damage or loss of signs attached to the building.	A violent windstorm blows the sign off your building, breaking the front window.
Utility Interruption	Covers loss from failure of gas, electric, water, or communications services.	A break in the gas supply turns of your furnace, causing the water pipes to freeze and burst during a cold night, then to flood the salon the following warmer day.
Business Interruption	Provides income in case the business has to be closed because of any insured issue.	Any or all of the above events occur, causing your salon to be closed for days or weeks.

However you find one, the main thing to remember about insurance brokers is that they are primarily "suppliers" as opposed to "advisers." Even the best-intentioned, most ethical brokers cannot be objective about the amount of coverage you need, since they are paid by commission—the more insurance you buy, the more they get paid. You have to decide for yourself, based on your experience and research, how much insurance to buy.

Once you've made that decision, you can be sure to get a good price by shopping around. Many insurance websites provide online quotes. If you are in a business with unusual or particularly high risks or you just need independent professional advice about insurance, you can hire a **risk management consultant**. These are professional advisers on risk and insurance requirements who neither sell insurance themselves nor are they associated with insurance providers. Licensing or registration requirements for risk management consultants vary from province to province.

risk management consultant
An independent (usually licensed) adviser on property and casualty insurance risks and coverages.

Security and Loss Prevention

You can lose your assets not just by being sued—assets are also at risk from those who would wish to steal them. No one likes to get ripped off, and good entrepreneurs plan to reduce risk from the more obvious methods of theft:

- **Pilfering**: Pilfering is the theft of small amounts of materials, usually by employees, suppliers, or transport people. It is a bigger problem in retail and wholesale businesses, but even in small offices, office supplies can disappear at an alarming rate. The primary defences against pilfering are tight inventory control (perhaps by having employees sign for supplies) and employee training (awareness of the costs and consequences of pilfering).[7]

pilfering Theft of small quantities committed by employees.

shoplifting Retail theft by stealth, committed while the store is open for business.

embezzlement Theft by a person entrusted with handling a company's cash or other assets.

burglary Theft by breaking into a business at a time when it is closed.

robbery Theft by force or threat of violence.

fraud Theft by deceit or trickery.

☑ **Memory Check 2.20**
True or False? Pilfering is committed by employees.

☑ **Memory Check 2.21**
True or False? Insurance brokers are the best advisors to assess your insurance needs.

■ **Shoplifting:** If you plan on having a retail store that sells anything smaller than refrigerators, plan on encountering those who will try to walk off with inventory. The greatest number of perpetrators are juveniles,[8] but the hardest to protect against are the professionals. The more economical defences against shoplifting include a highly visible store layout, trained employees (who know what to watch for and how to respond), mirrors, and even security cameras (which have dropped in price over the past few years).

■ **Embezzlement:** Embezzlement is when someone entrusted with your (or your company's) money puts that money to their own use. Embezzlers can be professional service providers such as lawyers or accountants, or employees such as bookkeepers or cashiers. Protections against embezzlement include using only bonded or insured professionals and implementing strict cash handling and auditing procedures.

■ **Burglary:** Burglary is when your place of business is broken into either by vandals or by professional thieves. Defences against burglary start with a good set of locks and can include alarm systems, window bars, or security services. Obviously, the level of burglary protection will vary widely from the simple "no valuables" office to the high-end jewellery store.

■ **Robbery:** Certain types of businesses are much more prone to robbery (all-night gas stations and convenience stores, retail jewellers, businesses with lots of cash on hand). Visibility, security cameras, "no-cash" signs, and a non-confrontational plan for dealing with would-be robbers are your best bets.

■ **Fraud:** You are more likely to be defrauded when participating in something slightly shady or high-risk, with the apparent potential to win big. For example, you might be offered twice your usual rate for a very large contract or order, but on the condition that you give extended payment terms. When it sounds this tempting, be suspicious: Go by the book, get it in writing, check up on customers and suppliers. These are your major defences against fraud.

Related to loss prevention is the problem that many new businesses face when they extend credit terms to their customers. Some customers don't pay on time and some customers just don't pay. This can be devastating for a new company, tight on cash and dependent on money coming in from customers who have already received goods or services. (See Chapter 5 for a complete discussion on how a small firm can protect itself from problems with collections.)

⭐ Head Start Exercise

2.8 Write down the type of theft that would be most likely to affect you or your business. Identify the ways you will protect against this. List any start-up or ongoing expenses involved (1/3 page maximum).

Intellectual Property

Intellectual property laws are designed to protect your work in areas of the arts, communication, design, or applied research, but the actual enforcement of these laws is left to you. If someone steals your work in these areas, you have to take them to court and prove that the work was yours. Registering your work with the appropriate government office is the best—and, in some cases, only—acceptable proof. Digital technologies have certainly created some problems for protecting intellectual property. Photographs from social media sites, anecdotes from blogs, videos, and music are frequently copied illegally. It is a tradition of the internet that as fast as new technological protection measures can be created, someone finds a way to get around them. Currently, the government is under pressure to strengthen intellectual property laws and provide severe penalties for overcoming these technological protection measures.[9]

You can protect yourself only in the areas specifically covered by the intellectual property laws: patent, copyright, trademark, industrial design, and microchip design. *Ask yourself: How do these forms of protection differ?* You may have a great idea, but even if you're the one who thought of it first, anyone is entitled to "steal" it from you if it doesn't fit into one of these categories. You can't protect just an idea.

Patent protection is for an **invention**. Let's say you invent a new kind of light bulb that uses salt crystals to produce light. (Hey, it could happen!) This would be a new technology, and if you applied for a Canadian patent you would be granted exclusive rights to your invention for 20 years in Canada only. Later, if you invented a way to use your salt-light as an electronic switch, this would be a new application of your technology and a second patent could be granted. You can use your Canadian patent application to file for patents in over a hundred other countries through the Patent Cooperation Treaty, of which Canada is a member. Protecting foreign patents can be expensive and complex, but you can get help in this area from a **patent agent**.

Copyright protection covers software and works of art including writing, music, and visual arts. The creator of a work (or an employer who contracts the work) automatically owns the copyright. No registration is legally required, but you can register a work for additional protection. It is also a good idea to indicate your ownership of copyright on creative works as a warning to others that they may not possess, use, or copy the material without your permission. (Check the warnings on this text and make sure you don't violate the copyright.) Coverage is worldwide and normally extends for the life of the creator plus an additional 50 years.

A **trademark** protects a word, phrase, or symbol that identifies your company and its products. Trademarks are registered by country, and in Canada provide protection for 15 years, but this protection is renewable indefinitely. Large companies depend heavily on their trademarks (the Coca-Cola name, the Nike "swoosh," the McDonald's Golden Arches) and these companies rigorously enforce against anyone else infringing on them. So be careful not to violate their trademarks or you could find yourself in court—at a great disadvantage against such large firms.

Industrial design protection applies to a pattern, a shape, or an ornamental design of mass-produced manufactured products. Examples would include the shape of a spoon handle or the ornamentation on a table leg. Protection must be applied for and lasts for 10 years, although a renewal fee must be paid at the five-year mark.

Microchip design is the only other kind of intellectual property specifically protected by law. Technically, it's called **"integrated circuit topography" (ICT)** and, unless you're in the business of designing microchips, you don't really need to know about it. If you do need to know, registration of a chip design is done on a country-by-country basis, although Canada now has reciprocal agreements with many other countries (20 at the time of writing). In Canada, protection lasts for 10 years. The designer of the microcircuits or the employer of the designer may apply for this protection.

Check the website of the Canadian Intellectual Property Office (www.cipo.gc.ca) for information on patent, copyright, trademark, industrial design, or ICT. There are other forms of intellectual property not clearly protected by specific laws, such as the details in your business plan or the secret recipes for your restaurant's cocktails. These are called trade secrets and attempts to protect them generally include non-disclosure agreements and reliance on the trust responsibilities of professional advisers, who would see your confidential information. Even though employees have some responsibility to an employer,[10] rights to trade secrets are certainly more difficult to enforce in court than protected forms of intellectual property.

patent Exclusive rights to a useful invention, granted by a government for a specified period of time.

invention A new technology or a new application of an existing technology.

patent agent Someone trained in engineering and law and registered with the federal Commissioner of Patents. Patent agents can assess inventions and assist with the patent application process. Visit the Intellectual Property Institute of Canada website at www.ipic.ca.

copyright Protection against anyone (other than the creator, or someone authorized by the creator) reproducing a creative work such as a drawing, piece of writing, audiovisual production, and so on.

trademark A word, phrase, or visual symbol that identifies the products or services of a company.

industrial design Registered rights to the original, visually aesthetic elements of a manufactured product.

integrated circuit topography (ICT) The design of a microchip, which can be registered for protection of exclusive rights for up to 10 years.

✅ **Memory Check 2.22**
True or False? Burglary and robbery are interchangeable terms.

✅ **Memory Check 2.23**
True or False? Copyright protection is "automatic" in that it does not legally require registration.

A Music Business in the File-Sharing Era

KIMBERLY LEE PHOTOGRAPHY

Marty Bernie was in his second year of a Contemporary Music degree program when he started teaching music. Teaching was not a career path that Marty wished to follow, but it provided a way to get money without being employed in the traditional sense. His experience with jobs had taught Marty that they involved "too little pay for too much time and energy"—time and energy that he needed for his passion: making music. So at the beginning, entrepreneurship for Marty Bernie was just a necessary evil.

During his third year, Marty was teaching a variety of different students at a variety of locations as well as taking sub-contract work from an established music school. It was not particularly profitable and Marty was wasting time and energy travelling between students. At this point, he had decided to specialize in composing and producing music tracks for film and video. He was able to showcase his work by providing free music tracks for student films in the hope that the filmmakers, when they moved on to bigger

budget productions, would hire him to write and produce their music.

In his fourth year, Marty competed for and won a grant from Humber's New Venture Seed Fund that provided him with $8000. He used the money for some electronic equipment and a membership in the Canadian Screen Composer's Guild. This gave Marty some much-needed contacts in the industry. He was promoting the idea that he could prepare soundtracks in a wide variety of genres and at different levels of complexity. A small trickle of money was starting to come in from this work, but not enough to be considered profitable. He was also toying with the idea of gaining experience by becoming an assistant composer to someone established in the industry. This would mean preparing smaller sections of music tracks, working in the style of another composer. But it was at this point when Marty decided to take a more business-like approach to this art.

First, he decided to concentrate on producing his own brand of "electro" music, what Marty calls his "musical obsession." He would create his own tracks and provide his distinctive style of remix for other bands. Next, he focused his teaching on a small target market of young professionals who could afford musical tutoring for their kids and who all lived in the same small geographic area. Finally, Marty decided to promote his brand of music (and generate cash) through DJing at clubs catering to the young, urban target for his music. Marty also realized that his music and his business would need to be protected.

Marty set about trying to learn everything he could about intellectual property. He knew it was a hugely complex area of law, but it is the basis for making money in the music industry. Copyright is the only means of protecting his compositions and recordings, plus it puts limits on his own privileges in using the music of others, for teaching, or for DJing. At the same time, copyright laws are struggling to keep up with the many new technologies for sharing music.

Today, for Marty, entrepreneurship is no longer the "necessary evil." "I see the $25 000 plus that a music degree costs as an investment in my business," he says. Marty's advice to others pursuing a career in the music business is "You always have to be doing two things. One is your musical obsession and one is making money. And you have to give time and energy to both." Sample Marty's musical styles on his website: http://martyberniemusic.com.

Revising Your Plan

Once you have gathered the information and worked through the decisions for Section 2 of your business plan, you may find that you now have to go back and revise some of the decisions you made in Section 1. Figure 2.4 demonstrates how some elements of feasibility may affect your business model.

Figure 2.4 The Business Plan Revision Process

Answers to Memory Check Questions

2.1 F   2.2 T   2.3 F   2.4 F   2.5 T   2.6 T   2.7 T   2.8 T
2.9 F   2.10 F   2.11 T   2.12 T   2.13 F   2.14 F   2.15 T   2.16 F
2.17 T   2.18 F   2.19 T   2.20 T   2.21 F   2.22 F   2.23 F

Questions for Discussion

1. Identify a highly successful consumer retail or service business in your area. What are the advantages of this firm's physical site? What could be improved?
2. Identify a retail site in your area that is empty and available for lease. Was there previously a business there that failed? How might the site have contributed to this failure?
3. What would be an appropriate target market for a home-based hair salon? What features would the home ideally need? What would be an inappropriate target for a home-based information technology consultant? Why?
4. Try to find a commercial lease consultant who provides help to small businesses in dealing with their landlords. Why is there a need for these kinds of firms? How can they help a small business that has an existing lease?
5. What is the danger of being in an industry where the market potential is growing, but your firm is staying the same size?
6. Imagine you are thinking of starting a laptop computer repair service for the students at a local college. How would you define the market potential? If you were going to find this market potential using a questionnaire (primary research), what questions would you ask a sample of students?
7. Identify several popular songs that sound closely alike. Discuss why so many cases of copyright infringement in the music industry end up in court.
8. Why is it that, historically, so many inventors ended up penniless? Who makes money from their inventions? Discuss the fairness of this.
9. Who owns the copyright on pictures you post on Facebook? What does your agreement with Facebook have to say about this?
10. Discuss the idea that insurance is really "betting against your own success." Is insurance an investment?

Case for Discussion

Omar Ramesh made his first lamp in his high school industrial arts class. Then, he started making novelty lamps just for the fun of it. He sold a few to friends, charging just enough to cover his costs of materials. Eventually he was able to make a small profit on custom orders he received through referral.

By the time he was in college, studying Business Management, Omar did not have the time to make his own lamps, so he started buying novelty lamps from Asian manufacturers and selling them at arts and crafts fairs around his hometown of Victoria, BC. His fastest selling items were the newest LED smart lamps, even though they were by far the most expensive (and most profitable) items that Omar carried. These new lamps were just starting to come in a variety of shapes and sizes. All used the newest LED bulbs. Some involved fibre optics and others were programmable. Omar understood that, like other new technologies in the past, the price of these items would start to come down and the variety would increase as would the demand. And so, a little light bulb went on over Omar's head and his idea for a specialized lamp store in downtown Victoria was born.

But would the idea work? Omar knew that the first indicator would be the market potential. In other words, how much money was his target market spending on his type of product?

It only took about five minutes of searching the web for Omar to find a government survey of household spending in BC. This showed that the average household expenditure for lamps and lampshades was only $21 per year. From the Statistics Canada website, Omar found that Victoria had just under 150 000 households, which meant the whole city was spending roughly $3.2 million every year on lamps and lampshades ($21 $\times$ 150 000). Omar had found his market potential.

Now he had to find out how much of that market potential his business could get: his sales forecast. Omar was able to identify eight small, independent lighting stores in the city of Victoria. These would be his direct competition. His indirect competitors, however, would be all of the furniture and department stores that also sold lamps, including giant retailers like Walmart and Canadian Tire. In total, he could find 30 retailers in Victoria that sold lamps. Including his own store, this would mean 31 competitors sharing the $3.2 million, or an average of $103 000 each. This was a disappointing estimate for Omar's sales forecast. It would not be nearly enough sales to cover costs and expenses for the store he envisioned.

There was one small lighting store in downtown Victoria that was similar in size and style to the one Omar pictured for himself. He paid $25 to a commercial credit reporting agency to buy a profile of the company. The report showed that the store had annual sales of $480 000. Omar was delighted, believing it was a more reasonable forecast of what his own store could do. But then again, this was an established store.

Omar felt frustrated. He knew he should try and get a better estimate of the sales for his business, but didn't know what else to do.

1. Numbers aside, does Omar's idea for a lamp store that specializes in LED lamps sound like a good one? Why or why not?

2. Is Omar's estimate of market potential valid? What would be the difficulty if he wanted to find out the expenditures on LED lamps only?

3. Discuss Omar's attempts at estimating his future sales. How accurate are they likely to be?

4. What other methods could Omar use to get an estimate of his future sales? Spend five minutes on the web and see what relevant data you can come up with.

5. What other issues should Omar consider in deciding whether to move ahead with his business idea?

6. If Omar decides to continue developing his business idea, what are the next steps he should take?

The Business Plan, Section 2:
FEASIBILITY

Location Analysis

1. Explain the general area where your business will be located, describing the surrounding population of potential customers (provide numbers).

2. Describe any other factors in your choice of location, such as your proximity to transportation, suppliers, or relevant services.

Site Analysis

3. Describe the site of your business, including any relevant details such as parking, neighbouring firms, visibility, and traffic (provide numbers).

4. Explain why this choice of a site is appropriate for what you are selling and appropriate for the customer groups to whom you are selling.

Site Expenses

5. If you are leasing your business premises, outline the major provisions of the lease including all rental and maintenance fees and renewal terms.

   Or

   If your business is home-based, calculate what percentage of the home (square footage) will be used exclusively for business purposes. Explain the ownership or leasing arrangements of the home.

Market Potential

6. Clearly define the market potential you will be estimating. In other words, you will be calculating the annual expenditures of which group of potential customers on what product or service?

7. List all the relevant data you have gathered, indicating the sources. (If the information is extensive, attach the list of sources as an appendix.)

8. Clearly explain any calculations or logic involved in estimating the market potential, and indicate the dollar value of your estimate.

Competition

9. Name, locate, and briefly describe any direct competitors to your business. Provide an estimate of the sales of each, explaining your sources of information.

10. Name, locate, and briefly describe any indirect competition.

11. Describe any advantages you will have over the competition.

Sales Forecast

12. Make as many sales forecast estimates as you can, using different methods. Rank the different estimates to show the range of sales you might expect.

13. From the information above, choose or calculate a single conservative estimate of sales that you will use for planning your business. Explain your choice.

Protecting the Business

14. Briefly describe any business insurance you will carry, explaining the coverage, the premiums, and the payment schedule.

15. Explain any techniques you will use for protection against theft or other dangers to which the business could be subject (e.g., security systems or operating policies).

16. Describe any intellectual property of the business and how it will be protected.

Chapter 3

Marketing: How Will I Get Customers?

So far, your business plan has explained exactly

- who you are;
- what you will sell and to whom you plan on selling it;
- where you plan on doing business;
- what your business will mean legally;
- how much of your kind of business is out there (market potential);
- how much of the total market you can reasonably expect to get (sales forecast);
- how your business can be protected.

Now it's time to explain, in detail, how you plan on getting customers. Not just the selling or advertising involved—**marketing** means more than that. You will be explaining how you will specialize your business for your particular target customers. This chapter will help you answer the following questions:

marketing The process of selecting groups of potential customers, identifying their needs, and developing a strategy to satisfy those needs.

- **How Will I Become a Specialist?**
- **What Combination of Things Will I Sell?**
- **What Prices Will I Set?**
- **How Will My Products or Services Get to the Customer?**
- **How Will I Inform and Persuade Customers?**

Learning Objectives

On completion of this chapter, you should be able to:

1. Discuss four ways a business can project its image.
2. Compare service/product strategies among businesses.
3. Discuss the three basic pricing strategies.
4. Outline a simple distribution chain.
5. Compare at least four advertising media for advantages and disadvantages.
6. Explain six steps in the selling process.
7. Discuss the potential risks of at least four sales promotion techniques.
8. Prepare the marketing portion of a business plan.

HOW WILL I BECOME A SPECIALIST?

Image

The first step in developing a strategy for getting customers is to decide on your image. This is the perception people will have about what your business is like—what some marketers would call your *brand*. Of course, if you personally are the business, then we're talking about your personal image, or your personal brand. You are going to have an image whether you intend to or not. So, it's better that your business image is one that you intend—one that is appropriate for what you are selling and to whom you're selling it.

To be more precise, your company will have two images: a **projected image** and an **expected image**. The projected image will be the impression of your firm, which is given by everything you do: how you or your employees dress, talk, act; what your place of business looks like, where it is situated, how it is decorated; where and how you advertise; whether you call people by their first name.

If you dress in blue jeans and athletic shoes, you may be projecting a casual image. If you are located in the fanciest shopping district, you are likely projecting an exclusive image. If you drive a Volvo, you are projecting a reliable image. If the people working for you have purple and orange hair, your image may be creative or wild—but it is certainly not conservative. *Ask yourself: What image do I personally project?*

The expected image of your business is the perception of your firm that people carry in their heads even before they encounter your company—in other words, an idea of what they expect your business to be like. People expect an expensive jewellery store to be formal and elegant. They might expect the owner of a catering firm to look clean and perhaps wear chefs' whites. People don't expect a mural painter to be wearing a cocktail dress, or the director of a children's theatre troupe to be telling inappropriate jokes.

Now, we can often get people to sit up and take notice when we do things a little out of the ordinary. This is a keystone of successful advertising. But if we stray too far from the image that customers expect of us, it produces a kind of psychological discomfort in the customer. This discomfort is called **cognitive dissonance**. People tend to avoid it and, logically, to avoid businesses that make them experience it.

How would you feel about engaging a roof repair contractor who is wearing a $1200 suit and driving a Mercedes? How would you feel about a doctor whose washroom is always unclean? On the other hand, the messy washroom at a used tire dealer probably wouldn't bother you as much. It has to do with the images you expect.

There is nothing wrong with setting a tone for your business that is new or out of the ordinary. But this image must always be tempered by what your customers expect. *Ask yourself: What adjectives describe the image that customers will expect from my company?* Obviously, different customer groups will have different expectations. If you work as a travel consultant who specializes in seniors' bus trips, your image may have to be reliable, inexpensive, kindly, and caring. A travel consultant who works for professional sports teams must also have a reliable image, but in addition will need to be precise, tough, responsive, elitist, and expensive. It's what these clients would expect.

Your image need not be totally clean, honest, and reliable—or even accurate. Think of the New York street hawker who rips open a packing case at a busy intersection and starts selling brand-name pantyhose on a quick, cash, no-questions-asked basis. Tourists, glancing over their shoulders, rush forward to make their purchases and quickly disappear back into the crowds. The street hawker's slightly crooked image may be far from the reality. Most likely, the vendor is fully licensed and has a credit account with the pantyhose wholesaler, pays all taxes, and is totally legal. But that's not the image that would work for these particular customers, excited by the adventure of a seedy deal. Naturally, a disreputable image would never work for a company that installs security systems. *Ask yourself: Have I ever seen a business that prospers by having a "seedy" or disreputable image?*

---

projected image The impression of your business created in the minds of potential customers by everything you do.

expected image An impression carried by potential customers of what your business should be like.

cognitive dissonance The psychological discomfort felt when trying to hold two opposing ideas in the mind at the same time.

✅ **Memory Check 3.1**
True or False? Every business has an image of some sort.

✅ **Memory Check 3.2**
True or False? The expected and projected images of your business must not be extremely far apart.

❓ **Get Help 3.1**
Ask friends or associates to come up with single words describing what your company should be like.

✅ **Memory Check 3.3**
True or False? A company's image is the perception of the firm held in the mind of the company's owner.

3.1 Make a list of adjectives that describe the image your company will project (1/8 page maximum).

Once you have decided on an image for your company, it's time to apply your image decisions.

✔ **Memory Check 3.4**
True or False? A company's image should never be unwholesome or unreliable.

Naming the Business

Most people have worked out a name for their company long before this point in the business plan, probably because choosing a name is one of the more fun aspects of starting a business. But if you haven't done it yet, now is the time—and if you have done it, now is the time to do it properly. Doing it properly means considering what you're selling, to whom you're selling it, and the resultant image you wish to project.

Names chosen only for their personal meaning to you will not boost sales. If your last name is Goldstein and your partner's last name is Hornsby, you and your partner might think that "Goldhorn Bathtub Repair" is a great name for your company. It's not. It has meaning only for you and it doesn't sell.

Choose a name that will

- get attention;
- be easy to remember; and
- project the image you want.

But choosing the name is a balancing act. Naked Sex Clock Store will surely get attention—and people aren't likely to forget it—but is it the image you want to project? Whatever name you choose, you should be able to explain, in your business plan, how the name works to project the appropriate image for your company.

☆ Head Start Exercise

3.2 List at least five possible names for your business and note how they project different images. Identify the one that best satisfies your image needs (1/3 page maximum).

✔ **Memory Check 3.5**
True or False? Selecting a name should be the first step in planning a business.

Marketing Strategy

How you project your image—how you make yourself appear different from your competitors—is with your marketing strategy, or what professional marketers call the **marketing mix**. Over the years, a fairly standard method has evolved to explain a firm's marketing mix, and this is probably the best way to describe it in your business plan. The marketing mix is typically broken down into the following elements:

- product or service strategy
- pricing strategy
- distribution strategy
- promotion strategy

The better you get to know your market, the more accurately you will be able to tailor your business to give customers what they want—what they really want, not the superficial or the impossible.[1] Customers may *seem* to want the impossible: the highest quality, fastest service, longest warranty—all at impossibly low prices. You must develop a marketing strategy that will give customers not everything, but those things that are most important to them.

marketing mix The particular combination of marketing elements that a business uses to find and satisfy its customers; the marketing strategy, usually described in terms of its product/service, price, distribution, and promotion elements.

❓ **Get Help 3.2**
If consumers will be your customers, get some secondary information on trends. For example, read recent copies of *The Trend Letter*. This U.S. publication covers current trends in marketing, demographics, and technology, and is available online at www.thetrendletter.com.

Figure 3.1 Marketing Mix

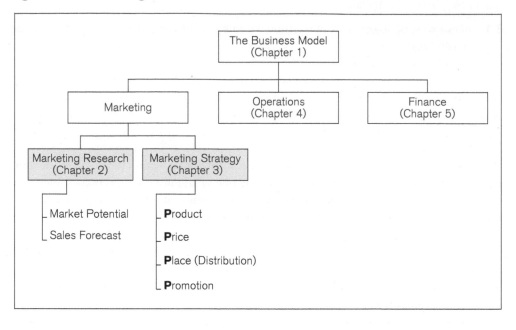

⭐ Head Start Exercise

3.3 Make a prioritized list of the things that are most important to the kind of customers you will have (e.g., price, atmosphere, speed, accuracy). If you cannot identify their priorities based on your experience, then do some research to identify them. (1/3 page maximum).

To put *marketing mix* into context, think of business as being made up of several different functions. The first of these functions is deciding the overall business strategy or model —the topics covered in Chapter 1. Then, *marketing* itself can be thought of as two functions: marketing research (Chapter 2) and marketing strategy (Chapter 3). In Figure 3.1, notice that marketing strategy, or marketing mix, is broken down into *product, price, distribution*, and *promotion*. Distribution is conveniently referred to as *place*, giving us the commonly used expression "the 4P's of the marketing mix."

As businesses grow, the functions shown in Figure 3.1 tend to become separate departments. So, that in a larger company, for example, there might be a president in charge of overall business strategy, then a vice president of marketing, a VP of operations, a VP of finance, and many managers for the separate activities shown.

> **Note:** If it seems that we're going into a lot of detail on *marketing*, that's because it's important. Many business professors would argue that marketing is the primary activity of any successful organization.

WHAT COMBINATIONS OF THINGS WILL I SELL?
Service/Product Strategy

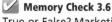 **Memory Check 3.6**
True or False? Marketing mix and marketing strategy mean the same thing.

The particular combination of things you sell is your product or service strategy. It describes the variety and quality of goods and/or services you provide. The fewer different things you sell, the more specialized your business will be—and specialization is profitable. However, the choice of things you sell is another balancing act that depends on your chosen market. You must try to ensure that you are offering everything your customers expect of you. (You don't want them to go to competitors for some of their needs, which could end up with you losing the customer.) On the other hand, you don't want to tie up your money or energy in a huge variety of products or services that won't make profit for you.

Imagine you are a software training consultant who sells courses and seminars to government departments and agencies all over your province. You specialize in web design courses, but have a very broad information technology background. From your training experience, you know that the first time you teach something new you spend about four hours outside the classroom in preparation for every hour you spend inside the classroom. The second time you teach the same course, the ratio is about two hours outside for every one hour in class. The third, fourth, and subsequent times, the ratio can fall below one-quarter hour of preparation for every hour of teaching.

Now let's say you charge $800 per day for six hours of instruction. If you keep teaching the same old web design course over and over (even allowing time for customizing and improvement), you'll be making lots of money. On the other hand, if you teach web authoring software one week, database the next, graphics the next, and office software after that, life will be less boring but you will have little profit to show because of too much time spent preparing new material. Besides, if you present yourself as the "web training specialist," you will be a more obvious choice for this type of training compared to someone who is seen as a generalist. Usually, small firms that are more specialized in their product or service offerings perform better.[2]

This specialization of your product or service works only if it is appropriate for the kinds of customers you are chasing. Being a photographer who specializes in taking pictures of horses is fine provided that you are targeting horse owners or trainers in your area. And when you specialize your service or products, you have to keep the other elements of the marketing mix in mind. For example, if you open a bakery that sells only bagels, you will have a problem when customers can get similar bagels at a competitor's location, where they can also pick up bread, doughnuts, and other items they might be looking for. In this case, being the "bagel specialist" will work only if your product is clearly different in terms of quality or price or some other feature.

Your product/service strategy includes not only the basic services and products you will offer, but also the variety of additional things you may do for your customers that will cost you money and time. *Ask yourself: What might I do for my customers that will add value to the product or service?*

Will you accept payment by Visa or MasterCard? Will you give your customers credit terms? Will you provide free installation? Will there be a warranty attached to your service or product? Will you supply free estimates? Free delivery? Free bags to carry home your product? Will you provide advice by telephone?

All these added services will provide value to the customer, and will cost you money. The decision about which extra services you will provide must also be part of your overall strategy in catering to your chosen market groups and differentiating yourself from your competitors. The ability to give more personalized service is one of the competitive advantages of small firms over larger ones.[3] Nevertheless, the general rule for a new business is to offer relatively few products or services (compared to the competition), especially when you are just starting up. At the beginning, keep it simple. Then, later on, your business can grow by expansion of your offerings (what you are selling) or going after new markets (to whom you are selling). It is always easier to add something new than it is to stop providing something that some of your customers have come to expect. A good exercise is to prepare a chart comparing the service/product mix of your proposed company to those of the competitors. (See the example in Figure 3.2.)

✓ **Memory Check 3.7**
True or False? Production is one of the "P's" of the marketing mix.

✓ **Memory Check 3.8**
True or False? Generally, it is more profitable for new businesses to specialize in fewer products or services than their competitors offer.

Get Help 3.3

Interview the owner of an established business in your chosen field. Ask how the products or services the company offers now are different from those originally provided. Has the company changed the type of customers it was originally targeting?

Figure 3.2 Services Comparison for Pet Grooming Companies

Product/Service	Me	Competitor 1	Competitor 2	Competitor 3
Dogs	X	X	X	X
Cats		X		X
Other pets				X
Shampoo	X	X	X	X
Styling	X	X	X	X
Nail trim		X	X	X
Store location		X	X	X
House calls	X			
Show-prep	X		X	X
Boarding			X	X
Transportation			X	
Obedience				X

⭐ Head Start Exercise

3.4   Create a chart (see Figure 3.2) showing the specific products or services you will offer compared to your direct competitors (1 page maximum).

WHAT PRICES WILL I SET?

Your pricing strategy is measured in comparison to your competition. There are only three basic pricing strategies:

- You can price lower than the competition.
- You can price higher than the competition.
- You can price the same as the competition.

   Ask yourself: How will I be priced compared to my competition? Why?

Pricing Low

Pricing lower than your competitors is often appropriate for a new business, especially when potential customers have established relationships with your competition. The most obvious reason for customers to give you a try is that you are offering the same (or better) services/products for less than they pay now.

   If this is your strategy, you have to be priced sufficiently lower than the competition so that it is worthwhile for customers to switch suppliers. But there are limits to how low you can go. *Ask yourself: How low can my prices go?*

   Pricing lower than the competition is what professional marketers refer to as **penetration pricing**, since it can be used as a technique to "penetrate" new groups of customers. However, selling something at a loss just to get your foot in the door is only a good way to operate at a loss. Remember, you are in business to make a profit. The best way to ensure that you make an overall profit is to profit on every single transaction you have with a customer. This means that the price of everything you sell must include your costs plus an amount to cover all of your operating expenses (including the value of your own time) plus some level of profit.

penetration pricing Setting prices lower than those of the competition.

Even though you are setting your prices now, you will better understand your costs after you have completed the financial section of the business plan, and may well revise your pricing.

Pricing High

It is a myth that "you always get what you pay for." But, like other myths, it is powerful because so many people believe it. Those who want the "best" often associate this with the "most expensive." Marketers often refer to a high pricing strategy as a **skimming** strategy, implying that it targets the upper-income segments (or "skims the cream") of a market. If you are dealing with customer groups who want only the highest quality products, service, guarantees, and prestige, then likely they also expect the highest prices and you will have to provide them.

Imagine you own a retail hat store in the high-rent shopping district. You cater to wealthy professional men who have offices in this area and your hat prices start at $100. One day, you find out about a wholesaler who is going out of business and is selling medium-quality hats for $5 apiece. You calculate that if you were to buy the hats and sell them for $30 each, you would still be making several times your usual markup and could move the hats quickly. Bad idea!

The customers you are targeting don't come to you for $30 hats. They want $100 hats. If you buy the $5 hats, you will still have to sell them in the $100 range, in line with your customers' expectations. The danger here is that one of your customers may see the same hats on sale at a lower-priced competitor in the $15 range. Seeing this, a customer who believes he or she has bought a superior product will experience serious cognitive dissonance and the consequences will not be good for your business.

Ask yourself: How high can my prices go? For the most part, you will be priced higher than the competition only when you are dealing with an upscale market and offering a hard-to-get or superior product. But even then, there are limits to what you can charge—there is a limit to "what the market will bear." Rolls-Royce and Rolex must do sophisticated analyses of the relationship between price and supply/demand to set their prices. They must also ensure that the price keeps their buyers in an exclusive category, without appearing to "price gouge." You will not have the same level of research as these companies and will have to rely on experience, observation, intuition, and asking a lot of questions. Make sure you can logically explain your specific prices in your business plan.

price skimming Setting prices higher than those of the competition.

Pricing the Same

Ask yourself: Why might I want to have prices pretty much the same as my competition? Being priced the same as your competition is technically referred to as a **competitive pricing** strategy. Even though the public takes "competitive" to mean lower prices, this is not what it really means—be careful not to make this mistake in your business plan.

Generally, you will use a competitive pricing strategy whenever trying to "sell higher" will cost you customers, but at the same time you are not in a position to sell lower because of your costs or the ability of competitors to win a price war. Lots of consumer goods and services are widely found to be competitively priced (such as milk, gasoline, and movie tickets) as are many professional services (such as dental fillings and minor legal services).

In some cases, even though you may be an independent business, the rates you charge could be set, or strongly influenced, by a professional association (accountant, paralegal, chiropractor). So you are automatically stuck with a competitive pricing situation.

Your prices might even be determined by a collective agreement. This could be the case if you were a contract sound mixer for network television productions. In such an event, you would have to convince producers to use you based on your experience, or the

competitive pricing Setting prices at the same level as those of the competition.

✓ Memory Check 3.9
True or False? A new firm should always try to price under the competition.

What's in a Name?

"Rocky River" is probably not the greatest name for a sign company, particularly one that's not even in Rocky River. But it's the name the company started with and is now so recognized that it would be difficult change. Besides, the company founder is happy with things the way they are.

Cameron Mahy was working for Canada's largest sign company when he got notice that he was being let go. Essentially, he and others were being replaced by new technologies. But Cam had no regrets, since the company and its artists from all over the world had trained him in the classic art of sign painting. The path ahead was clear, because Cam had been an entrepreneur for most of his life. As a kid, starting with a paper route, he had progressed to a lawn maintenance business by age 12, and even as a full-time employee he was painting signs on trucks for his own clients. So when he lost his job, Cam immediately signed up for a federally sponsored business start-up program, where

he learned to write a business plan. Thus Rocky River Sign Co. Inc. was born.

In the first two years, the business was growing, but there were many problems. Cam was a great designer and artist and good with the customers, but details like billing and accounting were not getting attended to. Then Cam's wife, Robin, joined the company and, with her background in banking and administration, she organized the operation to run smoothly and efficiently. Interestingly, over the years Robin has picked up more involvement in the design end of things, showing her own creativity with banner, vehicle, and even apparel designs.

These days, Rocky River Sign Co. targets primarily small local firms, providing them with a complete range of signs from illuminated storefront and rooftop signs to decals, window signs, billboards, vehicle signage, and even custom embroidery that lets customers wear their signs. Cam is recognized for some of his more visible work, which includes murals on major buildings and even the logos on the Astroturf field for the Grey Cup.

Typically, Robin works the five-day, nine-to-five work-week while Cam can put in 70–80 hours as the business goes through a growth spurt. The company has three employees now, and Cam expects it to grow to five over the next couple of years. Cam sees no disadvantage to working with his wife, whom he describes as "definitely my best friend."

And the company name? It comes from a nickname that Cam had has a kid. It doesn't mean much to new or prospective customers, but it is memorable and represents quality to those who know the company. Visit their website at www.rockyriversign.com.

---

fact that you use superior recording equipment, or some other advantage you have over your competitors.

It is perfectly fine to be priced the same as your competitors, provided you can explain why you are doing it and you can differentiate yourself from the competition by some other element(s) of your marketing mix: products/services, distribution, or promotion.

☑ **Memory Check 3.10**
True or False? Competitive pricing means trying to price lower than your competition.

⭐ Head Start Exercise

3.5 Make a chart listing the products or services you will offer that are the same as or similar to those of your direct competitors. List the prices that each of your direct competitors charge. Now do the same for indirect competitors (1 page maximum).

Negotiation

Ask yourself: How will I handle it if I have established my list of prices and then a potential customer offers me less than my set price for one of my services or products? Let's say you're a meeting planner who has been working for the local convention and tourist board on a three-month contract. You have done an outstanding job and are offered a two-month extension at the same daily rate. You feel that you should be paid at a higher rate, but don't want to risk losing the contract extension. It's time for **negotiation**, and that involves the following activities:

- *Doing your homework.* You must find out the going rates for your products/services, the market conditions, and, in some cases, your customer's circumstances. (For the meeting planner, that means how badly they might need you.)
- *Using a plan.* You must decide how much you will initially ask for, how much you really expect to get, and the least you will settle for. (In the case of the meeting planner, the least is what you're being paid now.)
- *Taking a co-operative approach.* You must sincerely try to get an agreement that will benefit both you and the other party. (In the case of the meeting planner, this could involve pointing out the cost savings to the convention and tourist board of not having to train a new planner, while you save the effort of not having to secure a new employer.)

In some businesses, a formal bidding process replaces negotiation. This is often the situation when large contractors are selling off smaller pieces of a project or when dealing with government. In such cases, doing your homework usually means checking the winning bids for previous similar contracts. The skill is in writing your bid or proposal.

In other kinds of business, active negotiation is constant. If you start a business selling used motorcycles, you will have a formal asking price based on your cost (which you have negotiated) as well as on market conditions. But realistically, you will expect to negotiate every sale.

Negotiation is a skill similar to salesmanship in that it involves an element of persuasion. There are lots of books with good negotiation advice that are worth reading, but you can't really learn a skill from a book. You have to practise it.

HOW WILL MY PRODUCTS OR SERVICES GET TO THE CUSTOMER?

The answer to this question is through your distribution strategy. **Distribution** is how goods and services actually get from a producer to the final user; in the business plan it is commonly broken down into **distribution channel** and **physical distribution**. *Ask yourself: What is the difference between distribution channel and physical distribution?*

Distribution Channel

Distribution channel refers to the legal or contractual elements of how goods and services get from the producer to the final consumer.

Imagine you are a trained hairstylist who would like to start a business that is somewhat different from other salons. You decide to become a visiting hairdresser, specializing in hospitals and nursing homes. The fact that you go to the customers is what makes you different from your competition, but this is only a physical element of the distribution. Equally important is the issue of whether you are working on a contract with the nursing home, which might pay you a single fee for cutting the hair of its patients. Or do you approach the patients directly and get paid by each of them personally? In either case, the actual hair being cut still belongs to the patients, and you are still working at the nursing home locale, but the channel (the customers you are contracting with) is different.

Most new small businesses use a "direct" form of distribution: You contract with and provide your services or products directly to the end-user. But let's say you start an interior

Negotiation The process used to arrive at the terms of an agreement.

Get Help 3.4
Check the library, where you will find many negotiation titles. A couple of old standards are *You Can Negotiate Anything* by Herb Cohen, and *Getting to Yes: Negotiating Agreement without Giving In* by Roger Fisher.

Memory Check 3.11
True or False? It is always best to take a co-operative approach when negotiating.

distribution A company's strategy for getting services or products from the producer to the end-user. Distribution is sometimes referred to as place, so that the elements of the marketing mix can be described as the Four P's: product, price, promotion, and place.

distribution channel The legal or contractual elements of how a service or product gets from the producer to the end-user.

physical distribution The chain of production storage and delivery that products move through, from producer to end-user.

Memory Check 3.12
True or False? The best way to learn negotiation is reading about the topic.

Acting as an intermediary, connecting — who arranges a deal between buyers and companies — not directly involved in the services being sold —

decorating business, specializing in decor for elevators. The real beneficiaries of your service are those who ride the elevators, but they are not your customers. Who is the real user of your service? Maybe you will be working directly for the building owners. Maybe you will be working through an intermediary—a larger design firm that is decorating the entire building but subcontracts the elevators to you. Maybe you are acting as an intermediary yourself, going out and getting the design contracts, then paying independent designers to do the work.

The owner of a business based on a new product must often choose among many channel options. What if you were to invent and patent a Teflon-type liquid protection for golf balls: Just rub it on and the balls resist grass or mud stains and cracking and—most importantly—they fly farther. But who would actually buy and apply your product: golfers themselves? Pro shops? Golf ball manufacturers?

And if the actual users are to be the golfers themselves, to whom do you sell? Will you have a store where the golfers can come to buy? Or will you sell directly to pro shops, which will, in turn, sell your product to the golfers? Perhaps you will sell to a sports wholesale company, which will then sell your product to sporting goods stores, hardware chains, and pro shops, and the golfers can buy from any of them. The choices are many, but the channel decision for getting the product to the end-user must be clarified in your plan.

In some cases you might be an agent (real estate, theatrical, travel), in which case you are an intermediary who arranges a deal between a buyer and a seller, but you do not get directly involved with the product/service being sold. As an agent, your customers are often both the buyers and the sellers, and you must have strategies for selling to both.

In Section 1 of the business plan you clearly defined your business: what you are selling and to whom you are selling it. But after the process of clarifying your distribution channel, you may wish to reassess and redefine who your customers really are—not necessarily the end-user of the product, but those to whom you are selling. For example, you may be publishing an electronic pet-care newsletter on the internet. You may have put a lot of research into understanding and measuring the potential readers of your product, but they are not your real customers. Those who pay you are the veterinarians and dog-food companies that advertise in your cyber-mag, so your channel of distribution is directly to these advertisers.

Memory Check 3.13
True or False? Agents do not own the services or products that they are selling.

⭐ Head Start Exercise

3.6 Clearly state in one or two sentences to whom you are legally selling your product or service. Is this the ultimate user? If not, explain. Are you an intermediary in providing your product or service? Make notes to explain (1/2 page maximum).

Physical Issues

Physical distribution commonly refers to the issues of moving tangible products, although elements of this topic still apply to service businesses. For product-based firms, it can involve many complex issues. Some examples are:

- **Inventory.** Will your strategy be to carry lots of inventory or little (compared to your competitors)? Which is appropriate for your customers?

- **Ordering.** Will you need special methods for ordering replacement inventory because of the length of time it takes to get, or the fact that it spoils quickly?

- **Storage.** Will you need to rent warehouse space because you will be selling seasonal products? Will you be dealing with customs brokers as an importer? Will you need special provisions for sorting products?

- **Order process.** Will you require complicated order forms or an electronic database that will automatically order from your suppliers for your customers?
- **Transport.** Will you do your own deliveries? Will you need to ship overnight by courier or will your strategy be to always send orders by the cheapest method?

Depending on your type of business, there is a wide variation in which of these factors might be pertinent to your business plan. It is increasingly common to use the term **supply chain** for describing all of the processes and inputs for both the channel and the physical elements of distribution. For large businesses, mapping and controlling complex supply chains has become an area of specialized study. For most new small firms, however, the method of physically getting the product or service to the user is simple and obvious. If you're starting an aromatherapy products store or an art gallery, the customers will come to you. If you're starting a tree-removal service or a bottled water delivery company, you will have a truck that goes to them. But in some cases, neither do you go to them nor do they come to you.

E-commerce Selling, delivering, and being paid for products over the internet are all components of e-commerce. These activities move a website from the more passive roles of advertising and gathering data to the more active role of distribution. Setting up e-commerce capabilities is more complex and expensive than simple website functions. But this set of tools is cost-efficient and reliable, especially for things like selling intellectual property (music, photographic images, software) and time-booked services (hotel rooms, theatre tickets, limousine services). Web users have been moving from buying small-ticket items (books, CDs, gifts) to include the purchase of big-ticket items such as furniture, computers, and even cars.

It is relatively easy to sell products and services on the web without having to build an expensive e-commerce capability of your own. This can be done through third-party virtual stores, where your products or services are displayed on the third-party site, often along with the products of other companies. eBay has traditionally led in this field, but there are many specialty online intermediaries. For example, on Scribd (www.scribd.com), authors can publish and sell their own works at their own prices.

E-commerce can be used for selling products to consumers, in which case it is often referred to as **e-tailing**. This is a form of non-store retailing (as are print catalogue systems, door-to-door selling, infomercial operations, etc.). E-tailing may be classified as **B2C e-biz** (business-to-consumer). Selling to other businesses via the internet may be referred to as **B2B e-biz**.

Distribution and Image

There is a close relationship between your company's image and physical distribution. The only impression future customers might have of your lawn maintenance business is the look of your truck when it pulls up to their neighbour's yard. The decor of your office or store is often the first means of projecting your image to new customers. In fact, one study shows that customers use the physical appearance of a business to judge its trustworthiness.[4]

The owner of a second-hand bookstore may be enormously wealthy, but would be foolish to use his money for sprucing up the store to make it look new and fresh. Used bookstores are better to look run-down because that's the kind of place where people expect to find cheap stuff—and that is the image that book bargain hunters will respond to. If your customers will be coming to you, you should explain in the business plan how the decor, fixtures, lighting, furniture, displays, and so on will contribute to projecting your image. Some of these decisions may require going back to the feasibility section of your business plan and rewriting the costs of leasehold improvements.

supply chain All of the contractual and physical aspects of bringing a product or service from its most basic components to the end-user.

e-commerce The selling, ordering, payment, and sometimes the delivery of products or services over the internet.

✅ **Memory Check 3.14**
True or False? The fact that a product might be sold to a wholesaler, then a retailer, then a consumer refers to "physical distribution."

e-tailing Selling products to consumers via the internet, without the use of a physical store.

B2C e-biz Selling products or services from a business to consumers via the internet.

B2B e-biz Selling products or services to other businesses via the internet.

❓ **Get Help 3.5**
Industry Canada's website has many helpful articles on e-commerce. Go to www.ic.gc.ca and use the search tool.

3.7 Make notes to explain any decor or physical set-up of your place of business that will have an impact on customers (1/3 page maximum).

HOW WILL I INFORM AND PERSUADE CUSTOMERS?

promotion strategy The approach a business uses to inform and persuade its customers, including techniques of advertising, publicity, personal selling, and sales promotion.

Promotion strategy means the methods you will use to let prospective customers know about your business and to persuade them to buy from you.

Ask yourself: How am I likely to promote my business? "By relying on word of mouth" is definitely the wrong answer to this question! Many new businesspeople, especially those in some form of self-employment or contract work, are not comfortable with aggressively promoting themselves or their business. Perhaps they associate it with ideas of bragging or hucksterism. Their solution to the problem of promotion is to take a passive approach, to rely on others to talk about their superior skills or products. These entrepreneurs often say they will rely on *word of mouth* to promote their services/products. However, this is an approach almost guaranteed to fail. It is an abdication of the entrepreneur's responsibility for promoting the business. It is basically a decision not to promote.

Business history is full of contests between entrepreneurs with superior products versus entrepreneurs with superior promotion. Superior promotion usually wins. So you are well advised to have a plan for actively promoting your business—a plan that projects your chosen image.

In a business plan, it is convenient to have the promotion strategy broken down into the following components:

- advertising media
- advertising content
- publicity
- one-on-one selling
- sales promotion

Advertising Media

advertising The attempt to persuade through mass communications media.

Advertising for your new business must be entered into cautiously: A huge proportion of the money spent by small firms on advertising is wasted. *Ask yourself: What advertising medium might I use?* For advertising, most mass media charge according to the number of people who will see or hear the ad. So, most TV and radio stations or big city newspapers charge more for advertising space or time than a small, new business can afford to pay. Even if you can afford it, in many cases it isn't sensible, particularly if you are specializing in a narrow customer group. Why pay to advertise to a huge group of people, most of whom will never consider dealing with you? So the problem becomes one of finding an advertising medium that will target your chosen market segment. And no medium is better at targeting than the internet.

✅ **Memory Check 3.15**
True or False? New businesses are best to rely on "word of mouth" for promotion.

Websites Today, the website is the primary advertising tool for many small firms. A website can be an efficient, cost-effective tool only if it is being accessed by the market segment you are targeting. To ensure this, you may need the help of a professional web developer. Issues to be negotiated with the web developer include:

1. *Host selection.* Identify the company that will hold the data for your website on its computers and the fees you will pay. This may be the same company that acts as your web developer.

2. *Domain name.* An example of a domain name would be "studententrepreneur.com." Webpages and email addresses are attached to a domain name. It's not necessary to register your own, but it projects a more successful professional image if you do. And if your domain name contains keywords relevant to your business, it makes it easier for customers to find your site with a search engine. Your web hosting service is commonly used as the agent to apply for a domain name. Alternatively, you can visit the Canadian Internet Registration Authority (www.cira.ca) for a list of Canadian certified domain name registrars.

3. *Site design.* All the details of how your site will function, how it will be updated, and how data will be gathered from it must be planned.[5]

4. *Tracking programs.* You must select the particular software that will measure the activity of your website as well as gather specific information about its users. Web researchers are often concerned about the **clickstream** pattern of users, the series of selections that brought the user to the point of a purchase selection.[6]

clickstream The total series of selections that a web user makes leading up to a particular page or purchase.

5. *Search engine strategy.* Having a great website does not help your business unless you are able to drive potential customers to the site. You do this through other advertising media, through your linking strategy (below), and through your search engine strategy. This involves the selection of the key words that search engines use to match sites with customer queries. It can also involve paying search engines to give priority to your "sponsored" site and might also involve bidding on keywords used in searches. Optimizing your search engine strategy usually requires professional help.[7]

Get Help 3.6
Check your local college to see if it offers a program in webpage design or internet management. The program co-ordinator may advise you on set-up costs or refer you to a senior student who will assist you at a reasonable price.

6. *Linking strategy.* Getting potential customers to your website will also involve links from social media sites, blogs, online magazines, consumer advice sites, referral agency sites, or any other type of website that your potential customers would be likely to view. In some cases the links will be free. In some cases you can offer a reciprocal linking arrangement. (They display your link, you display theirs.) But typically, for commercial sites, you pay for the link. There are a variety of ways to pay for advertising your website on other sites, including:

   - pay-for-impression (you pay each time someone views your ad)
   - pay-for-click (you pay each time someone clicks on your link)
   - pay-for-purchase (you pay a commission each time someone buys)[8]

Get Help 3.7
To find a competent web developer, what better way than by a web search using the terms "web developer" and the name of your city, neighbourhood, or region? You can make an initial assessment by comparing the quality of the web developer's own site against the website criteria outlined in this section.

7. *Design contract.* The details of your deal with the web developer must be spelled out, including all fees, warranties, payment schedules, and follow-up service.

   Some general principles of web design are that sites should be

- *Simple.* Any lack in clarity or difficulty of use will only serve to frustrate the customer.
- *Fast.* Downloading time should be short.
- *Consistent.* Choose a pattern of fonts and graphic styles and stay with it throughout, so readers do not think they have strayed to another site.

Website content should also adhere to the general principles of advertising content (discussed below).

The Canada Business Network is a co-operative effort among Industry Canada, other federal departments, provincial and territorial governments, and private sector partners. It is a great starting point for up-to-date information on how small business can use web technologies, and it serves as an excellent example of a well-designed site. The homepage for Canada Business Network is pictured in Figure 3.3.

⭐ Head Start Exercise

3.8 Sketch the layout and explain the features of the homepage for your company's website (1 1/3 page maximum).

Figure 3.3 Canada Business Network Home Page
www.canadabusiness.ca/eng/

Source: Canada Business Network Website, www.canadabusiness.ca. Reproduced with the permission of the Minister of Public Works and Government Services Canada, 2013.

Social Media Social media allow people to communicate in groups or one on one using text, video, voice, and photography, or some combination of these media. Members of a particular social media group are usually self-defined by interest in some particular topic, common endeavour, or some pre-existing social connection among the members. For example, you might belong to a Facebook group based on the school you attended. Or you might sign up to receive **tweets** on your smartphone from your favourite singer or a politician you support. They may also allow users to form branching connections such as opening a dialogue with the contact of one of your existing contacts.

The most important advertising use of social media is to drive prospective customers to your website. But these services are also great sources of information on your competitors, industry trends, and what others are saying about your company and your services and/or products.

New social media platforms are being developed constantly. The few discussed below were among the most popular at the time of writing.

Blogs A blog is a website that primarily contains the writings of one person often on one particular topic. The writer can post new commentary (or pictures, links, music, etc.) on a regular or irregular basis. Readers of the blog may be able to post comments for others to see. Blogs have many business applications. For example, you might own a small wholesale operation selling organic vitamin supplements. But the blog you write is about tips on running retail health food stores (a topic of interest to your customers.) Or let's say you're a freelance fashion writer working for various newspapers and magazines on an ad-hoc basis. You may also keep a blog that chronicles your travels to fashion shows, provides industry gossip, and talks about articles you are working on and when they will appear. In this way, you can develop and maintain your own fan base even though you do not have a regular column.

Facebook Facebook is the most widely used social network in the world, with over a billion users. There are many ways to use Facebook to promote your business, including

tweet A short message (140 characters or fewer) posted via Twitter social networking website.

Memory Check 3.16
True or False? A good website will use a broad variety of fonts, colours, and graphic styles.

highly targeted ads that connect directly to your website. You can also create a business fan page, where your customers can register. As you post updates to your page, they will automatically flow to the news feeds of your fans. As well, entrepreneurs can use the site to maintain a profile in a target community and stay up to date on the competition.

Twitter Twitter allows a user to post text messages or very short blogs. Users (with the permission of the posting writer) can subscribe to these posts and receive them in their Twitter feeds. Let's say you own a small restaurant in the business district of town. You encourage regular customers to follow you on Twitter, and every morning, you send out tweets about that day's lunch specials. This is timely, targeted advertising. Twitter is also an excellent way to find out what others are saying about your company.

YouTube YouTube allows users to post short video clips as well as to share videos within network groups. Highly popular videos on this site can be viewed by millions around the world. It is the ambition of many small entrepreneurs to promote their company by creating a **viral video** on YouTube—one that thousands of viewers will be recommending to millions of their friends. In reality, however, only a tiny percentage of postings ever "go viral," and these are most likely to have been created by a well-financed team of advertising experts. Even for those that become wildly popular, the broad exposure may not translate into sales for the posting company. But imagine that you have a business as a public speaking trainer. You might try posting a funny video of public speaking bloopers (one that you have created or have copyright permission to use). At the end of the video, you could direct viewers to the website where you sell your services.

> **viral video** A short video that viewers email to their friends who, in turn, will email it to others and ultimately millions of viewers.

LinkedIn LinkedIn is the only major social media platform that has a majority of male users. Primarily business-oriented, it allows members to build contact networks, with a set of rules for introducing new contacts. Users can post résumés, job postings, or business profiles. LinkedIn also allows you to buy "ads" where you can post text and small images advertising your company's products or services. This service would be valuable if your business was training sales forces on using the more complex features of their smartphones. You would try to build contacts with sales managers, human resource directors, vice presidents of marketing—the kind of people who would be likely to contract for your service.

Pinterest Pinterest allows users to upload, share, and display visual images. Users create boards, usually based on certain themes, where they pin images uploaded or copied from other Pinterest users. Businesses can create their own pages to promote their goods or services. For example, you might pin a picture of each pair of shoes in your high-end shoe store, and shoe lovers could display on their own boards the items that they purchased from you.

Ask yourself: Are social media websites effective promotion tools for small businesses? The only way to know for sure is by measuring. As in any form of promotion, the entrepreneur must calculate the cost-effectiveness of the effort to know whether it is worthwhile. (See the discussion at the end of the advertising section on page 64.)

⭐ Head Start Exercise

3.9 Outline a plan for how you could use social media to promote your business (1/2 page maximum).

> **direct mail** A form of advertising that communicates individually with large numbers of potential buyers through postal or electronic mail.

Direct Mail/Email Of the many advertising media available, the one most overlooked by small firms but potentially the most valuable for those who specialize is **direct mail**. Direct mail can mean a lot of different things. It can involve sending out letters (hard copy or email), web links, brochures, flyers, or catalogues to individuals or organizations—precisely of the kind you are targeting. Direct mail can be addressed personally to the customer, and even though some of it is classified as "junk mail," people do read it and respond.

In most cases, the mailing piece you prepare is distributed using one of the following methods:

- **Customer lists.** Once you have actually started your business, your most important future customers will be your past customers. Think about it. People repeat the same behaviours over and over. Of all the people in the world, the ones most likely to buy from you are those who already have. Sure, there are a very few exceptions, but the vast majority of enterprises rely on repeat business. This being the case, it only makes sense that you maintain a list of the names, addresses, and phone numbers of your past customers. They are the ones you most want to send your future advertising to. It is also possible, in some cases, to buy or rent someone else's customer list when they have the same target customers as you but are not in competition.

- **Subscription lists.** Most publishers of trade journals, magazines, or newsletters are willing to rent out the names and addresses of their subscribers, or the email addresses, either directly or through a mailing list company. If everyone in your target group is likely to read a particular periodical, that's the list for you. In many cases, the publisher is willing to send the list only to a third party (called a letter shop or mailing house) that will inexpensively label, print, sort, and deliver your promotional piece to the post office, or email it directly to the prospect. The third-party involvement is so you don't make an actual copy of the subscription list, and, therefore, will have to rent it again the next time you wish to use it. Similarly, you can rent lists of members in particular organizations, delegates to particular conventions, subscribers to cable TV, and so on.

- **Compiled lists.** Compiled lists are lists specifically put together for your purposes. You can do it yourself or hire a mailing list company to do it for you. There are so many databases around these days that mailing list companies can "merge and purge" to produce a list of just about any possible customer group. The narrower the list, however, the more expensive it will be to compile. In fact, compiled lists can run up to several dollars per name. There is software available that can help you compile your own lists of email addresses for potential customers. These email extractors can work from many different types of files (e.g., CDs with information on participants at particular conferences) or they can comb the internet looking for particular types of websites and extract addresses from these. Naturally, the effective use of **email extractors** depends on the skill of the user in choosing appropriate search parameters.

- **Postal tracts.** If you are going after customers that are all in the same geographic area, you will be able to draw your target area on a map as a postal tract. It is a simple matter to get a postal code directory and find the postal codes where your customers are located. The post office can deliver your mailing piece to every business or home within those codes at bulk mailing rates. Alternatively, you can enlist an independent handbill delivery company or bulk mailer—or you can even do it yourself.

Let's say you're a retired professor of accounting and wish to work as a financial adviser targeting college professors in your city. Knowing that the vast majority of professors use email, you could check the websites of the various colleges in your area, access the internal phone books, and save the email addresses of everyone with the title "professor." You now would have the perfect list to merge with your promotional letter.

Newspapers For most small businesses, it's just too expensive to have even a small ad in one of the large mass-circulation daily newspapers. Even a listing in the classifieds can be prohibitive—and, in most cases, you would still be paying to advertise to a wider audience than your own target customers.

Unlike using the big dailies, by advertising in smaller **community newspapers** you could hit your entire market at a low cost. This happens when the customers you are targeting all live within the same geographic area that is serviced by the paper.

---

customer list A database of the names, addresses, phone numbers, purchases, and so on of those who have purchased from a company.

subscription list The names and addresses of customers for particular publications or services. These can be rented (at relatively low cost) for the mailing of advertising pieces.

compiled list The names and addresses of prospective customers that have been gathered to meet the specifications of a business. Compilation is usually an expensive process.

email extractor Software that will compile lists of email addresses from electronic files or websites.

postal tract A geographic area that is made up of a series of adjacent postal code districts.

? Get Help 3.8
For information on postal tracts, visit the Canada Post website at www.canadapost.ca.

✓ Memory Check 3.17
True or False? Women are more likely than men to use most forms of social media.

community newspaper A smaller-circulation newspaper targeting a specific geographic area, often published weekly.

You may be targeting customers who live in different geographic areas but all have the same ethnic or language background. For example, you may be starting a language school that will teach English to recent immigrants from China. It's a pretty good bet that all your potential customers will read the Chinese newspaper in your area, so that particular **specialty newspaper** is the place to run your ad.

There are other sorts of newspapers that specialize in people who attend the same college, who are involved in business finance, who are retired, who are of a particular religion, who are in the computer field, and so on. If your target market coincides with one of these publications you may be able to communicate with all your potential customers inexpensively. *Ask yourself: Which specialty newspapers do I read? Is the advertising in them aimed at people like me?*

Magazines The line between newspapers and magazines is becoming increasingly blurred. While newspapers can often publish your ad within a day or two, many magazines require the ad to be ready a full three months before readers will actually see it. With internet publishing, however, online magazines can offer an almost instant response to advertisers.

The most important magazines for small, new specialty businesses are **trade journals** (not the mass-market consumer magazines). Trade publications are written for those involved in specific industries. There are literally thousands of such magazines and they are widely used by those within the industries they serve. For example, a freelance clothing designer looking for contract work might run an ad in *Canadian Apparel Manufacturer*, knowing that pretty much everyone in the industry reads this publication. A computer parts importer knows that his or her potential customers read *Computer Dealer News*, and a custom lamp designer knows to advertise in *Lighting Magazine*. Magazine advertising can be expensive, but cost is geared to circulation. *Ask yourself: Are there any publications that my potential customers will subscribe to?*

Directories There is a proliferation of online directories, some effective, some not so. Today, most people searching for a business online rely on their browser as the primary directory. For example, you may have a disposal business for used electronics in the city of Mountview and someone tries to sell you a listing in the Mountview Preferred Business Online Directory. *Ask yourself: Should you list?* If you do, you are relying on the effectiveness of the search engine strategy that the directory will use. In fact, it may be better to put the same money into optimizing the search engine strategy for your own website.

For many years, the Yellow Pages was the obvious directory for small firms to list in. Yellow Pages usage has been declining steadily over the past few years, but both online and hardcopy versions are still necessary for some industries. People tend to use directories like this for infrequently used services—tow trucks, taxis, florists—services that are used so irregularly that most people don't have a normal supplier. So a restaurant in the downtown tourist district (where people from out of town don't know where they should eat) may find a directory ad useful. A suburban restaurant where people typically go because they have seen it in the neighbourhood or because it has been recommended may be wasting money on a directory ad.

In industries where most of the practitioners work freelance (professional photography, motion picture arts, theatre arts), online **directories** are available for use by industry professionals only. In some of these industries, it may be almost mandatory to have a listing in these directories.

Outdoor Advertising Advertising media such as transit cards and billboards tend to be too expensive for a micro-enterprise, but other forms of **outdoor advertising** may be appropriate: posters, handbills, vehicle lettering, sandwich boards, and so on.

specialty newspaper A smaller-circulation newspaper targeting customers who have a particular interest or are of a particular ethnic background.

Memory Check 3.18
True or False? The most valuable mailing lists for most companies are their own customer lists.

trade journals Magazines written for people involved in specific industries; for example, a commercial fishing publication or a professional teachers' magazine.

directories Published lists of suppliers for particular goods and services; for example, a trades directory, an antique dealers directory, a directory of professional actors.

outdoor advertising Visual promotion aimed at passing vehicle and pedestrian traffic.

If you are starting a retail business, your most significant piece of advertising may be your business sign. Illuminated store signs are expensive, so plan to have it for a long time. Make sure the sign clearly identifies the store and clearly projects the image you wish to send out. Don't forget: The sign will often be the first impression potential customers have of your business.

⭐ Head Start Exercise

3.10 Identify the primary advertising technique you will use in your first year. Make an estimate (call around) of what this will cost you (1/4 page maximum).

Advertising Content

Writing advertising copy (for websites, letters, newspaper ads, telemarketing pitches) is an area where many people seem to think they have some talent. It's one of those things that you may believe is easier and cheaper to do without outside help—after all, you have been exposed to advertising your whole life. But thinking that this means you know how to prepare advertising is like thinking you know how to cook just because you have been eating your whole life. At the very least, you should have as many other people as possible read anything you've written (even letters). And don't get defensive when your writing is criticized! Instead, carefully weigh the comments of your proofreaders.

All of your advertising activities should try to achieve the following:

- **Grab attention.** This is most easily done by mentioning something specifically important to the viewer or reader. For example, seniors and college students tend to have different priorities in life. Starting an ad by talking about *pension cheques* will get the attention of one group while mention of *serious partying* will appeal to the other.

- **Project the right image.** This applies not just to what you may have written, but to how it was sent, the speed of download time or the type of paper, the colour, even the font. Keep in mind the potential for cognitive dissonance, discussed earlier in the chapter.

- **Entertain.** There is an informal contract between media consumers and advertisers that the viewer will lend their ears and/or eyes to the advertiser in return for being entertained. So, if you are a tattoo artist, you may write a blog on "Goth Ink," which readers will come to in order to read about the latest trends in black-and-white tattoos. They will not be entertained if most of your blog is about how great your tattoo shop is and why they should come there. Yes, you must imply or mention these things at times (after all, the purpose of your blog is to sell) but most of the blog must be about things that will entertain and inform the reader.

- **Get action.** This is most easily done by directly telling people what you want them to do: "Drop by today for a free estimate," "Please call as soon as you have seen my portfolio," "Click on the order form below."

If you choose to advertise, you should be prepared to explain in your business plan your choice of media, why they are likely to be effective, and how you will know whether you are spending your money wisely. This means measuring and keeping records. Indicators of advertising effectiveness you will want to keep track of include:

- **Activity.** How much did your advertising increase the number of calls you get, people coming into the store, website hits, or the number of order forms coming in?

- **Sales.** Did you bring in more dollars when advertising? If activity went up but sales didn't, you can see that the advertising had an effect, but you need to adjust some other element of your marketing mix, such as your product/service offering.

- **Profit.** Never lose sight of profit as the purpose of all your business activity. If your advertising increased your sales, but after the cost of the advertising there was no new profit, you may have to adjust your prices or other aspects of your marketing mix.

⭐ Head Start Exercise

3.11 Make a list of ways you will measure the effectiveness of any advertising you do (1/4 page maximum).

Publicity

Publicity means free advertising—a misleading definition because, as you know, nothing is free and that includes publicity. In the case of publicity, you pay, but only indirectly.

Let's say you start a service to help plan and organize weddings: Bride's Aid Wedding Planners. You might then mount a campaign (letters, clippings, brochures, free T-shirts) trying to convince the producer of a local radio call-in show that you would be an ideal guest for a show about wedding disasters. If the producer goes for it, you get to be on the show answering questions, giving comments, and generally demonstrating the value of having someone like you plan a wedding. You hope that the host of the show will work in, as often as possible, the fact that today's guest is "the owner of Bride's Aid Wedding Planners, located at. . . ." Now this is valuable exposure which you did not pay for, but it did cost you time and money to convince the producer and appear on the show.

Giving a free talk at the local public library (and later handing out your business cards), writing an unpaid article (which clearly identifies you and your business) for a local community newspaper, donating your product or service to a school or volunteer fire department (which ends up with you being interviewed on the local TV news)—these are all examples of valuable publicity.

⭐ Head Start Exercise

3.12 Make a list of at least three ways you could get publicity (1/4 page maximum).

One-on-One Selling

Traditionally, **personal selling** has meant dealing physically, one on one, with a salesperson. But since the growth of telemarketing and online communications, the lines between advertising and personal selling are becoming less clear. Nevertheless, salesmanship—the skill of meeting potential customers and convincing them to buy your service or product—is the key to success for many entrepreneurs. At the same time, for many it is the most dreaded aspect of being in business. *Ask yourself: Can I see myself in the role of salesperson?*

Many new entrepreneurs are uncomfortable with the idea of themselves as salespeople, preferring to see themselves as professional service providers. As a result, when it comes to developing a promotional strategy for the business plan, they wrongly choose to rely on some form of advertising. In some cases, this is just a way of avoiding the discomfort of calling on prospective customers. Even when some alternative promotional tool is properly employed, however, for most new enterprises the entrepreneur must, to some extent, act as the salesperson in order to foster the relationship with the customer.[9]

If you feel that you have no selling abilities, keep in mind that selling is a skill, and as such you will improve with practice. Before you can get the practice, however, you must

✅ **Memory Check 3.20**
True or False? Direct mail tends to be a relatively good promotional investment for small firms.

publicity Promotion by spreading information about a company, product, or service without directly paying for the use of media space or time.

✅ **Memory Check 3.21**
True or False? The name of your company on the side of your van is a form of outdoor advertising.

personal selling Promotion of services/products through person-to-person interaction between the supplier and the potential customer.

overcome any initial fear. As with public speaking for some, going to the dentist for others, or skydiving for most of us, the process of overcoming fear is pretty much the same:

- Analyze what you're really afraid of (rejection? failure? embarrassment? responsibility?).
- Imagine the worst-case scenario (your worst fears coming true).
- Decide to accept and live (or die) with the worst-case scenario (should it come about).
- Go ahead and do what you're afraid of (it won't be that bad!).
- Do it again! (Already you can see improvement.)

The steps in the personal selling process are quickly learned, and you'll do best by sticking to the basics. But knowing the steps is not a substitute for building your skill through practice. The selling steps are:

- **Prospecting.** This means finding prospective customers. Other types of promotion (when people respond to your advertising or when you talk to delegates after your publicity presentation) are ways of accomplishing this. Referrals (sometimes paid for) can come from existing customers or businesses that are complementary to yours. Sometimes, however, it comes down to manually building a list of prospects by checking through directories (such as the Yellow Pages) for your kind of potential customer.

- **Approach.** The first contact with your prospect can come with the prospect's response to your ad. It is also possible to have other people (such as telemarketers) generate leads and set up appointments for you. For new businesses, however, it is often a matter of cold calling, where, with no previous contact, you phone or visit the prospect, introduce yourself, and explain why you are contacting them.

- **Qualifying.** You don't want to waste a minute of your selling time talking to people who are never going to buy from you. Qualifying means finding out whether your prospect really is the kind of customer who could benefit from your product or service, whether they are in a position to buy, and whether you are in fact dealing with someone who has the authority to make the buying decision. You qualify the prospect by asking questions—lots of questions.

✓ **Memory Check 3.22**
True or False? Owners of new service businesses should avoid personal selling as a promotion technique.

- **Presentation.** A good sales presentation should explain to the prospect the benefits of your service or product as quickly as possible—for the sake of your time as well as the prospect's. And it must be flexible. New salespeople face the danger of rigidly sticking to a sales presentation (especially if it's one they're proud of) when the customer is bored (already knows the information) or even when the customer is trying to interrupt in order to buy.

- **Closing.** Getting the customer to actually agree to buy is what we mean by closing. It seems so obvious an objective. Nevertheless, new salespeople are known for making an elaborate presentation, thanking the prospects for their time, and leaving without ever asking "So, will you buy?" "Do we have a deal?" "When would you like delivery?" "Can we set a date to start the work?" or "Will you sign the contract for that amount?" All of these are closing questions, and you should never leave the prospect without asking one.

❓ **Get Help 3.11**
For information on selling, start at the library. An introductory marketing textbook (it doesn't have to be new or even particularly recent) will explain the basics of salesmanship and sales management. Avoid slick popular works that promise miraculous sales results.

- **Managing objections.** If someone has a legitimate objection (a reason why they cannot buy from you), you want to find it out as quickly as possible so you won't be wasting time. But it's part of human nature to avoid making decisions (including the decision whether to buy your service or product), and prospects will typically come up with reasonable (but untrue) objections so they can avoid decision making. Your job as the salesperson is to deal with the objection by requalifying the prospect (asking more questions) or by using the objection to close the deal. "So, the reason you don't want to buy is that you feel the price is too high? Well, if I could give you a lower price, would you sign the contract today?" After a few sales encounters, you'll have heard most of the objections you're likely to encounter and you will develop an appropriate closing response for each.

3.13 List the steps in the selling process. Identify which will be the easiest and which will be the most difficult for you, personally. Explain why (1/2 page maximum).

Preparation should involve rehearsing your sales presentation (find a willing critic) and organizing tools to assist you. Sales aids can include everything from your business card to samples, an order book, a laptop computer (for demonstration or ordering), your portfolio, résumés, a cell phone, overhead transparencies, and so on.

If personal selling is the logical way of getting business from your type of customers, don't try to get around it by looking for promotional alternatives. If you can't learn to do

Business Reality 3.2 addrenaline Media
Selling E-Marketing, the Old Fashioned Way

Using his skills as a designer and communicator, Kyle Hosick was working for a company in the events management business. The firm successfully created and managed conferences, trade shows, and other large events for their clients. At the time, Kyle thought that the systems and techniques used by the company were too reliant on old paper-based methods. He proposed to his boss that they shift to fully web-based methods for managing and promoting their events. The boss didn't agree that it was time for this transition, so Kyle decided to go out on his own. (Kyle and the ex-boss are still friends and, with hindsight, she recognizes that decision as a mistake.)

A year later, working from his kitchen table, Kyle started finding clients he could design web applications for. Over the next few years, he moved to new offices, acquired partners, moved again, bought out the partners, and moved again, all the while building his expertise and his client base. Today, the business is housed in a modern open space in a newly refurbished building. There are six employees and the main activity of addrenaline Media is to design more effective websites for a wide range of clients.

In 2007, Kyle was closely watching the rise of Google and realized that a major focus of his work would be in the area of search engine optimization for client websites. "The old hard copy Yellow Pages are gone," says Kyle, who sees the website as the primary listing for any company. While web design has been a major focus, the company has also been building expertise in e-commerce applications, advertising, branding, and business strategy. Now, almost half the company revenue comes from secondary marketing services provided for web design clients.

The big marketing challenge faced by addrenaline itself is to move its pricing upward to reflect its increased levels of expertise. As the company has become more successful, Kyle has even had to "fire" clients who could not adjust to the new positioning of the firm. He also sees a certain irony in that to help the growth of his company, which specializes in electronic media, Kyle had to hire a full-time salesperson. This decision came with the realization that electronic communications are no substitute for personal contact with clients and prospects. As well, as the contracts become bigger, there is more emphasis on the sales function for things like responding to proposal requests.

Kyle's first piece of advice for would-be entrepreneurs is to "believe in your own ideas and don't be discouraged by the nay-sayers." His second piece of advice is to "be cautious when taking on debt."

it yourself (although you probably can without too much trouble), the options are hiring a salesperson, getting a partner who can sell, or changing your distribution strategy (provided there is an alternative).

If you decide to hire a salesperson, you are now into the role of sales manager. This may involve decisions about territory, compensation, training, and motivation for the salesperson. It is much easier to manage salespeople if you have some selling experience yourself. However, an introductory marketing test will tell you the basics of getting others to sell.

Sales Promotion

Sales promotion is not some sort of discrete marketing activity. Instead, it's just a convenient way of lumping together any kind of promotional activity that is not clearly in the categories of advertising, publicity, or personal selling. Sales promotion is a big grab bag of creative promotional techniques, which are fraught with dangers for the new entrepreneur. Proceed with extreme caution when using any of the following techniques:

- **Giveaways.** These include items like pens, mouse pads, lighters, fridge magnets, and T-shirts printed with your company name and likely the phone number. The problem with giveaways is that much of it (that you will have paid for) ends up in the hands of people who are not part of your target market and will never buy from you. *Ask yourself: Do I own any pens showing the names of companies that I have never otherwise heard of or am extremely unlikely to ever deal with?*

- **Coupons.** The idea behind coupons is to get new customers to deal with you once, see how good you are, and then become regulars. Let's say you're a hairdresser, targeting elderly women in the neighbourhood of your salon. You distribute coupons for "$25 off the price of a perm" to the entire neighbourhood, trying to get new customers. But it could turn out that almost all of the coupons that come back to you are from existing customers, who are now paying $25 less for a perm that they would have bought anyway at full price.

- **Premiums.** Two-for-one deals, buy something and get something else free, the second entrée at half-price—these are all means of using premiums to promote your business. The danger, as in coupons, is giving away something that established customers would have paid for anyway. At the same time you are unsure if you are bringing new customers in. There is some evidence to show that retail price promotions are generally of more benefit to the manufacturer than to the retailer.[10]

- **Events.** Having skydivers land in your parking lot, a book signing by a celebrity, a face-painting contest—these are all promotional events. They often involve high cost and high risk: The weather may turn bad, the celebrity might be a no-show, a bigger event somewhere else may kill your turnout.

- **Trade shows.** If all of your potential customers annually attend a particular trade show or conference, you will be able to economically contact your entire market at one time,[11] provided you can afford the fee to rent a booth. Depending on the size of the show and the location, a two- to three-day booth rental can run from a few hundred dollars to many thousands—and this will not include the actual cost of setting up your display and providing handout material. The major risks are that the traffic won't appear (especially with shows that are not established), that your booth will be outclassed by the competition, or that your service really requires personal selling and you won't have time to talk to many customers.

- **Displays.** This usually means providing displays for someone else to sell your service. For example, you may be a pilot offering charter fishing flights to tourists visiting your town. You get customers by paying a commission to local hotels and travel agencies and you provide them with your company's brochures, maps, and price lists along with a display rack to put them in. But the display rack that you paid for could end up in the back room holding magazines or be used to display your competitor's brochures advertising a dinner theatre.

- **Free samples.** Remember the "image" issue of something being worth what you pay for it? If you're selling a professional service, free samples will not help your image, where a money-back guarantee in your contract might. On the other hand, for some businesses you cannot promote your product without samples. For example, if you plan on selling frozen perogies to restaurants, you have to let them taste the product first and try it out on their clientele.

Because of the high risk involved in most forms of sales promotion, if you decide to use one of these techniques, as in advertising, you should predetermine a method to measure the cost-effectiveness of your campaign.

⭐ Head Start Exercise

3.14 Identify any sales promotion techniques you might use and make notes to justify your choice (1/4 page maximum).

Keep in mind that your marketing strategy is a series of trade-offs or compromises that will give you the best mix of product, price, distribution, and promotion for the particular kind of customers you are specializing in. Learn from the most profitable businesses: Tim Hortons arguably does not have the best coffee. Canadian Tire does not consistently offer the best prices. Leon's does not have the greatest number of furniture outlets. But they all owe their success to having the right marketing mix for the customers they target.

Revising Your Plan

Once you have gathered the information and worked through the decisions for Section 3 of your business plan, you may find that you now have to go back and revise some of the decisions you made in Sections 1 and 2. Figure 3.4 demonstrates how some elements of marketing may affect previous sections of the business plan.

Figure 3.4 The Business Plan Revision Process

1 Model	2 Feasibility	3 Marketing	4 Operations	5 Finances
Product/Service	Market Potential	Name/Image		
Target Customer	Competition	Service/Product Mix		
Location	Sales Forecast	Pricing		
Legal Form	Insurance	Distribution		
Agreements	Intellectual Property	Promotion		

Answers to Memory Check Questions

3.1 T   3.2 T   3.3 F   3.4 F   3.5 F   3.6 T   3.7 F   3.8 T
3.9 F   3.10 F   3.11 T   3.12 F   3.13 T   3.14 F   3.15 F   3.16 F
3.17 T   3.18 T   3.19 T   3.20 T   3.21 T   3.22 F

Questions for Discussion

1. Discuss how the average person misuses the term "marketing." Try to identify the reasons for this.

2. Pick several small businesses in your area and discuss the types of image that the names of those companies imply. Are these images appropriate for these firms? Suggest better ones.

3. Explain why cognitive dissonance is a "weirded-out" feeling. Why does the behaviour of politicians or sports heroes sometimes produce cognitive dissonance?

4. Do *brand* and *image* mean the same thing? When are they used interchangeably? When are they used differently?

5. Discuss the *product mix* of dollar stores. Why might this be appropriate for their target market?

6. Identify some businesses that promote themselves as having low prices when in fact their pricing strategies are competitive. Why do they use this approach? What are the dangers?

7. Do you negotiate all or most of your retail purchases? Discuss reasons for people's reticence to negotiate lower prices on consumer purchases.

8. Imagine your business is producing custom-made clothing for women in your city who are immigrants from South Asia. Specifically, how could you use social media to promote your company? Why might this technique fail?

9. Find a piece of "junk mail" addressed to you. Are you an appropriate prospect for the goods or services being sold? Speculate on how the advertiser got your mailing information.

10. Identify the reasons that most new entrepreneurs are reluctant to engage in personal selling. How can an entrepreneur overcome this reluctance?

11. Check your collection of pens and pencils for one that has a company name on it (not the name of the company that made the pen). Are you a good prospect for the products or services of this company? How did the pen get into your hands? Is the pen going to make you more likely to buy products or services from this company? Why do you think the company is using this form of promotion?

Case for Discussion

Michael Cruz had thought that selling his service was going to be the easiest part of starting a part-time business. He was in for a big surprise.

Michael had been working full-time as a painter and general repairperson for the local board of education. It was an 8:00 a.m. to 4:00 p.m. job, Monday to Friday. He lived in a small bungalow in a subdivision of small bungalows, close to the board offices. The exterior paint on Michael's house (window frames, eaves, and soffits) had been fading and flaking, consistent with the age of the house. Michael's next-door neighbour had recently hired a firm to paint the same areas on his house at a cost of $650.

Michael thought this was hilarious. He went to the paint supplier used by the school board and paid $35 for enough high-quality exterior paint for his house, and completed the work himself in less than six hours on a Saturday. Looking around at his neighbourhood, Michael realized there were hundreds of potential customers whose houses were the right age for painting. He could easily do two houses every weekend, could charge a fair price (a lot less than his neighbour had paid), and still make lots of money. The first thing he did was get online and register his business with the provincial government. Best to start off properly. Besides, maybe this could turn into a full-time business.

Michael had hundreds of half-page flyers printed up and hired two kids with bicycles to put one in every mailbox in the neighbourhood:

CHEAP PAINT JOB FOR YOUR HOUSE
Windows, soffits, eaves and downspouts for

$350

Here is my phone number: 855-555-3213
Done in one day. Good Work

He didn't get a single call.

Only slightly discouraged, Michael decided he would have to sell his service by personally going door-to-door. He approached each customer with a big smile and his hand ready to shake. "I'm Michael, and I noticed the exterior paint on your house is a real mess," he would begin. When that got no positive responses, Michael began varying his approach: "Hey, how are you? Look, you want a really good paint job for cheap?" Or: "You interested in saving some money on paint work?"

At most houses he would be met with a polite refusal (only one slammed door) and the same list of objections to his offer:

"Thanks, but my husband (or wife) makes those decisions about the house and he (or she) is away right now."

"No, thanks, I do my own repairs and painting around the house."

"No, we have our own guy we deal with for that kind of work."

"No, I don't mind how it looks. It's not really bad enough to repaint yet."

After five days of house-to-house canvassing, Michael only managed to get one customer. When the work was completed, the customer tried to pay Michael with MasterCard. Michael explained that he only worked for cash, but they finally settled on a personal cheque. Over the next few days, the customer called Michael twice to come back because of "problems" the customer had spotted. In both cases, the problem was related to flaws in the framing or the metal and had nothing to do with Michael's work.

Michael was starting to wonder if his business idea was such a good one.

1. Identify any services Michael should be providing other than painting. Explain.

2. Discuss Michael's pricing strategy. Where would you put the price for his service? Why?

3. Critique the advertising piece that Michael is using. Write a better one.

4. Critique the sales approach Michael is using. Suggest alternatives.

5. What sort of signage should Michael use? Explain.

6. How could Michael encourage his one customer (and any future customers) to get referral business for him?

The Business Plan, Section 3:
MARKETING

Image

1. Describe the image that your company will project and explain why this is appropriate for your services or products and the expectations of the customer groups you are targeting.

Business Name

2. Give the name that your business will be operating under and explain how this name projects the appropriate image for your products/services and customer groups.

Service/Product Mix

3. Provide a detailed explanation of the products or services you will offer, comparing your range to that of your major competitors. Explain why this strategy is appropriate for your type of customers.

4. Explain any added value services you will offer and why they are appropriate.

Pricing

5. Outline the pricing strategy you will be using and explain how it fits in with the rest of your marketing mix.

6. Prepare a price list showing the specific products or services you will offer and the prices you will charge. Indicate any discounts you will offer for specific types of customers or volumes, or any ranges within which you will negotiate prices.

Distribution

7. Explain clearly who the ultimate users of your products/services are and where your business fits into any chain of distribution. Identify your "legal" customers and the details of any contracting arrangements.

8. Explain how your service or product will physically get to your customer. If the customer is coming to you, describe in detail the set-up, decor, and tone of your site. Explain how the site design is in keeping with the image you wish to project.

Promotion

9. Identify any advertising medium you will use, the nature of the advertising piece, and the frequency of advertising.

10. Explain any publicity you will get and how you will arrange this exposure.

11. Describe any personal selling you will engage in, explaining how you will get your prospects, how you will approach them, and any sales aids you will use.

12. Explain any sales promotion techniques you intend to use and any risks involved.

Promotion Evaluation

13. Explain how you will measure the effectiveness of the promotional means you have chosen, and outline any backup plans for redirecting your promotional efforts.

Chapter 4

Operations: How Will I Organize the Work?

So far in your business plan, you have explained what business you're getting into, you have presented evidence of why it will work, and you have explained the marketing strategy you will use. Now, in Section 4, you will give the specifics of what you will do on a day-to-day basis. You will answer the following questions:

- How Will I Manage the Space and Equipment?
- How Will I Manage the Process?
- How Will I Manage Information?
- How Will I Manage Myself and Others in the Firm?
- How Will I Manage the Government?

Learning Objectives

On completion of this chapter, you should be able to:

1. Discuss how retail, office, and manufacturing spaces differ in layout.
2. Discuss the two main objectives of purchasing systems.
3. Employ four techniques for outlining the processes in a business.
4. Discuss the need for setting and enforcing quality standards.
5. Outline the importance of managing information in a small business.
6. Explain five techniques for effective leadership.
7. Discuss three ways in which government influences small business.
8. Prepare the operations portion of a business plan.

HOW WILL I MANAGE THE SPACE AND EQUIPMENT?

Acquiring Necessities

Most of us enjoy shopping. On top of that, we like new "toys": the thrill of unpacking them, setting them up, and (for a few of us) reading the instruction manuals. So it's no wonder that one of the strongest urges for the new entrepreneur is to get out there and start buying fun things for the new business.

Slow down! A business is not a hobby (even though the idea may have started out that way). Business decisions are based on profit, not fun (even though entrepreneurs consider it fun to make profit). Any equipment acquisitions should be appropriate for what you are selling and appropriate for satisfying the needs of those to whom you are selling. If you're starting a recording studio that will make demo CDs for amateur bands, top-of-the-line equipment might be what you want. But for your market, it is not necessary, and you could go bankrupt trying to pay for it. Don't acquire anything more than you have to.

Ask yourself: What are the problems that arise when you treat your business as a hobby? When buying the things you really need, keep in mind that the equipment doesn't have to be new. Newspaper classifieds, sales by **tender**, and auctions (remember all those businesses that go bankrupt?) are good places to look for used equipment.

Items you already own but will use in your business are considered part of your investment in the company. This is important for claiming depreciation expenses on your tax return and for demonstrating to lenders how much of an investment you have made personally.

☆ Head Start Exercise

4.1   Make a list of all the personal belongings that you could invest into a new business (e.g., a desk, car, computer, filing cabinet, tools, etc.) (3/4 page maximum).

In many cases, when acquiring equipment, you will have a choice between leasing and buying.

Frequently, the **lease** deals available to small firms (for items like computers, vehicles, construction equipment, or machinery) are just another way of financing the purchase. Instead of you borrowing the money and going out and buying items in the name of your company, the leasing company buys it and title stays in the leasing company's name, while you use the equipment and make monthly payments.

In a great many of these leases, however, you are actually agreeing to buy the equipment by paying a final fee at the end of the lease. For these types of leases, careful comparison will often show that it is actually cheaper to finance the outright purchase of the equipment from the beginning. In fact, the requirements to borrow the money are likely no more stringent than the requirements for leasing.

So, shop carefully and keep in mind that lease prices, just like purchase prices, are negotiable.

☆ Head Start Exercise

4.2   Make up a list of any equipment you will have to buy for your business, along with ball-park prices. The prices are important for Section 5 of your plan (1/2 page maximum).

Office Set-Up

Almost all enterprises have some sort of office, which is really just a place for processing and storing information. As such, an orderly arrangement of communication devices, work areas, and filing equipment is only to be expected. But most of the real processing of information (the planning and the decision making) takes place inside the head of the entrepreneur. Therefore, the office set-up must take into consideration your personal work habits, idiosyncrasies, and needs. Other office issues include:

- *Efficiency.* Self-employed people can spend a huge amount of their time on the phone, yet relatively few invest in an inexpensive headset (better than a speaker phone) that will keep both hands free for the computer or other work. Frequently used information (phone lists, current projects) should be close to hand, and work areas should reflect the process or flow of work.

- *Flexibility.* As office equipment becomes more portable (laptops, printers, hand-held communication devices) the actual office space itself can become more fluid and portable.[1]

- ***Ergonomics.*** If your business operations basically consist of you sitting at a computer, your productivity (and even your long-term health) could depend on a design that reduces eye, joint, and muscle strain, not necessarily the most comfortable. An ergonomic study of laboratory seating clearly showed a relationship between productivity and correct seat height.[2]

- *Visitors*. Visitor space is only important if customers, and to a lesser extent suppliers, come to your site. Considerations for the visitor might include issues of a comfortable reception or waiting area and on-site displays or advertising. In addition, you may need meeting space separate from your work areas to maintain confidentiality of your records and materials.

⭐ Head Start Exercise

4.3 Make a quick sketch of the office set-up you might need (1 page maximum).

Retail Set-Up

For a retail store, the business plan should outline the organization of storage and work areas. It should also show (using drawings) the layout for actual selling space, with the objectives of minimizing cost and maximizing sales in mind.[3] Considerations for use of the store space include:

- *Volume of shelf space allocation.* Since the business will have limited shelf space and some items take up more room than others, the question becomes how much space will be allocated for each item sold. These decisions can depend on the rate of sale (for restocking), shipping quantities, and the profitability of the item.

- *Positioning of merchandise.* Putting items in the more visible and easier-to-reach spaces will, on average, increase the sales of those items. Logically, the more profitable items and impulse items (things the customer did not intend to buy, but may decide to after seeing the item) would receive the prime positions. In addition, similar items should be stocked together to make it easier for customers to find them.

- *Security.* For many retailers, it is important to have the cash register positioned so the operator can see the entire store and at the same time monitor the entrance. It may also be important to keep the cash area well lit and visible to the street or mall traffic. *Ask yourself: Why might it be wise to place cash registers so they are visible to the street?*

Keep in mind that the overall tone of the store has been established in your marketing strategy (Section 3 of the business plan). Therefore, the actual layout, fixtures, and decor should be selected to project the image you have already decided on. Even security issues (like the placement of cash registers) should be in keeping with your image.

✔ Memory Check 4.2
True or False? A healthy investment for the small office is likely to be the most comfortable chair you can find.

❓ Get Help 4.2
If you are starting a retail operation, it is worth spending some time on the website of the Retail Council of Canada at www.retailcouncil.org.

⭐ Head Start Exercise

4.4 Make a preliminary sketch of any selling space, product demonstration, or display areas (1 page maximum).

Manufacturing or Wholesale Set-Up

Both manufacturers and wholesalers must carefully plan the shipping and receiving functions to allow for the orderly movement of raw materials or parts in and the rapid dispatch of products out.

The storage set-up is a balance between maximum use of the space and maximum ability to locate and access materials and finished products when they are needed. Let's say a wholesaler imports hang glider kits from Europe for distribution to the North American market. The kits would be fairly large, but there would be relatively few models and the boxes would be labelled. So, even though lots of space would be needed, the organization might consist of just piling the boxes on top of each other, label facing out. On the other hand, a business that builds and repairs custom guitar amplifiers would require very little storage space even though it might have hundreds of tiny electronic parts. Here, a complex labelling and ordering system would be needed.

⭐ Head Start Exercise

4.5 Make a sketch of any storage areas you will need for holding materials or finished products (1 page maximum).

Manufacturers of custom, made-to-order products generally use a **process set-up**, grouping together types of equipment that perform similar functions. However, businesses that mass-produce the same items over and over are likely to use a **product set-up**, where machinery and equipment are lined up in the order they are used for production. For example, in a small, custom furniture plant all the sanding machines will be together—a process set-up. On the other hand, a wood shop that mass-produces table legs may have one sanding machine near the beginning of the line (to smooth the wood after shaping on the lathe) and another one near the end (to sand between coats of lacquer)—a product set-up.

Let's say you want to custom-make model trucks as gifts for truck drivers. (You will provide a scale replica of the rig the trucker actually drives.) It sounds simple, but to make it pay you may need a fairly complex manufacturing process that has part of your shop devoted to a process set-up (which will make large numbers of popular brands of trucks that will be stored) and part of your shop devoted to a product set-up (that will take the correct model of truck from storage and modify and paint it for the individual client).

Manufacturing firms, like this example, will need some kind of manufacturing plan. This will normally include a floor plan, an analysis of machinery use, and a detailed explanation of costing and scheduling methods. In the future, a flexible manufacturing space could be ideal, so that the set-up can be changed for different types of orders, seasons, and so on. So far, this is generally not economical, although there is some research looking for ways to make manufacturing space more dynamic.[4] Remember, however, that offering both mass-produced and custom-made products is generally a bad idea for a start-up business; it is more profitable to specialize in one or the other.[5]

⭐ Head Start Exercise

4.6 Make a sketch of any production set-up you might need, labelling all equipment and showing (with arrows) the direction that products will follow as they go through your process (1 page maximum).

Service Set-Up

This category could include everything from construction contractors, to dry cleaners, to music schools, to psychotherapists. The category is defined as a service, since most of the cost involved in what you're selling comes from labour and expertise as opposed to the cost of some physical product (even though a physical product may be an important part of what you're selling).

For many service firms, the only space and equipment considerations will be for an office. For others, such as restaurants and garages, your explanation of equipment and space use may include all the components of office, retail, and manufacturing set-ups.

For example, someone with a background involving theatrical makeup and hairdressing might decide to start a business making custom wigs for cancer patients. In this case, the business plan would have to include sketches of the set-up for the area where clients

---

process set-up A manufacturing layout that groups similar types of equipment or activities into separate areas.

product set-up A manufacturing layout that places machinery and equipment in the order that they are used for producing a particular product; an assembly line set-up.

❓ Get Help 4.3
Industrial engineers (not to be confused with industrial designers) have expertise in designing maximum efficiency workplaces for manufacturing and storage. There are also several software programs to assist with layouts. (See www.instantplanner.com.)

✅ Memory Check 4.3
True or False? A product set-up is laid out like a traditional assembly line.

✅ Memory Check 4.4
True or False? A firm may be selling a physical product and still be classified as a service type of business.

Boarders won't be Bored with this Layout

Tropical North in Barrie, Ontario, is recognized locally as the cool place to buy a board. The store sells snowboards, skateboards, surfboards, and sailboards, but much of the revenue these days comes from selling clothing and accessories popular with the "boarder" crowd. This subculture, originally a small group of extreme sports enthusiasts, shares tastes in apparel, footwear, and even music. Brands are important to this group because of their traditional concern for equipment quality. The segment has expanded in numbers and age range over the past few years, to the point where it has become increasingly mainstream. But a larger market also means more competitors. When it comes to boarder apparel, large malls have chain stores, like West 49, with huge purchasing and advertising power competing for Tropical North's customers. The company has responded by concentrating more on boards and other specialty items, expanding its product lines to include stand-up paddle boards, kite boards, windsurfing boards, long boards, and wake boards. As well, Tropical North has increased its web presence and sells its specialized boards online.

The location of the business—Barrie, Ontario—has proven to be excellent because of the city's explosive growth over the past few years, as well as its proximity to several ski resorts and cottage country. Young middle-class families have been moving into the city's new subdivisions, doubling the population over a 10-year period. Like many smaller cities, the downtown area has been rejuvenated with specialty stores and services that do not compete directly with the chains and big box stores. The site for Tropical North offers excellent visibility with high levels of pedestrian and auto traffic. The older buildings in this section, however, make layout a challenge. The long, narrow store is set up with the cash register two-thirds of the way toward the back, pulling buyers in to see the entire inventory. There are lots of impulse items at eye level around the cash register and at other strategic spots in the store. The high ceilings are used to excellent advantage with maximum display of inventory.

Pulling this off, of course, takes experience. Owner Jeff Borgmeyer's advice to would-be store owners is to "get a minimum of three years' experience in retail, working for someone else, before going on your own." Visit the company's website at www.tropicalnorth.ca.

will be dealt with (identifying reception area, chairs, mirrors, storage areas, equipment, and lighting), as well as the workshop area where the wigs are made (showing moulds, work benches, tool areas, etc.).

HOW WILL I MANAGE THE PROCESS?

It's not enough that your business plan explains what goes where. It must also show that you have worked out the details of how you will do things.

Logistics

The term **logistics** originally applied to the planning and carrying out of military movements. Large manufacturing firms eventually adopted it, primarily to describe the transportation and storage of products. Large firms also came to believe that their profits were more and more linked to their ability to cut inventory costs, especially with **just-in-time** delivery systems. Many small firms have also tried to follow this trend, but with less success.[6] Over the years, the meaning of logistics has broadened to include issues of purchasing, production planning,

logistics The study and management of the planning, procurement, transportation, and storage of products.

just-in-time An inventory management system that plans to have products delivered shortly before they are required in order to reduce storage costs.

and customer service. At the same time, a greater emphasis on logistics has taken place in the wholesale and retail sectors, and even service industries have adopted many logistics concepts. Often the term *logistics* is used interchangeably with **supply chain management**. The supply chain, mentioned in Chapter 3, involves both the channel and physical elements of distribution.

In Canada, the study of logistics has become more formalized, with many post-secondary courses available. The Logistics Institute confers a professional designation (P.Log.) for trained practitioners in the field. These logisticians are experts in developing systems that ensure the supply of products, when they are needed, as profitably as possible. You are applying many of the principles of this discipline as you figure out the most economical way to secure and manage materials.

If your business must manage high volumes, or a wide variety of materials, or if it has a complicated distribution process, it may be necessary to get the advice of a professional to prepare this part of your business plan, especially considering that smaller firms tend to be poor at more formal approaches to logistics.[7] *Ask yourself: Are there elements of my business that will need logistics planning?*

For most new ventures, however, it is sufficient to show some basic logic in your plan for keeping your business supplied in an economical fashion.

Get Help 4.4
Look in the Yellow Pages under "business consultants" for specialists in the area of logistics. See also the website of the Logistics Institute at www.loginstitute.ca.

Purchasing

The topic of purchasing is not about the one-time purchase of equipment at the start-up of a business. Rather, it is about the ongoing buying of materials, supplies, and services that your business will need on a regular basis. The idea is that every time you buy or contract something for the business, you don't want it to be a big decision-making exercise. Instead, you will have figured out a system for making purchases in advance.

The purposes of your purchasing system are

- to prevent your business from running out of inventory or supplies (you can't make money if you don't have the supplies needed for your service); and

- to reduce your costs by keeping as little inventory as possible (you don't want to spend money financing and storing inventory that you don't need).

Ask yourself: Which is the lesser of two evils, to have too much inventory or to have too little inventory? Obviously, you have to strike a reasonable balance between these two objectives. But the general rule is this: better to have too much (you can reduce prices to move the stock) than too little (and risk losing the customer as well as the sale).

How much work you put into this issue will depend on the nature of your business. If you plan on being a yoga instructor, your ongoing purchases will be only minor supplies—and going too heavily into business cards won't bankrupt you. But if you plan on opening a vegetable market, cases of unsold rotting avocados could be your undoing.

If your business depends on inventory, your business plan must show your method for knowing when to order stock and for knowing how much to order at one time. Small entrepreneurs often explain that knowing these things comes from experience. But a careful analysis of their "experience" really shows that most have worked out a purchasing system (often informally) that is based on things like the following:

- the rate of use of a particular product
- the amount of storage space available
- the order quantities offered by suppliers
- the delivery cost of an order
- the amount of time it takes to get replacement stock
- the rate at which the stock spoils

Get Help 4.5
Manufacturers and some retailers often depend on economic order quantity formulas for their purchasing decisions. Purchasing textbooks offer lots of these formal methods, and there are excellent articles on inventory management at www.inventoryops.com.

Memory Check 4.5
True or False? One of the objectives of a purchasing system is to maximize the amount of inventory.

Memory Check 4.6
True or False? The terms *logistics* and *supply chain management* are commonly used interchangeably.

- the peak-demand times of the year
- the production schedule

⭐ Head Start Exercises

4.7 If your business will depend on any specific supplies, make a list of the factors that will affect your ordering decisions (1/3 page maximum).

4.8 If your business will be carrying products for resale, estimate how much inventory you will need to carry, what this stock will cost you, and how often it will have to be replaced (1/2 page maximum).

Even if your business doesn't purchase products, it may have to buy services from other professionals or businesses. Before starting up, new entrepreneurs may get a wide variety of outside help for the preparation of their business plan. Advisers may include teachers, bankers, engineers, accountants, marketing consultants, lawyers, appraisers, and so on. Many of these resources will provide free advice, but others will charge hefty professional fees. Don't hesitate to ask how much someone intends to charge for advice or assistance, and then compare those prices. Even though professional bodies publish suggested fee schedules, you may still find a huge variation in the price two different law firms will charge to register a simple corporation. Always try to negotiate (you may even be able to **barter** your own services in lieu of cash), and be prepared to challenge any bill that seems too high.

> **barter** The exchange of goods and services in lieu of cash payment. (This term is also synonymous with negotiation, but the former definition is the more common in a business context.)

⭐ Head Start Exercise

4.9 Make a list of any paid advisers or consultants that you might need to hire in order to prepare your business plan. Estimate what this will cost you (1/3 page maximum).

Once their businesses are running, self-employed people typically use the **accounting** services of **accountants** or **bookkeeping** firms on a regular basis. Other consultants tend to be used as required, although some entrepreneurs (especially in fields where contract disputes are likely to arise) will pay **retainers** to particular law firms to keep their services available.

Your business may also purchase the services of other businesses on an ongoing basis. For example, you may have a landscape design firm where you create layouts for home gardens. Some of your customers will also want porches, gazebos, or other structures, and you could have a deal with an architectural engineer to prepare all of your drawings in order to get building permits. Or, if you work as a personal image consultant to senior executives, you could have subcontract arrangements with a tailor, a hairdresser, a public speaking consultant, and a fitness trainer, any of whom you will bring in as needed. With each of these service suppliers, you must have already worked out a price at which they will provide their services through your company.

> **accounting** The recording, classifying, analyzing, and reporting of financial information.
>
> **accountant** A person holding one of several professional designations who oversees, reports on, and makes recommendations on financial decisions.
>
> **bookkeeping** The clerical or mechanical elements of accounting.
>
> **retainer** An amount of money paid to a professional adviser (such as a lawyer) before any services have been given. This amount ensures that the services of the retained professional will be available when required, and charges for service are then deducted from the retainer.

⭐ Head Start Exercise

4.10 Make a list of any advisers or subcontractors you will have to use on a regular basis once the business is running. Estimate the total monthly expense for their services (1/3 page maximum).

Procedures

For most of us, it doesn't take very long to perform the morning chores of washing, grooming, getting dressed, and getting ourselves to work or school. But these apparently simple

> ✅ **Memory Check 4.7**
> True or False? It is possible to make business deals with customers or suppliers that do not involve the exchange of money.

tasks could fill hours and hours if we had to make new decisions on how to proceed at each step of the process:

- Brush the teeth before or after showering?
- Put the toothpaste on before or after wetting the brush?
- Start with the front teeth? With the outside surfaces of the teeth?
- Work in which direction?

Memory Check 4.8
True or False? *Bookkeeping* and *accounting* are interchangeable terms.

We don't have to spend time making any of these decisions because we have worked out a system that we follow the same way each day. Similarly, the major tasks of your business should be worked out in advance to ensure that they are performed efficiently.

There are a variety of ways that you can demonstrate in your business plan that you have worked out orderly procedures. Typical techniques include sequential lists, bar graphs, flow charts, and continuity charts.

Lots of businesses will follow the same linear process for each job or customer. This is true for many retailers, consultants, and contractors who merely have to explain what they will do first for the customer, what they will do second, and so on.

For example, a company that paints parking lots for building owners might follow the procedures shown as a **sequential list** in Figure 4.1.

Businesses that involve overlapping activities or that have various jobs in progress at the same time may use a **bar graph** to plan and track those activities to completion. This type of graph, when used to show both "scheduled" and "completed" activities, is known as a Gantt chart. In the business plan, however, it only needs to show the planning process. For example, a conference planner can rely on this type of chart to ensure that all steps in the process have been completed on time. See the example in Figure 4.2.

Some businesses require the customer to make specific choices leading to different paths that a service will take. These optional routes are usually offered in a specific order and can be outlined in a **flow chart**. The example in Figure 4.3 is for a day spa that offers a series of different aesthetics packages to its customers. Note that the hair removal option is not available with some of the other services, either because of scheduling or possible irritation to the client's skin.

Another method to graphically show a sequence of procedures over time is a PERT chart (*p*rogram *e*valuation and *r*eview *t*echnique) or CPM (*c*ritical *p*ath *m*ethod)—both of which show more details of time use. These **continuity charts** can be very useful in the business plan for "project" sorts of activities. For example, a theatrical costume designer may demonstrate a four-month costuming project as shown in Figure 4.4.

sequential list A simple, chronological ordering of procedures that will be followed by a business.

bar graph A chart that can be used to monitor and control project activities, showing time along the *x*-axis and business activities along the *y*-axis.

flow chart A map showing the various services offered by a business and the different routes that can be taken through these services.

continuity chart A graph of the sequence of procedures and the time frame for each that must be followed for a project.

Figure 4.1 Parking Lot Painting Procedures

1. Schedule job with client and confirm new parking lot markings.
2. Divide lot into sections equal to one day's painting work.
3. Notify lot users of date on which their spaces will be unavailable.
4. Barricade section to be painted before lot opens.
5. Black out previous lines/markings.
6. Survey lot section for new lines/markings.
7. Place guides.
8. Paint new lines.
9. Stencil new markings.
10. Remove/transfer barricades.
11. Repeat steps 4-10 until job completion.

Figure 4.2 Conference Countdown

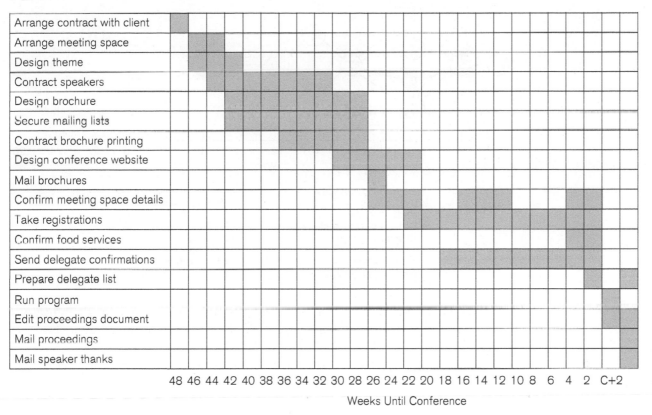

	48	46	44	42	40	38	36	34	32	30	28	26	24	22	20	18	16	14	12	10	8	6	4	2	C+2
Arrange contract with client	▓																								
Arrange meeting space		▓	▓																						
Design theme		▓	▓																						
Contract speakers			▓	▓	▓	▓	▓																		
Design brochure					▓	▓	▓	▓	▓																
Secure mailing lists						▓	▓	▓	▓																
Contract brochure printing								▓	▓	▓															
Design conference website										▓	▓	▓	▓												
Mail brochures													▓												
Confirm meeting space details																▓	▓	▓							
Take registrations														▓	▓	▓	▓	▓	▓	▓	▓	▓			
Confirm food services																			▓	▓					
Send delegate confirmations																▓	▓	▓	▓	▓	▓				
Prepare delegate list																							▓		
Run program																								▓	
Edit proceedings document																								▓	▓
Mail proceedings																									▓
Mail speaker thanks																									▓

Weeks Until Conference

For very simple endeavours, the business plan may require only a short paragraph or two to explain your procedures. Extremely complex processes may require a detailed operations manual attached as an appendix. (See Chapter 11, "Systemization" for a more detailed look at making processes more efficient.)

Figure 4.3 Time Out Day Spa | Service Options

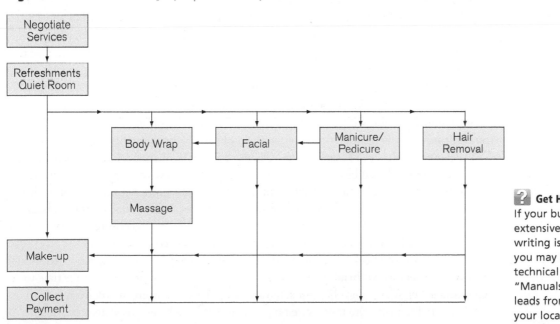

Get Help 4.6
If your business plan requires extensive technical detail (and writing is not your strength), you may have to hire a technical writer. Search for "Manuals Preparation" or get leads from writing programs at your local college.

Figure 4.4 Costuming Process

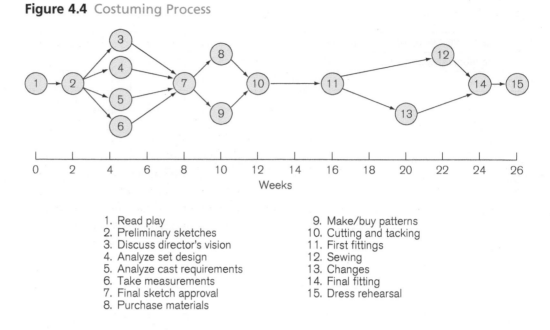

1. Read play
2. Preliminary sketches
3. Discuss director's vision
4. Analyze set design
5. Analyze cast requirements
6. Take measurements
7. Final sketch approval
8. Purchase materials
9. Make/buy patterns
10. Cutting and tacking
11. First fittings
12. Sewing
13. Changes
14. Final fitting
15. Dress rehearsal

Quality and Customer Service

Ask yourself: Am I committed to giving my customers the highest possible quality? Perhaps you shouldn't be. Lots of businesspeople talk about their "commitment to quality," always implying the "best" or "highest" quality. But your commitment should be to the "right" quality: right for the customer groups you are targeting. Some customers will demand stringent quality standards and control methods.[8] Additionally, true quality control is about ensuring not only that you do not fall below your standards, but also that you do not exceed them at unnecessary cost.

Let's say you're in the business of making novelty candy for special events. It may be important that you do not ship any of your 100-gram chocolate animals that are below the promised size. On the other hand, you can't make money by giving away an extra 25 grams of chocolate on each animal. You have to have a method for setting lower and upper weight limits along with a system of checking that each product falls within those limits.

Ask yourself: What will my standards of quality be? For your custom chocolate animals, you may decide that quality means a particular weight range, a particular standard of appearance (no smudged bits, no extra bits), and a particular standard of taste (no bitter flavour).

Some entrepreneurs think they are ensuring quality with their personal guarantee that they will correct any complaints "to the satisfaction of the customer." This approach dumps the responsibility for checking quality onto the customer: The customer has to complain for it to work. But what about those unhappy customers who don't complain—the ones who just go somewhere else with their business and bad-mouth you for the rest of their lives? You can't rely on the customer to complain. You have to check quality yourself.

Ask yourself: How will I check quality? Quality control is all about checking. This applies not just to product-based businesses, but equally to services. Anyone going into business as a flight instructor would be acutely aware of this. The most significant measure of quality in aviation training is safety, and the control system to ensure safety (quality) is the checklist. Pilots live by checklists (literally). The checklist can be adapted to ensure quality for businesses as diverse as moving companies, nightclubs, and pest control services.

Other means of checking quality can range from a simple visual inspection to formal, detailed customer surveys. In most cases, however, it's simply a matter of setting aside time to ask the customer: "How's your meal?" "Just calling to check that everything was delivered on time," or "We wanted to make sure there were no problems with the basement waterproofing job."

HOW WILL I MANAGE INFORMATION?

What appointments will you have to keep? To whom do you owe money, and who owes you? What remains to be done on each of your jobs/projects? Whose phone calls do you have to return? How much inventory do you have on hand? How much is your next tax payment? Which letters do you have to send? These are just a few examples of the things you have to know when you're in business for yourself, and since you can't remember them all, you need systems to keep this kind of information at your fingertips. *Ask yourself: How well organized am I? Am I good at writing down important things I have to remember?*

✓ **Memory Check 4.9**
True or False? An entrepreneur should strive to always deliver the highest quality product or service possible.

Keeping Records

For some new entrepreneurs, the habit of good record keeping comes the hard way: only after losing a legal dispute, losing a customer, or paying more taxes than would otherwise be necessary. Get into the habit of good record keeping right from the very first day you even consider working for yourself. If you drive somewhere to buy a small business magazine, save and file the receipt and record the date and mileage of your trip. These are legitimate business expenses, but only if they are properly recorded and saved.

Ask yourself: For how long do I have to save my records? Popular lore maintains that a business has to keep important records for seven years before they can be destroyed. But in some cases, even this will not meet the legal obligations of the business owner. Especially for a new business, a better rule is: When in doubt, don't throw it out. Better to set up some sort of permanent storage file for items such as business registrations, basic employee information and deduction records, tax returns, contracts, financial statements, and anything else with legal or tax implications.

Just as you organize your personal workspace, you must develop a system for recording and saving information, a system that you will come to use by habit. For some, a simple appointment calendar and shoebox for receipts will be enough. For others, it will take a filing cabinet with separate files for all the functional areas of the business, a large desk calendar that includes appointments, and a to-do list. And for many, the entire record-keeping system will be computerized using desktop, notebook, or handheld computer equipment, or some combination of these.

Small-Business Software

Over the past few years, small-business computer programs have been evolving, becoming increasingly more comprehensive in the types of tasks they handle for the independent businessperson.

Today, the most commonly used programs are integrated office management packages incorporating word processing, email, fax, list management, graphics, database, web, video, and calendaring; some packages even include business plan and financial statement templates along with numerous other capabilities. Examples are Microsoft Office and iWork.

✓ **Memory Check 4.10**
True or False? In Canada, all business records can be thrown out after seven years.

Many software packages that started out as programs to manage small-business accounting have evolved into comprehensive management information packages; these programs include QuickBooks and Microsoft Small Business Accounting.[9] Increasingly, these have the capability to integrate with office software packages that typically offer the following features:

- Word processing
- Email
- Web authoring
- Database
- Presentations

Word processing commonly includes templates for letters, invoices, reports, quotations, and so on for hard copy or email transmission or faxing from the computer screen. But even though today's inexpensive software has the capability for letterhead macros and embedded pictures, you may not have the capability because you haven't had time to learn it all. Few independent businesspeople can afford the time to develop high levels of software expertise unless this is specifically how they make their money. For most of us, the main consideration is whether it is easy to use. *Ask yourself: How computer literate am I?*

Email is now viewed as the most important business communication tool. It's fast, it's cheap, it can be secure, it documents your communication, and it works from hand-held devices. At times, it may seem easier to use the phone since most businesspeople have a mobile device. But if you deduct the time you might spend on hold and consider the advantages of being able to edit your words and attach pictures and graphs, email is an area where it is worth building some skill.

Office packages also provide **web-authoring** capability, but if your business has a sophisticated website or you use e-commerce transactions you will likely need advanced web management software and a higher level of expertise to use it.

These are features that help with both decision making and actually doing the work. Doing-the-work software can include everything from forms design (templates are available for a wide variety of forms) to purchase orders to job tracking and project management charts. Specific time-tracking and billing programs are available for many professions.

Many of the decision-making tools are database applications. **Database software** can record large amounts of information in particular files (e.g., customer files) with many pieces of information in each file, stored in particular fields (e.g., customer name, product order, or customer postal code). Information can be retrieved from the database by combining any number of files and it can be presented in many different formats (e.g., sales reports, inventory reports, or customer rankings) as well as different styles of graphs and charts.

Setting up a database management system involves a fairly long learning curve—or, more likely, bringing in expert help. However, a number of database templates are commercially available for specific businesses such as restaurants, machine shops, and retail stores, and the list will continue growing.

In some cases, your web browser can be used as a tool to help you find prospective customers, and your own website can be a form of advertising. Mailing lists for fax, hard copy, or email are fairly easy to develop and these can be used for a variety of direct mail approaches. (See "Advertising Media" in Chapter 3.)

Presentation software helps you create professional sales presentations with dramatic audiovisual effects. Some software includes job costing and estimating forms that are especially good for manufacturers, contractors, and various types of consultants. This information can be automatically transferred to quotations and ultimately invoices. For large contracts, it is also relatively easy to develop your own proposal outlines and contract templates.

web authoring The creation of documents and other media using the necessary language and protocol for transfer via the World Wide Web.

database software A program that stores many pieces of information in the form of tables, allowing the information to be sorted and reported in many different formats.

presentation software Programs that help to create a series of "slides" or pages of information that can be viewed on a computer screen, computerized projector, over the web, or in hard copy. Typically used for training and promotion, the most widely adopted program is Microsoft PowerPoint.

For a business that relies heavily on one-to-one selling, quality software is available that will help you manage your sales time with calendars, customer contact files, and summaries of sales information. For a discussion of e-business technologies, see Chapter 12, "What are the Recent Challenges for Small Business?"

How much of your own record keeping and accounting you choose to do will depend on

- the financial complexity of your business activity;
- your own abilities and training;
- how much you can afford to pay an accountant to do the work; and
- your accounting software (if any).

Ask yourself: How much do I know about accounting? Some self-employed people do no more record keeping than putting all of their receipts in one location and writing down all their deposits, withdrawals, and payments in a chequebook. Then, typically, they will sit down with their accountant on a monthly basis and explain each of the transactions while the accountant enters the data. The accountant will provide monthly, quarterly, and/or annual reports and prepare the necessary tax returns. Sounds simple, but this is an expensive and time-consuming way to handle what is largely a matter of routine bookkeeping.

It is better to have your accountant help you set up a software (or paper) accounting system where you (or an employee who costs a lot less than the accountant) regularly record all of the transactions. This way, the accountant is just there to check reports and handle non-routine occurrences.

The first step in organizing your accounting system is to set up a **chart of accounts**. This is a list of specific categories in which your business will have transactions. For example, almost all businesses will have a cash account (money in the bank) and an **accounts payable** account (that shows bills owing). But a freelance writer is unlikely to have an **employee deductions** account, whereas a restaurant most likely will. A furniture dealer will have an inventory account, but a lawyer likely will not. Typical charts of accounts for many specific kinds of businesses are included in small-business accounting software.

A **general journal** is a tool that records each of your financial transactions in chronological order, noting which of your accounts the transaction affects. With some minimal training in bookkeeping you can probably record your own transactions (buying something, paying a bill, depositing a cheque), saving the money you would have had to pay your accountant for this job. The software takes care of updating the individual accounts that are affected by each transaction. You must decide your own capabilities in this area.

The status of a company's accounts is reflected in the financial statements. (See Chapter 5 for a complete discussion of financial statements.) The **financial statements** show a company's profitability and its position as far as what it owns and what it owes. A major advantage of accounting software is that the entrepreneur (with a little expertise) can see up-to-date financial statements at any given time.

Accounting software also includes planning tools, which can be used for **cash flow** planning. This is one of the most valuable spreadsheet applications for entrepreneurs. The rows and columns of financial information on the spreadsheet can produce instant calculations, allowing the entrepreneur to play what-if games for planning purposes; for example: "What if half my customers are two months late in paying their bills? How will this affect my bank balance?"

In selecting computer software, try to choose a package that has all the features you want. But use only those features you need. You don't have to adopt any package in its entirety (and end up having the software shape the operation of your business). For example, your accounting package may offer a slightly cumbersome on-screen personal organizer that would take you 15 minutes to update each day. But if working with a small pocket calendar is more efficient for you, there is no need to commit to its computerized counterpart.

Memory Check 4.11
True or False? Database and presentation software are typically part of office management packages.

chart of accounts A list of the particular financial categories in which a business will have transactions. The chart assigns a name and number to each financial area, or "account."

accounts payable A list of the bills a business owes that will have to be paid in the near future.

employee deductions Money taken from the gross pay of employees to pay for such things as employee income tax, employee pension contributions, and employee benefit contributions.

general journal A book or computer document that forms part of a company's accounting system, in which all financial transactions of the firm are recorded in chronological order.

financial statements Accounting reports that summarize the position of a business and the financial changes that have taken place over a period of time.

cash flow The analysis of how money comes into and goes out of a business and the factors that affect the cash balance.

Get Help 4.7
For information on employee deductions, see the Canada Revenue Agency webpage at www.cra-arc.gc.ca/tx/bsnss/menu-eng.html. Click on payroll.

Pick and choose your tools. (For a more complete discussion of small business software, see the section "E-Business Technologies for Small Firms" in Chapter 12.)

HOW WILL I MANAGE MYSELF AND OTHERS IN THE FIRM?

management The setting and achieving of a company's goals and objectives, often through the work of others.

Management really means "getting people to do work." But what if there are no people other than yourself? This is the situation for lots of self-employed people.

Ask yourself: If I have no employees, am I still practising management? What about in the case of a partnership? Are the partners managing each other? The simple answer is that many of the techniques and principles of managing others can be applied equally well to managing yourself, partners, subcontractors, suppliers, and, at times, even customers. Management is about answering the questions:

- What are we trying to accomplish?
- Who will do what?
- Is the plan working?
- How can we accomplish more?

Planning: Goals and Objectives

goals Things to be achieved in the long term, usually expressed as broad concepts.

objectives Things to be achieved in the short term, usually expressed as specific numbers with specific dates.

The first question (what are we trying to accomplish?) involves the management function of planning: setting **goals** and **objectives** and communicating them to those being managed. In fact, that's exactly what you've been doing by creating a business plan. You have been explaining exactly what you wish to achieve and setting it down in a format that can be understood and referred to by partners, lenders, or outside investors—even yourself.

As an entrepreneur, clearly your goal is to make money. But you will ultimately achieve this by accomplishing a whole series of small objectives along the way: You will have a customer list completed by Tuesday; you will be making a particular number of sales calls per day next month; you will have so many dollars in sales by the end of six months; and so on.

There is no point in telling an employee that the goal is to help you make money and leaving it at that. Clearly, you must agree on a series of realistic objectives (involving numbers and a time line) that you expect the employee to achieve. This can be easily documented in a confirming memo: "Just to confirm our decision of this morning: we agreed that. . . ."

Planning is rarely a solitary activity and should more often involve those affected by the planning process: partners, employees, customers, and suppliers—getting the necessary agreement to make the plan work.

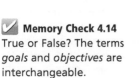 **Memory Check 4.12**
True or False? Your accounts payable represents money you expect to collect from your customers.

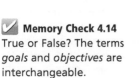 **Memory Check 4.13**
True or False? A business owner with no employees can still be considered a manager.

Dividing the Tasks

In a new one- or two-person business, you can expect to do everything from unloading the truck to strategic planning to negotiating a contract to cleaning the washroom—whatever needs to be done. However, there is an unfortunate tendency for entrepreneurs to hire help on the same basis: "Working for me, you'll do a little of everything. Whatever needs to be done." *Ask yourself: What's wrong with that?*

Doing "whatever needs to be done" is not what employees want. They want a clearly defined job: salesperson, secretary, janitor, installer, proofreader, instructor. It is unreasonable to expect an employee to function as an entrepreneur; that's your role. Besides, there is some evidence that small firms with clear organizational structure perform better.[10]

The best way to handle this is to start thinking of your business as a collection of different specific jobs, right from the start. True, you may be the only employee, but think

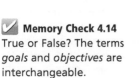 **Memory Check 4.14**
True or False? The terms *goals* and *objectives* are interchangeable.

of yourself as alternating between jobs as the marketing director, the accountant, the repairperson, the writer, the computer programmer, and so on. Thinking of your business this way makes it easier to divide up the work among partners (partners can each take responsibility for several specific jobs), and as the business grows it becomes clear which specific jobs you will hire new people into. *Ask yourself: Which specific jobs could my business be made up of?*

A very complex business will have lots of jobs, and these will have to be represented on an **organization chart**. It is perfectly reasonable to show an organization chart with more jobs than there are actual people working in the company. In this sense, the chart is a planning tool (for when you are finally in a position to hire people for all the jobs). For example, three plumbers might get together to form the No-Leak Plumbing Company Inc. Delvina, the largest shareholder, will run the company, and her two partners, Alexis and Bhupinder, will each have specific management responsibilities. All three, however, will continue to perform the actual plumbing tasks. If they hire two other employees, Roland (to act as accountant and receptionist) and Waylan (as apprentice), there will be five people in total in their company. The start-up organization chart for this company (shown in Figure 4.5), nevertheless identifies nine positions. In this case, the shaded boxes indicate jobs for which new people will be hired in the future.

An organization chart only names the jobs and shows any reporting relationships (i.e., who will be whose boss). It does not actually explain the function of each job. For that you need job descriptions.

Like an organization chart, a **job description** can be an excellent planning tool and it can even form the contract between the employer and the employee.

A good job description can be written on a single page. It should state the general **responsibilities** of the job, or those things that the employee is obligated to look after. It should also outline the **authorities** of the job, specifying the areas where the employee has the right to make decisions. In addition, it should provide some indication of the job's **accountabilities**, or those things on which the employer will judge the performance of the employee. See the sample job description for a rock band Road Manager in Figure 4.6. If you work with partners you can still use job descriptions, likely having more than one apiece. But the "who does what" question should also be addressed in your partnership agreement. Remember, the more detailed your agreement, the fewer partnership disputes you will have.

organization chart A graphic representation of the structure of an organization, showing who is whose boss.

job description A statement of the duties, responsibilities, and other issues pertaining to a particular job within a company.

responsibility The task that an employee is obligated to complete.

authority The specific area within which an employee has the power to make decisions.

accountabilities Those duties on which an employer judges the performance of an employee.

Figure 4.5 No-Leak Plumbing Company Inc. | Organization Chart

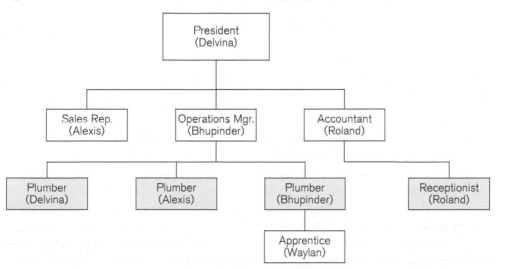

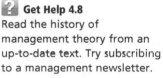 **Get Help 4.8**
Read the history of management theory from an up-to-date text. Try subscribing to a management newsletter.

Figure 4.6 Job Description

Position: Road Manager

Reports to: Band Manager/Agent

Supervises: Drivers, set-up labourers, and technicians

General: The road manager travels with the band on tour and arranges the transportation and set-up of all staging and promotional materials. Co-ordinating with the musicians, sound engineer, lighting director, stage manager, and tour promoter, the road manager handles the logistics so that all of these other functions have the equipment and materials they have requested when and where they are needed.

Accountability: The road manager is expected to meet all deadlines for delivery and deployment of equipment and materials within the budget negotiated with the band manager. In addition, the road manager is expected to prepare and carry out contingency plans for predictable failure of equipment and contractors, as well as respond effectively to unpredictable occurrences on the tour.

Responsibilities and Duties:

- identifying the transportation requirements for the tour
- costing transportation for equipment and materials as well as the accommodation and other expenses of the road manager's staff
- negotiating a logistics budget with the band manager and managing that budget
- keeping the band manager informed of progress and problems in organizing and logistics for the tour
- hiring, training, and supervising drivers and set-up labourers and technicians
- developing set-up and break-down plans for all equipment that will meet the needs of the other managers and departments
- scheduling all equipment and material transportation.

Authority: The road manager generally has control over the hiring of drivers and set-up staff as well as selection of and contracting with transportation suppliers and transport equipment suppliers within the budget approved by the band manager.

Leadership: Accomplishing More

leadership The motivational aspects of management that encourage greater productivity from employees.

Memory Check 4.15
True or False? It is possible for a small business to have more jobs on its organization chart than there are people working for the company.

Memory Check 4.16
True or False? Accountability refers to those things on which a person's performance will be measured.

Ask yourself: If management is about getting people to work, then what is leadership? **Leadership** is about getting people to work harder. It is about motivating to achieve. Leadership may be more skill than science, but there is a huge body of research on the effects of different management practices on things like productivity, employee turnover, and absenteeism. From these works of applied psychology, we can get many practical ways to improve our own leadership style. The following are five practical leadership tips:

- *Measure behaviour.* You can't know if your management approach is improving things (getting your employees to make fewer errors, increasing your own sales rate, having your partner be more punctual) if you don't actually measure and record specific behaviours.
- *Reward improvement.* Look for employees, associates, and yourself doing something right (better); then, reward that behaviour. It doesn't take much to be a powerful reward—a thank-you, some recognition, or a small treat usually works well. And when you reward improvement, the result is that you get more improvement—at an accelerating rate.

Sharing Values with Valued Customers

Nupur Gogia and Carrianne Leung are very busy women. Both have completed their Ph.Ds, and between them juggle careers in wholesale management, motherhood, and teaching. But they still find time for their shared passion of healthy, sustainable food as partners in Multiple Organics. Looking like an old-time neighbourhood grocery store, Multiple Organics carries the same lines as most grocery stores: produce, meats, dairy products, dry goods, canned goods, cleaning supplies, and health and beauty products. The difference is that Multiple Organics specializes in locally produced, environmentally responsible, safe products. And the emphasis is on "food; delicious food."

The company has to rely on labelling requirements and the Canada Organic Office of the Canadian Food Inspection Agency to keep up to date on the various types of product certifications. Minimizing waste is both an environmental and business objective of Multiple Organics, and this is accomplished by careful attention to ordering and inspecting the inventory. And working with suppliers close to the store is a major priority. For Nupur and Carianne, supporting local producers is not just ethically important in that it reduces the carbon emissions from long-distance shipping; it is also the key to fresher, tastier produce. And, of equal importance, it is a way in which the business is integrated into its community.

The drawing area for Multiple Organics customers is a dense urban neighbourhood of older detached and semi-detached homes with lots of public transit. The people are a complex mix, including recent immigrants of many ethnic backgrounds. And increasingly, young educated families are moving into the area, people who are concerned about healthy lifestyles and the environment. These are values that Nupur and Carrianne share with their customers. "The vast majority of our customers get to the store on foot or by bicycle," explains Nupur, "and we know about 80 percent of our customers by name. This is what differentiates us from the large grocery chains." But knowing the customers on a personal level is about more than marketing strategy for this business; it is about personal relationships with those customers. In fact, it is not unusual for the owners to extend informal, short-term credit to some of the regular customers.

Even a store like Multiple Organics, however, with its small-town feel and close customer relationships, still gets its share of problem customers. When this does happen, according to Nupur, it usually involves a new or infrequent client making one of the owners or employees a "target of their bad mood." The response at Multiple Organics is to "just be as polite as possible and get them out door as quickly as possible."

See the website for the store at www.multipleorganics.ca.

- *Take responsibility for employee well-being.* Paternalism from entrepreneurs toward employees is certainly out of fashion. Studies consistently show, however, that employees highly value (more so than wages) the security provided by group benefit packages. Even more important might be taking a personal interest in your employees ("Are your kids getting over the measles?"), as it encourages loyalty and productivity.

- *Provide opportunity.* Everyone, to varying extents, needs recognition, challenge, or some definition of success. As an entrepreneur you may recognize these needs in yourself, but fail to recognize them in others. Even though the opportunities for promotion,

✓ **Memory Check 4.17**
True or False? Authority, accountability, and responsibility all have the same meaning.

✓ **Memory Check 4.18**
True or False? Leadership and management are interchangeable terms.

recognition, and prestige are documented as potent motivators, entrepreneurs are notoriously selfish about allowing employees to participate in even token ownership of the business. British tycoon Richard Branson, however, attributes his enormous wealth to giving others the opportunity to get rich.

- *Practise dynamic leadership.* The best leaders are those who can change their leadership style to meet the changing requirements of the circumstances, the employees, and the business. This means at times giving orders, at other times seeking group consensus, and sometimes letting others make decisions. It also means continuously growing and learning new skills as a leader.

Getting Paid

The issue of who gets paid how much and when can be an employer/employee issue, it can be an issue between partners, or, if you're on your own, it can be a personal budgeting issue.

Ask yourself: How much should I pay my employees and on what basis? When it comes to compensation, small business owners are often victim to two false beliefs:

- that money is the strongest motivator for employees
- that small firms cannot afford to pay the same rates as large firms

Studies have shown time and again that money rarely motivates employees to work above a minimal effort: Money is not a motivator. But it can be a potential demotivator.[11]

Ask yourself: In your current job, would you be prepared to work 15 percent harder for an additional 15 percent in pay? If you answer honestly and you're like most of us, the answer is no. But let's say you have a job working for a uniform supplier, doing clothing alteration. One day, you encounter several other people doing basically the same job as you do and through them you learn that you are being paid about 5 percent less than any of them. The next day, your boss asks you to put in an extra effort for a particularly large order. If you stay late, you will be paid overtime rates. *Ask yourself: How motivated would you be to put in extra effort? Even to stay late for overtime pay? What if the boss promises you a promotion for handling this order well?* The fact that you now feel underpaid will hamper any other efforts to motivate you. In this sense, the issue of money has become a demotivator.

So the trick, as an employer, is not to overpay employees (you'd just be wasting your money), but rather to make sure that they feel they are paid fairly. At that point, you can then go on to motivate them to higher productivity by other means.

Ask yourself: If I should pay employees fairly, it should be fair compared to what? Employees want to feel that they are paid fairly compared to others in the same firm (based on relative responsibility, job requirements, experience, and seniority) as well as compared to others doing the same job in different firms (i.e., the going rates). You can get information about industry averages from trade sources and various salary surveys.

Equally dangerous to viewing money as a motivator is the myth of the small employer being unable to compete with big firms when it comes to compensation. Skilled labour is a commodity, like oil or lettuce. Is it reasonable for a small manufacturer to expect to pay less for electricity than General Motors does just because of size? If you try to rationalize underpaying employees "because you can't afford the going rates," expect serious motivation problems.

This same principle holds when it comes to **employee benefit** packages, including extended health care, dental care, drug plans, disability insurance, and so on. True, the large employers can usually buy group benefits more cheaply because of their size, just like Wendy's gets a deal on their lettuce that an independent sandwich shop can't get. However, insurance companies are increasingly offering benefit packages for self-employed people and small-business owners at competitive rates. (See "Small Business Insurance" in Chapter 2.)

? Get Help 4.9

Up-to-date salary survey information showing the pay range for a wide selection of job categories in your area is often available from the local chamber of commerce. Major newspapers such as *The Globe and Mail* periodically publish national salary surveys. Also, look up specific jobs and check out the salary information on www.jobfutures.ca.

? Get Help 4.10

If there is a business association for your field, call and ask if they offer a group benefit plan for members and their employees.

employee benefits The non-monetary compensation of employees, through items such as pension plans, extended health care, and other insurance programs.

Remember that benefit packages satisfy the employee's need for security, and therefore become powerful motivators.

⭐ Head Start Exercise

4.13 Calculate the monthly amount you will have to pay for employees, including the expenses for any employee benefits or required employer contributions (1/2 page maximum).

If you are working as a sole proprietor or in a partnership, the money the business operates on is considered the personal funds of you or of you and your partners, so money that you pay to yourself is really your own cash that you are drawing out of the business activity. This is referred to as **drawings**.

Sometimes your business will have more cash in the bank than at other times, and there is an unfortunate tendency to take out more money for your personal use at these times. But cash is not the same thing as profit, and you must carefully consider whether the money you decide to pay yourself should be earmarked for other purposes, such as paying bills that haven't come due yet.

A safer approach is to treat drawings like a regular salary. Predetermine how much you need to pay yourself and take a standard amount on a regular schedule, keeping your personal finances separated from the business finances.

In the case of a corporation, your personal finances are legally separate from the business finances and you would normally set up a regular salary payment for yourself or other working partners. But you also have the option of paying to yourself the business profits (or any part of the profits) in the form of dividends. When a business makes profit, there can be tax advantages in how you split your remuneration between salary and dividends.

Be cautious at start-up. Many ventures are extremely cash-hungry at the start and take a long time to show a profit. Early on, it's easy to be overly optimistic about how profitable working for yourself can be at the beginning. A safer approach is to rely on little or no cash from the business until you have established a clear pattern of growth.

⭐ Head Start Exercise

4.14 Estimate how many months you can survive without having to rely on the business for income. After that period, how much would you have to pay yourself each month? (1/8 page maximum)

HOW WILL I MANAGE THE GOVERNMENT?

The largest common source of irritation among those who work for themselves is "the government": the government as regulator, the government as taxer, the government as the place where you wait on hold trying to get information. It may come as a surprise when you become newly self-employed just how much of your life you will spend trying to find out what the government wants you to do and then how much time you will spend doing it. During that time you are doing things that don't make you any profit, but you must do them just to stay in business. On top of all that, you have three different levels of government to deal with: federal, provincial, and municipal, each for different issues.

Ask yourself: How will I handle the frustration of dealing with government? Step one is to remind yourself that your competition must deal with the same governments and the same frustrations. Step two is to start building some skill in efficient government dealings. This includes learning to be patient and assertive and to talk to the right person.

✅ **Memory Check 4.19**
True or False? It is better for business owners to pay themselves regular salaries than to take personal money from the business as needed.

✅ **Memory Check 4.20**
True or False? Salary is classified as an employee benefit.

drawings Cash withdrawals from a business by an owner of the company and intended for the personal use of the owner.

❓ **Get Help 4.11**
Paying yourself is another area where you will likely rely on your accountant. You can, however, make decisions on the best way to pay yourself by using tax return software and running a series of different compensation scenarios.

❓ **Get Help 4.12**
A valuable resource for dealing with the federal and provincial governments is the Scott's Government Index published by Southam Inc. This is a listing of government administrators (by name or department) with full names, titles, phone numbers, and email addresses. This up-to-date loose-leaf service can be found in larger libraries or purchased online at www.scottsinfo.com.

Licences and Permits

Depending on the nature of your business, licences and permits may be required from any of the three levels of government, although this is most commonly a municipal issue. Municipalities can require a variety of permits, from general vendor's permits, to trade contractor licences, to specific retail and service licences for businesses like bars, dry cleaners, taxis, street vendors, and restaurants. In addition, you will likely need building permits (for any remodelling you do to your place of business), sign permits (if you have any public signage), and parking permits (if your business is in a major urban area). Check the blue pages of your phone book for the licensing or clerk's office in your municipality.

Provinces affect most businesses in the area of transportation, requiring driver's licences and motor vehicle permits. As well, provinces may require licensing for a host of other endeavours, such as real estate sales, travel agencies, motor vehicle sales, nursing homes, daycare centres, and collection agencies. Find the provincial ministry that issues licences, using your search engine.

Federal licensing is most likely to affect the independent entrepreneur in the area of import and export licences or if you are involved in aviation or an industry using radio frequency communications.

? Get Help 4.13
For an overview of import permit requirements, call the automated customs information line at 1-800-461-9999. For information on export assistance, see the Industry Canada website at www.ic.gc.ca. Select "Just for Businesses" then select "Do Business Across Borders."

✓ Memory Check 4.21
True or False? Building and sign permits generally come from the provincial level of government.

Taxation

Not only does a businessperson have to pay his or her own taxes, but in many cases the businessperson is also the designated tax collector working on behalf of the government to collect, record, and remit taxes from those they do business with. Examples would be provincial sales taxes or the federal goods and services tax (GST). (You must collect GST if your sales are more than $30 000 per year, so get a GST number from Canada Revenue Agency right away. This number is being used for an increasing number of other government registrations.) Another example is the federal excise tax on manufactured goods. You are also the collector for employee income taxes, Employment Insurance, and Canada Pension (and/or provincial pension) contributions. Don't try to get around this by having true employees bill you for services as though they were sub-contractors. Check with your accountant. Manufacturers may also have to pay federal excise tax.

Federal income taxes are easiest to deal with when you are a sole proprietor or general partner, since your business income calculation is part of your personal income tax return. The federal government collects for most provinces as well as itself, but the rules change a little every year. Even if you are competent with tax return software (your accounting package may include this), it is still a good investment to have an accountant make sure you are paying no more tax than necessary.

If you're incorporated, things become a little more complicated. You have to pay your corporate income tax to the province and the federal government separately, and this is also separate from your personal income taxes (which may include salary and dividends from the corporation). *Ask yourself: Now do I think I need an accountant?*

Depending on your deal with your landlord (if you have one), your business activities may also have to deal with property or service taxes levied by the municipality. (This also includes your business's share of property taxes on a home where you have your business.)

? Get Help 4.14
Canada Revenue Agency has a valuable small business information section on its website at www.cra-arc.gc.ca.

Regulations

Sole proprietorships and partnerships must register in the province where they are operating. This is a fairly simple and inexpensive process involving the filling out of forms and a **name search** at the provincial business registration office. Your registered business certificate can now be used for obtaining licences and permits or opening business bank accounts.

If you're starting a corporation, you have the choice of whether to incorporate provincially or federally. If you know that you are going to be operating in more than one province, then it may be easier in the long run to incorporate federally. Do-it-yourself software, books, and kits are available, although many people prefer to have a lawyer set up their corporations.

There is a large body of law that governs the function of businesses and the conduct of entrepreneurs. There are federal laws concerning contracts, competition, shareholders, and lenders, as well as laws that govern the relationships between employers and employees. These laws rarely affect the small businessperson. Even if you have employees, your business is likely to be covered under provincial employment law. (The exception here is if you are in a federally regulated business, such as aviation or radio broadcasting.)

Provincial employment laws in the areas of employment standards (hours of work, holidays, minimum wage, etc.), health and safety (including office environments), and human rights (including pay equity) are those most likely to affect the small employer.

Pamphlets or webpages summarizing the provisions of the applicable laws are generally available from the provincial ministries.

Municipal regulation of businesses can cover zoning, land use, hours of operation, and even issues such as the appearance of retail storefronts. A local chamber of commerce can often help provide direction on these issues.

Professional and Industry Associations

Professional and industry associations are not owned or run by the government, although in some cases they form a type of government themselves to oversee the regulation and licensing for a profession. For example, there are self-governing bodies for the different types of accountants, for lawyers, for engineers, and for different classes of health care professionals.

Most associations, however, do not have control over the practices of their members. Rather, they exist to provide information and services to people in particular endeavours. There are organizations representing car dealers, funeral directors, hairdressers, artists, musicians, writers, grain farmers, commercial travellers, insurance agents, actors, marketing researchers, ice suppliers, and hundreds of other industries. (There's even an association for people who run associations.)

A significant, sometimes unofficial, function of both the regulating and non-regulating associations is to act as government lobby groups on behalf of the specific industry they represent. When legislation that would directly affect your business is pending, you are most likely to be kept informed about it and have the opportunity to influence such legislation through your industry association. There is also an organization that lobbies on behalf of independent entrepreneurs right across the country: the Canadian Federation of Independent Business.

Revising Your Plan

Once you have gathered the information and worked through the decisions for Section 4 of your business plan, you may find that you now have to go back and revise some of the decisions you made in Sections 1, 2, and 3. Figure 4.7 demonstrates how some elements of operations may affect previous sections of the business plan.

---

name search An inexpensive check, by computer, to make sure that a business is not being registered under a name already in use.

? Get Help 4.15
There is a Canada Business Service Centre in most major cities, with information on federal, provincial, and municipal regulations. Check the Canada Business Network website at canadabusiness.ca.

✔ Memory Check 4.22
True or False? For a sole proprietorship, business taxes are calculated as part of the personal tax return.

? Get Help 4.16
The Canadian Federation of Independent Business is a major source of information about issues affecting entrepreneurs: see www.cfib.ca.

Figure 4.7 The Business Plan Revision Process

1 Model	2 Feasibility	3 Marketing	4 Operations	5 Finances
Product/Service	Market Potential	Name/Image	Space/Equipment	
Target Customer	Competition	Service/Product Mix	Logistics	
Location	Sales Forecast	Pricing	Methods/Process	
Legal Form	Insurance	Distribution	Systems	
Agreements	Intellectual Property	Promotion	Organization Structure	
			Regulations	

Answers to Memory Check Questions

4.1 F   4.2 F   4.3 T   4.4 T   4.5 F   4.6 T   4.7 T   4.8 F

4.9 F   4.10 F   4.11 T   4.12 F   4.13 T   4.14 F   4.15 T   4.16 T

4.17 F   4.18 F   4.19 T   4.20 F   4.21 F   4.22 T

Questions for Discussion

1. Discuss the human tendency to buy things that we really don't need. Use personal examples and explain how entrepreneurs can guard against this.
2. How is the virtual office taking the place of the physical office? Which elements of the physical office are still superior to their electronic equivalents?
3. How is a classroom an efficient layout for the activities of teaching and learning? Find improvements for the room you are in now.
4. Identify a retail business where the layout is poorly designed. What are the problems and what are the solutions?
5. Compare the offices of doctors and dentists. Which has better layout from the patient's viewpoint? Why? Account for this difference.
6. How could a Gantt chart be a good tool for students to plan and track their assignments and tests? Why are these not used by most students?
7. "If you build a better mousetrap, customers will beat a path to your door." Discuss why this old saying is a business myth.
8. Discuss some of the dangers in using email as a business communications technology. What precautions should be taken?
9. Why are many students and entrepreneurs "accounting phobic"? How can this be overcome?
10. Speculate about why small entrepreneurs are slow to adapt new methods and systems for efficient ordering, delivery, and inventory control. What advantages do they have over larger competitors?
11. What is the difference between managing employees and manipulating them? How do modern employees expect to be managed?
12. Discuss whether money can be a motivator for employees and under what circumstances. What are the most powerful employee motivators?
13. Typically, the federal cabinet has a minister responsible for small business. Why not just have a minister for business? What special concerns would governments have around small business?

Case for Discussion

Wish Levine was furious with the government. They were picking on her, trying to put her out of business; and all over a few little regulations, most of which she hadn't even known about.

Four years ago, Wish started a business going into people's homes and making video recordings of customers' possessions. She provided the customers with a copy of the recording as well as an itemized inventory, and she kept a copy of each in safe storage. The idea was that if any customer had an insurance claim for loss of items through theft, fire, or flood Wish would be able to provide the insurance company with the details and proof of the loss. Wish had a lawyer set up the business as a corporation so that it would sound more professional (Levine Asset Records, Inc.).

Business was good from the start, and within a couple of months Wish had to hire two other videographers just to keep up with sales. A friend advised her that instead of hiring the videographers as employees, she could treat them as subcontractors and avoid a lot of government paperwork. Her new helpers agreed that they would use Wish's equipment, but their own vehicles, and she would pay them a flat rate of $60 for each video job they did. The videographers would cover their own transportation costs and file their own tax returns.

The business grew so quickly that Wish was working night and day to deal with customers, produce the inventory lists, schedule appointments, and still do some of the video work herself. Her helpers seemed to enjoy their jobs; they never complained. And Wish had lots of money pouring into her bank account, but she was just too busy to spend any of it except for her basic living costs. She knew that she had not been keeping up with her accounting and she was getting weekly reminders about tax returns and corporate returns unfiled. (Wish wasn't sure if those were the same thing or different things.) But she felt that as long as she was saving most of what went into her bank, then she still had more than enough to pay whatever she owed the government.

When she finally went to see an accountant, she was told that Canada Revenue Agency (CRA) would not be able to process her tax returns because Industry Canada had dissolved her corporation for failure to send in her corporate returns. (Now Wish understood they were different things.) There was, however, a process to get the corporation reinstated, but it would take some time and a lot of paperwork for Wish to complete. In the meantime, CRA was threatening legal action over unpaid taxes.

At the same time, another branch of CRA called Wish regarding the fact that she had failed to collect HST from her customers. Wish explained that she was under the impression that only retail stores had to collect this. "Wrong," she was told, and was further informed that she was responsible to pay 13 percent of all the revenue she had made in the form of HST—immediately. When she called the accountant for help, she was told that HST filings could not be processed because the corporation had been dissolved.

The same week, the provincial labour board sent a summons for Wish to appear. She was accused of paying one of the videographers less than minimum wage (after time spent on the job and transportation costs were figured in). And it turned out that the other videographer had not been paying his taxes. So yet a third branch of CRA was holding Wish responsible for this. It was explained to her that despite any contract she may have had, the videographers were in fact employees for whom she should have been deducting income tax, CPP contributions, and EI contributions, all of which Wish would now have to pay, along with possible fines.

1. Is someone in the government picking on Wish? Why is this all happening at the same time?

2. Why should Wish have consulted an accountant when setting up her business? What sort of procedures could the accountant have set up?

3. How could Wish have managed her time to keep up with the requirements of government regulations? Who could help?

4. What sort of regulations come under provincial jurisdiction? Federal? Identify the websites where you can find details on the business regulations in your own province.

5. Were Wish's videographers employees or sub-contractors? What are the rules around this? Where is the place to find out?

6. What should Wish do now? Why?

The Business Plan, Section 4:
OPERATIONS

Space and Equipment

1. Briefly list all the equipment, furniture, and vehicles you will need to run your business. Include both the items you already own and those you need to acquire. Justify your needs.

2. If yours is a retail or consumer service business, sketch a layout of the store identifying entrances, windows, displays, cash, and so on. If there is a wholesale or manufacturing component to the business, sketch a layout of the work and storage areas, identifying all equipment and explaining the use of each area.

Logistics

3. Explain your systems for buying, ordering, and storing any supplies that your business will depend on.

4. Identify any subcontractors or suppliers you intend to use. Explain the services or products they will provide and the details of contracting arrangements you will have with them. Be sure to include any professional advisers you may use, such as accountants or lawyers.

Methods and Procedures

5. Briefly explain and/or chart the process you will use to complete a typical client or customer transaction.

6. Explain any methods or systems you plan to have for ensuring quality and handling customer complaints.

Systems

7. Explain the paperwork and/or software systems you will use to control your business in terms of scheduling, inventory, billing, work progress, client records, and accounting.

Organization

8. If more than one person will be working in the business, explain who will do what, who has what authorities, and who is whose boss. If you have one or more partners, refer to details in the partnership agreement. If you will have employees, attach an organization chart along with one-page job descriptions for each major job as appendices.

9. Explain how and when you, any partners, and employees will be compensated (hourly, salary, drawings), and any payroll deductions or contributions you will make for taxes, benefits, and so on.

Regulation

10. Identify any registrations, licences, or permits you will be required to have for your business.

11. Identify any professional groups or business associations you will belong to and explain the reason for your membership. (Note any fees.)

Chapter 5

Finances: How Will I Manage the Money?

Organizing the finances is the last step in the basic business plan. For many, it is the easiest part of the business plan to prepare, since much of the work has already been done in the first four sections. Now, it is only a matter of organizing and working with the numbers that have come from those parts of the plan. This chapter will show you how to accomplish that by answering the questions:

- How Will I Explain the Business Finances?
- How Will I Track the Finances?
- Where Will I Get the Money?

Learning Objectives

On completion of this chapter, you should be able to:

1. Explain the purpose of three types of financial statements.
2. Create a simple balance sheet.
3. Create a simple income statement.
4. Apply the concept of "break-even" in calculating a break-even point.
5. Explain the need for credit and collections policies.
6. Discuss the need for cash flow planning.
7. Prepare a simple cash flow projection.
8. Compare at least three sources of start-up financing.
9. Complete the *finances* portion of the business plan.

HOW WILL I EXPLAIN THE BUSINESS FINANCES?

You don't have to know a lot about accounting to run your own business. Chances are you will have an accountant you can go to for help. In fact, the more you get advice from your accountant, the better for the business.[1] However, if you're going to talk to other businesspeople (banker, investor, consultant) about the finances for your venture, you have to acquire some basic accounting vocabulary. This is where it gets just a little confusing because accountants often have more than one term for each accounting idea. Don't worry. You don't have to know all the financial jargon in order to understand the financial concepts.

Don't underestimate how much you already know about business finance. It's really no different from personal finance, and most people have some experience in that area. The issues are simple: You own some things; you owe some money; you have money that comes in; you have money that goes out. What you want is more coming in than going out so that you can own more and owe less. It's the same with business.

Financial Statements

The standard way of explaining the finances of any business is with financial statements. These are documents that show what has happened to the business financially over a period of time and where the business stands at a particular moment in time. There are a variety of different documents that can be called financial statements, but a business plan is usually only concerned with the three main types:

- **Balance sheet**. This outlines where the business stands in terms of what it owns, what it owes, and how much investment the owners have in the business. It is the statement of the financial position of a business at a particular point in time.

- **Income statement**. This shows the sales of the business over a period of time (e.g., a year), what it cost to conduct business during that period, and how much profit (or loss) resulted during that period. It is the statement of a business's profit or loss over a given period of time.

- **Cash flow statement**. This represents the same period as the income statement and gives details of cash coming into the business, cash going out of the business, and how these have affected the bank balance of the business. This is usually broken down on a monthly basis.

Ask yourself: If a business doesn't yet exist, how can it have financial statements? The business plan for a brand-new venture must use **projected financial statements** to explain the financial plan for the business. These represent your expectation of what's going to happen financially over the first three (or more) years of business activity.

- *Projected balance sheets*. You will have several of these. They will show where the business will stand financially on opening day, at the end of the first year, at the end of the second year, and at the end of the third year.

- *Projected income statements*. You'll have three of these, one for each of the first three years of business. They will show the year's expected sales, costs, expenses, and profit (or loss). In a sense, they will explain why the balance sheet (the company's financial position) will have changed each year.

- *Projected cash flow statements*. There will be three of these covering the same periods as the income statements. By planning when cash comes in and goes out of your business, you will demonstrate that you will always be able to pay the bills that are due.

Even when you have an accountant prepare the statements for you, the actual planning decisions are yours. Furthermore, it is not economical to pay an accountant to ask you all the little details about the finances of your venture. Instead, you can organize all the information needed for the projected statements before you start paying for the accountant's time. All you have to know are a few basic terms; for example, assets, liabilities, and equity.

Assets

You or your accountant will need information about **assets** in order to complete the opening-day balance sheet. *Ask yourself: What are my assets?*

You may consider the fact that you're physically strong or particularly good-looking to be an asset. But when it comes to finance, an asset is something that is owned, rather than a personal attribute. It must also have some monetary value. You may have legal title to the 15-year-old Chevrolet with no engine sitting in your backyard. So you own it. But it's not an asset because it has no monetary value—it's going to cost more to tow it away than you could sell it for.

Doubtless, you will need some assets to operate in business. For a math tutoring business, the assets are little more than a telephone and some pencils and paper. For a building

---

balance sheet A statement of the financial position of a business at a particular point in time.

income statement A statement of a business's profit or loss over a given period of time.

cash flow statement A statement of cash going into and out of a business over a given period of time, and how this has affected the cash balance.

projected financial statements Statements predicting what the financial performance and position of a business will be in the future. Sometimes called pro forma financial statements.

? Get Help 5.1
Many small accounting firms specialize in working with small businesses or self-employed people. Ask some entrepreneurs for referrals. In some cases, you can get help from a senior student—ask a business teacher at your local college.

assets Things that are owned and have monetary value.

Table 5.1 Worksheet (Kidproofers)

Material and Operating Cash Needs (for Start-Up)

Materials and Cash (Current Assets)	$ Value	
	Already Have	**Need**
Inventory (Locking devices)		$1400
Inventory (Monitoring devices)		2800
Inventory (Gates)		400
Office Supplies	$ 100	
Insurance Prepayment	950	
Operating Cash	5000	

foundation contractor, assets may be vehicles, heavy equipment, and cash. Some of the assets you might already have; others you will have to acquire.

Assets are traditionally divided into two categories. Those that tend to be more permanent in value (vehicles, equipment, machinery, land, buildings) are called **fixed assets**. Others are less permanent in value, or more liquid. They tend to be used up or change their form quickly (within a year) and are called **current assets**. Current assets include office supplies, inventory, prepaid expenses (like insurance or licences), any money that your customers owe you (this is called **accounts receivable**—but you shouldn't have any of these on opening day), and, of course, the cash you will need in your bank account to run the business.

Table 5.1 is an example of a worksheet that can be used to identify the current assets needed for your new business. The one shown here is for Kidproofers, a start-up one-person company that will go into homes and install various safety devices such as gates, cupboard locks, and video monitors to make the home safer for children.

⭐ Head Start Exercise

5.1 In the business plan template at the end of this chapter, complete Table 5.6 to indicate the materials, supplies, insurance, cash, inventory, and so on that you will need to come up with before your business can open. (Do not include equipment or machinery.) Estimate the monetary value of each item and enter it into the appropriate column to indicate whether you already own it or must buy it (1 page maximum).

When listing your current asset requirements, you will only be guessing how much cash you will need on hand to run the business. Later, when you look at how cash will come into your business and when bills will be due, you can more accurately predict how much of a cash cushion you will need to stay operating.

Table 5.2 is a worksheet that can be used to list the fixed assets the business will use. The example here is for BackLight, a small start-up that will install emergency lighting systems in older commercial buildings. Worksheets like this are not generally part of the body of the business plan, but may be attached as appendices at the back of the plan.

⭐ Head Start Exercise

5.2 In the business plan template at the end of this chapter, complete Table 5.7 to list the fixed assets you will need in your business. Estimate the monetary value of each item and enter it into the appropriate column to indicate whether you already own it or must purchase it. Do not include items that will be leased or rented for the business (1 page maximum). (Refer to Section 4 of your plan.)

fixed assets Things that are owned and that tend to keep their value or form for long periods (in excess of a year). Examples are buildings, machinery, and equipment.

current assets Things that are owned and tend to be impermanent in value or form. Examples are cash, inventory, and prepaid expenses.

accounts receivable Assets in the form of money that is owed to a company by its customers.

☑ **Memory Check 5.1**
True or False? The principles are the same for both personal finances and business finances.

☑ **Memory Check 5.2**
True or False? The balance sheet is an example of a financial statement.

Table 5.2 Worksheet (BackLight)

Equipment Needs (for Start-Up)

Equipment (Fixed Assets)	$ Value	
	Already Have	**Need**
Van	$14 000	
Hand Tools	980	
Laser Level		$190
Lawn Sign		160
Computer & Printer		800

Liabilities

liabilities Legal debts; money owed by a business.

Now that you've listed the business assets (things owned), you must consider the **liabilities** (things owed). It's not a liability to owe a favour to your unemployed brother-in-law (whom you may consider to be a liability himself). We're talking here about legal debts, with monetary value.

current liabilities Short-term debts that will have to be paid off within a year.

Like assets, liabilities come in two varieties: **current liabilities** and long-term liabilities. It's not critical that you know the difference, but it will save time (and money) when explaining your anticipated debts to your accountant. Current liabilities are any debts that will be paid off within a year. This would include things like short-term loans, credit terms from suppliers, and even the final 12 months' worth of payments on a long-term loan (because it will now be paid off within one year).

✓ **Memory Check 5.3**
True or False? Cash is an example of a current asset.

⭐ Head Start Exercise

5.3 Write down any credit terms you expect to get from suppliers. Would you expect to owe anything to suppliers on the first day of business? How much? (1/3 page maximum)

long-term liabilities Debts that will have to be paid off within a period greater than one year.

Long-term liabilities are debts that will take more than a year to pay off and include things like long-term loans for buying vehicles or equipment as well as mortgages on land and buildings. By this point in your planning, you will have an idea of whether you will have enough money to buy everything you need to get into business. You might also need some extra cash to run things at first, before you get regular income from customers. If you (and your partners or investors) won't have enough of your own money, you may have to borrow. Expect to revise your thinking on this several times while refining your plan.

⭐ Head Start Exercise

5.4 Make a note of any long-term loans you think you will need, indicating what the money will be used for (1/8 page maximum).

Equity

equity The amount of claim an individual has on an asset; or the measure of an individual's wealth.

Equity is the amount of financial claim an owner has on an asset. It measures wealth. *Ask yourself: Who is a rich person I know? How rich are they?*

Perhaps you are thinking of someone who lives in a $600 000 home and drives a brand-new $80 000 Cadillac. That's $680 000 worth of assets right there. But think of someone else who lives in a $200 000 home and drives an older, used car that's worth only $10 000. *Ask yourself: Which of these two people is richer?* Well, you don't know. You can't judge how rich someone is by their assets alone. You must also consider their liabilities.

Let's say the Cadillac driver purchased his or her home with a 25 percent down payment and still owes $450 000 on a mortgage. If the house were sold for $600 000, $450 000 would go to pay off the bank and the owner would only get to keep the $150 000. So, this person only has a $150 000 claim, or *equity*, in the home. If the Cadillac was bought with a $5000 down payment, $75 000 would still be owing on the car and the owner would only have the $5000 as equity. This would give the Cadillac driver a total equity of $155 000.

But let's say our used-car owner owns the $200 000 home outright, with no mortgage owing. This person paid cash for the $10 000 car, and has no other debts. This used-car driver's equity, or wealth, totals $210 000. This is the richer one. How rich someone is, or their equity, is not just a measure of the assets they own but also of the debts they owe— their liabilities. This can be expressed as an equation:

$$\text{Equity} = \text{Assets} - \text{Liabilities}$$

This equation can also be expressed in a slightly different way, with the assets on the left:

$$\text{Assets} = \text{Liabilities} + \text{Equity}$$

If you don't know enough mathematics to understand that these equations are the same, just accept it. It's true. And it is this second way of expressing the equation that is important to your accountant, because this is the **accounting equation**.

It means that the value of all the "stuff" in the business (assets) is equal to the amount of money owed by the business (liabilities) plus however much the owners have invested of their own money (equity). For example, you may be a musician with a $5000 sound system (assets), but you still owe $1000 to a finance company (liability) from the purchase. Therefore, you have a $4000 investment (equity) in your business.

$$\$5,000 = \$1,000 + \$4,000$$
$$\text{(asset)} \quad \text{(liability)} \quad \text{(equity)}$$

accounting equation The basis for the balance sheet, showing that the value of assets is equal to the sum of the values of liabilities and equity.

⭐ Head Start Exercise

5.5 Estimate how much equity you will have in your new venture by adding up the value of any cash or assets that you already own that will be used in the business (1/4 page maximum).

Balance Sheet

The information you have put together in Head Start Exercises 5.1–5.5 is all that's needed to assemble an opening-day balance sheet. When you give the information to your accountant you will be saving him or her lots of time (and yourself some money) since the information is already organized.

You may want to save even more by creating the balance sheet yourself and just having the accountant check it over. This won't be hard since you already know the basis for the format of the balance sheet—the accounting equation, or

$$\text{Assets} = \text{Liabilities} + \text{Equity}.$$

Just as the left side of the equation must balance with the right side of the equation, the left side of the balance sheet must balance with the right side.

Figure 5.1 is the balance sheet from a new company that installs video surveillance equipment. The company has $21 179 worth of assets (on the left) and this same amount

☑ Memory Check 5.4
True or False? The accounting equation is "assets = liabilities – equity."

Figure 5.1 Open Eye Equipment | Balance Sheet

(Date)					
CURRENT ASSETS			**CURRENT LIABILITIES**		
Cash	$ 4 000		Accounts payable	$ 122	
Inventory	2 100		Total	122	$ 122
Accounts receivable	nil				
Prepaid expenses	1 106		**LONG-TERM LIABILITIES**		
Office supplies	73		Car loan	$ 8 400	
Total	7 279	$ 7 279	Bank loan	2 750	
			Total	$11 150	$11 150
FIXED ASSETS					
Automobile	$11 300		**TOTAL LIABILITIES**	$11 272	$11 272
Computer equipment	1 700				
Furniture/fixtures	900		**OWNER'S EQUITY**		$ 9 907
Total	13 900	$13 900			
Total Assets		**$21 179**	**Total Liabilities and Owner's Equity**		**$21 179**

is the value of the liabilities and equity (on the right). They have to be the same because a balance sheet must balance.

Typically, balance sheets no longer divide the page into left and right; rather, the right side just follows along below the left side, as in the example for a formalwear rental business shown in Figure 5.2. Nevertheless, people still talk about the "left" and "right" sides of the balance sheet. The date on the balance sheet is critically important because it shows how the company stood at a particular moment in time: The following day supplies could be used up and customers might pay some bills, so the balance sheet would change.

Costs and Expenses

Ask yourself: Is there a difference between costs and expenses? In regular usage, the terms *cost* and *expense* are used interchangeably. For the purposes of the business plan, however, we will need to distinguish between the two.

As much as possible, *cost* should refer to what we pay for something that we resell to our customers. This is referred to, more precisely, as **cost of goods sold**.

Cost of goods sold is a critical element of the income statement. The sales of a business minus the cost of goods sold equals the **gross profit**. For example, a store selling Western hats may have had $300 000 in sales last year, but the owner of the store paid $140 000 (cost of goods sold) for those same hats. So, this has produced a gross profit of $160 000. The owner of the store cannot go out and buy a vacation condo with the $160 000, however, because much of that money must be used to pay for rent, insurance, advertising, and so on. These are the operating **expenses** of the business.

If the hat business has expenses totalling $110 000, the owner now has $50 000 net profit to do with as he or she sees fit (after paying taxes, of course). This is the essence of the income statement, as shown in Figure 5.3.

For many straightforward, service-type operations, the only money to be paid out will be in the form of expenses, since there are no goods to be resold. If your business is reselling goods, you already have a sales forecast and you should have a rough idea of what your

Memory Check 5.5
True or False? Referring to Figure 5.1, the owner of Open Eye Equipment has a personal investment of $9,907 in the business.

Memory Check 5.6
True or False? Referring to Figure 5.1, at the time of the balance sheet, no one owes money to Open Eye Equipment.

cost of goods sold What a business paid for the goods that it purchased and resold over a given period of time.

gross profit The sales of a business minus the cost of goods sold over a given period of time.

expenses All the money a company pays out (other than cost of goods sold) in order to stay in business. This includes things like rent, utilities, supplies, advertising, salaries, and so on.

Figure 5.2 Tres Hot Formals | Balance Sheet

Opening Day	(Date)	
ASSETS		
CURRENT ASSETS		
Cash	$ 2 010	
Rental inventory	14 500	
Prepaid expenses	2 230	
Supplies	400	
Total current assets		$19 140
FIXED ASSETS		
Store fixtures	$ 4 250	
Equipment	1 000	
Vehicles	9 950	
Total fixed assets		$15 200
TOTAL ASSETS		**$34 340**
LIABILITIES		
CURRENT LIABILITIES		
Accounts payable	$ 1 080	
Short-term loans payable	3 500	
Other current liabilities	nil	
Total current liabilities		$ 4 580
LONG-TERM LIABILITIES		
Long-term loans payable	$ 8 000	
Other long-term liabilities	nil	
Total long-term liabilities		$ 8 000
OWNER'S EQUITY		
Total investment		$21 760
TOTAL LIABILITIES AND OWNER'S EQUITY		**$34 340**

Figure 5.3 Hat Business | Income Statement

For the One-Year Period Ending (Date)	
Sales	$300 000
Cost of Goods Sold	$140 000
Gross Profit	$160 000
Operating Expenses	$110 000
Net Profit	$ 50 000

Get Help 5.2
You can look up the average percentage that cost of goods sold represents of sales for your industry (or a similar industry) in the small-business profiles published by Statistics Canada. These are available in many libraries. Or, check Industry Canada's Small Business Benchmarking Tool at www.sme.ic.gc.ca.

products will cost you (as a percentage of your selling price). It won't be hard to estimate, from your sales forecast, your cost of goods sold for the first year of business.

⭐ Head Start Exercise

5.6 If you will be selling tangible products, estimate your cost of goods sold for your first year of business. Base this on your sales forecast from Section 2 of your business plan (1/4 page maximum).

As you have been preparing all the elements of your business plan to date, you have been identifying your various operating expenses. Since you have identified the site for your business, you are now able to figure out how much you will have to pay each year for your rent, utilities, property taxes, and so on. Since you have identified your advertising techniques, you can add up what you will pay to advertise for a year. You also know what you will have to pay for insurance, salaries, and so on. Next, you will go through your plan thus far and estimate what your annual operating expenses will be in each area.

But there is one important expense you have not yet considered: **depreciation**. Depreciation is the loss in value of an asset over time. Let's say you invest $1000 in a lawn mower that you will use to start a lawn maintenance business. This is your equity. If you pay all your basic expenses and then spend the "profit," at the end of two years you will find that your lawn mower is totally worn out and must be replaced. You have essentially "spent" the equity in your business and will need another $1000 to buy a new mower if you are to keep operating. Instead, you should treat the wearing out of the lawn mower as an operating expense. In this way, you can set aside money to replace depreciating assets.

Assets decline in value not just from getting worn out. They also become obsolete.[2] Let's say you buy high-quality video editing software for your business at a price of $1000. Two years later, the software may be working exactly as it did on day one, but in the meantime better software has become available for only $300. What is your asset worth now? It has depreciated because it is obsolete. This depreciation is an expense to your business.

Table 5.3 shows a worksheet that can help to summarize the various costs and expenses and translate them into an annual fee. The one shown here is for a small software retailer

Table 5.3 Worksheet (Software Solvers)

Ongoing Costs & Expenses

Expense	Payment Period (monthly or Other: Specify)	Amount per Period	Annual Amount
Inventory	every 2 months	$10 200	$61 200
Rent	monthly	900	10 800
Utilities	monthly	215	2 580
Drawings	weekly	865	44 980
Insurance	twice per year	890	1 780
Deprecation	annual		8 400
Interest	annual		860
Prof. fees	twice per year	900	1 800
Advertising	quarterly	1 625	6 500
Supplies	quarterly	75	300
Travel	monthly	350	4 200

that expects to get some of its revenue from software sales and the rest from program set-ups and customizing work. This information can be used later to help produce an income statement.

⭐ Head Start Exercise

5.7 In the business plan template at the end of this chapter, complete Table 5.8 to estimate all of your operating cost and expenses for the first year (1 page maximum).

Income Statement

In order to prepare a projected income statement it is necessary to figure out what your sales will be. You have already done this in Section 2 (Feasibility) of your business plan. You have now listed your cost of goods sold and your operating expenses, so there is sufficient information for you or your accountant to draft projected income statements. You will likely need one for each of your first three years of business. Figure 5.4 is a typical projected income statement for the first year of business.

Figure 5.4 Software Solvers | Income Statement (Projected)

For the First Year of Business		
SALES		
Product sales	$110 000	
Programming services	35 000	
Total sales income	$145 000	$145 000
COSTS		
Cost of goods sold		$ 61 000
GROSS PROFIT		
Gross profit		$ 84 000
EXPENSES		
Rent	$ 11 000	
Utilities	2 600	
Salaries/drawings	45 000	
Insurance	1 560	
Depreciation	8 400	
Interest	840	
Professional fees	1 800	
Advertising	6 500	
Supplies	300	
Travel	4 200	
Total operating expenses	$ 82 200	$ 82 200
NET PROFIT		
Net before income tax	$ 1800	$1 800
Income tax		600
Net Profit after Income Tax		**$1 200**

✅ **Memory Check 5.8**
True or False? Assets can depreciate even if they are not being used in a business.

A Small Grant Helps a Big Idea

It started as a brilliant idea for a smartphone app; one that would prevent the destruction of countless trees, save the environment from certain toxic chemicals, provide tremendous convenience to shoppers, and present huge marketing opportunities for merchants.

Vincent Panepinto and Nicholas Wiktorczyk had realized that cash registers all over the world were cranking out hundreds of kilometres of paper receipts, many of which were using toxic non-biodegradable inks and non-recyclable paper. As well, a great many of the receipts would be lost or discarded by the customer long before they were needed for budgets, expense reports, or warranty purposes. Their idea was to use the capabilities of smartphones and modern cash registers to provide the customer with an instant digital receipt, stored in the cloud and which the customer could access at any time via cell phone or computer. The possible tie-ins were endless: budget analyzers to show consumers where and how they were spending, the ability to photograph and upload old paper receipts, permanent records supporting tax returns, merchant capability to customize receipts with promotional offers and rewards, and so on.

At the time of brainstorming these ideas, Wiktorczyk and Panepinto had graduated from the University of Western Ontario and were studying global business management at Humber College in Toronto. They had learned how to write a business plan and a professor suggested they enter their business concept in Humber's New Venture Seed Fund Competition. The fund would provide a grant of $8000 toward start-up expenses to get the company going. But a lot more funding would be needed to develop the concept.

An angel investor provided over $100 000 to bring things to the next stage, and Wiktorczyk and Panepinto managed to get accepted as a client of MaRS. MaRS is a not-for-profit organization that was originally set up to help commercialize medical discoveries. Eventually, it expanded into helping entrepreneurs in a broader range of technologies by providing work space, training, and links to venture capital. However, the technology for merchants to offer point-of-sale digital receipts was going to be very expensive to build and install. And Wiktorczyk and Panepinto realized that the company would have to quickly start generating cash flow if it were to continue developing.

So, like many new firms, the business model had to deviate from the original concept. Today, their company, Spently.com, is primarily providing a system to merchants which enables merchants to offer email receipts that they can easily customize to promote their brands, include social media links or advertise special offers. This has led Spently.com to partner with other firms like Shopify, which has over 30 000 online merchants. At the time of writing, Vincent and Nicholas are working out of office space provided by the Centre for Social Innovation, free for one year. This is another not-for-profit organization, one that supports concepts that are making a positive change in the world. Now, with Spently.com as a going concern, Wiktorczyk and Panepinto can keep working toward a world of paperless receipts.

HOW WILL I TRACK THE FINANCES?
Break-Even

Ask yourself: Why would I be interested in just breaking even, when the goal of my business is to make a profit? The purpose of financial statements is to help you plan and track what is going on in your business, ultimately to make sure you make a profit. But these are complex tools, and often difficult for the average self-employed businessperson to use. It's not unusual for business owners to look at their financial statements only at the end of each quarter or, in some cases, only at the end of the year when they have their personal tax return completed.

But if you have to wait months to find out if you're making a profit, you may already be out of business by the time you get the news. What you need is a tool that will help you gauge on a monthly, weekly, or even daily basis whether you are making a profit. What you need is a break-even number.

Break-even is the point at which all of your costs and expenses are covered and where you are starting to make a profit. It can be expressed in dollars, or sales units, or as a percentage. For example, if you are a safety consultant you might know that you have to bring in $3600 worth of billings each month before you are making any net profit. If it's the fifteenth of the month and you have only brought in $1250, it's time to either get nervous or make a lot of phone calls to potential customers. As a bicycle shop owner, you may know that you must sell 12 bikes a week in order to break even. If you have 15 bikes sold by Thursday afternoon, you know it's going to be a good week. As a bed-and-breakfast owner, you may know that you must have a 30 percent occupancy rate to be profitable. If your place has been at least half full every day for the past month, you know you're making money. *Ask yourself: What measurement would be the most appropriate way for me to think of break-even? Dollars? Number of units sold? A percentage of my capacity? What period is most important for me to consider break-even in: Monthly? Weekly? Daily?*

Break-even is a guideline—it is not a very precise tool, but still can be extremely valuable in helping you track your performance. It can be expressed as a single number or shown on a chart where you can see your amount of profit at different sales levels. You can calculate an annual break-even amount using the information on your income statement. On most income statements, the operating expenses are broken down into two categories:

- **Fixed expenses**: These are the expenses that do not vary with sales. In other words, things you would have to pay whether or not you had any sales. These would include rent, insurance, utilities, and so on, and are normally shown first in the expenses area of the income statement.

- **Variable expenses**: These tend to vary with your sales (or go up as your sales go up). Examples are packaging, delivery, travel, casual labour, and often advertising.

To calculate an annual break-even value, you must first figure out the contribution ratio. This just means the portion of each sale that is left after paying its cost of goods sold and variable expenses. This is the amount that can be used to either pay off the fixed expenses, or, when they are paid off, can be kept as profit.

$$\text{Contribution ratio} = \frac{\text{Gross profit} - \text{Variable expenses}}{\text{Sales}}$$

You can now calculate break-even as a dollar value.

$$\text{Break-even} = \frac{\text{Fixed expenses}}{\text{Contribution ratio}}$$

This is only one formula to calculate break-even. There are lots of methods. You may wish to include this valuable tracking tool in your business plan.

Credit and Collections

As an entrepreneur it is important to know whether you are making profit. It is also important to know whether you are actually getting your hands on the money you are making. Unfortunately, some clients are slow or reluctant to part with money, even when it is properly owed to suppliers. This is a danger against which you must try to protect yourself.

If your business sells to ordinary consumers, payment isn't much of a problem since you will likely accept cash, debit cards, cheques (guaranteed by phone, using companies such as Telecredit), credit cards, or other third-party credit. For example, you could sell furniture from your antique store, where you also arrange finance contracts for your customers (you do the paperwork) with a local bank or finance company. The finance deal, however,

break-even The point at which a company starts to make a profit; the point where sales are sufficient to cover all of the costs and expenses of a company.

Get Help 5.4
A competent business or accounting student should be able to help you quickly calculate a break-even point.

fixed expenses Expenses of a business that tend to remain constant, regardless of the sales level of the business. Examples include rent, utilities, and permanent salaries.

variable expenses Expenses of a business that tend to fluctuate with sales. Examples include supplies, packaging, and delivery expenses.

Figure 5.5 Example Collections Policy

Time Overdue	Action
7 days	• a reminder phone call.
14 days	• a reminder phone call and • a follow-up letter.
30–45 days	• a visit to the company to discuss the problem and • a follow-up letter.
45–60 days	• stop supplying the company and • a phone call offering to pick up a cheque for outstanding payments.
75 days	• a formal letter from a lawyer demanding payment, threatening legal action and • a phone call offering to pick up a cheque.
90 days	• sell the debt to a collection agency or • commence legal action.

remains between your customer and the finance company and you will get the cash. Rarely can small retailers afford to get into the business of extending their own credit to customers.

But let's say you start an executive limousine service where you work on contract for large corporations. They expect to be billed on a monthly basis for your service. This puts you in the business of granting credit. Even if your monthly invoice says "payable on receipt," you have already allowed up to a month's worth of delayed payment. Furthermore, many companies will ask for another 30 days from receiving the invoice because of their internal payment systems. Now you could be waiting as long as 60 days to get paid. And what happens when their system breaks down and you have to wait still another month? What if payment is more than three months overdue?

You can't wait forever to take action. Instead, you should have a series of increasingly serious steps planned for dealing with delinquent accounts. The steps should be appropriate to the nature of your industry. For example, you may take your first action when an account is seven days overdue. Figure 5.5 shows one kind of collections policy you might implement.

Ask yourself: What happens if a client who owes me money gets into financial trouble and might be going bankrupt? This is one of those cases where an ounce of prevention is worth a ton of cure. Small creditors of a bankrupt business rarely get much of the money they are owed—and the little they do get, they have to wait for.

The only real defence here is to try to avoid this problem in the first place. Before extending credit, get credit reports. (These come from credit reporting agencies such as Dun & Bradstreet or Equifax/Creditel. They include information such as the sales of the firm, the amount of assets and debts it carries, and the speed at which it usually pays its bills.) Set limits of credit for individual customers and stick to these limits, regularly checking to see who owes you and how much. Your credit and collections policy and how you enforce it will have a big influence on when money comes into your business. This is important for you to be able to plan your cash flow.

Cash Flow

Ask yourself: Is there a difference between "cash flow" and "profit"? Lots of potentially profitable business ventures go **bankrupt**, not because they can't make a profit, but because the entrepreneurs fail to plan for the way the money comes in and goes out. For most businesses, **revenue** comes in on one schedule but bills become due on a totally different schedule. Because of this, you could find yourself in a position where you are making a profit, but the

Memory Check 5.9
True or False? Giving a customer time to pay what they owe you is the same as giving them credit.

Memory Check 5.10
True or False? A break-even number is a very precise financial tool.

bankruptcy When a business does not have sufficient assets or earning power to repay its debts and legal action is taken to dissolve the company and compensate the creditors as much as is possible.

revenue The income of a business from sales.

cash has not yet come in from your customers. At the same time, your **creditors** are taking you to court for non-payment.

In a situation like this, there is little use in running to the bank asking for money to tide you over, because few loan officers will feel comfortable lending money to someone who is being chased by creditors, even when the borrower can demonstrate his or her profitability on paper. The trick is to plan for any future cash shortages before they happen. You must arrange for any financing needs well in advance, when it's not urgent, and when your reputation is intact. You do this with **projected cash flow** statements. These are also called cash budgets and they represent the same periods as your projected income statements. Typically, they are broken down into 12 monthly columns, with rows of information showing

- the expected sales;
- the cash expected to come in;
- the cash that will have to go out; and
- the changes in the bank balance.

Lots of rows of information make cash flow look a little complicated at first, but most of the rows just explain these four basic pieces of information. The example shown in Figure 5.6 is for an upholstery shop that gets about half of its business from consumers who pay with cash, and the other half from business customers who can take up to two months to settle their accounts. If you're looking at a cash flow projection for the first time, don't panic. Just concentrate on one column, one item at a time, as you try to make sense of it. And remind yourself that it's only a tool to check that you won't run out of cash when your bills are due. It will become more clear as you assemble the information that will go into it.

The first task in preparing a cash flow projection is to look at your annual sales forecasts and then break these down into monthly forecasts. This is part guesswork, part experience, and part logic. Virtually all businesses have some seasonal fluctuation. For example, December, July, and August are big vacation months, which means lots of income for tourist restaurants. However, there is also a decrease in new project starts or capital expenditures by larger organizations during these months, so it might be a slow time for an architectural firm. Many businesses have their own unique patterns. An ice sculptor may be extremely busy in the summer (wedding decorations) and February (winter carnivals) but really slow the rest of the year. A florist may sell more roses around Valentine's Day than during all the rest of the year put together.

For a new business, the problem of monthly fluctuations is compounded by the expected pattern of growth. This issue was examined when you prepared your sales forecast and now must be considered again when you look at sales by month.

Table 5.4 shows a worksheet that can be used to break down the annual sales forecast (this was completed in Section 2 of the business plan) into monthly forecasts. The one shown here is for a company that wholesales high-end imported snowboards to sporting goods retailers. The business is opening on February first. Therefore, February is Month 1, March is Month 2, and so on. September (Month 8) will be the biggest sales month, since this is when retailers are stocking up for the build up to Christmas sales. The chart also takes the growth of the business into account.

⭐ Head Start Exercises

5.8 Write down the main issues that will affect how your business will fluctuate monthly throughout the year. Also write down the issues that will affect the initial growth of your business (1/4 page maximum).

5.9 Using Table 5.9, Projected Sales Income by Month (in the business plan template at the end of this chapter), take the sales forecast from Section 2 of your business plan and break it down into monthly sales predictions for the first three years of business. Keep the issues of growth and seasonal fluctuation in mind (1 page maximum).

---

creditors Those to whom a business owes money.

projected cash flow A statement predicting how money will flow into and out of a business during a given period in the future. Also known as a cash budget.

✅ **Memory Check 5.11**
True or False? Credit reports can be purchased for individual companies.

❓ **Get Help 5.5**
Check trade journals for your industry, looking for articles on seasonal fluctuations in business.

✅ **Memory Check 5.12**
True or False? The first step in a collections policy should be to stop supplying the debtor.

✅ **Memory Check 5.13**
True or False? *Cash flow* and *profit* are interchangeable terms.

Figure 5.6 Projected Cash Flow | First Year of Operation, New Look Upholstery

MONTH	May	Jun	Jul	Aug	Sep	Oct	Nov	Dec	Jan	Feb	Mar	Apr
Sales	$1 000	$3 000	$5 000	$8 000	$12 000	$16 000	$20 000	$10 000	$15 000	$15 000	$20 000	$25 000
CASH IN-FLOW												
Cash sales	500	1 500	2 500	4 000	6 000	8 000	10 000	5 000	7 500	7 500	10 000	12 500
Account payments received	–	–	500	1 500	2 500	4 000	6 000	8 000	10 000	5 000	7 500	7 500
Cash borrowed from line of credit	–	–	1 600	2 700	1 600	–	–	–	–	–	–	–
Total Cash In-flow (a)	500	1 500	4 600	8 200	10 100	12 000	16 000	13 000	17 500	12 500	17 500	20 000
OPENING Cash Balance (b)	14 000	7 000	2 050	100	100	70	330	1 690	210	7 690	10 370	15 420
CASH OUT-FLOW												
Rent	800	800	800	800	800	800	800	800	800	800	800	800
Utilities	200	200	200	220	230	240	240	240	260	260	250	240
Vehicle expenses	200	250	250	280	300	300	300	240	260	260	300	300
Supplies	800	200	300	400	600	800	800	400	600	500	800	1 000
Loan payments	–	–	–	100	100	1 500	4 400	–	–	–	–	–
Payroll/drawings	4 500	4 500	4 500	4 500	7 500	7 500	7 500	10 000	7 500	7 500	9 500	9 500
Advertising	1 000	500	500	500	600	600	600	200	600	500	800	800
Taxes	–	–	–	1 400	–	–	–	2 600	–	–	–	8 200
Total Cash Out-flow (c)	7 500	6 450	6 550	8 200	10 130	11 740	14 640	14 480	10 020	9 820	12 450	20 840
CLOSING Cash Balance (a + b – c)	7 000	2 050	100	100	70	330	1 690	210	7 690	10 370	15 420	14 580

Table 5.4 Worksheet (ColdSports)

Projected Sales Income by Month

Month	Year 1	Year 2	Year 3
1	$ 10 000	$ 12 000	$ 14 000
2	12 000	14 500	19 000
3	14 000	17 000	20 500
4	6 000	7 000	8 000
5	1 000	1 000	15 000
6	10 000	12 000	14 500
7	18 000	23 000	27 500
8	20 000	24 000	29 000
9	19 000	23 000	28 000
10	18 000	21 500	26 000
11	16 000	19 000	23 000
12	14 000	17 000	21 000
Total Sales Forecast	$158 000	$191 000	$245 500

Go back and make sure that your totals are the same as your annual sales forecasts shown in Section 2 of your business plan, and that they also match any figures you have used for your projected income statements. If the totals don't match, it may be time to rewrite one or both components.

For many businesses the cash comes in as soon (or almost as soon) as the sale is made. These include businesses that accept payment by credit card, debit card, cheque, or automatic withdrawal, as well as actual cash money. In these cases, the cash flow will show exactly the same information in the *sales* row as in the *total cash in* row.

But let's say you give your customers 30 days to pay and you know from experience that only half of them will pay within the 30 days. The others will take between 30 and 60 days to actually get the money to you. If your sales are $10 000 in your first month, none of that money will flow into the business during that month. Half of it, $5000, will come in during the following month, and the other $5000 will arrive two months after the sale. This situation is shown in Table 5.5.

The cash in during Month 3 is made up of half the sales from Month 1 ($5000) and half the sales from Month 2 ($6000). *Ask yourself: How complicated can it get to predict the cash coming into my business?* Imagine that some of your customers will pay cash at the time of sale, some will get 30 days to pay (with a third of those taking 60 days to pay), and some will get 60 days (with some of those actually taking 90). It would become a very complex chore to figure out how much money would be coming in each month. *Ask yourself: Do I want to reconsider my credit-granting policy?*

☑ **Memory Check 5.14**
True or False? Almost all businesses have some form of seasonal fluctuation in sales.

☑ **Memory Check 5.15**
True or False? Cash flow projections rely on sales forecast.

Table 5.5 Worksheet (ColdSports)

Cash Coming in

	Month 1	Month 2	Month 3	Month 4
Sales	$10 000	12 000	14 000	6 000
Cash in		5000	11 000	13 000

⭐ Head Start Exercise

5.10 Outline your credit and collections decisions. Write some notes that will explain any time gap between when your sales are made and when the cash will come into your bank account (1/3 page maximum).

expenditures The money a business pays out in a given period for costs and operating expenses.

The cash that you put out for costs and expenses is called **expenditures**. In planning for your projected income statements, you have already listed the ongoing costs and expenses you will have to pay for a full year. In order to plan your cash flow, however, you will have to provide some more detail about when you will actually pay these bills. And unfortunately, many of your bills won't come due in nice equal monthly amounts.

For example, you may have to pay insurance of $1000 per year (as shown on your income statement), but the insurance company might require that you pay six months in advance. That means that you will have prepaid $500 before opening the business (this will show as a **prepaid expense** on your balance sheet), but you will have to pay another $500 every six months. So your cash flow projection will show a $500 payment in your sixth month of operations and another $500 payment in your twelfth month.

prepaid expenses Expenses of a business that must be paid in advance, such as insurance and legal retainers. The value of the prepaid expense shows as an asset on the balance sheet and the value goes down as the value of the expense is used up.

You may plan to run a weekly ad in your local Saturday newspaper, and the paper will bill you on a monthly basis. This means you won't have any advertising expense to pay in your first month, because the first month's advertising bill won't arrive until the second month. Simple. Unfortunately, not all months have four Saturdays; some have five. So when it comes to planning your advertising expense, you will have to sit down with a calendar and plan for a bigger bill in the months following the months with five Saturdays. Not so simple. The people who are best at financial planning are imaginative thinkers—those with the ability to visualize the future comings and goings of money. Use your imagination for this process when you write down each of your conclusions about when bills will have to be paid.

After you (and likely your financial adviser) have completed your first draft of the cash flow, you will probably want to go back and reassess how much cash you will need on hand at start-up to ensure that you will be able to continue paying your bills through the growth period. *Ask yourself: Approximately how much cash do I think I'll need at the start of my business?* Typically, new entrepreneurs will underestimate their need for operating cash and the cash flow projection will demonstrate this by showing a negative bank balance. There are two ways to fix this, of course:

- Re-plan the expense portions of your business plan, coming up with ways to do things more cheaply.
- Find a way to get more money (from lenders or investors) to be able to cover your planned expenses.

In fact, you may well do some of both, which leads to the final big question of planning to work for yourself. *Ask yourself: Where will I get the money?*

WHERE WILL I GET THE MONEY?

This is the last big question to answer in preparing a basic business plan. It is only here at the end of the planning process that the question can be answered. Until this point, there was nothing to get money for. But now there is a clear plan to be financed; the next step is to look at the different sources of funding. *Ask yourself: What are my options for getting start-up money?*

Personal Sources

Sometimes a business starts with no financial input from the entrepreneur, but this is rare. More commonly, the new business owner contributes materials and equipment or personal cash, or puts up other personal assets as **collateral** for borrowing money. Many new entrepreneurs risk pretty much everything they have. At first, this sounds pretty daunting—especially when you consider the high rates of new-business failure. But it's not nearly as bad as it sounds. A business failure is not necessarily a bankruptcy. Lots of entrepreneurs find that they aren't making any money with their venture and close the operation down before losing very much of their personal assets.

Risking your own money in a business is critically important if you plan on asking others to risk theirs. Potential lenders and investors want to know how much you're risking; not just as a percentage of the total investment, but also as a percentage of everything you've got in the world. For example, you may ask someone to invest $25 000 in a business that you are putting $5000 into. If they find out that you are worth $100 000 (you might have this much equity in your home), how would they feel? On the other hand, if they find out that $5000 is everything you've got in the world (you had to sell your TV to get some of the money), they are going to feel a very different sense of commitment on your part. In both cases, however, you're still only investing $5000.

Your own cash is not the only personal source of funding. A significant portion of the start-up (or "seed") money for new businesses is borrowed from family and friends. In Canada, this is one of the major sources of start-up capital. This may be due in part to our immigration policies, which give priority to family reunification, the likelihood of immigrants living in an extended family unit, and the fact that immigrants are more likely to start new businesses than are native-born Canadians.

Ask yourself: Who in my family would be able and likely to lend me money for business purposes? This source of seed capital is referred to as **love money** because it is largely loaned on the basis of the relationship as opposed to the strength of the business plan or the amount of collateral. Interestingly, the ease of access to love money seems to be culturally related, with some ethnic groups setting a higher priority on family entrepreneurship.[3]

Just because love money might be available to you doesn't mean you'll take it. You may choose other sources, such as banks or partners, since there can be potential problems with love money. Family members with little business background often cannot distinguish between debt and equity. They might lend you money thinking that this makes them your partner. Not only might they wish to interfere in the operation of the business—but also, in some cases, the debt will be never-ending, even after it has been long paid back: "See where she is today? She owes everything to me. I'm the one who got her started. Without me, she'd be no place." *Ask yourself: Does this sound like any of my relatives?*

The fact that your uncle will not require a business plan before lending you money is not all good news. The very process of creating the plan increases your chance of a successful start-up and in the long run could save your relationships with family members. In addition, any loans from family should still be formalized with a written agreement explaining all the terms and conditions.

⭐ Head Start Exercise

5.11 If you plan on borrowing money from family members or close friends, make a note of the contract terms that you will try to negotiate and how these will avoid potential "love money" problems (1/2 page maximum).

Government Programs

Many millions of dollars are earmarked each year by the federal and provincial governments to assist small entrepreneurs in one way or another. But politicians and bureaucrats are much like managers in other large institutions: They need to prove their accomplishments with statistics. The best kind of stats for entrepreneurial funding programs show lots of activity generated at low administrative cost to the taxpayer. And the administrative

collateral Assets of a borrower that are pledged to a lender in the event of non-payment of a loan.

love money Money that is borrowed from relatives and/or friends for a business venture.

☑ **Memory Check 5.16**
True or False? Collateral refers to assets that are protected against claims by lenders.

❓ **Get Help 5.6**
There are a number of publications (available in many libraries) that list government funding programs for business. One of the best is the CCH Government Assistance Manual, since it is a loose-leaf service that is updated frequently. For additional information try www.cch.ca.

cost for making a small loan is just about the same as it is for making a large loan. So if it comes to a choice between making lots of small loans or fewer but larger loans, the big loans win.

This explains the frustration sometimes felt by new entrepreneurs looking for small loans. At times it looks easier for an existing business to borrow $500 000 than it is for a new venture to get $30 000. This has always been a problem when dealing with banks (a problem for which many politicians have criticized the banks), but the same problem is true of government funding.

The other major problem with government programs is that they are always changing. Some programs expire, others run out of money, and for some the rules change. Sometimes a change of government means the end of a program that is brought back to life under a new name. It's hard to keep track. But all that aside, there has been a steadily growing commitment at all levels of government to encourage entrepreneurship, and it is worthwhile for anyone planning self-employment to see what assistance is available.

The **Business Development Bank of Canada (BDC)** is a financial institution owned by the federal government. BDC offers excellent assistance to entrepreneurs through lending, investing, and reasonable-cost consulting programs. For early-stage and established businesses they have loan programs going all the way up to $5 million. In addition, they offer numerous specific programs (e.g., loans to help companies create a web or e-commerce component of a business or loans for Aboriginal or exporting ventures). They even have a growing Venture Capital initiative where they can hold equity in certain businesses. This federal government agency is highly innovative in the many flexible repayment programs it has created. The mandate of BDC allows it to make loans with less emphasis on collateral than would be typical of banks. Check out BDC's website at www.bdc.ca to find the office closest to you.

If you want to borrow money for the purchase of fixed assets, you may consider a loan under the **Canada Small Business Financing Program (CSBF)**. These loans are negotiated through a regular bank but are like a student loan in the sense that repayment is mostly guaranteed by the federal government. You can borrow up to 90 percent of the value of the assets at reasonable repayment rates, although there are usually some administration fees. You can get information on CSBF loans from branches of most banks.

In addition to loans, there are some government grants available for specific purposes. These usually come in the form of tax credits or payments to third parties for specified services. (It's rare to get cash from the government that you could use to purchase tangible assets.) More typically, the money is available for staff training, technical research, tourism development, or export market development. If you have to do some of these things anyway, be sure and check if any of this "free money" is available to you.

If your business is based on some technical innovation or adaptation, there may be financial or expert assistance available from one of the programs of the National Research Council or Industry Canada. As well, Export Development Canada offers various forms of financial assistance to firms that will be exporting products and services from Canada.

Human Resources and Skills Development Canada (HRSDC) has for some time offered the Self-Employment Benefit Program through various private-sector partners. (This program was still available but under review at the time of writing.) This is one of the most extensive grant programs for new entrepreneurs and can include personal income support for up to a year as well as training and other support. HRSCD finances numerous other programs, especially in the areas of employee training and counselling services.

For Aboriginal entrepreneurs there are several federal initiatives offering training and financial support. In addition, some Canadian Aboriginal bands offer financial assistance to their own members who become entrepreneurs. Visit the Aboriginal Business Canada website at www.ainc-inac.gc.ca.

The federal government supports a number of regional programs (Atlantic Canada Opportunities Agency, Federal Office of Regional Development—Quebec, Federal

Business Development Bank of Canada (BDC) A federal government agency charged with lending money to small and medium enterprises, under reasonable terms.

Canada Small Business Financing Program (CSBF) The Canada Small Business Financing Program provides federal government guarantees to banks that lend money to small and medium enterprises for the purchase of fixed assets.

Human Resources and Skills Development Canada (HRSDC) Human Resources and Skills Development Canada is the department of the federal government concerned with training and employment. It has various programs that support entrepreneurship and provide training assistance to small business.

Economic Development Initiative for Northern Ontario, Western Economic Diversification Canada) that offer specific regional support to entrepreneurs. As well, there are numerous provincial programs, municipal programs, and co-operative programs involving more than one level of government. Provincial governments produce many free guides on business start-up and often have toll-free information numbers that can direct you to provincial funding programs. Carefully check the blue pages of your phone book to identify provincial offices that offer information about small-business funding.

Government should represent more than an information source or source of funding for the new entrepreneur. You may consider government as a group of potential customers—big customers who can always pay their bills. Governments buy a huge range of goods and services and a firm government contract can be an important advantage when seeking other forms of funding.

Chartered Banks

Banks basically lend money to small entrepreneurs in two ways:

? **Get Help 5.7**
You can register to be a supplier to the federal government by calling your regional office of Public Works and Government Services Canada (check the blue pages) and asking for an application for registration, or by logging on to http://buyandsell.gc.ca.

1. *Term loans.* These are loans given with a fixed repayment period, usually for fixed assets at a fixed interest rate. They are typically used for things like store fixtures, vehicles, or equipment.

2. *Lines of credit.* These allow a borrower to "overdraft" a chequing account up to a pre-set amount. Typically, the borrower pays back a portion of the outstanding balance each month at a variable interest rate. The amount the borrower has access to is often a percentage of inventory or accounts receivable.

Banks make their lending decisions based on the viability of the business plan, the strength of any collateral you offer, and your personal credit history. The lending decision is made within the bank's policies, but usually it is the person you are dealing with at the branch level who has the final say. The loans officer or branch manager may find it more convenient to imply that some decisions (like loan refusals) are made anonymously at head office, but in most cases you are negotiating with a person holding the necessary authority. And, as you know, everything is negotiable, from interest rates to the amount of collateral needed.

It is normally difficult for new ventures to get bank financing. But just because a bank turns you down, it doesn't mean you can't get the money. There are lots of competing banks. Try them all. But be sure to always clarify the reasons for a refusal. It may be a matter of restructuring your business plan or it may be an issue related to your credit history—the bank gets this information from a **credit bureau**.

credit bureau An organization that gathers and reports information on the financial status and borrowing and repayment histories of consumers and businesses.

Credit bureaus are provincially regulated and in most provinces may not show your file to anyone without your permission. In addition, you must have access to your own file should you want to check the accuracy of information. And if you plan on borrowing money you should check your file before applying for a loan. Then you can attempt to have any inaccuracies corrected. Because of the millions of credit transactions taking place daily, mistakes happen—lots of them. Credit bureau files are full of inaccurate entries and you don't want an error to prevent you from being able to secure financing. Check first.

Investors

When someone invests in your business operation, it means that they will have an equity position—they will own part of the business. They may or may not be active partners in the business. If you have a general partnership, however, don't forget that any partner you may bring in will have the right to be involved in managing the business. In this case, the decision to bring in a partner is far more than an issue of securing funds. *Ask yourself: Other than for investment money, do I really need a partner?*

? **Get Help 5.8**
To get a copy of your credit report, call Equifax Canada (www.equifax.ca) at 1-800-465-7166 or TransUnion Canada (www.transunion.ca) at 1-800-663-9980.

angels Wealthy individuals who invest in independent small businesses and who are not related to the business owners.

crowdfunding Web-based methods for small donors/ investors to provide money for business start-ups or social enterprises.

indirect financing Methods whereby a business has the use of assets for which it has not paid.

If you're set up as a corporation, however, it will be easier to maintain control of the business after you bring in investors (as long as you keep at least 51 percent of the shares). Don't forget that there are strict limits on selling the shares of a privately held corporation to avoid the highly regulated and expensive area of publicly traded shares.

You can bring in formal investors in the form of venture capital companies, although it is extremely rare (it does happen) for them to invest in start-up ventures. These firms are large pools of money (from their own investors) intended for investing in other firms. Generally, they are looking to invest substantial amounts (millions) in companies that are "high-tech" and that offer high rates of return (30 percent or more). However, if you are starting a business based on the proprietary rights for a product or technology (i.e., you have a patent or the Canadian distribution rights), then you may wish to investigate this source.

More likely, any corporate investors you get will be of the informal variety: **angels**. These are relatively wealthy individuals (often senior or retired professionals) who enjoy taking some risk with a portion of their capital by investing in small business, especially those where they can see themselves providing advice.[4] Most angels seek an opportunity to personally contribute to the venture, at least in an advisory capacity. This implies that asking for advice may be a significant tool of persuasion when it comes to recruiting an angel. You are most likely to find an angel investor through personal contact or an introduction by some other professional such as an accountant, lawyer, or investment dealer. Ask around. Also, be cautious of websites offering to hook you up with an angel, especially if the website wants you to submit your business idea/plan or charge a fee.

Other Sources

A highly innovative and still-evolving source of capital is known as **crowdfunding**. The idea here is to solicit money from "investors" often without providing any equity in return. Instead, the so-called investors might receive some other sort of promised benefit. For example, a band that doesn't have the money to produce its next CD may ask fans to pre-purchase the album before it is made and those who do will receive a special edition autographed copy of the recording. A promised seat for a gala premiere might be offered in return for contribution to a documentary film production. An inventor might offer patrons early production models of some product for their donations toward manufacturing the product. There are a number of organizations that run crowdfunding websites, or platforms, some for profit (they keep a portion of the money they help entrepreneurs raise) and some not-for-profit (usually helping to raise money for charitable or social enterprises.) Most of the most well-known crowdfunding sites, like Kickstarter, RocketHub, and Indiegogo, are based in the United States but operate globally. At the time of writing, security regulations in Canada's provinces and territories restrict these kinds of websites.

One of Canada's best resources for writing a business plan comes from the Canadian Youth Business Foundation. The website of this not-for-profit organization (www.cybf.ca) offers great advice and many valuable links, including a wide variety of business plan examples. The organization also has an outstanding loan program for new entrepreneurs between the ages of 18 and 34. Unsecured loans of up to $15 000 are available in conjunction with a free mentoring program.

There are many small local programs available involving prizes for great business plans and entrepreneurship awards. Also, some ethnic communities offer financial help to their own entrepreneurial members, and various service clubs and educational institutions have entrepreneurial awards. It can take a lot of digging to turn up these sources, so keep asking and spend time in the library.

Indirect financing can also be a source. This would include such things as negotiating generous terms from suppliers (difficult at start-up), helping to get you inventory that hasn't yet been paid for. In rare cases (e.g., an art gallery), it could even mean getting

A Case of Creative Financing

After Dave Johnson graduated from Ryerson, he was working in road construction and had absolutely no experience running a farm. But he knew that farming was what he wanted to do. With his own savings, the investment of two partners, and a big mortgage, he was able to buy a small dairy farm. Then Dave's partners set up a limited partnership to invest in high-quality purebred Holsteins, and Dave's farm was paid to board the cows. The limited partnership received certain tax advantages and the deal gave half the offspring of these cows to the farm. In this way, Dave was able to start building a very high-quality herd that he could never have financed otherwise.

According to Dave, "Canadian cattle have always had a high reputation internationally for quality and health." This, combined with the lineage and high milk production of Dave's cows, meant that he could profitably export breeding cattle all over the world. Then in 2003, mad cow disease was found in Canada, and the United States immediately closed the border to all Canadian cattle. Eventually the border was re-opened for Canadian beef, but the ban had effectively killed Dave's exports, not only to the United States but also to Mexico and Latin America (Canadian cattle could not travel through the United States to these destinations), as well as to many other countries that follow U.S. leads on import restrictions.

Despite all this, Dave still sees advantages in being a Canadian dairy farmer, partly because of Canada's marketing board system. Marketing boards (they may have different names in different provinces) have the authority to control and regulate the production, distribution, and pricing of specific commodities such as milk. They buy all of the production of milk, paying the farmers a fair return, and sell to the processors. The production is generally controlled to about equal the consumption so there are no wild fluctuations in supply and price. Because of this, dairy farmers can count on predictable, reliable cash in-flow. Currently, however, some marketing boards around the country are being dissolved or are under attack. So, Dave's advice to would-be farmers is: "Marry a teacher. You get a steady income and good benefits."

inventory on **consignment** (where your supplier lets you display the item and, when you sell it, you share the proceeds with your supplier). Indirect financing can also mean leasing equipment rather than buying, to reduce any down payment or deposit.

Once you have examined all the possible sources of finance and identified which are available to you, you must start approaching them with your business plan. Don't expect this to be a one-shot deal. You may have to change your plan to meet the requirements of potential investors or lenders. You may have to change the scope of your ideas to fit within the financing available. You may have to do both. Often, it is a tedious, back-and-forth process of negotiation that will involve considerable rewriting of the business plan.

consignment When an item is taken into inventory and held for sale by a business, but still remains the property of the supplier to the business. The proceeds of any sale are split between the supplier and the selling business.

Revising Your Plan

The process of rewriting (and rewriting and rewriting) may be more necessary for the financial section of the business plan than any other. Every other planning decision you make will have some financial implications. And the financial summaries you see in Section 5 of the plan may indicate that you have to go back and revise earlier parts. For example, problems you see in your cash flow might indicate that you should go back and change your credit policies. Or an inability to borrow the capital you want might mean that you will have to bring in partners. This means going back and changing your legal form and creating partnership agreements. Figure 5.7 shows some of the possible implications.

Figure 5.7 Business Plan Revision Process

1 Model	2 Feasibility	3 Marketing	4 Operations	5 Finances
Product/Service Target Customer Legal Form Agreements Location	Market Potential Competition Sales Forecast Insurance Intellectual Property	Name/Image Service/Product Mix Pricing Distribution Promotion	Space/Equipment Logistics Methods/Process Systems Organization Structure Regulations	Start-up Needs Investment Loans Fin. Statements Credit Policy Cash Flow

Memory Check 5.20
True or False? Angels are wealthy people who lend money to their family members.

Fortunately, by the time you get to this point, most of the work for the basic business plan is completed. Congratulations. The rest of this text is about variations in the business plan for different circumstances and how the business plan is a tool for the ongoing management of a business. All of this is built on the foundation of the basic business plan (the first five chapters) that you have completed.

Answers to Memory Check Questions

5.1 T   5.2 T   5.3 T   5.4 F   5.5 T   5.6 T   5.7 T   5.8 T
5.9 T   5.10 F   5.11 T   5.12 F   5.13 F   5.14 T   5.15 T   5.16 F
5.17 F   5.18 F   5.19 T   5.20 F

Questions for Discussion

1. Take a poll of how many in the group suffer from "accountingphobia." Discuss the reasons for this and methods of overcoming it.
2. "An accountant is always the most important adviser to an entrepreneur." Discuss ways in which this statement might not be true.
3. Identify as many businesses as you can that could be started with very little in the way of assets. Why might you be reluctant to start one of these businesses?
4. How much equity must you have to be considered "wealthy" in Canada? How important is wealth in determining a person's happiness?
5. How fast do cars depreciate? What are some myths and rules of thumb in this area? What are the factors affecting automobile depreciation?
6. When someone owes you money in Canada, what steps are you allowed to take in order to collect the debt? What sorts of actions are prohibited? Why?
7. Why are the cash flow projections in a business plan so important to lenders and investors? What common mistakes might new entrepreneurs make in their cash flow planning?
8. "Banks only lend money to those who don't need it." Discuss the truth of this old saying.
9. "Lending or borrowing money is the fastest way to end a friendship." Discuss this statement in the context of "love money" and your own experiences.
10. Why are there so many government programs to support entrepreneurship? What sort of checks and safeguards might be built into these programs?
11. Discuss methods for building a strong credit history. Why might this be important, even if you have no intention of ever borrowing money?

Case for Discussion

Cassandra had spent five years as a struggling personal yoga instructor before concluding that she was never going to make a decent living that way. When her friend Jenny offered Cassandra a full-time job as a receptionist in one of her three hair salons, Cassandra jumped at the chance of having a steady income, at least for a while. Cassandra envied Jenny's success as an entrepreneur and since the reception job was not particularly demanding, Cassandra had lots of time to work on her own idea for a business.

Cassandra planned to use her yoga expertise to develop an iPhone app for people in desk jobs. The app would interrupt the sedentary worker every 45 minutes to provide four minutes of yoga stretching and exercise. The computer or phone screen would show a four-minute video (starring Cassandra as the yoga coach) that would remind the user of the health and productivity benefits of exercise, then lead them through the short workout. The app would take the user through a series of 50 different videos, each increasing in intensity the longer the viewer had been using the app.

After weeks of planning, Cassandra used some of her savings to have a lawyer set up her company as a corporation: "Yoga Master Coaching Inc." Then she spoke to an acquaintance in the video business about shooting the 50 short videos (200 minutes of video in total). To finance the $20 000 in production costs, she used her remaining $6000 of savings, then put her car (worth about $15 000) in the name of the business and, using that as collateral, managed to borrow another $14 000 from a local car loans company. Cassandra felt that she could handle the $290 monthly payments on the loan out of her receptionist salary, just until the app was generating cash flow. But now she had to get money for developing the app.

She was shocked to find out that a firm of local software engineers wanted $40 000 in development costs to build the iPhone app. The bank that Cassandra went to would not accept the app itself as collateral, so Cassandra asked her boss/friend Jenny for advice. After a series of discussions, Jenny offered to put up the $40 000 plus an additional $10 000 in operating cash in exchange for 55 percent of the company shares. Cassandra agreed.

The app worked well, but one year after launch, it had been downloaded only 1285 times, producing only $899.50 of revenue for the company. (Apple kept 30 percent of all revenue.) During that time, the company had spent $9000 to promote the app through YouTube, other social media, and attempts at getting publicity.

1. Was the share split between Jenny and Cassandra fair? Explain. Who could have advised the pair on this?

2. Create a rough income statement for Yoga Master Coaching Inc. for the first year of operations. What does this indicate?

3. Create a rough balance sheet for the end of the first year of operations for Yoga Master Coaching Inc. Why could the value shown for the video and app software be wrong?

4. What was wrong with Cassandra's financial planning? How should she have gone about it? What should she do now?

The Business Plan, Section 5: FINANCES

Start-Up Requirements

1. Complete Table 5.6, indicating all the current assets you will need to come up with before your business can open. This list will include things like office supplies, inventory, prepaid expenses (like insurance or licences), and the cash you will need in your bank account in order to run the business. (Attach this chart to your plan as an appendix.)

Table 5.6 Material and Operating Cash Needs (for Start-Up)

Materials and Cash (Current Assets)	$ Value	
	Already Have	Need

2. Complete the equipment needs worksheet in Table 5.7 by reviewing the list you have made and establishing prices for what you need or the value of things you already have. (Attach this chart to your plan as an appendix.)

Table 5.7 Equipment Needs (for Start-Up)

Equipment (Fixed Assets)	$ Value	
	Already Have	Need

Owner(s)'s Investment

3. Briefly explain how much you, your partner(s), and any other investors (angels, venture capitalists) will be contributing in order to start the business. (Do not include any borrowed money.) Be sure to include the value of those things you already own (cash, equipment, or materials) that will be used exclusively for the business. Also include any expenses you have already paid.

Borrowed Money

4. Indicate any money your business will have to borrow. Identify the lender(s), the interest rate, and the repayment terms. (This amount may have to be estimated for a first draft, then recalculated after completing the balance sheet, and again after completing the cash flow.) Indicate any collateral that may be required.

Balance Sheet

5. Prepare a balance sheet for the opening day of your new business (Figure 5.8). After you have completed the rest of the financial section, prepare projected balance sheets for the end of the first, second, and third years (Figure 5.8a, 5.8b, and 5.8c, respectively) of business to indicate how the financial position of the firm will change.

Figure 5.8 Balance Sheet

Opening Day	**(Date)**	
ASSETS		
CURRENT ASSETS		
Cash	_____	
Accounts receivable	_____	
Inventory	_____	
Prepaid expenses	_____	
Other current assets	_____	
Total current assets		_____
FIXED ASSETS		_____
Land and buildings	_____	
Fixtures	_____	
Equipment	_____	
Vehicles	_____	
Other fixed assets	_____	
Total fixed assets		
Total Assets		_____
LIABILITIES		
CURRENT LIABILITIES		
Accounts payable	_____	
Short-term loans payable	_____	
Taxes payable	_____	
Other current liabilities	_____	
Total current liabilities		_____
LONG-TERM LIABILITIES		
Mortgage payable	_____	
Long-term loans payable	_____	
Other long-term liabilities	_____	
Total long-term liabilities		_____
OWNERS' EQUITY		
Total investment		_____
Total Liabilities and Owners' Equity		_____

Figure 5.8a Balance Sheet (Year End, Year 1)

(Date)

ASSETS

CURRENT ASSETS

Cash   _____

Accounts receivable   _____

Inventory   _____

Prepaid expenses   _____

Other current assets   _____

Total current assets   _____

FIXED ASSETS

Land and buildings   _____

Fixtures   _____

Equipment   _____

Vehicles   _____

Other fixed assets   _____

Minus accumulated depreciation   (_____)

Total fixed assets   _____

Total Assets   _____

LIABILITIES

CURRENT LIABILITIES

Accounts payable   _____

Short-term loans payable   _____

Taxes payable   _____

Other current liabilities   _____

Total current liabilities   _____

LONG-TERM LIABILITIES

Mortgage payable

Long-term loans payable

Other long-term liabilities

Total long-term liabilities

OWNERS' EQUITY

Capital investment   _____

Retained earnings   _____

Total owners' equity   _____

Total Liabilities and Owners' Equity   _____

Figure 5.8b Balance Sheet (Year End, Year 2)

(Date)

ASSETS

CURRENT ASSETS

Cash _____

Accounts receivable _____

Inventory _____

Prepaid expenses _____

Other current assets _____

Total current assets _____

FIXED ASSETS

Land and buildings _____

Fixtures _____

Equipment _____

Vehicles _____

Other fixed assets _____

Minus accumulated depreciation (_____)

Total fixed assets _____

Total Assets _____

LIABILITIES

CURRENT LIABILITIES

Accounts payable _____

Short-term loans payable _____

Taxes payable _____

Other current liabilities _____

Total current liabilities _____

LONG-TERM LIABILITIES

Mortgage payable _____

Long-term loans payable _____

Other long-term liabilities _____

Total long-term liabilities _____

OWNERS' EQUITY

Capital investment _____

Retained earnings _____

Total owners' equity _____

Total Liabilities and Owners' Equity _____

Figure 5.8c Balance Sheet (Year End, Year 3)

(Date)

ASSETS

CURRENT ASSETS

Cash _____

Accounts receivable

Inventory _____

Prepaid expenses _____

Other current assets _____

Total current assets _____

FIXED ASSETS

Land and buildings _____

Fixtures _____

Equipment _____

Vehicles _____

Other fixed assets _____

Minus accumulated depreciation (_____)

Total fixed assets _____

Total Assets _____

LIABILITIES

CURRENT LIABILITIES

Accounts payable _____

Short-term loans payable _____

Taxes payable _____

Other current liabilities _____

Total current liabilities _____

LONG-TERM LIABILITIES

Mortgage payable _____

Long-term loans payable _____

Other long-term liabilities _____

Total long-term liabilities _____

OWNERS' EQUITY

Capital investment _____

Retained earnings _____

Total owners' equity _____

Total Liabilities and Owners' Equity _____

Costs and Expenses

6. Complete the ongoing costs and expenses worksheet (Table 5.8) by carefully reviewing all the earlier parts of the business plan and estimating how much you will need to pay annually, as well as on a regular monthly basis, to operate the business. For costs or expenses that are paid on an irregular basis over periods longer than monthly, provide notes to indicate approximately how much and when these items would be paid for—examples might include semi-annual licence fees or large inventory purchases. Be sure to fill in both the annual and monthly (or other period) columns. (Attach this chart to your plan as an appendix.)

Table 5.8 Worksheet

Ongoing Costs and Expenses

Expense	Payment Period (Monthly or Other: Specify)	Amount per Period	Annual Amount

Income Statement

7. Using the above information and your sales forecast from Section 2, prepare projected income statements for the first, second, and third years of business (Figures 5.9a, 5.9b, and 5.9c, respectively).

Figure 5.9a Income Statement (Projected) First Year

For the One-Year Period Ended: (Date)		
SALES		
Sales from source #1	_____	
Sales from source #2	_____	
Total sales income		_____
COSTS		
Cost of goods sold		_____
GROSS PROFIT		
Gross profit		_____
EXPENSES		
Rent	_____	
Utilities	_____	
Equipment/lease	_____	
Salaries/drawings	_____	
Insurance		
Depreciation	_____	
Interest	_____	
Maintenance	_____	
Professional fees	_____	
Advertising	_____	
Supplies	_____	
Delivery	_____	
Travel	_____	
Total operating expenses		_____
NET PROFIT		
Net before income tax		_____
Income tax		_____
Net Profit after Income Tax		_____

Figure 5.9b Income Statement (Projected) Second Year

For the One-Year Period Ended: (Date)

SALES

Sales from source #1   _____

Sales from source #2   _____

Total sales income   _____

COSTS

Cost of goods sold   _____

GROSS PROFIT

Gross profit   _____

EXPENSES

Rent   _____

Utilities   _____

Equipment/lease   _____

Salaries/drawings   _____

Insurance   _____

Depreciation   _____

Interest   _____

Maintenance   _____

Professional fees   _____

Advertising   _____

Supplies   _____

Delivery   _____

Travel   _____

Total operating expenses   _____

NET PROFIT

Net before income tax   _____

Income tax   _____

Net Profit after Income Tax   _____

Figure 5.9c Income Statement (Projected) Third Year

For the One-Year Period Ended: (Date)

SALES

Sales from source #1 _____

Sales from source #2 _____

Total sales income _____

COSTS

Cost of goods sold _____

GROSS PROFIT

Gross profit _____

EXPENSES

Rent _____

Utilities _____

Equipment/lease _____

Salaries/drawings _____

Insurance _____

Depreciation _____

Interest _____

Maintenance _____

Professional fees _____

Advertising _____

Supplies _____

Delivery _____

Travel _____

Total operating expenses _____

NET PROFIT

Net before income tax _____

Income tax _____

Net Profit after Income Tax _____

8. Take the sales forecast from Section 2 (feasibility) of your business plan and break it down into monthly predictions (Table 5.9). (Attach this chart to your plan as an appendix.)

Table 5.9 Projected Sales Income by Month

Month	Year 1	Year 2	Year 3
1	$	$	$
2			
3			
4			
5			
6			
7			
8			
9			
10			
11			
12			
Total Sales Forecast	$	$	$

9. Give logical reasons for this monthly breakdown, considering items like seasonality and growth of the business.

10. Specify any credit or payment terms you will provide to your customers and when you expect them to actually pay. Explain the pattern of when cash will actually be received for your sales. Describe any policies and methods you will use for collecting outstanding accounts.

11. Describe any credit or payment terms you will expect from your suppliers or subcontractors and note how this will affect your cash disbursements.

12. Prepare projected cash flow statements for each of the first three years of business, broken down by month (Figures 5.10a, 5.10b, and 5.10c, respectively).

Figure 5.10a Cash Flow

PROJECTED CASH FLOW

FIRST YEAR OF OPERATION: (date)

MONTH	1	2	3	4	5	6	7	8	9	10	11	12
Sales												
CASH IN-FLOW												
Cash sales												
Payments received												
Other cash received												
Total Cash In-flow (a)												
OPENING Cash Balance (b)												
CASH OUT-FLOW												
Equipment purchased												
Inventory purchased												
Rent paid												
Utilities paid												
Loan payments												
Salaries/drawings												
Supplies purchased												
OTHER expenses paid												
Total Cash Out-flow (c)												
CLOSING Cash Balance (a + b − c)												

Figure 5.10b Cash Flow

SECOND YEAR OF OPERATION: (date)

PROJECTED CASH FLOW												
MONTH	1	2	3	4	5	6	7	8	9	10	11	12
Sales												
CASH IN-FLOW												
Cash sales												
Payments received												
Other cash received												
Total Cash In-flow (a)												
OPENING Cash Balance (b)												
CASH OUT-FLOW												
Equipment purchased												
Inventory purchased												
Rent paid												
Utilities paid												
Loan payments												
Salaries/drawings												
Supplies purchased												
OTHER expenses paid												
Total Cash Out-flow (c)												
CLOSING Cash Balance (a + b − c)												

Figure 5.10c Cash Flow

PROJECTED CASH FLOW

THIRD YEAR OF OPERATION: (date)

MONTH	1	2	3	4	5	6	7	8	9	10	11	12
Sales												
CASH IN-FLOW												
Cash sales												
Payments received												
Other cash received												
Total Cash In-flow (a)												
OPENING Cash Balance (b)												
CASH OUT-FLOW												
Equipment purchased												
Inventory purchased												
Rent paid												
Utilities paid												
Loan payments												
Salaries/drawings												
Supplies purchased												
OTHER expenses paid												
Total Cash Out-flow (c)												
CLOSING Cash Balance (a + b – c)												

Chapter 6

The Purchase Alternative: How Do I Buy (or Buy Into) an Existing Business?

In this chapter, we look at the process of becoming an owner, or part owner, of a business that is already up and running. Just like starting a new business, this method of getting into business requires a business plan. This plan includes the topics covered in Chapters 1 through 5, and answers the following questions:

- Is Buying a Business Right for Me?
- What Is Involved in Buying a Business?
- What Should the Purchase Agreement Include?
- How Much Should I Pay?

Learning Objectives

On completion of this chapter, you should be able to:

1 Discuss at least three advantages and six risks of buying a business.

2 Describe the processes of *buying into* and *breaking off* a business.

3 Explain the difference between purchasing shares and purchasing assets of a business.

4 Outline five major provisions included in a purchase agreement for a business.

5 Apply the *return on investment* concept to pricing a business.

6 Distinguish between *asset* and *income methods* of business valuation.

7 Plan a method for negotiating the price of a business.

8 Prepare alternative components of the business plan related to buying a business.

IS BUYING A BUSINESS RIGHT FOR ME?

Personal Circumstances

On average, buying a business is a less risky option than starting a brand-new business (buying a franchise is even lower risk). So, the selection of a start-up method will likely have something to do with your tolerance for risk. This is partly a reflection of your own personality, but it can be influenced by factors like the risk tolerance of your spouse or any business partners. Commitments, such as supporting family members, or assets you wish to protect can also influence the amount of risk you are willing to take. *Ask yourself: How much risk am I willing to take?*

Your financial circumstances may also be a factor in how you go about becoming an entrepreneur. Buying an existing business is usually more expensive than starting a brand-new company. That's because when you start a new business, you can shrink the idea down to any size necessary to fit your available financing. For example, if you wish to start a new specialty dessert restaurant, but can't arrange financing, you may be able to finance a gourmet ice cream stand and build from there. But if you want to buy an existing specialty restaurant, you will have to buy the whole business as it exists. So, generally, those buying existing businesses have access to more personal financing than those starting new firms.

Sometimes, you just find yourself in circumstances where there is an opportunity to buy a business, and you have to make the decision whether to pursue that opportunity. Some examples are:

■ You hear that the owner of a business is retiring or has died. This could be a business you are working for or have some other association with (customer, supplier), and you may be approached directly or hear of the opportunity informally.

■ You may be part of an **employee stock ownership plan (ESOP)**, where you have been accumulating shares of the company as part of your retirement plan. An opportunity may arise to significantly increase your holdings by buying additional shares from the principals or other employees.

■ You are approached by other managers of the company where you work and asked to participate in a **management buyout** of the company. This usually involves each of the management team giving personal guarantees on a loan used to purchase a controlling interest in the company. There are lenders that specialize in financing management buyouts.[1]

Most of these circumstantial opportunities imply that you must make a quick decision on whether to pursue the opportunity. However, after you have declared your intentions, you do not have to rush the research and negotiations leading to a final agreement.

Merits of Buying

Ask yourself: What's the big advantage of buying an existing business? When you buy an existing business, you are usually buying one that has proven it can make money. In addition, the time-consuming, often frustrating, start-up work has been done for you, resulting in:

■ *Efficient methods and procedures.* Presumably, company systems have been refined over time for some measure of efficiency that you would not have when starting a new business. In a new business there are many decisions (and many mistakes) to make—the best place to put the cash register; how often to buy inventory; how to set up the bookkeeping. . . . The owners of the existing business should have already made (and corrected) most of the mistakes.

■ *Defined markets.* Through trial and error, there should have come about a clear understanding of which particular customer groups are most likely to buy from this business.

■ *Established customers.* The base of existing customers and the likelihood of their remaining as customers is primarily what we mean by the **goodwill** of a business. The past purchases of these customers form the basis of predictions for the future performance of the business.

■ *Established suppliers.* Established suppliers are important, not just because of their proven reliability, but also because of any credit terms that are in place with them. When you start a new business, suppliers are reluctant to extend credit terms, but when you take over an existing company it is often possible to continue any favourable payment terms that were established by the previous owner.

■ *Trained employees.* Having employees in place not only keeps the business going and generating cash, but these employees can also serve as a resource to help train you as the new owner.

All these components contribute to a documented financial history of the company that can be used for making decisions about its future—including the decision of whether or not to buy it.

☑ Memory Check 6.1
True or False? Starting a brand-new company is, on average, higher risk than buying an existing business.

employee stock ownership plan (ESOP; also employee share ownership program) Allows employees to purchase shares in the company where they work as part of their retirement packages. Shares may be held within pension plans or registered retirement savings plans (RRSPs), with the associated tax benefits. In some cases provincial tax credits are also available.

management buyout A group of employees, led by a management team, arranges to purchase a controlling interest in a company. Some merchant bankers and venture capital funds specialize in funding this type of purchase.

☑ Memory Check 6.2
True or False? Starting a brand-new business is, on average, more expensive than buying an existing business.

☑ Memory Check 6.3
True or False? Buying an existing independent business is lower risk than buying a franchise.

goodwill The amount paid for a business in excess of the value of its assets. The value given to a business's ability to make profit because of its established customer base. Sometimes considered an intangible asset of the business.

☑ Memory Check 6.4
True or False? Goodwill refers to the intentions of business sellers to treat prospective buyers fairly.

6.1 Briefly explain why buying a business is the most appropriate start-up method for you and your circumstances (1/2 page maximum).

6.2 Briefly describe the history of the company you are buying. Note: Students who are using the Head Start Exercises as class assignments will each have to interview an entrepreneur whose business they will use as an example for the exercises in this chapter (1/3 page maximum).

Risks of Buying

It is easy to underestimate the amount of work involved in buying a business—that is, if you're going to do it properly. The amount of research required and the complexity of the business plan will likely exceed that required for a new start-up because

- You are likely dealing with a larger entity than a start-up business, since the business you are buying will have gone through some growth since its own start-up.

- There is extensive investigation required in figuring out how much to pay for the business.

There are many potential problems associated with buying a business:[2]

- *Overvalued assets.* The problem of overvalued assets may be the single biggest danger for the naive business buyer. You may, for example, be buying a shirt store with an inventory of $25 000 worth of shirts. Your accountant will confirm that the store did, in fact, pay $25 000 for the shirts, but that's not necessarily what they are worth. Many of them may be obsolete styles or inferior quality, worth far less than the value showing on the balance sheet. Or, you may be buying a business with equipment that has been depreciated to 30 percent of its original value. But the equipment may be totally worn out, worth nothing. *Ask yourself: How could I deal with this problem?* Every asset of a business must be carefully inspected, and where you cannot accurately assess value yourself you should bring in professional appraisers.

- *Redundant assets.* **Redundant assets** are things that a company owns that are not necessary for it to function at its current or expected income levels. For example, you may be considering buying a garden centre that has three pickup trucks for delivery, but two trucks are more than sufficient to deliver all the sales that the store can handle. In buying the business, why should you buy a truck you don't need? *Ask yourself: How could I deal with this problem?* In setting a price for the business, you should deduct the value of any redundant assets and perhaps give the vendor a chance to liquidate them before the sale.

- *Lease problems.* Escalator clauses and inability to renew are major problems associated with leases. You may be looking at a business whose success depends on the site, but the lease for the property runs out in three years. *Ask yourself: How could I deal with this problem?* You will not be able to secure loans that must run longer than the existing lease, so you must deal with the landlord before buying the business and attempt to negotiate a lease that is conditional on your making a deal on the business. Alternatively, you can first make an offer on the business that is conditional on your being able to negotiate an acceptable lease.

- *Impending loss of key employees.* Sometimes the success of a business depends on the knowledge and skill of one or two employees. You might be considering the purchase of a trail mix packaging company. The old-but-working machinery for mixing and packaging is maintained and operated by two brothers, who each have 30 years of experience in the job. Your fear is that with a change in ownership, the brothers might retire. *Ask yourself: How could I deal with this problem?* If retirement is imminent, you may be able to contract with these employees to train replacements before they leave.

- *Impending location/site changes.* Retail and consumer service businesses depend heavily on location for their success, and changes in the geographic area (zoning changes, roadway changes, deteriorating neighbourhood) could be disastrous. *Ask yourself: How could I deal with this problem?* Research is the first step, usually conducted by visiting the planning department of your City Hall and asking a lot of questions. If planned changes will dramatically alter the traffic patterns around the business site, you may rethink your decision to buy.

- *Negative image.* Some businesses have a bad reputation among their potential customers. Even minimal research will turn up a company's bad image. But you may decide to buy anyway if you can get a bargain price. *Ask yourself: How could I deal with this problem?* Trying to reverse a negative image is among the most difficult of marketing problems. You can change the company name, but if you're buying a neighbourhood retail store, the old name will persist. You can put up "under new management" signs, but they can't stay up forever. You can redecorate, hire new staff, and send out letters. It is possible to change a negative image, given enough time and effort, but it is difficult to assess how much this will ultimately cost.

- *Non-transferability of contracts.* Some of the revenue for a business may come from particular contracts that are not transferable to the new owner(s). For example, you may want to buy a television repair service that makes much of its profit from servicing patient TVs in local hospitals. After buying the business, you find out that the hospital contracts are **personal services contracts** with the previous owner and give you no rights to the hospital business. *Ask yourself: How could I deal with this problem?* This is another issue that has to be dealt with in advance of buying the business, first by carefully checking all contracts with your lawyer. In a case like this, options include setting a price for the business that excludes revenue from personal service contracts, or making an offer to buy the business that is conditional on your being able to secure the contracts.

Memory Check 6.7
True or False? It is relatively easy to change an existing negative image of a small business.

personal services contract
An agreement contracting with an individual rather than a company to perform particular services that is generally not transferable to another individual or business.

⭐ Head Start Exercise

6.3 Briefly identify any potential problems or areas of concern relating to the business for sale. Note how you will address these concerns (1/3 page maximum).

WHAT'S INVOLVED IN BUYING THE BUSINESS?

Assessing the Business

Many of the risks in buying a business can be minimized by properly assessing the business. The assessment should logically cover most of the factors in the business plan, looking at whether the business is satisfactory in each area as well as identifying things you could improve if you owned the business. The business assessment checklist in Table 6.1 is a thorough list of the topics you would want to investigate. *Ask yourself: What is the most important question to ask about a business for sale?* The key question to ask anyone selling a business is, "Why are you selling?" Surprisingly, the answer is very often a lie. It may well be plausible and have an element of truth to it:

- "I'm 74 and been in this business for 40 years; it's about time I retired."

- "I need the money from the business to invest in a great new opportunity."

- "I'm moving to Florida."

Table 6.1 Business Assessment Checklist/Notes

✓	Factor	Description	Potential for Improvement
	Business Definition		
	Existing business plan		
	Clearly defined products/services		
	Clearly defined market segments		
	Business Feasibility		
	Advantageous location		
	Advantageous site		
	Acceptable terms of lease		
	Appropriately estimated market potential		
	History of accurate sales forecasting		
	Clearly identified competitors		
	Accurately estimated market share		
	Appropriate levels of insurance		
	Intellectual property protection		
	Full transferability of customer contracts		
	Marketing		
	Appropriate image for target market		
	Appropriate product/service mix		
	Appropriate pricing strategy		
	Appropriate distribution channel		
	Effective physical distribution		
	Appropriate promotion methods		
	Effective advertising techniques		
	Effective sales techniques		
	Operations		
	Acceptable condition of fixed assets		
	Efficient space utilization/layout		
	Efficient purchasing system		
	Effective quality control systems		
	Appropriate record keeping systems/software		
	Up-to-date records		
	Clear lines of authority (organization chart)		
	Clear job descriptions		
	Effective management policies		
	Appropriate salary levels for staff		
	Appropriate salary levels for owner(s)		
	Appropriate employee benefits		
	Up-to-date licences and permits		
	Full legal compliance		
	Beneficial association memberships		
	Finances		
	Up-to-date financial statements		
	Acceptable financial statement audits		

Table 6.1 (*Continued*)

✓	Factor	Description	Potential for Improvement
	Healthy key ratios		
	Healthy credit report		
	Healthy relationship with creditors		
	Sale/Purchase Issues		
	Appropriate asking price		
	High level of personal accord with seller(s)		
	High level of seller negotiating flexibility		
	Acceptable involvement of intermediaries		
	Acceptable involvement of advisers		
	Reason for selling		

It could be that all of these statements are true, but they are not necessarily the underlying reasons for selling. *Ask yourself.*

- *If the business was good enough for 40 years, why not 41?*
- *Why is your new opportunity better than your current business?*
- *Why move to Florida now?*

Perhaps business sellers fear that their real reasons for selling are reasons that would prevent you from buying. Regardless, you must try to investigate the reasons for sale. Suppliers, employees, bankers, and neighbouring businesses are all potential sources of information.

Admittedly, you may never identify the real reason for sale. But if you do, you can have a strong negotiating advantage because you will understand how badly the seller wants to sell. And the real reason for selling may not be a reason that would prevent you from buying. For example, you may want to buy a barbershop that is situated across the street from a retirement community, close to a new college campus. The owner has told you only that he is moving from the area, but you find out from neighbouring businesses that in reality he is worried about losing his many senior citizen customers, who have several competing shops to choose from. The seniors have been complaining about the loud and unruly behaviour of college students who hang around in front of the barbershop. For you, this could be great news because your intention for the shop is to target the college students—none of the other shops in the area has pursued this market. Here, the seller's reason for selling is not a reason that would prevent you from buying, and now you have the negotiating advantage.

> **Memory Check 6.8**
> True or False? The critical question to ask the owner of a business for sale is, "What is the price?"

⭐ Head Start Exercise

6.4 Note the reasons for sale given by the owner(s) and briefly speculate about alternative reasons (1/4 page maximum).

Buying In

Sometimes when a business is in trouble the owners will look for new capital to keep the business afloat until things turn around. This scenario most often indicates a failing business and any new capital will just keep the business alive a little longer until it eventually fails, taking the new partner's money with it. If you are buying part ownership in a business, it should be because

- the business is growing and needs capital for well-planned expansion, and/or
- you have some particular expertise that would be an advantage to the business, and the current owners are willing to give up some equity in order to get you.

If you are buying just a portion of a company, the most common way to do this would be with the company set up as a corporation and with you buying a certain percentage of the shares. The expression **buying into a company** usually implies buying a minority share ownership (less than 50 percent), while buying a majority share ownership is usually referred to as taking over a company. If you are **taking over a company**, you essentially have full control to run the company as you see fit (as long as you look after the interests of the other shareholders). When you buy into a company, you may be doing so as an outside investor, with no active participation in the company, other than voting as a shareholder. More typically, with small businesses, you will be buying in with some particular active management role in the company.

Whether you are buying into a company as a general partner or as a working shareholder, you will need a partnership agreement. The agreement should cover issues such as:

- the amount of capital you are contributing and the percentage of equity (or shares), liability, profits, and losses that will be apportioned to you and each of the other partners
- specific areas of management responsibility and restrictions on authority for each of the partners
- rules for transferring ownership (or shares) in the business
- specific salaries and benefits for the partners as well as rules for agreeing on paying out profit (as drawings or dividends) or equity to the partners
- rules for dissolution or sale of the business
- dispute settlement mechanisms to be used by the partners

The partnership agreement is critical when you are buying into an existing partnership, because you are already at a disadvantage as the new person in the relationship. Your ultimate guarantee of fairness and equality within the partnership is the strength of your written agreement. Also, if you are buying all of an existing business in conjunction with a new partner, you must be careful not to focus on the purchase agreement to the exclusion of your partnership agreement. This partnership agreement will be at least as important to your long-term success as an entrepreneur. For more information on partnerships, see "Do I Need a Partner" in Chapter 1.

Breaking Off a Piece of a Larger Firm

Large companies tend to go through cycles of expansion (adding to their products and services and widening their target markets) and contraction (where they become more specialized in their products/services, markets, and the kinds of activities they actually perform). During these contraction phases organizations sometimes sell off divisions or departments of the organization in order to concentrate more on the **core business**. At the same time, they will try to **outsource** various supplies and services if it is more economical to do so. In times of reorganization like this, companies may entertain proposals—by employees, suppliers, or others—to take over some of the activities of the companies as separate firms.

buying into a company Purchasing less than 50 percent ownership of a company.

taking over a company Purchasing more than 50 percent ownership of a company.

core business The particular products and services and market segments that produce the majority of a company's profit.

outsource Find suppliers outside of a company to provide certain products or services that the company formerly produced internally.

Let's say you work for a large fast-food chain that uses plastic buckets for delivering liquid muffin batter to its franchisees. At a site separate from the main plant, the company has a department that brings back the empty buckets to clean and sterilize for reuse. A history of mechanical breakdowns and labour friction has made this department a problem area for the company. The company may consider selling off this division to you as your own business. This is most likely if the company is in a contraction phase and if the company can be convinced that by doing so it will have

- a secure source of supply under a long term contract;
- a reliable quality of service; and
- a cost saving by outsourcing to you.

Memory Check 6.9
True or False? Buying into a business typically means taking a majority ownership in the firm.

Ideally, you might be able to get the original company to accept payment for the assets you are purchasing over an extended period of time. This is most likely if you can demonstrate that the company will not be putting out any additional cash to do so, and if you can present a business plan showing your ability to pay off the assets within a reasonable time.

The starting point in taking over such a company is to write the mission statement for the new firm (what the company sells and to whom it sells) as an independent company, not as a former department. For example, in the bucket sterilizing business mentioned above, you would describe your market as *fast-food chains* as opposed to specifying your former owner and only customer. Thus, right from the beginning, you are seeing your business as an independent venture having growth potential.

Intermediaries

Real estate agents working on a commission basis sell many small businesses. There are also specialized business brokers who arrange purchases of slightly larger businesses (rarely the smaller "mom and pop" operations), sometimes as part of corporate buyouts. Brokers may provide other professional services such as evaluation on a fee-for-service basis.

Get Help 6.3
The Canadian Real Estate Association's commercial real estate website (www.icx.ca) is easy to use for finding businesses for sale by geographic area.

If you're looking for a business for sale, you can go to a real estate agent who will search the Multiple Listing Service to find a prospective business of the sort you are looking for. Then your agent will represent you in the negotiations by dealing with the seller's agent. If a deal can be reached, your agent will receive half of the commission paid by the seller. But the reality is that once negotiations start, your agent has little incentive to represent your best interests (ethical considerations aside) by perhaps advising you to walk away from the deal. The most economical use of the agent's effort is to try to persuade you to accept the deal on the seller's terms. And the higher the price, the higher the commissions.

An alternative strategy is to search the papers or internet on your own to find a prospective business for sale. (This is not a difficult task.) Then, deal only with the listing (seller's) agent. In this case, when it comes to final negotiations, the agent's financial interest will be in working to convince the seller to accept your offer. That's because this agent may get to keep all of the commission if the seller sells to you, whereas the listing agent may only get half if selling to buyers who are represented by agents of their own. In fact, when negotiations get tough, a listing agent may even be willing to forgo a portion of the commission to put a one-agent deal together.

⭐ Head Start Exercise

6.5 Briefly describe the role of any intermediaries that will be involved in your purchase transaction (1/4 page maximum).

WHAT SHOULD THE PURCHASE AGREEMENT INCLUDE?

Shares vs. Assets

When a business is a sole proprietorship or partnership, the assets and debts of the business are, technically, the personal assets and debts of the owner(s). So, in buying such a business, you are really purchasing the assets of the company, which you will be using (in a legal sense) in a brand-new business. The store, factory, or office will look the same and the company may have the same name and the same employees, but it will be a different legal entity consisting of you and any partners you may have.

When you are buying a company that is incorporated, you have a choice:

- You can buy the assets of the company.
- You can buy the shares of the company.

When you buy only the assets, the original corporation still exists as a business entity and any debts or legal liability related to the past actions of the company remain with that corporation. When you buy the shares of the company, the corporate entity, even though it has a new owner, is still responsible for any liability resulting from past actions. For example, you might have bought a business whose taxes from two years ago were reassessed and the tax bill was increased by $4000. If you had purchased the shares of the company, you would now be responsible to pay this bill. If you had purchased the assets of the company, you would not.

When buying assets, you would ideally wish to purchase them on a *free and clear basis*. This means having the seller agree to discharge all **liens** before the finalization of the sale. It will be your lawyer's responsibility to make sure this has been done. In some cases, you will be agreeing to take over certain liabilities from the seller as part of the purchase arrangements. In either event, you will have to negotiate any **warranties** provided by the seller. Assets may be sold on an as-is basis, where you must accept them in whatever their condition on closing the deal. Or you may have them fully warranted, where the seller has promised that they will be in good working condition. A warranty may be important if you are buying a business that depends on a particular piece of expensive equipment. For example, if you were buying a business that made oil pans for car engines and the main asset was a large metal stamping machine, which the seller has told you will be good for at least five more years, you may try to get that in writing (as a promise that if the machine needs major repair or replacement before that time, the seller will pay for it.)

Payment Options

In many cases, the seller will wish to have full payment due on the finalization of the sale. But if the seller is having trouble finding a buyer who can arrange this, or if there is a tax advantage to the seller, it may be possible to arrange payment—at least for part of the business—over an extended period; in essence, to have the seller help finance your purchase. This would mean having the seller extend you a loan for a portion of the purchase price of the business, and the loan would be secured against the assets of the business.

Rather than holding a loan against the business, some sellers may be persuaded to retain a minority share position in the company. This is more likely if the prospects for profits are high for the next few years. Such an arrangement may include a specific time frame for ultimately selling the minority shares to the new owner.

When a business for sale owns the property where it is situated, it may be possible to negotiate an arrangement with the owner to buy the other assets of the business but have the owner retain the property and lease it to you. At the end of the lease, depending on the profitability of the business, you may choose to negotiate to buy the property or to move

lien The right of a creditor to take over a particular asset if a particular debt has not been paid as agreed.

warranty The legal promise that an asset will be delivered in the condition described in a contract.

✅ **Memory Check 6.10**
True or False? It is possible to buy the shares of a sole proprietorship.

✅ **Memory Check 6.11**
True or False? Compared to buying shares, buying the assets of a company provides greater protection against being sued for past actions of the company.

✅ **Memory Check 6.12**
True or False? The right of a creditor to take over a particular asset because of an unpaid debt is referred to as a lien.

the business. Such arrangements are often decided by the situation of the seller and where tax advantages lie. This kind of arrangement can also apply to other fixed assets, such as heavy equipment.

Another option is to have an agreed-on price that is payable on closing, but with the possibility of additional payments that can be made if the business achieves certain levels of profit over the next few years. This approach can help make the deal when the buyer and seller cannot agree on the profit potential of the firm. It can also be used when someone is buying into a business as an active partner, as long as the additional payment levels are not so high as to take away the new partner's incentive to maximize the company profit.

The past relationship between the buyer and the seller, the financial/tax position of the seller, and the ease with which the business can be sold are all factors that can affect the kind of financing arrangements you can make with a seller. Getting the details of these kinds of complexities on paper is a job for a lawyer, one familiar with business buy-sell agreements.

Non-Competition Issues

Purchase agreements will often include restrictions that prevent the old owner of a business from entering into any form of competition with the business. These usually specify a geographic range (five kilometres, for example) or a time limit (such as five years). The need for such a restriction is obvious if the business has involved the personal services of the owner. For example, you could buy an automobile repair shop from a mechanic who has a long-standing relationship with most of the customers. Shortly after you buy the shop, the seller could open a competing shop close by, taking all of the customers that you paid for as the goodwill value of the business. Non-competition clauses have to be carefully drafted, because certain laws make any unreasonable restriction on a person's right to earn a living unenforceable.[3]

Disclosure Issues

You will want to have a disclosure clause in your purchase agreement. This basically says that the seller agrees to tell you about anything that might adversely affect your decision to buy the business. This covers all of the items listed in "Risks of Buying" on page 136. For example, you might buy a successful carpet store where, unknown to you, the two top salespeople had plans to marry and start their own business. Or, let's say you bought a glass-blowing business where no one told you that the furnace was showing symptoms that it would soon have to be replaced. The idea here is that if the business turns out to be less profitable than expected because of such a problem, the door is open for you to sue the seller. To be successful in your lawsuit, you will have to provide evidence that the seller knew about the problem before the finalization of the purchase deal. You certainly do not plan on spending your time and money to take the seller to court, but it is important to have this clause, because it makes it in the seller's best interest to tell you everything the seller knows that might even possibly be a problem.

The negotiations to buy a business can also involve issues of non-disclosure. For example, if you have expressed interest in buying someone's business, you expect to be able to see financial statements, customer lists, operating methods, and anything else that will help you assess the business. The seller does not want you to learn all the intimate details of the business, change your mind about buying it, and then tell everything you know to the competition. Therefore, you will likely be required to sign a non-disclosure agreement before having access to confidential information about the company. Non-disclosure can also be required of the seller. If you buy the business, you will not want the seller to reveal confidential information to competitors—including the selling price or financing arrangements.

Get Help 6.4
You will need your lawyer's time as you discuss specific provisions that you or the seller want in the purchase agreement. You can cut down on this time (and expense) by studying a purchase agreement template, which you can buy for a few dollars at an office supply store. An example is the Buy–Sell Agreement Kit from Self-Counsel Press. See www.self-counsel.com.

Memory Check 6.13
True or False? A non-competition clause restricts a seller from disclosing company secrets to a competing firm.

Continuing Assistance

It is a fairly common practice to have the old owner of a business remain with the business as an employee or adviser, often for an extended period after the business is sold. This can be arranged as a condition of the purchase agreement, usually with some form of salary payment involved. The old owner is able to help the ownership transition by

- training the new owner
- keeping the business running and creating cash flow during the transition
- introducing the owner to customers, suppliers, and employees to help transfer these critical relationships

Ask yourself: What problems could arise from these types of arrangements? It sometimes happens that deals keeping the old owner in the business must be renegotiated to a shorter time period. This is usually the result of personal conflicts that develop between the new and old owners of the business relating to

- *Supervision of employees.* The new owner is trying to establish authority while the old owner continues in the long habit of being the boss.
- *Changes in methods.* The new owner has bought the business with a view to improving things, while the old owner acts defensively to changes, interpreting them as a criticism.

When negotiating for the continuing help of the previous owner, it is wise to leave some flexibility in the planned duration of the arrangement.

☑ **Memory Check 6.14**
True or False? A disclosure clause in a purchase agreement requires the seller to tell anything they know about the company that might prevent the buyer from completing the sale.

☆ Head Start Exercise

6.6 Briefly note any provisions you would require in the purchase agreement (1/4 page maximum).

HOW MUCH SHOULD I PAY?

Valuation Concepts

A business is constantly changing and adapting to the marketplace, the environment in which it lives. It grows, it shrinks, it gets sick or healthy. And people can be very subjective, even emotional, about a business. It is impossible to set a definitive monetary value on any business since no two people will view it exactly the same way. But people do agree on certain general concepts and approaches to estimating the value of a business.[4]

Ratio Analysis You would never consider buying a business without having an accountant examine the financial statements for that company. The financial statements can reveal a lot about a company—is the firm profitable, is it able to pay its bills, does it have a good inventory turnover, and so on. The accountant doesn't draw these kinds of conclusions just by glancing at the numbers and relying on experience. Instead, the accountant will perform a ratio analysis. This means using the numbers on the financial statements to calculate certain **key ratios**, which will help to build a picture of the company's financial health.

These ratios describe the company in terms of

- *Profitability.* The most common measure of profitability is return on equity.

$$\text{Return on Equity} = \frac{\text{Net Profit}}{\text{Owners' Equity}}$$

- ***Liquidity.*** This liquidity ratio indicates whether a firm is in a position to keep paying the bills that are due.

key ratio A financial indicator for a company, obtained by dividing one specific value from the company's financial statements by another specific value from those statements.

liquidity The ability of a company to pay its short-term financial obligations.

Adelle McAfee owns A McAfee & Associates Insurance Brokers Ltd. Over a 17-year period, Adelle went from being part-time employee of the firm, to full-time employee, to half owner, and finally to full owner. This was all part of an orderly, planned succession for the business leading up to the retirement of the previous owner. And there is a succession plan in place for when Adelle retires. Today, the firm has eight full-time employees and one part-timer. At the time of buying the business, putting a value on the company was relatively easy. There is a pricing formula or multiplier that is widely used for

the insurance industry, based on the commissions generated by a brokerage, so negotiations tend to be minimal.

The insurance industry, by its very nature, tends to be conservative and slow to change, but during her time in the business, Adelle has seen significant changes in the market—less so in technology. Her firm is still using the primary software that it purchased almost 20 years ago, although the provider updates the program regularly for an annual maintenance fee. Additional, new software is used that allows the brokerage to provide online quotes for home and auto insurance.

Changes in legislation and more competition among financial service providers over the past few years have allowed for a greater range of products and insurers that Adelle can offer to her clients. It has also required greater knowledge on the part of the broker. This means constant training for Adelle and her employees. Part of this requirement comes from the provincial insurance brokers licensing and regulating body, which requires annual training in legislation as well as ethical issues. Then there is the huge amount of product and market information that has to be absorbed. "Education never stops, once you get into a profession," says Adelle.

Visit the website for A. McAfee & Associates at www.mcafeeinsurance.ca.

$$Current\ Ratio = \frac{Current\ Assets}{Current\ Liabilities}$$

Another ratio that tests liquidity is called the quick ratio, or sometimes the acid test ratio. In this case, inventory is not counted as a current asset because it may take some time to turn inventory into cash.

$$Quick\ Ratio = \frac{Current\ Assets - Inventory}{Current\ Liabilities}$$

- *Management efficiency.* These profitability ratios also indicate how efficiently the company is able to use its assets, as well as its purchasing and sales efficiency.

$$Return\ on\ Assets = \frac{Net\ Profit}{Total\ Assets}$$

$$Gross\ Margin = \frac{Gross\ Profit}{Sales}$$

- *Debt management.* These ratios indicate the **solvency** of a company. The debt-to-equity ratio indicates how much a firm relies on borrowed capital compared to capital invested by the owners.

$$Debt\ to\ Equity = \frac{Total\ Liabilities}{Owners'\ Equity}$$

? Get Help 6.5
Financial ratios are available, classified by industry, on Industry Canada's SME Benchmarking site at sme.ic.gc.ca. You can access the site free of charge. Statistics Canada also sells ratio information in its document Financial Performance Indicators for Canadian Business, which you may be able to access through your library or accountant. Key ratios are often difficult to read because they are sometimes expressed as percentages and sometimes as fractions. You may need the help of an accountant.

solvency The ability of a firm to pay all of its financial obligations (short- and long-term).

How much debt a company carries can affect profits because of the related interest expense. Most industries have their own standard for what is considered a healthy debt ratio.

$$\text{Debt Ratio} = \frac{\text{Total Liabilities}}{\text{Total Assets}}$$

■ *Cash management.* How long it takes a company to collect money that is owed to it can affect its ability to pay its own bills.

$$\text{Average Collection Period} = \frac{\text{Accounts Receivable}}{\text{Average Sales per Day}}$$

Key ratios by themselves still tell you relatively little about the financial health of a company. It is only when these numbers are compared to the averages for your industry that you can see a company's relative liquidity, profitability, or efficiency.

Rate of Return In estimating the rate of return to expect from a company, ratio analysis will show you the past rate using the return-on-equity ratio. But other ratios are also important here, because things like the relative efficiency or debt management of a company give hints about the likelihood of that particular level of profitability continuing.

Imagine you have inherited some money that you would like to invest. You know that the higher the risk associated with any investment, the higher the return on investment (ROI) you should expect. You also know that the more liquid the investment (the easier it is to get your money back in cash), the lower the return. For example, if you put your money into a daily interest savings account, your money is insured and guaranteed (up to a maximum of $100 000 at the time of writing). The money is also totally liquid, in that you can take it out of the account at any time. But with such low risk and high liquidity, the return (the annual interest rate) will only be a percentage point or two.

Putting your money into Canada Savings Bonds is also low risk. But these are a less liquid investment, in that you have to wait for the bonds to mature in order to get your interest. So, they should give a higher return. For the sake of the example, let's say that the bonds will be paying around 3 percent this year. If you would like to assume more risk, you could look to the securities markets, where you might be able to find a mutual fund that has a pretty consistent return of, let's say, 6 percent. Ultimately, there are no guarantees with such an investment, but based on past performance you might still consider the risk to be moderate.

Ask yourself: What if I were to invest in a small business? What rate of return would I want from such a risk? The high failure rate of small firms means that this tends to be high risk. Also, your investment has very low liquidity in that you can get your money back only by selling the business, which could take some time. So you certainly wouldn't be willing to accept a return of 1 percent or 3 percent or even 6 percent. Perhaps you will decide that if you are going to take the risk of buying a business, you will want a return of 15 percent. But this is only a general decision on your part.

The specific rate of return that you will want from any particular business will depend on the risks associated with that business. The higher the risk, the higher the return you must expect. Risk factors include

■ how long the business has been established

■ the stability of the particular market

■ dependence on individuals in the firm who may leave

■ growth in the competition

■ rate of change in technology

and many other factors that you will investigate while assessing the business.

Memory Check 6.15
True or False? The return-on-equity ratio is an indicator of a company's profitability.

Memory Check 6.16
True or False? The quick ratio is an indicator of a company's management efficiency.

Memory Check 6.17
True or False? The collection period indicates how long, on average, it takes a company to get money owed to it by customers.

6.7 Choose a rate of return that would be acceptable for your investment in a business. Explain your choice (1/4 page maximum).

Present Value The concept of present value starts with the idea of future value. If you were to invest $100 today at an annual interest rate of 5 percent, at the end of one year you would have $105. And at the end of two years, because the interest is compounded, you would have $110.25. At the end of five years, you would have $126.63. So if you entered into a deal with someone who was going to pay you $126.63 at the end of five years, you know that's not the same as getting paid $126.63 today. The present value of that $126.63 (considering 5-percent annual growth) is only $100. There is a formula to calculate the present value of any future amount of money you are expecting:

$$PV = \frac{FN_n}{(1+i)^n}$$

where:

PV = Present value
FV_n = The amount of money to be received in year "n"
n = The number of years in the future that the money is to be received
i = The annual interest rate at which the money will grow

Try the formula using FV_n = $126.63, i = 0.05, and n = 5, just to test your math skills. The application of present value is appropriate when you can reasonably predict the future profit of a business and then calculate the present value of that profit at some reasonable growth rate. This gives you an indicator of what that future profit is worth today, or how much you might be willing to pay for a business that would make that future profit.

Valuation Methods

Most small business owners have no idea what their business is worth in objective terms.[5] This is despite the fact that there are many formal methods of putting a value on a business and many professional consultants to help do this. There are two main considerations in putting a monetary value on a business:

- the value of the assets you are buying
- the projected value of the future profits of the business

Each of these considerations has its own set of methods for determining business value: asset methods or income methods. Within these two groups of methods, there are lots of specific techniques for setting a value on a business. A broad sample, but certainly not all of these techniques, is presented here.

Asset Methods Asset methods for setting a value on a business are also known as balance sheet methods, since it is the balance sheet that provides the information for their calculation. Imagine you are considering buying A-Brand Spray Tan Equipment Distributors, whose recent balance sheet is shown in Figure 6.1. This supplier of commercial spray tan booths sells several brands of beds to spas and tanning studios throughout your province. In addition, A-Brand Spray Tan has just secured the exclusive Canadian distribution rights for a new type of booth that provides a more even spray. We will look at four asset methods for establishing the value of A-Brand Spray Tan:

- liquidation value
- book value

✓ **Memory Check 6.18**
True or False? The lower the liquidity of an investment, the lower the expected rate of return should be.

✓ **Memory Check 6.19**
True or False? The higher the risk of an investment, the higher the expected rate of return should be.

❓ **Get Help 6.6**
Present value can be calculated by formula or by using a present value table. These tables are often found in business math and accounting textbooks, or can be downloaded from the internet. For example, the business and legal publisher CCH has a Business Owner's Toolkit site at www.toolkit.cch.com/tools/tools.asp, where you can click on Present Value Tables.

✓ **Memory Check 6.20**
True or False? Present value calculations are based on the idea that an amount of money is more valuable if received now rather than later.

Figure 6.1 A-Brand Spray Tan Equipment Distributors | Balance Sheet

December 31, 20XX

ASSETS

CURRENT ASSETS

Cash	$ 4 752	
Accounts receivable	16 228	
Inventory	72 225	
Prepaid expenses	1 005	
Total current assets		$ 94 210

FIXED ASSETS

Land and building	$ 262 000	
Warehouse equipment	12 210	
Office equipment	4 160	
Truck	22 750	
Total fixed assets		301 120
Total Assets		**$395 330**

LIABILITIES

CURRENT LIABILITIES

Accounts payable	$ 29 994	
Short-term loans payable	3 946	
Taxes payable	10 620	
Total current liabilities		$ 44 560

LONG-TERM LIABILITIES

Mortgage payable	$ 177 252	
Long-term loan payable	14 418	
Total long-term liabilities		191 670
Total Liabilities		**$236 230**
Owners' Equity		**159 100**
Total Liabilities and Owners' Equity		**$395 330**

- adjusted book value
- replacement value

Liquidation value is the lowest possible value for a business and is more valid for a failing business than it is for a **going concern**. The liquidation value estimates what the value of the assets would be if they were sold at auction (or otherwise quickly disposed of) and deducts from this amount the liabilities of the business. The remainder represents the liquidation value of the company. Using the A-Brand Spray Tan example, Figure 6.2 shows the value of the company's assets, as appraisers and an auctioneering firm have estimated their quick-sale value.

going concern An operating business that is expected to continue operating into the foreseeable future.

From the liquidation value of the assets ($288 987) the value of the company liabilities ($236 230) is deducted. This leaves $52 757 as the liquidation value of the business.

Figure 6.2 Liquidation Value of Assets for A-Brand Spray Tan Equipment Distributors

	Balance Sheet (Book) Value	Liquidation Value
CURRENT ASSETS		
Cash	$ 4 752	$ 4 752
Accounts receivable	16 228	3 245
Inventory	72 225	28 890
Prepaid expenses	1 005	0
Total current assets	$ 94 210	$ 36 887
FIXED ASSETS		
Land and building	$262 000	$225 000
Warehouse equipment	12 210	8 700
Office equipment	4 160	1 900
Truck	22 750	16 500
Total fixed assets	$301 120	$252 100
Total Assets	**$395 330**	**$288 987**

Obviously, this is far from any fair market value for the business. However, it is important to calculate this value to show the range of possible values for a business—especially for the buyer, who may use this information in negotiations.

The *book value* of a business is the value of its assets, as shown on the balance sheet, minus the value of its liabilities—in other words, the owners' equity. So, in the case of A-Brand Spray Tan, the book value would be $159 100. The main problem with book value is that the value of assets stated on the balance sheet may be quite far from any market value of the assets. For example, companies have choices in how they can depreciate assets for maximum tax advantage, but this could result in assets being undervalued on the balance sheet.

Adjusted book value attempts to correct for problems with book value by trying to represent all assets and liabilities at fair market value. For example, in Figure 6.3 you can see that for A-Brand Spray Tan, the following figures have been adjusted:

- *Accounts receivable.* Further investigation showed that two of the accounts still carried on the books had been outstanding for some time and were from companies known to be in deep financial trouble. Since there was little chance of ever collecting on these, they were deducted from the receivables.

- *Inventory.* A careful inspection of the inventory revealed some old stock, including a couple of models of a tanning bed that was considered obsolete. Because of safety considerations, there was no hope of ever selling these beds and they could not be returned for refund since the manufacturer was out of business. Their value was, therefore, deducted from the book value of the inventory.

> **Memory Check 6.21**
> True or False? Liquidation value is typically a lower amount than book value.

Figure 6.3 Adjusted Value of Assets for A-Brand Spray Tan Equipment Distributors

	Balance Sheet (Book) Value	Adjusted Value
CURRENT ASSETS		
Cash	$ 4 752	$ 4 752
Accounts receivable	16 228	7 000
Inventory	72 225	63 000
Prepaid expenses	1 005	1 005
Total current assets	$ 94 210	$ 75 757
FIXED ASSETS		
Land and building	$262 000	$287 000
Warehouse equipment	12 210	16 500
Office equipment	4 160	5 500
Truck	22 750	25 200
Total fixed assets	$301 120	$334 200
Total Assets	**$395 330**	**$409 957**

- *Land and building.* This asset was revalued upward to reflect steady increases in real estate prices and because of a building inspection that revealed the structure and facilities to be in excellent shape.

- *Warehouse and office equipment.* These also were revalued upward. The accounting system used by A-Brand Spray Tan had depreciated both assets at the standard capital cost allowance rates indicated by Canada Revenue Agency on tax returns. The equipment, however, had been well maintained and was worth much more than the book value. Because of an active market in both used warehouse and office equipment, it was easy to establish fair market values.

- *Truck.* Recent increases in new-vehicle prices also resulted in increased market value for used vehicles. In addition, this particular truck had logged very few kilometres and was in excellent condition, resulting in the new higher value.

The adjusted value of the assets ($409 957) minus the value of the liabilities ($236 230) gives an adjusted book value of $173 726.

Replacement value is a useful technique for comparing the cost of buying a business with the cost of starting a similar business from scratch. Assets are revalued at what it would cost to replace them—not necessarily with brand-new assets. But even available used assets will almost always cost more than the depreciated book value of existing assets. Figure 6.4 shows the assets of A-Brand Spray Tan at their replacement cost.

Obviously, the value of assets like cash and accounts receivable will remain unchanged. Assets like inventory and prepaid expenses are valued higher because prices will likely have gone up between the time these things were purchased and the present. The replacement value of assets like buildings and equipment is generally higher than the adjusted value because replacing assets can include fees like real estate transfer taxes, legal fees, or delivery

Figure 6.4 Replacement Value of Assets for A-Brand Spray Tan Equipment Distributors

	Balance Sheet (Book) Value	Replacement Value
CURRENT ASSETS		
Cash	$ 4 752	$ 4 752
Accounts receivable	16 228	16 228
Inventory	72 225	74 500
Prepaid expenses	1 005	1 060
Total current assets	$ 94 210	$ 96 540
FIXED ASSETS		
Land and building	$262 000	$297 900
Warehouse equipment	12 210	16 800
Office equipment	4 160	5 700
Truck	22 750	28 300
Total fixed assets	$301 120	$348 700
Total Assets	**$395 330**	**$445 240**

and installation costs. The $445 240 replacement value of the assets minus the $236 230 in liabilities produces a business replacement value of $209 010.

Income Methods Income methods put a value on a business based on the ability of that business to earn money. Many of the income techniques require you to predict the future earnings of the business, which is arguably a more fair way to assess value. But it can also be a less accurate way, since the value is no more accurate than your ability to predict the future. We will look at four income methods for establishing the value of A-Brand Spray Tan:

- capitalization of earnings
- capitalized cash flow
- discounted cash flow
- earnings multipliers

The *capitalization of earnings technique* for pricing a business starts with establishing your desired rate of return. For example, you might want at least a 15 percent return on any business that you would buy. But you must decide on the relative risks of this particular business. You know that the business has been established for many years and has shown a steady growth in sales and profit. Your ratio analysis shows that the business is financially healthy and well managed. The only outstanding risk you can identify is the potential for health problems related to spray tans. You know that there have been widespread warnings by dermatologists over many years against tanning beds, but spray tans have been considered safe. Recently however, some doctors have been concerned that some chemicals used in spray tanning might cause lung damage. You know, however, that there are several choices in spray tan solutions and expect that most will be safe.

Memory Check 6.22
True or False? Replacement value is an asset method of business valuation.

Memory Check 6.23
True or False? Adjusted book value is an income method of business valuation.

After careful discussions with your advisers, you may settle on 15 percent as an acceptable return on any investment you would make in A-Brand Spray Tan. You can then compare this figure to the profits of the business (the return) to calculate a price for the business (the investment). For example, look at the income statement of A-Brand Spray Tan Equipment Distributors shown in Figure 6.5.

Last year's net profit before tax was $30 210, and let's say that the average profit over the past few years has been around $30 000. You are looking for an ROI of 15 percent. Another way of writing this is:

$$\frac{R}{I} = \frac{15}{100}$$

Since you already know that the return (profit) will be $30 000, you can substitute that into the equation:

$$\frac{\$30\,000}{I} = \frac{15}{100}$$

Figure 6.5 A-Brand Spray Tan Equipment Distributors | Income Statement

For the One-Year Period Ending December 31, 20XX

SALES

Equipment sales	$602 015	
Installations and repairs	104 725	
Total sales		$706 740

COSTS

Cost of goods sold		$331 110

GROSS PROFIT

Gross profit		$375 630

EXPENSES

Salaries/benefits	$287 865	
Depreciation	12 135	
Building maintenance	11 055	
Utilities	8 190	
Professional fees	6 100	
Advertising	6 328	
Supplies	5 922	
Insurance	7 445	
Miscellaneous expense	380	
Total expenses		$345 420

Net Profit Before Tax   **$30 210**

Now all you have to do is solve the equation for I, the investment: I = $200 000. This tells you that if you want a return on investment (ROI) of 15 percent and the return is $30 000, then you should be willing to pay $200 000 for the business.

Capitalized cash flow is another income method. In this context, it refers to net profit that has been adjusted by adding back in

- *Depreciation.* This expense does not use up actual cash of the business.

- *Extraordinary salary, benefits, or "perks" received by the owner.* This solves the problem of properly accounting for these forms of earnings as discussed under valuation concepts.

- *Extraordinary one-time transactions.* This would include settlement of a lawsuit, a one-time licence fee, or some kind of windfall that would not be normal for the business but could dramatically affect the profit in the year it occurred.

In the income statement shown for A-Brand Spray Tan, the only adjustment would be for the $12 135 of depreciation. So, let's say that this business had an average cash flow over the past three years of $30 000 + $12 000 = $42 000. Dividing this cash flow by your expected return of 15 percent would give you a price of $42 000/15% = $280 000 for the business. This is the same math as in the previous example, just expressed in a shorter form.

Discounted cash flow is yet another income method. This way of pricing a business depends on your ability to predict future cash flow of the business by using the same projection techniques used throughout your business plan to project sales costs and expenses. If cash flow for A-Brand Spray Tan has been growing at roughly 10 percent a year for the past few years, you may decide to project this same growth rate for the next five years (this is the outside length of time considered feasible for small-business projections). In the past year, cash flow was $42 000, so next year it will be 110% × $42 000 = $46 200, and so on. And if we look up the 15 percent ROI that we want (also called a **discount rate**) on a present value table, we will find the present value factors for each of the years shown in Figure 6.6.

discount rate The yearly rate of return that is used to calculate the present value of future cash inflows.

This figure shows us that the present value of the cash flow the business is expected to produce (at a 15 percent ROI) is $184 145. Assuming that your projections are correct, this is the amount you should be willing to pay for the business based on this method.

Get Help 6.7
The Canada Business Network offers several methods of valuing a business at www .canadabusiness.ca/eng/ guide/1398.

Earnings multipliers represent another method of pricing a business. If you knew the selling price of several recently sold firms in your industry, as well as the profits of those companies, you would be able to calculate a ratio between the selling price and the earnings. For example, on average, the companies may have sold for five times their earnings (before-tax net profit). It would then be a simple matter to multiply the recent average earnings of the company you are pricing by five (the multiplier) to get an estimate of the current market value of the firm. *Ask yourself: Where could I get the information to calculate an earnings multiplier?*

In all likelihood, sale price information will be based on your own experience and observation, insider information, or industry gossip. Corporate directories and credit reports will also give earnings information, and it is possible to deduce selling prices from them by comparing before and after sale reports. You can also get an indication of the multiplier for your industry by using the average **price–earnings ratio** of publicly traded companies in

price–earnings ratio (P/E) The ratio comparing the current market price of an ordinary share of a company with the profit per share for that company over the past year.

Figure 6.6 A-Brand Spray Tan Equipment Distributors | Discounted Cash Flow at Discount Factor of 15 Percent

	Year 1	Year 2	Year 3	Year 4	Year 5	Total
Projected cash flow	$46 200	$50 820	$55 902	$61 492	$67 641	
Present value factor	0.869565	0.756144	0.657516	0.571753	0.497177	
Present value	$40 174	$38 427	$36 756	$35 158	$33 630	$184 145

your field. This information is easily available but will apply to companies that are many times larger than the small firm you are pricing. Keep in mind that this number will change with volatility in stock prices, so the price–earnings ratio should be averaged over some period of time.

Earnings multipliers are considered to be a **rule-of-thumb pricing** method. Many industries have their own traditional rule-of-thumb methods for setting values on companies. Primarily based on profit, rule-of-thumb pricing can also use factors such as sales income, units sold, or assets to produce the ratio with price. For example, gas stations might be priced, on average, at $0.30 multiplied by the number of litres of gas sold each month. Some industry associations and periodicals track and publish current information about multipliers for calculating business prices.

Other valuation techniques include

- adjusted tangible net worth
- discounted future earnings
- capitalization of after-tax earnings
- discounted after-tax discretionary cash flow

And there are many, many variations on all of the techniques listed.

⭐ Head Start Exercise

6.8 Outline the business valuation techniques you plan to use to put a price on the business. Identify any professional advisers you will use (1/3 page maximum).

Negotiating Price

In spite of the many objective methods of valuing a business, ultimately the value of a firm is whatever price can be negotiated between a buyer and a seller.[6] In determining a price to pay for a business, however, it is only prudent to use a variety of different techniques for estimating the value of the firm. These will produce a variety of values, which you can use to help establish

- a fair market price for the business;
- the lowest reasonable price you think the business could be purchased for; and
- the maximum amount you are personally willing to pay for the business.

These are the numbers you need to prepare for your price negotiations.

One method for establishing a fair market price is to use a weighted average of your different business values. You may have used several techniques to estimate the value of the business, but some of those techniques are more valid than others. So you may have a discussion involving your accountant, perhaps a business valuation specialist, and some other advisers, where you come to a consensus about the relative weight that each of your valuation methods should be given—maybe on a scale of 1 to 10. For example, you may decide, as a group, that the liquidation value has little validity since the business is financially sound. You may weigh book value at 5 since it does not take the established goodwill of the company into account. You may decide that discounted cash flow deserves a 10 weighting because of the steady historical growth in cash flow that the company has shown, and so on. As shown in Figure 6.7, the weighted values are averaged to estimate a fair market value for the business.

$$\text{Weighted Average Business Value} = \frac{\$9\,005\,836}{46} = \$195\,779$$

This process can now help you plan for negotiations by first determining the lowest reasonable value that you think the business could be sold for. This should be your opening offer.

---

rule-of-thumb pricing Using a ratio showing a relationship between the average price of a business in a particular field and some other factor such as profit to calculate the price for a specific company.

❓ Get Help 6.8
Various financial services and other companies offer websites that give stock information, including P/E information for the shares of specific companies traded on Canadian exchanges. For example, see Google Stock Screener at www.google.ca/finance/stockscreener.

❓ Get Help 6.9
Accountants who specialize in establishing the value of businesses often carry the CBV designation, showing that they have been certified by the Canadian Institute of Chartered Business Valuators. The institute's website, at www.cicbv.ca, can help you find a business valuation specialist in your area.

✅ Memory Check 6.24
True or False? Many industries have their own rule-of-thumb pricing methods using multipliers.

Valuation Technique		Business Value ×	Weighting	= Weighted Value
Asset Methods	Liquidation Value	$ 52 757	1	$ 52 757
	Book Value	159 100	5	795 500
	Adjusted Book Value	173 727	7	1 216 089
	Replacement Value	209 010	4	836 040
Earnings Method	Capitalized Earning	200 000	5	1 000 000
	Capitalized Cash Flow	280 000	6	1 680 000
	Discounted Cash Flow	184 145	10	1 841 450
	Earnings Multiplier	198 000	8	1 584 000
Totals			46	$9 005 836

Using the A-Brand Spray Tan example, you may decide to set the opening offer close to the book value of the business, with only a token amount ($6000) included for the goodwill of the business—let's say, $165 000. This leaves you more than $20 000 of negotiating room to get to your fair market value of $195 779, but you are still within the range in which the business could conceivably sell.

Business Reality 6.2 Kutters Hairstyling
From Employee to Partner

Melanie Graham bought Kutters Hairstyling, an upscale hair salon in Whitehorse, Yukon, 10 years ago after working there as an employee for seven years. Melanie had started working for Kutters part-time when she was 13 years old. To buy the business, she was able to secure a bank loan, and since that time the salon has expanded from the original 3 employees to 12. It has also expanded in the range of services that it offers, which now include aesthetics, tanning, and massage. The change in ownership went smoothly, with all of the former employees remaining with the business.

At the time of the buyout, the agreement included a provision for the original owner to work in the salon on a "chair rental" basis, keeping her own fees and clientele but paying Melanie for the space and services. The other stylists (and all of the new hires since then) have worked as employees on a commission basis. This arrangement makes it more conducive for Melanie to invest in the training of "her team." In fact, Melanie's reputation for the training and development of her staff helped her win the Business Development Bank of Canada's Young Entrepreneur Award in 2001. Melanie emphasizes training not only to keep her staff on the "cutting" edge of hair fashion, but also as a team-building activity. In fact, Melanie has been known to take her employees on a "training cruise," combining a holiday perk with serious development.

Recently, Kutters moved to new premises in the heart of downtown Whitehorse. Melanie formed a partnership with her brother to buy the building, which is then leased back to the salon. The site is ideal for maximum pedestrian traffic and visibility and will allow for future expansion. Melanie Graham's advice to new entrepreneurs is to "really try to learn the finance. Even if it's a simple business and even if you have a bookkeeper or accountant, you should still try to know as much as you can about finance and accounting."

Visit Kutters Hairstyling's Facebook page at www.facebook.com/kuttershairstyling.

The next step is to set the maximum amount you are willing to pay for the business. You would certainly not want to pay above your assessment of a fair market value. But if you have come this far in the buying process, you have already invested a considerable amount of your time, effort, and no doubt money for professional fees in buying the business. Let's say you estimate the cost at $2500. If you don't make the deal, not only are you out by this amount, but you also will have to spend it all over again on the next business you consider buying. So, in an effort to avoid going through the process again, you can add this amount to your fair market value and get your maximum price of $198 279. You now have the settlement range that you will negotiate within ($165 000 to $198 000), working hard to keep the price as low as possible by moving, when necessary, in very small increments.

The starting point for price negotiations is usually the asking price for the business.[7] Be careful not to let the asking price influence your opening offer.[8] The asking price itself tells you nothing about the value of the business. It does, however, give you some small indication about the negotiating style of the seller and about the nature of the final agreement. For example, if the asking price is ludicrously high, it could indicate that the seller has a totally unrealistic sense of the value of the business—in which case, the negotiating challenge for you is to educate the seller. Or, it could indicate a seller who is looking to mislead a naive buyer into paying too much—in which case, you should be suspicious of everything the seller tells you and wary of all the seller's tactics. Careful questioning of the seller and checking their references and reputation are your best bets for distinguishing between the two reasons for such high pricing.

An unreasonably low asking price could be a warning sign that the seller is trying to hurry you into snapping up a bargain before you do a thorough investigation of the business. But it could also mean a seller who is in distress and needs to sell quickly. If this is the case, the seller will probably be looking for a short closing (a short time to the finalization date of the deal). The low asking price could also indicate a seller who truly underestimates the value of the business. This is more likely to be the situation when the seller does not have competent professional help to assist with the sale. Either of these last two situations presents an opportunity for a real bargain. *Ask yourself: Would I have a moral problem in taking advantage of a distressed or incompetent seller?* There is certainly an ethical line between negotiating a great deal and deceiving someone who is vulnerable because of a personal crisis or bad advice. Most ethical businesspeople would want to make sure that the distressed seller had full knowledge that a higher price could be secured by waiting. And it would be unethical to actively mislead a naive seller, even by confirming misinformation the seller may have received from advisers. Besides, an incredible bargain of a deal, even after it is long closed, could still end up in court if there is evidence of deception.

An important principle of price negotiations is to bargain based on the documented verifiable facts only, not on something the seller may tell you off the record. For example, you may be negotiating to buy a golf course and the seller privately confesses to **skimming cash** for rounds of golf that require no receipts to the tune of $20 000 a year. The implication here is that you too can benefit by this illegal activity and that the business is really worth more than the value that the financial statements indicate. In such a case, you must remember that you do not know that the business has an additional $20 000 in revenue. All you know for sure is that the seller is a thief. *Ask yourself: What are the chances of a thief also being a liar?*

A second negotiating principle you should adhere to, as the buyer, is to negotiate for the business as it is—not as how you could make it. Beware when the seller is constantly pointing out that the business has this potential or that possibility of improvement. These are potentials that the seller did not take advantage of, improvements that the seller did not make. As a result, the seller is not entitled to compensation for them. Improvements to a business are worth money only if they have been implemented.

skimming cash The illegal removal of unreported cash from a business in order to avoid paying tax on that income.

In buying a business or a share of a business, price is only one issue to be negotiated. But it cannot be separated from the other issues. For example, you will likely have to pay more if you can get the seller to agree to payment terms that favour you. On the other hand, if the seller wishes to retain the right to open a competing business within the next few years, this should reduce the price of the business. There will be many non-monetary issues that have to be negotiated, and the best way to deal with them is to set a monetary value on each of them in your negotiation planning. This may be more of a subjective process than actual calculation, but each issue can be priced. For example, if you would prefer to close the deal on May 30, but the seller would prefer April 30, you must estimate what it will cost you in cash and inconvenience to have to run around and hurry your preparations to advance the date—say, $1000. This means you will reduce your opening offer (or any offers currently on the table) as well as your maximum price by $1000.

To simplify the negotiating process, it is often a good tactic to seek agreement, in principle, on as many non-monetary issues as possible before discussing price. This reduces the number of times that you will have to recalculate your price position during the talks. (For additional ideas on negotiation, see Chapter 3, "What Prices Will I Set?")

> **Memory Check 6.25**
> True or False? Cash skimming by the previous owner should be factored into the price of a business.

⭐ Head Start Exercise

6.9 Briefly list the negotiating tactics you will use in arranging the purchase agreement (1/4 page maximum).

Answers to Memory Check Questions

6.1 T   6.2 F   6.3 F   6.4 F   6.5 T   6.6 T   6.7 F   6.8 F   6.9 F   6.10 F
6.11 T   6.12 T   6.13 F   6.14 T   6.15 T   6.16 F   6.17 T   6.18 F   6.19 T   6.20 T
6.21 T   6.22 T   6.23 F   6.24 T   6.25 F

Questions for Discussion

1. What are the personality differences between entrepreneurs suited to buying a business versus those suited to starting their own new business?
2. What is the cheapest way to get into business for yourself? The most expensive? Outline some scenarios where buying a business could be the cheapest.
3. Identify some instances where you have bought something and ended up feeling cheated. How could these situations be similar to buying a business?
4. Identify some businesses that suffer from having a negative image. What steps could be taken to turn this image around? Is the situation ever hopeless?
5. Have you ever sold anything and not disclosed your reason for wishing to sell? Did you indicate some other reason for wishing to sell? Why?
6. What problems are likely to arise when you buy a minority share in someone's business? What if a business is owned by two people who are willing to sell you a 1/3 share in the company?
7. Is it possible to buy a business with little or no cash? Outline any stories you may have heard of this happening. What could you negotiate instead of cash for taking over a business?
8. If you were buying a retail store, should you base the price you offer more on asset valuation methods, or more on income methods? What if you were buying a construction company? A restaurant? A rental apartment building? A real estate brokerage?
9. Other than information found in the financial statements, what is the single most important thing to find out before buying a business? Argue your position.

10. Have you ever negotiated the price of something where you ended up getting a great bargain? What was the key to your successful negotiation?
11. Discuss the issue of skimming cash. How prevalent is this among small businesses? Which businesses would be ideal for this practice? How can it be discouraged?

Case for Discussion

Nelson worked as chief installer for a small chain of floor-covering retailers, All Floors Inc. Most of the company's installers specialized in just carpet, or ceramics, or hardwood, but Nelson had experience in all types of installations and he was also skilled at measuring and costing installation jobs.

One day the owner of All Floors, Hugette, came to Nelson and explained that the company was going to stop doing its own installations and, in future, sub-contract out that work. Nelson was immediately worried. Losing his job meant that he would not be able to pay the mortgage on his house. But Hugette went on to explain that All Floors would sell off its installation department, including its trucks and tools, as a separate company. This new separate company could get most of All Floors's installation work as well as work from other flooring retailers. She said it was a great opportunity to make money and that Nelson, with his broad experience, would be the ideal owner of the new company.

Hugette knew that Nelson's only major asset was his house, but she suggested that Nelson could borrow money against it. And if that wasn't enough to cover the cost of buying the installation department, Hugette might be willing to loan Nelson the difference, which he could repay out of his profits. She suggested that if he was interested, he should go to his bank and see how much he could borrow.

Nelson and his life partner, Morgan, discussed the situation, agreeing that it was a risk to go into business, but both were excited about the idea of owning their own company. The bank agreed to give Nelson a second mortgage on the house of $200 000, and he had another $20 000 that he could take out of his registered retirement savings plan.

When Nelson met with Hugette, he told her that he could arrange finance of up to $220 000. Hugette said that All Floors' accountant had been working out a value for the installation department. She said the cost of buying used trucks and tools similar to what would be sold off would come to around $150 000. She also indicated that the installation department was already a going concern with trained employees, established systems, and customers. She said that this goodwill was worth another $150 000, for a total value of around $300 000. Hugette said that if Nelson wanted to buy the department as his own company, she would be willing to let him have it for $290 000, and she would loan him the $70 000 that he was short. Nelson quickly agreed to the deal and Hugette said she would have her lawyer draw up a contract.

Two years later, Nelson was bankrupt.

Nelson had renamed his spin-off company Nelson Floor Installations. And for the first few months, the new company was profitable, subcontracting from All Floors as well as two or three other carpet retailers. Nelson paid himself a small living allowance and gave the rest of the profit to Hugette in order to get that loan paid off as quickly as possible. During this time, two new installation companies started to compete with Nelson, and their business was growing rapidly as they were able to undercut Nelson's price by paying lower wages to their employees. Nelson believed that because all his installers were experienced, it would be difficult to pay them less than the rates established by All Floors.

During this time, three of the trucks that Nelson had purchased from All Floors turned out to need such extensive repairs that he decided to replace them with new vehicles. Also, over the next few months, one by one, the carpet companies Nelson was getting business from left him for his cheaper competitors, and he was unable to find new customers. The final blow came when Hugette regretfully informed Nelson that she, too, would be turning to cheaper installers. When Nelson reminded her that she had a contract with his firm, Hugette explained that their contract obligated Nelson to supply installation services at their previous rates, but did not obligate her to buy from Nelson.

Nelson managed to hang on for several more months, able to pay his employees, but with other unpaid bills piling up. Eventually he was forced into bankruptcy and a court-appointed trustee seized the assets of his company. The bank took Nelson's house, and all his remaining equity in it was used up by legal and administrative costs. Ironically, it was Hugette who purchased the assets of Nelson's business from the trustee for a sum of $75 000, including the new trucks Nelson had replaced her old ones with. Using those trucks and the other equipment, she re-opened her own installation department at All Floors, hiring new installers at cheaper rates than she had previously paid.

1. Suggest reasons why Hugette likely wanted to sell off the installation department. How could Nelson have investigated these reasons?

2. What method had Hugette's accountant used to value the assets of the spin-off department? What other methods should have been used? Explain why.

3. What mistakes did Nelson make? What were the likely reasons that he was not more diligent?

4. What advisors should Nelson have used before making the purchase? For what specific areas of advice?

5. How could Nelson have responded to the competition?

6. How could he have dealt with the employees?

7. What is the most important lesson to be learned from Nelson?

The Business Plan, Alternative Module:
BUSINESS PURCHASE

Entrepreneurs buying or buying into an existing business should complete Sections 1 to 5 of the business plan as well as this portion.

1. Briefly describe why buying or buying into a business is an appropriate start-up method for you and your personal circumstances.

2. Describe the history of the company you are buying (or buying into) and any specific advantages of buying now.

3. Describe the investigation methods you used to assess the business and to get the information for completing Sections 1 to 5 of the business plan.

4. Briefly describe the reason for sale by the owner(s) as determined by your investigations.

5. Generally describe your purchase transaction in terms of what you are buying (a piece of a business, a partnership role, a whole business) and from whom you are buying it. Attach, as an appendix, a draft of any partnership or shareholder agreement that will apply.

6. Briefly identify and describe the roles of any intermediaries in arranging the sale.

7. Briefly outline the main provisions of your purchase agreement and attach a draft of the agreement as an appendix.

8. Describe the financial health of the company being purchased, referring to the analysis of the key business ratios.

9. Identify what you consider an acceptable rate of return for investing in a business. Give your rationale.

10. Identify a fair market value for the business. Briefly explain your valuation methodology and sources of assistance. Attach, as an appendix, a detailed valuation of the business using several techniques from both asset and income methods.

11. List your opening offer and the maximum price you are willing to pay for the business. Explain your rationale.

12. Describe your plan for conducting negotiations.

Chapter 7

The Franchise Alternative: How Do I Buy a Franchise?

Buying a franchise is an increasingly popular way of getting into business for yourself. Every year some portion of Canadian franchises fail. But buying a franchise is, on average, a lower-risk start-up method than either starting a brand-new business or buying an existing business. Because of this, franchising has grown at a very high rate over the past two decades, to somewhere between 80 000 and 90 000 franchise units in Canada. And during this time, what we mean by *franchise* has grown to cover an assortment of legal arrangements and product/service distribution systems. Just a tiny sample of the kinds of franchises for sale includes home inspection services, schools, funeral homes, water delivery services, employment agencies, driver training centres, management consulting firms, computer retailers, logistics companies, accounting firms, car repair shops, and, of course, fast-food outlets. There are even franchises that help people to buy franchises.

If you decide to buy a franchise, you will need a business plan that includes all of the topics covered in Chapters 1 to 5. As well, your business plan will need to address the topics covered in this chapter:

- **How Does Franchising Work?**
- **Is Franchising Right for Me?**
- **How Do I Choose a Franchise?**
- **How Can I Finance a Franchise?**
- **What Are the Contract Issues?**

Learning Objectives

On completion of this chapter, you should be able to:

1. Name and describe five franchising formats.
2. Assess your own suitability as a franchisee.
3. Summarize a typical process of arranging to buy a franchise.
4. Explain five major issues in assessing a franchisor.
5. Estimate the cash requirements for financing a franchise.
6. Describe and discuss three major provisions commonly found in franchise agreements.
7. Prepare alternative components of the business plan related to buying a franchise.

HOW DOES FRANCHISING WORK?

Franchise Types

The word **franchise** refers to a set of rights (the right to use a company's name, products, trademarks, copyrights, design, and style of business) that are sold by a **franchisor** to a **franchisee**. But within that definition, there are still lots of different things that we call

---

franchise The particular set of rights that are sold by a company, allowing others to use its products, intellectual property, and style of doing business.

franchisor A company that sells the rights to duplicate its system and style of doing business or to distribute its products and services. (Note U.S. spelling: franchiser.)

franchisee An individual or company that purchases the rights to distribute the products of or use the intellectual property and business style of another company.

franchising. The field of franchising is changing so rapidly that there has not been time for a standard classification system to evolve. Nevertheless, by using the following five broad categories you will be able to communicate sensibly with other businesspeople about franchising issues:

- licensing
- dealership franchising
- conversion franchising
- multi-level marketing
- business format franchising

Licensing
A traditional franchising format—**licensing**—is where the franchisor sells the right to produce and sell the franchisor's products or services, using the franchisor's name and trademarks. Soft drinks and frozen treats are often franchised this way. The franchisee is often not bound to producing the franchisor's products exclusively and may have licences from more than one franchisor (usually not in direct competition). At the same time, the franchisee may even produce products under the franchisee's own brands.

Dealerships
Dealerships are generally retailers operating under the trade name of the franchisor, which is the manufacturer and/or wholesaler of products carried by the franchisee. Car dealers, hardware stores, snowmobile dealers, and gas stations can all be examples of **dealership franchising**. Some franchises in this category are not limited to carrying only the brands of the franchisor, or necessarily only products supplied by the franchisor. For example, hardware franchisors generally offer relatively few products under their own house brands, while they may distribute many competing national brands. Car dealers may be obliged to carry new models manufactured by their own franchisor only, but a Chrysler dealer will certainly have used Fords on the lot for sale.

Conversion
A long-standing trend in dealership franchising has been **conversion franchising**. This is where an independent business converts to becoming a franchise. So, an independent gas station and garage called Jim's Garage could become a Petro-Canada station, a franchise still owned by Jim. This would involve putting up the Petro-Canada sign and carrying the Petro-Canada products. At the end of the franchise agreement, Jim would have the opportunity to renew the franchise, return to independent status, or convert to another franchisor's brand.[1]

Traditionally, dealerships afforded generous management freedom to franchisees, which resulted in considerable variation among individual franchises. For example, at one time you could find substantial individuality among Canadian Tire dealerships or Shell stations. Over the past few years, however, as franchisors have refined their retailing systems, they have insisted on greater conformity in decor, layout, and merchandising systems. As this trend continues, it blurs the line between dealerships and business format franchises (see below).

MLM
Multi-level marketing differs from other forms of franchising in that there are usually minimal selection criteria for the franchisees and rarely a true franchise agreement or fee. However, there are usually start-up costs relating to sales kits and initial inventory. MLM is a method of selling the franchisor's products through independent salespeople (usually working from their homes) who sell directly to consumers, often in the customers' homes or via telephone. Typically MLM is used to sell household cleaning products, cosmetics, giftware, kitchen products, vitamin/herbal supplements, books, jewellery, and even long-distance telephone service. As an MLM franchisee, you make some profit by selling

---

Memory Check 7.1
True or False? The word *franchise* refers specifically to a fast-food outlet, typically found in a high-traffic suburban area.

licensing The selling of the right to produce and distribute a particular brand of product or service.

Memory Check 7.2
True or False? A franchisor is a buyer of a complete method of doing business.

dealership franchising When a retailer has the rights to carry the products of and operate under the trade name of its supplier.

conversion franchising The adapting of an independent small business to become a franchise outlet.

Memory Check 7.3
True or False? The manufacture and sale of Popsicles uses a form of franchising called licensing.

multi-level marketing (MLM) A form of franchising where products are distributed through independent direct sellers (franchisees), who can recruit subordinate levels of sellers (sub-franchisees) and earn commissions on the sales of those subordinate levels.

the franchisor's products or services. However, you can also make commissions on the sales of new salespeople that you recruit. And, ultimately, you can make a commission on the sales of new sellers recruited by your recruits and so on for several levels of commission.

This is the draw of MLM—it is often touted by the franchisor as a road to wealth by having multiple levels of salespeople making money for you. And there is no doubt that a small minority of people involved with MLM do get wealthy. But these people are the exception. They are often people involved early in a new market or at the start of an industry's growth cycle. However, these are the examples held up by the franchisors to recruit new sellers. A good tip-off to the approach of an MLM franchisor is to check the company's website and see if it emphasizes the quality and benefits of its products. Or does it tell you to stop being a loser and join a team of rich happy winners?[2]

Most franchisors using other, traditional formats are reluctant to recognize MLM as a type of franchising, largely because of its history involving now-outlawed **pyramid selling** schemes. Some of the pyramid selling elements still prevail in MLM. For example, training is often heavily motivational, as opposed to informational, with franchisees sometimes paying to attend expensive conferences and seminars put on by the franchisor. There certainly are cases of MLM franchisors with quality products, reasonable prices, and longtime franchisees who make a reasonable living and enjoy the work. But many people who enter into MLM put in long hours in saturated markets and end up working for less than minimum wage before leaving in frustration. Because it is so easy to get into, there is a tendency to avoid any research in favour of just seeing how it works out. Even minimal research, though, could save you a great deal of time and effort if the MLM venture you are considering is less than it promises.

pyramid selling Illegal forms of multi-level marketing involving participants buying the right to recruit salespeople and being forced to buy unreasonable amounts of inventory.

Memory Check 7.4
True or False? Petro-Canada uses dealership franchising to distribute its products.

Business Reality 7.1 Guardian Security
A Franchise "Authorized" to Run Its Own Show

Guardian Security is centred in Mount Pearl, Newfoundland. Owner Rodney England started the company in 1998, working by himself selling alarm systems and monitoring services to homes and businesses as an ADT dealer. Within four years he had built the firm to more than 80 employees, and since then he has been carefully following his own plan for expansion.

Authorized dealerships or distributorships tend to be at the lower end of the franchise spectrum in terms of franchisor control. Typically, the dealer will contract with a manufacturer for training and the rights to sell and service a product. The authorized dealer sells and installs the product to the standards prescribed by the manufacturer, but otherwise dealers run their company as they see fit. In the case of Guardian, it sells ADT security equipment and ADT monitoring services, but in addition it offers security guards, surveillance, secret shoppers, closed-circuit TV, patrols, anti-bugging, bodyguard services, and many other types of security products and services.

This industry has grown dramatically over the past few years, partly because of technical innovation reducing security system costs. As well, there has been increased legislation for things like smoke and natural gas detectors, and an aging, more vulnerable but wealthier population that can afford such services. These conditions plus Rodney England's own strategic approach to growth have produced Guardian's rapid expansion. According to Rodney, the first expansion priority now is to "grow geographically because we can just reproduce a system we've got down pat." Following this approach, he opened branches in Grand Falls and Corner Brook. Visit the company website at www.guardian-security.com.

Business Format Sometimes called full-business format, or entire business format, this is the most common form of franchising. Usually targeting consumer markets, this type of contract has the franchisor prescribing, in great detail, the marketing and operational procedures of all franchisees to the point where, to the customer, each outlet seems virtually identical. Even within **business format franchising**, however, there are many possible variations of the franchise agreement. Some examples are:

■ *Single-unit franchise.* This is the simplest franchise arrangement, where the franchisee operates a single outlet or provides service to a defined geographic area. For example, you could have a lawn maintenance franchise and operate several trucks from a single garage within one particular suburban territory.

■ *Multi-unit franchise.* This is where a single franchisee purchases more than one franchise site or territory from the same franchisor. This situation may arise when a successful franchisee is given the opportunity to buy additional sites or territories as they become available. In some cases, additional franchises could be planned for in the original franchise contract. For example, you could buy a photo shop franchise in a fast-growing suburban area. You know that a new mall is planned for several years in the future a few kilometres from your shop. So, your franchise contract gives you the right of first refusal on buying any franchise that the franchisor grants in this mall, or even any area adjacent to your territory. Some franchisors encourage multi-unit deals because they give expansion opportunities to franchisees, producing greater commitment to the franchisor.[3] As well, it can reduce training costs and minimize conflict among adjoining franchisees.

■ *Multi-brand franchise.* As franchisors have become bigger and bigger corporate entities, there has been a tendency toward takeovers of complementary franchise companies. For example, at the time of writing, Yum Brands! Inc. owns the Pizza Hut, KFC, and Taco Bell brands. So, if you were looking to buy a fast-food franchise for a tourist gas-stop, Yum may be willing to sell more than one franchise brand to you, a single franchisee.

■ *Territory franchise.* For this type of contract, the franchisee buys the rights to service a geographic area with the franchisor's products or services. The franchisee has the responsibility to open as many outlets, or hire as many service people, as the territory requires.

■ *Master franchise.* In this arrangement, the master franchisee buys the right to sell franchises to others within a given territory. Commonly, the master franchisee provides the training, support, and administration for the individual franchisees. This set-up works well for American franchisors, which can sell a master franchise for all of Canada or for specific regions. The Canadian master franchise can then modify the marketing and operational approaches of the American franchisor to fit the Canadian market or regional markets.

⭐ Head Start Exercise

7.1 Identify the franchisor and briefly describe the format of the franchising system you will be buying into (1/3 page maximum). Note: Students who are using the Head Start Exercises as class assignments will each have to interview an individual franchisee whose business will be used as an example for the exercise assignments in this chapter.

Legal Issues

Compared to the United States (which has strict federal legislation as well as some state laws), franchising in Canada has been very poorly regulated. At the time of writing, only Alberta, New Brunswick, Ontario, Prince Edward Island, and Manitoba have laws that

business format franchising
Buying a complete method of doing business under the trade name of, and with the products and systems of, the franchisor.

❓ **Get Help 7.1**
For information about MLM and other business practices, visit Canada's Competition Bureau website at www.competitionbureau.gc.ca.

✅ **Memory Check 7.5**
True or False? A significant majority of direct sellers in multi-level marketing eventually become wealthy.

✅ **Memory Check 7.6**
True or False? Pyramid selling is an outlawed activity.

✅ **Memory Check 7.7**
True or False? Wendy's uses business format franchising.

specifically regulate the sale of franchises, and legislation is being prepared in some other provinces. The Canadian Franchise Association, an organization of franchisors, does have a code of ethics that its members agree to follow. The major provisions of the code are:

- freedom for franchisees to form and join associations that promote their own interests

- reasonable training and management support of franchisees

- reasonable notice of, and opportunity to correct, any franchisee **defaults** on franchise agreements

- reasonable effort to solve complaints from or disputes with franchisees

- encouraging prospective franchisees to contact existing franchisees for research purposes

- full disclosure to the franchisee of all relevant information about the franchisor (including past and present **litigation**), and about the franchise agreement, within a reasonable length of time before the franchisee has to make a binding commitment

It is this last item, **disclosure**, that forms the key provision of the existing franchise laws. Without this, you could find yourself signing a franchise agreement with someone who has past convictions for defrauding franchisees. Or you could find out too late that most of the franchises sold by the company have failed. If you are in an area where there is no franchise legislation, you can still request that the franchisor supply you with all of the disclosure information that would otherwise be required. A refusal, naturally, should give you second thoughts about the franchisor. Be careful about relying on franchisor disclosure as a means of protecting yourself as a franchisee. Just because a franchisor is willing to disclose something about the company or the agreement does not render it harmless. In fact, disclosure can work in favour of an unscrupulous franchisor. That's because the franchisor, once having disclosed something in writing, cannot be accused of having misled the franchisee in that area. In this sense, disclosure requirements put the responsibility for protecting yourself as a franchisee squarely on your shoulders.

Buying a franchise in Quebec is subject to provincial language legislation: the Charter of the French Language. This means that the franchisor must be willing to prepare the franchise agreement in French. It may also require the translation of operations manuals and training and promotional materials. Signage must be either French or bilingual, with French clearly predominating. The province's Civil Code, based on the French system of law, may also require some revision of the franchise agreement's content to meet the Code's standards for clarity. For franchisors that operate on a nationwide basis, an even greater flexibility of language options may be required for New Brunswick and parts of Ontario, where there are large bilingual areas. If your franchisor is new to these areas, your negotiations with the franchisor may have to involve educating the franchisor on the cultural issues of the country.

The federal Competition Act can affect franchise operations across the whole country, especially in the area of price setting.[4] For example, if you own a motorcycle dealership, the franchisor can advertise a manufacturer's suggested retail price for each model of new bike you carry. But the franchisor cannot dictate to you a minimum selling price for any product, as this would inhibit competition. Franchises do, however, have many exemptions from the Competition Act because of the relationship between the franchisor and the franchisee. For example, Tim Hortons may run a national campaign advertising strawberry doughnuts at a particular price with every franchisee expected to use that price. This would not be a violation of the act because there is no significant impairment of competition—there are still lots of competing franchises where you can get doughnuts.

The contract, or Franchise Agreement, governs the relationship between the franchisor and the franchisee. Thus, the relationship is subject to the great body of contract law that has evolved, including various **precedents** resulting from past cases between franchisors and franchisees. But this murky area of the law is complex and expensive to

default Failing to fulfill the terms of an agreement.

litigation Being involved in a lawsuit, either suing or being sued.

disclosure The revealing of confidential information.

✅ **Memory Check 7.8**
True or False? A master franchise provides the right to sell franchises to others within a given area.

✅ **Memory Check 7.9**
True or False? When the same franchisee owns both a Harvey's and a Swiss Chalet at the same site, this is an example of multi-unit franchising.

❓ **Get Help 7.2**
The full Code of Ethics of the Canadian Franchise Association is available on its website at www.cfa.ca. You can also use this site to check whether a particular franchisor is a member in good standing of the association.

✅ **Memory Check 7.10**
True or False? Canada tends to have stricter franchising regulations than most of the United States.

precedent A decision by a court that will set the pattern for subsequent decisions on similar matters.

Get Help 7.3
You can see the disclosure document requirements for the Alberta Franchises Act on the website for the Alberta Queen's Printer at www.qp.gov.ab.ca. Search for Franchises Regulation.

Get Help 7.4
Some of the provincial and territorial law societies have lawyer referral services that you can access by telephone to get the names of lawyers in your area identified by specialty. Try the white pages of the phone book under "Law Society." As well, you may try the website for Canadian lawyer referrals: www.canlaw.com.

brand The name of a company or a trademark-protected word that identifies the company and that creates a specific image in the minds of consumers.

Memory Check 7.11
True or False? Members of the Canadian Franchise Association are franchisors.

Memory Check 7.12
True or False? Canadian federal regulations require franchisors to disclose all past litigation.

turn-key (also turnkey or turn key) Operations that are ready to go, with all set-up and preparation completed. You just "turn the key" and it goes.

pursue, especially when litigating against the deeper pockets of an established franchisor. To avoid going to court, get the help of an experienced franchise lawyer before you sign an agreement. Because of the growth in franchising and the increasing legal complexity, many lawyers have decided to specialize in this area. This becomes obvious when you use your search engine to seek any topic related to franchising; a large number of the results will be from law offices.

Head Start Exercise

7.2 Describe the level of disclosure your franchisor is committed to, either by legislation or code (1/4 page maximum).

IS FRANCHISING RIGHT FOR ME?
Merits of Franchising

Buying a franchise from an established, growing, and ethical franchisor can have a great many benefits that add up to reduced risk and potentially higher returns for your new business. These advantages come from

- *Marketing research.* Well-run franchisor operations spend a significant amount of their revenue on marketing research, both at the national level (for developing corporate strategy) and at the individual site level. As a potential franchisee, the research relating to your future location/site can be critical to your success. This is especially true for retail and consumer service businesses.

- *Brand strategy.* Established franchisors have developed in the minds of potential customers clear images of their company **brands**.[5] For example, most urban Canadians would easily be able to rank, in order of expense, the cost of a chicken dinner at KFC, Swiss Chalet, or the Keg. *Ask yourself: How do they rank?* Part of this strategy is the careful selection and targeting of market segments and a diligent monitoring of competitors' strategies.

- *Existing customers.* If you buy a franchise from an established national or regional franchisor, the day your franchise opens, you have existing customers. They have never actually bought anything from you, but they already see themselves as your customers and you didn't have to win them. This won't be the case, for example, if you open a brand-new independent coffee shop. Prospective customers will have lots of reasons to hesitate before buying from you: "Will the coffee taste okay?" "Is it clean inside?" "Is it expensive?" But if you open a Tim Hortons franchise, there is no such hesitation. And these existing customers mean that you are creating cash flow as soon as you open.

- *Training.* Some of the more sophisticated franchisors have their own training institutions, with various certificate and diploma programs for franchisees and their staff. Some manufacturing franchisors have long-term in-factory training programs for the franchisee's technicians. But generally, franchisors offer short, intensive training programs, for the franchisee only, running from one to six weeks, with the average at around three weeks. Additionally, there may be some on-site assistance to train new staff for start-up of the franchise.

- *Complete package.* Many franchisors advertise that they are selling **turn-key** packages, because a new franchise can be up and fully running in mere weeks. This also implies that the franchisor has determined the best way of doing things for the industry and worked out the bugs in the system. The efficient systems of the franchisor, especially in a business format franchise, provide much of the franchise's value. And a top-quality franchisor is constantly working to further refine these systems.

- *Advertising power.* Advertising may be the single biggest advantage of buying a franchise over owning an independent business. If you open your own independent sandwich shop, you may decide to set aside, say, 3 percent of your sales for advertising. For this amount you could perhaps run a weekly ad (one you wrote yourself) in your community newspaper. But if you had a Mr. Sub franchise, your 3 percent advertising fee would be combined with the 3 percent from each of the other Mr. Sub franchises. This would produce an advertising campaign that was not only quantitatively superior (a national multimedia campaign) but also qualitatively superior (written by professionals from a top agency). Knowing the importance of this advertising power has caused many franchisors to divide the royalties they charge into two distinct components: a general royalty and a separate advertising fee intended strictly for this purpose.[6]

✅ **Memory Check 7.13**
True or False? A legal precedent is a court decision that sets the pattern for similar cases in the future.

✅ **Memory Check 7.14**
True or False? A franchisor of tractor equipment may not dictate minimum selling prices to franchisees.

Drawbacks

For some, the drawbacks of being a franchisee outweigh the potential benefits. Because the franchisor holds the power in the franchise relationship, the benefits depend to a great extent on the ethical practices of the particular franchisor. Even with an excellent franchisor, however, there are some general drawbacks to buying a franchise:

- *Franchise fee.* This is a major start-up cost for which you do not get any tangible assets. One way of thinking of this fee is as a prepaid expense (prepaid for the entire duration of the contract) for renting the intellectual property of the franchisor.

- *Franchisor control.* Depending on the franchise agreement, the franchisee can have less decision-making authority than a mid-level manager in a large organization. In some cases, the franchisor can even limit the profit potential for a franchisee through things like changing supply prices, opening adjacent franchise territories, and raising lease prices for property and equipment. Thus, two of the great advantages of entrepreneurship are removed: the independence of being your own boss and the potential for unlimited profit. Despite this, one study of American restaurant franchises indicated that tight franchisor control policies helped reduce the failure rate of franchises.[7]

- *Royalties.* These must continuously be paid regardless of whether the franchisor re-invests any portion of this money in the development and promotion of the organization. Furthermore, there is some evidence that higher royalty fees increase the likelihood of franchise failure.[8]

- *Advertising.* A separate advertising fee can sometimes give a franchisee a false sense of security in the belief that this money is being spent on effective advertising. For example, most of the money could be spent advertising for new franchisees as opposed to advertising for customers who will bring revenue to you.

- *Lack of goodwill equity.* When an independent entrepreneur works to build a business, there is the satisfaction of knowing that the business is increasing in value beyond the mere book value. That extra value, the value of the business's goodwill, will be realized in cash when the business is sold. At the end of many franchise contracts, however, the goodwill that the franchisee has worked to build accrues entirely to the franchisor, unless there is a specific buy-back condition stating otherwise.

Personal Requirements

Ask yourself: What are the skills needed by a franchisee? Each of the different start-up methods has its own average risk, going from highest risk in starting a brand-new business to lowest in buying a franchise. So, too, each method has its own requirements in terms of business skills. Starting a whole new business requires mostly entrepreneurial skills like innovation,

Figure 7.1 Business Skills Continuum

Entrepreneurial Skills   Management Skills

⟵───⟶

Start Brand New   Buy Existing   Buy Franchise

motivation, and negotiation. Being a franchisee, on the other hand, requires mostly management skills, like organization, planning, and supervision. Logically, the requirements of buying an existing independent business would be somewhere in between these two, as shown in Figure 7.1.

Remember that you are not the only one to decide whether you and franchising are suitable for each other. Some franchisors have specific requirements in terms of skills, experience, and personality. Occasionally, a franchisor may ask you to take some kind of formal test, but most often your suitability will be evaluated based on your résumé and the formal and informal interviews you have with managers from the franchisor. A stable financial history, good communication skills, and a mature, patient, conformist personality can all score points with franchisors.[9] Management experience, ambition, and dedication are also important characteristics that franchisors look for in potential franchisees. But still, the most important issue is: Do you have the money?

For a more complete discussion of entrepreneurial characteristics, see "The Entrepreneurial Personality" in Chapter 1.

⭐ Head Start Exercise

7.3 Explain why buying this franchise is a good route to business ownership for you personally (1/3 page maximum).

HOW DO I CHOOSE A FRANCHISE?

The Process

Checking out franchise magazines, franchise shows, and websites, or talking with an existing franchisee, are common preliminary sources of information for anyone thinking of buying a franchise. But finding a franchise that is suitable for you is a much more difficult task than you would expect. It's not like buying a car, where if you want one with low fuel consumption you can, within minutes, find data to compare the gas mileage of every model of car for sale in Canada. In another few minutes, you can compare every car available for its warranty terms, and so on. Not so with franchises. There is lots of information about franchises for sale, but it is confusing and difficult to compare, partly because of the way franchises are promoted. Publishers gather information from franchisors using surveys where the franchisors report their own information. Different franchisors use different definitions of the reporting terms, so it becomes difficult to compare franchises based on published information. Here, for instance, are some commonly used terms that can be misleading:

- *Minimum investment.* Sometimes this term refers to the entire start-up cost of the cheapest franchise sold by that franchisor. Sometimes it refers to the amount of cash that the franchisee has to put up before being able to finance the rest of the costs.

- *Initial franchise fee.* In some cases this refers to the entire franchise fee for the entire term of the franchise. In others it is an initial payment with the rest due on closing the franchise agreement, or at some other time.

Memory Check 7.15
True or False? The ability to be innovative is an important characteristic for a franchisee.

Memory Check 7.16
True or False? It requires more entrepreneurial skill to take over an existing business than to operate a franchise.

- *Required capital.* Normally this refers to the minimum amount of unencumbered cash that a franchisee must have to invest in the franchise. Occasionally, it refers to the net worth of the franchisee.

The difficulty in getting clear information from franchise websites, publications, or even from a visit to a booth at a franchise show may well discourage some potential franchisees, since these are common first steps on the road to buying a franchise. If you are not discouraged, you may take the next step and request more information from franchisors, which will generally send you information kits and sometimes follow up with personal contact from sales representatives. This begins a series of contacts, each of which is designed to reveal a little more information about the franchisor while at the same time qualifying you as a potential franchisee as quickly as possible.

The information kit will likely tell you about the minimum financial and other requirements of the franchisor. It may also contain an application form, similar to a job application, but one that asks for your personal financial information—like a credit application. This approach can save the franchisor from wasting time on you if you are not qualified. But it also elicits some commitment from you on the basis of very little information from the franchisor. Your application could trigger several meetings with one or more representatives of the franchisor, serving as combination selection interviews and sales presentations, but without ever giving you the details of the franchise agreement.

During these meetings you may be asked to sign a non-disclosure agreement relating to any information you get from the franchisor or any franchisees you may interview. But before the franchisor actually gives you detailed financial information, any legally required disclosure information, or a copy of the franchise agreement, you may have to sign a conditional offer to purchase a franchise and pay a deposit. This offer is made conditional on the details of the franchise agreement being acceptable to you. Only then are you and your lawyer permitted to analyze (usually under time constraint) the details of the franchise agreement. If the agreement is acceptable, or if it can be negotiated to the point where it is acceptable, you will pay the rest of the franchise fee and set a closing date for the agreement. Then you must set up the franchisee company in a way that is compliant with the agreement.

In choosing a legal form for your franchisee company, all of the same considerations apply as for an independent new business. Because the business is a franchise, however, there may be some additional arguments for incorporation. This would be the case if you wished to protect personal assets that may be put at risk through franchisor policies. For example, you might own a fitness club franchise where one of your clients has been injured using a piece of exercise equipment and is suing for damages. It could be that the equipment was specified and supplied by the franchisor and that you maintained and supervised the equipment exactly as the franchisor trained you and specified in operations manuals. Nevertheless, you (and probably the franchisor as well) are being sued and, without incorporation, your personal assets could be at risk.

Assessing the Franchisor

Franchise magazines, which you can get in most bookstores, are a source of some basic information for contacting franchisors. But remember that these are essentially advertising vehicles for the franchisors. They are mainly published by franchise associations, which are trying to promote franchising in general as well as their individual members. So you will find mostly good news franchising stories—not exposés of franchisee abuse or editorials about high-handed franchisors. When it comes to assessing a franchisor, however, the best source is existing franchisees.[10] The checklist in Table 7.1 identifies the major areas you need to look at.

⭐ Head Start Exercise

7.4 Briefly describe the history of the franchisor you will be dealing with (1/3 page maximum).

❓ **Get Help 7.5**
For links to and lists of franchises for sale in Canada, try *Canadian Business Franchise* magazine at www.franchiseinfo.ca.

✅ **Memory Check 7.17**
True or false? The loss of unencumbered cash will not cause you to go bankrupt.

✅ **Memory Check 7.18**
True or False? It is relatively easy for the average student to find out the terms of a franchise agreement.

❓ **Get Help 7.6**
So You Want to Buy a Franchise, by Douglas Gray and Norman Friend, is an excellent book with detailed lists of questions for evaluating a franchise. It is published by McGraw-Hill Ryerson and is out of print but available in libraries.

Table 7.1 Franchisor Assessment Checklist/Notes

✓	Factor	Description	Potential for Improvement
	BUSINESS BACKGROUND		
	Clearly defined products/services		
	Clearly defined market segments		
	Growing market potential		
	Accurately estimated market share		
	History of consistent growth		
	History of franchisee success		
	History of litigation		
	History of accurate sales forecasting		
	Clearly identified competitors		
	Intellectual property protection		
	MARKETING		
	Appropriate image for target market		
	Brand recognition		
	Appropriate product/service mix		
	Appropriate pricing strategy		
	Effective distribution/delivery		
	Appropriate promotion methods		
	Effective advertising techniques		
	Effective sales approaches		
	OPERATIONS		
	Efficient space use in franchises		
	Efficient ordering system		
	Effective quality control systems		
	Appropriate record keeping systems/software		
	Effective management policies		
	Beneficial association memberships		
	FINANCES		
	Up-to-date financial statements		
	Healthy key ratios		
	Healthy relationship with creditors		
	Financial assistance program for franchisees		
	FRANCHISE ISSUES		
	Appropriate franchise fee		
	Appropriate royalty fees		
	Appropriate advertising fees/controls		
	Acceptable sales/information approach		
	Acceptable involvement of advisers		
	Positive feedback from franchisees		

Assessing the Opportunity

In addition to the general merit of the franchisor, the particular opportunity available to buy a franchise outlet or territory must also be assessed. This basically means conducting the feasibility analysis that makes up Section 2 of the business plan. This will include any marketing research information supplied by the franchisor on location and site. As the franchisee, you will be responsible to review and verify the franchisor's information and, if necessary, conduct your own research. Generally, you will look at

- *The location.* This includes population size, trends, and wealth, as well as issues of transportation and competition.

- *The site.* Access, visibility, parking, surrounding businesses, and building condition are all elements of the site analysis.

- *The market potential.* If the franchisor does not have an estimate of market potential for the specific territory or **drawing area** of the franchise, it may be estimated from other data supplied by the franchisor.

drawing area The physical location in which most of the customers of a business live or work.

- *The sales forecast.* Your main objective is to produce a reliable sales forecast and accurate projection of expenses. This will enable you to calculate the expected earnings for the franchise. The franchisor will likely offer you information on average sales and profits for franchises, but this information cannot be relied on to predict sales for your new franchise. For example, the average may be skewed by a very few outlets with exceptional sites. Or, the average may include franchisor-owned outlets whose management expenses are charged to the overall franchisor overhead, thus inflating the profitability of the outlet. Instead, you must try to get copies of actual financial statements for a sample of existing franchises that are as similar to yours as possible. Then you can make your predictions by performing correlations of sales, expenses, and net profit. For example, you could calculate the square footage of your proposed site and multiply it by the average sales per square foot of your sample to give you an estimate of sales. You could also estimate the total value of assets in your new site and multiply that value by the ratio of profit to assets calculated for the sample.

Get Help 7.7
The case for getting professional accounting help is very strong, not just because of the importance of the calculations but also because of the time restrictions for making a final decision that the franchisor will likely impose.

Only with these types of calculations will you be able to make an accurate estimate of the future earnings for the franchise. Then you can use that estimate to calculate the return on investment (ROI) that the business will provide. In this case, the likely ROI calculation will be

$$ROI = \frac{Projected\ Annual\ Net\ Profit}{Total\ Equity\ Investment}$$

Remember that the higher the risk and the lower the liquidity of an investment, the higher the return you should expect. Compared to other start-up methods, franchising tends to be lower risk, but your investment is far from liquid. You can get your money out only by selling the franchise, and this process is likely to be highly restricted by the contract. Remember also that if you are comparing different possible franchises, there is more than a single type of ROI calculation that you can use for comparison.

Head Start Exercises

7.5 Briefly summarize the kind of data that you expect to get from the franchisor, which will help you to calculate your sales forecast (1/3 page maximum).

7.6 Briefly identify what you would consider to be an acceptable rate of return on equity for investing in this franchise. Give reasons (1/3 page maximum).

Buying an Existing Franchise

Memory Check 7.19
True or False? Buying a franchise is an investment with low liquidity.

This special case is a combination of buying an existing business and buying a franchise. Because of this, you should use both Table 6.1, the checklist for assessing an independent business, and Table 7.1, the checklist for assessing the franchisor.

The legal complexity in a case like this can be very high since you may be dealing with an agreement to purchase from the current owner, as well as the franchise agreement. As in buying any existing business, the key question is: Why is the business for sale?

There are lots of potentially valid reasons for selling a franchise, but each one of them should give you at least a second thought:

Memory Check 7.20
True or False? Buying an existing franchise has greater legal complexity than buying a new franchise.

- The franchisor is forcing the sale because of poor management on the part of the current franchisee. If you are an experienced manager, this could be an opportunity for you to buy the franchise cheaply and turn it around. But, *ask yourself: Is this a case of an overly demanding franchisor that strictly enforces a tough contract?*

- The current franchisee is a partnership and one of the partners wants to get out, while the other will stay with you as the new partner. If the business is profitable, having a partner who knows the ropes could be to your advantage. But, *ask yourself: Is this a case of a partner who is difficult to get along with?*

- The franchise was started as a franchisor-owned outlet but the franchisor is in an expansion phase and selling off company-owned units. This could be an advantage since the unit is already up and running with a financial history. But, *ask yourself: Does this mean that there is more money in selling franchises than in running them profitably? What does this say about future franchise support?*

- The franchise agreement is up for renewal but the owner is retiring. This could be an opportunity to get the franchise for the remainder of the contract period at a lower price than you would have to pay for a new franchise. But, *ask yourself: Why is the franchisor not buying back the remainder of the contract and selling a full-term franchise? Are the facilities old and worn?*

There are plenty of legitimate reasons for selling and buying an existing franchise, but there are also reasons that spell trouble. Thorough research is your best hope for ensuring a good deal.

HOW CAN I FINANCE A FRANCHISE?

Financial Requirements

For a rough idea of the kind of franchise you might be able to afford, take a look at Figure 7.2. The "minimum cash equity" column shows how much debt-free cash you must personally have available in order to buy a franchise in each category. Of course, any lenders financing the rest of the franchise cost will have their own creditworthiness and security criteria. In addition, some franchisors require a certain minimum net worth that is in excess of the unencumbered cash investment you can make. This is the franchisor's own measure of financial stability. It can indicate how well you will be able to survive a temporary downturn in the industry or whether you might be able to afford future expansion of the franchise.

Get Help 7.8
Check the CIBC website (www.cibc.com). Use the search tool for National Franchise to locate a CIBC franchise specialist or links to other franchise information.

Sources of Finance

For many franchisors, new franchisees are strictly a source of cash (franchise fees plus the sale of equipment and inventory) and the franchisees are left to arrange their own financing. However, it is becoming more common that business format franchisors pre-arrange a financing package with a major lending institution.[11] The lender has already completed a risk analysis on the typical franchise and has a predetermined lending formula that can be quickly applied

Fun and Profit in Feeding Hungry Students

When Tao Jiang and his wife, Xin Yu Wang, came to Canada from China, Tao spent his first year here as a full-time college student in an information technology program. He abandoned school to work full-time, and eventually he and Xin Yu ended up working in Subway franchises, which both enjoyed. The challenge soon became to get one of their own. The couple worked in Subways for five years and along the way looked at other franchise options, but settled on Subway partly because of the expertise they already had. The other reason was their belief that compared to the competition, the firm offered a superior product in terms of freshness and choice.

In 2004, Tao and Xin Yu approached the Subway head office and were offered a chance to take over an existing franchise that had been in operation for 14 years. The location was between a college campus and a high school in an area of lower-middle-class medium-density population. The site was in a small strip plaza on a busy street with both on-street parking and a lot in front. Tao and Xin Yu were impressed and signed a 20-year franchise contract. Financing was a combination of the couple's own savings, a loan from Tao's sister, and a bank loan.

Typical of fast-food franchises, the franchisor leases the unit and sub-leases it to the franchisees, technically the numbered corporation owned by Tao and Xin Yu. As expected, the majority of customers are students (big sub eaters), creating a slow summer season for the business. But there has proven to be enough midday traffic (lunch is the busiest time for the chain) even when the schools are closed. The couple are pleased with the performance of the franchisor, even though there are constraints of the franchise contract (a handy ATM cannot be added to the store). Tao strongly feels that advertising power gives a huge advantage to franchises over independent sub shops. Tao's advice to those thinking of entrepreneurship is to "do something you enjoy because you spend so many hours in it." To explore Subway's information on franchises, go to www.subway.ca and click on Franchise Opportunities.

Figure 7.2 Typical Ranges of Canadian Franchise Costs

Category	Minimum Cash Equity[1]	Total Start-Up Costs[2]	Franchise Fee
Home cleaning services	$15 000–30 000	$20 000–90 000	$12 000–20 000
Lawn maintenance services (including fertilizer and weed spray)	$20 000–40 000	$35 000–100 000	$15 000–30 000
Hair and beauty services	$20 000–50 000	$35 000–140 000	$7500–25 000
Small fast-food restaurants (under 35 seating capacity)	$45 000–100 000	$125 000–250 000	$15 000–50 000
Automotive specialty services (e.g., muffler, transmission, lube)	$50 000–125 000	$150 000–275 000	$25 000–50 000
Large fast-food restaurants (over 75 seating capacity)	$150 000–350 000	$150 000–1 000 000	$45 000–55 000
Full-service restaurants (licensed dining rooms)	$200 000–800 000	$600 000–2 500 000	$40 000–75 000
Small commercial hotels (under 75 rooms)[3]	$600 000–900 000	$2 000 000–3 000 000	$35 000–60 000

1. The minimum amount of unencumbered cash that the franchisee must have available to invest in the franchise.
2. Not including real estate, unless franchisee ownership of the building is required by the franchisor.
3. Assumes building a new facility.

to individual franchisees. The Royal Bank has developed a specific program for this, realizing that the bank can also reap the benefit of providing other banking services to franchisees. The bank has designated a team of franchise specialists, with training and experience in this area, who also make referrals to lawyers and accountants specializing in franchised businesses.

Another area where franchisors may help with financing is inventory. For example, if you have a gasoline dealership, the franchisor will provide you with the gasoline, which is paid for only as it is used. Because of the volatility in retail prices of gas, this is generally necessary for franchisees since a major price drop could have serious financial consequences. (On the other hand, any windfall profit from a price increase will go to the franchisor.)

Somewhat similar arrangements, called **floor plan financing**, are often available for larger manufactured products. For example, if you are a franchised dealer of recreational products, such as snowmobiles or personal watercraft, chances are that your franchisor has set up a private finance company that lends you the money to buy this expensive inventory. You will pay interest on each vehicle in your inventory from the day you receive delivery until the day you sell it. **Title** to each vehicle, however, will remain in the name of the franchisor until the day you sell it to your customer. Title is transferred to you and then your customer on the same day. The advantage of this arrangement to the franchisor is that if your franchise goes bankrupt, the franchisor is not at risk of losing the inventory.

For franchisees arranging their own financing, all the sources that might be pursued for starting a brand-new business can also be accessed to finance the purchase of a franchise. The franchisor, however, may have some restrictions on, or have to be involved with, some of these sources:

- *Personal sources.* Money borrowed from family and friends—love money—is sometimes easy to access on an informal basis. The franchisor, however, may have some restrictions on how much money you can borrow to buy the franchise, stipulating a maximum debt-to-equity ratio.

- *Government programs.* Government programs typically do not differentiate between franchised or independent small businesses. There are a few exceptions, such as some franchise restrictions on student business loans from the Business Development Bank of Canada.

- *Banks.* Before lending you money to buy a franchise, banks may require information about average franchise performance that you have agreed to keep confidential, so the franchisor will have to agree to the release of this information. As well, a bank loan may have requirements that in the case of your franchise's failure the bank has first priority on the assets of the franchise. This may contradict your franchise agreement and so will also require the permission of the franchisor.

- *Investors.* Bringing in partners or investors will require a partnership or shareholder agreement that will likely need the approval of the franchisor for a variety of reasons. For example, your franchise agreement might require the appointment of a single individual from the franchisee company as the responsible party for the franchise. At the same time, your shareholder agreement might have a buy/sell clause, which allows another partner to take over in case of the death of the first. This means that the franchisor would have to pre-approve all partners as potential replacements for the designated responsible party. Similarly, the franchisor would likely wish to restrict the bringing in of future partners without the franchisor's approval.

(For a more complete discussion of start-up capital, see Chapter 5, "Where Will I Get the Money?").

⭐ Head Start Exercise

7.7 Briefly outline your sources of finance to buy the franchise (1/4 page maximum).

Sidebar

✅ **Memory Check 7.21**
True or False? It requires about $40 000 personal net worth to purchase a McDonald's franchise.

floor plan financing A technique of lending money to a retailer for purposes of buying inventory, where title to the inventory remains with the supplier.

title Registered or legal ownership.

✅ **Memory Check 7.22**
True or False? Government lending programs generally treat franchises differently from independent small businesses.

WHAT ARE THE CONTRACT ISSUES?

Lawyers working on behalf of the franchisor prepare the franchise agreement to ensure that every sentence of every paragraph benefits and protects the franchisor. As a result, the contract emphasizes the responsibilities of the franchisee but gives all the authority to the franchisor; even to the extent that the franchisor can often unilaterally change the contract merely by amending its operations manual. For an established successful franchisor, there will be little willingness to negotiate the terms of the franchise. So, as a potential franchisee, your interest in the contract is to

1. make sure that you understand the implications for each of its provisions, and
2. decide whether or not you are willing to accept those conditions.

Territory and Site Issues

If the contract provides a protected territory, the contract should also include a map, or detailed description, clearly showing the geographic boundaries where you will have exclusive rights. Ideally, you would also like to have adjoining territories indicated and, if they are undeveloped, the right of first refusal for opening new franchises in them. Also, when the adjoining territories are undeveloped, some identification of the point at which they could be opened (e.g., when the population reaches a certain number, or when your sales surpass a certain level) would help to protect your franchise.

Some franchisors like to be, and some insist on being, the landlords for their franchisees. This means that the franchisor either owns the property where the franchise is to be situated or leases it and then sub-leases to the franchisee. The logic behind this approach is that it allows the franchisor to ensure that the site will remain available throughout the life expectancy of the franchise and that a third-party landlord will not be able to endanger the viability of the franchise through operating restrictions or unsupportable rent increases. If your landlord is your franchisor, however, you will have to ensure that the terms and conditions of your lease match those of the franchise agreement. If they don't match, it could give the franchisor the right to take an increased share of your profit. For example, if you have a 10-year franchise term and a 5-year lease, when it comes time to renew your lease the franchisor could raise your rent by an amount equal to the majority of your profits.

If your landlord is a company or individual other than your franchisor, the lease terms will probably require the approval of the franchisor. This is partly to ensure that your lease does not give your landlord the right to dictate your operating hours or other aspects of your business that may put you in violation of your franchisor's policies. But the franchisor will be primarily reviewing the lease with regard to specific rights (e.g., entry onto the premises) for the franchisor. You will have to check the lease to protect yourself and your franchise. For example, you must be careful of how the terms for renewal of your lease are written. Let's say you have a 10-year lease with a 5-year renewal option in order to match the 15-year term of your franchise. You could notify the landlord that you are exercising the option to renew, expecting a modest increase in rent. The landlord, however, may advise you that there will be a 100 percent increase in your rent. If you cannot negotiate an agreement on the new rent, depending on how the renewal conditions are written, you may have to go to arbitration. If the landlord can present a case for increased costs, you may end up with a rent far more than you can afford. It would be better to have a renewal option that is geared to the increased sales of the franchise.

> **✓ Memory Check 7.23**
> True or False? Franchise contracts tend to be written in favour of the franchisor.

> **✓ Memory Check 7.24**
> True or False? Major franchisors tend to be very willing to negotiate the terms of their franchise contracts.

Supply and Inventory Issues

Items in the franchise agreement may require you to buy certain supplies or products from the franchisor exclusively. This should be fine with you as long as there is assurance that

Memory Check 7.25
True or False? A franchisor will want the right of approval for a franchisee's lease agreement with an independent landlord.

Get Help 7.9
An excellent book on franchising, which contains a good sample franchise contract, is *Franchising in Canada: Pros and Cons* by Michael M. Coltman. Older editions published by the Self-Counsel Press may be available at the library. A current edition is published (but not widely distributed) by the Parkland Community Futures Development Corporation in Manitoba (www .communityfuturesparkland.ca).

you will get the supplies at some reasonable market value or better. A provision allowing you to use other sources of supply (as long as the quality is acceptable to the franchisor) should be included.

The contract may also give the franchisor the right to set minimum inventory levels for certain products and supplies. You must ensure that this cannot be done arbitrarily or merely to improve the franchisor's cash flow. Rather, the contract provision must specify that all inventory levels must be set for reasonable turnover rates for the industry. Let's say, for example, that you own a chicken wing franchise where the franchisor requires you to maintain an inventory of 100 kilograms of frozen wings at all times. If neither you nor any of the other franchisees have ever run out of wings, but the franchisor nevertheless increases the inventory requirements to 200 kilograms, this would be considered unreasonable.

Note that the real test for the reasonableness of a contract provision is how important you think it is for being used against other franchisees (ones who are less competent and ethical than you). If you think a provision could stop some other franchisee from endangering the image of the franchise, then it is probably reasonable.

Renewal and Termination Issues The carrot and stick combination that the franchisor uses to control the franchisees is the hope for renewal of the contract (by being in good standing) and the fear of termination from being in default of the provisions of the contract. The conditions of renewal should be spelled out in the initial contract, although it may not be under the same conditions as the original contract. For example, the renewal period may be shorter than the original contract, or you may be required to sign any new standard agreement that the franchisor has adopted since the original contract.

The franchisor will likely have the right to terminate the franchise if you are in default of the contract or for other good cause. The agreement will give the franchisor the right to inspect your franchise to ensure compliance with the contract, which will include all of the regulations in the operations manual. The contract should allow you a reasonable amount of time to correct any deficiencies that the franchisor has found and given you notification of. However, the franchisor would have the right to terminate the contract without notice for some gross act of negligence, fraud, bankruptcy, or anything else that would fall under the heading of good cause.

Ideally, you would like to have a provision that when the agreement is terminated—or runs out and is not renewed—you will be compensated not just for the value of the business assets but for the increased value of the business due to its growth. So if the franchisor sells the business, or takes it over as a company-owned outlet, you will still be compensated for your work in developing the business.

Training and Assistance Issues The nature and duration of training should be specified in the contract. Otherwise, you may find out that the training consists of letting you work, without pay, at another franchise or company-owned outlet for several weeks. True training should be active in nature with a specific training plan. The contract should specify if there are any additional training costs or if all costs are included in the franchise fee. The contract should also indicate whether the cost of training materials and manuals is included.

The manner of any ongoing assistance should also be specified so that it isn't just a case of "call us if you have any problems." Help lines, regular meetings, seminars, conferences, publications, and websites to assist franchisees and their staff should be listed, along with any associated costs. Start-up training for a new franchisee and ongoing franchisor support are two of the main advantages of buying a franchise. As a result, they should be specified in detail in the contract.

Answers to Memory Check Questions

7.1 F   7.2 F   7.3 T   7.4 T   7.5 F   7.6 T   7.7 T   7.8 T   7.9 F   7.10 F
7.11 T   7.12 F   7.13 T   7.14 T   7.15 F   7.16 T   7.17 T   7.18 F   7.19 T   7.20 T
7.21 F   7.22 F   7.23 T   7.24 F   7.25 T

Questions for Discussion

1. Which types (in terms of products or services) of franchises do you feel have reached the point of market saturation? Give reasons. Which types of franchises do you feel have plenty of opportunity to continue growing? Give reasons.
2. How has the internet affected franchising in terms of the relationship between the franchisor and the franchisee as far as efficiency and control?
3. How has the internet affected franchising in terms of the relationship between the franchisor and the customer? How does this affect the franchisee?
4. Would you rather buy a franchise with a lower franchise fee and higher royalty, or one with a higher franchise fee but a lower royalty? Discuss.
5. What issues of complaint would a franchisor be likely to have about a franchisee? How could these be resolved?
6. Franchisors tend to be secretive about the terms and conditions in their contracts. Speculate on why this is the case.
7. If you had a successful independent business and wanted to expand, would it be better to expand by opening new locations that you owned, or better to sell franchises? What factors might influence the decision either way?
8. If you were a franchisor, what characteristics would you look for in potential franchisees? What characteristics would you avoid?
9. What issues of complaint would a franchisee be likely to have about a franchisor? How could these be resolved?
10. If you were buying a coffee shop franchise, in what specific areas would you expect the franchisor to provide you with training? Why?

Case for Discussion

When Seth Mosely was in his graduating semester of Environmental Engineering, he attended a job fair at his university. One of the exhibitors was a company called EnerPeek Audits. EnerPeek was looking for qualified environmental engineers to buy franchises. The company was setting up franchised consulting offices across Canada to provide energy audits for home owners and businesses. The EnerPeek consultant would go into a house or company and conduct a detailed assessment of its energy use, producing a report on how the firm or homeowner could reduce energy costs and operate in a more environmentally friendly way.

Seth was immediately excited by the opportunity. He knew that this was a fast-growing field. Seth's parents were willing to co-sign a loan for the $25 000 franchise fee and another $15 000 in office start-up costs. EnerPeek gave Seth contact information for several existing franchisees, all of whom offered positive assessments of the company. Seth contacted a friend, a recent graduate from law school, for help reviewing the EnerPeek franchise contract. After four hours of reading the contract, Seth's friend advised him that he couldn't see anything wrong with it, but given his limited experience, Seth would be better off to engage a lawyer who was a specialist in franchises. Seth decided that there wasn't time for this if he was going to make it into the first training session for new EnerPeek franchisees, right after his final exams.

Two years later, even though Seth was running a profitable EnerPeek franchise, with two other engineers working for him, he was frustrated and unhappy. He was locked into a contract that still had 10 years to run, and he felt that every day, this contract limited his ability to function as an engineer and entrepreneur.

Seth's franchise gave him a territory that was the eastern half of the city. (Another franchisee owned the western territory.) Seth had sold energy audit services to several companies that had properties in both sides of the city. The contracts were for auditing all of their properties, but, according to the franchise contract, Seth's franchise was allowed to service only those in his territory. So, some of the work that Seth had sold went to another franchisee.

The franchisor charged Seth a 15 percent royalty on any work that was referred to his franchise from the company's head office or from the main website. Seth only had to pay a 10 percent royalty on business when he found and sold to the client himself. But he had sold energy audits to one client that had buildings across the entire country. He could only service the client's two buildings within his own territory, on which he paid the 10 percent royalty. The client's other 20 buildings were audited by other franchisees and EnerPeek collected a 15 percent royalty on all of those, with none of it going back to Seth, since this was how the contract worked.

All of EnerPeek's franchises had to use the same pricing software, provided by head office. It was a complex formula based on the type of business, number of employees, type and amount of space, and many other factors. Seth felt that the formula worked well for commercial and industrial clients but calculated prices for personal houses that provided much less profit. In fact, he wanted his own franchise to specialize in just commercial and industrial audits, but since this was not allowed by the franchise contract, he had to keep doing less profitable audits for houses.

Seth considered trying to sell his franchise, but according to the contract, anyone he sold it to would have to be approved by EnerPeek. And if he started his own independent business in this field, there was a non-compete clause in the contract that said he could not practice within 50 kilometres of his current franchise for the next seven years. And Seth did not want to move that far from his home. On the other hand, he was not sure he could last for another 10 years, the way things were now.

1. As a new graduate, what might have been a better career approach for Seth? Explain.

2. Search online for information about franchise operations similar to this one. Is the information generally positive or negative? Who is providing this information?

3. Are the royalty rates mentioned in the case typical for this kind of franchise operation? What information can you find online? Why is it difficult to get this kind of information?

4. Is the non-compete clause in the franchise contract legal? Is it enforceable? What legal opinions can you find about this online?

5. How could the franchise contract be changed in ways to make Seth happy? What problems would this present for the franchisor?

6. What options are available to Seth? What steps would you recommend that he take? Why?

The Business Plan, Alternative Module
FRANCHISE PURCHASE

Entrepreneurs who are buying a franchise should complete Sections 1 to 5 of the business plan, as well as this portion.

Franchise Type

1. Identify the franchisor and briefly describe the format and nature of the franchising system you will be buying into.

2. Briefly describe any legislation, codes, or franchisor practices that will govern the franchisor's dealings with you.

The Fit

3. Explain why buying a franchise is an appropriate business start-up method for you and your personal circumstances.

Opportunity Assessment

4. Describe in detail the history of the franchisor, outlining the franchise rates of success/closings as well as any history of litigation. (Note: Franchisor permission may be required before disclosing this portion of your business plan.)

5. Describe the strength of the franchisor's brand recognition and the overall marketing strategy of the company.

6. In general terms, describe the nature and efficiency of the systems provided by the franchisor.

7. Prepare a short analysis of the financial health of the franchisor and describe any financial assistance that is provided to franchisees. (Note: Franchisor permission may be required before disclosing this portion of your business plan.)

Financing the Franchise

8. Outline the entire cost of setting up the franchise, your amount of equity investment, the franchise fee, and the rate at which you will have to pay royalties and any other franchisor charges. (Note: Franchisor permission may be required before disclosing this portion of your business plan.)

9. Using information from Section 5 of your business plan, calculate the return on equity that you expect to get, and explain why this is appropriate considering the risk and liquidity of your investment. (Note: Franchisor permission may be required before disclosing this portion of your business plan.)

The Franchise Agreement

10. Briefly outline the major provisions of your franchise agreement including provisions for territory assignment, sources of supply, inventory requirements, contract renewal, termination, assignment, and franchisor assistance. (Note: Franchisor permission may be required before disclosing this portion of your business plan.)

Chapter 8

The Family Firm Alternative: How Do I Take Over My Family's Business?

This chapter examines the third alternative method of becoming an entrepreneur: taking over a family business. When you take control of a business that has been owned by members of your family, you will need a business plan that includes all of the topics covered in Chapters 1 to 5. As well, your business plan will need to include the additional topics covered in this chapter:

- **What Is the Family Business?**
- **How Do I Prepare for Running the Business?**
- **How Do I Help Prepare Retiring Family Members?**
- **What Are the Legal Issues?**
- **What Takeover Problems Will I Face?**

Learning Objectives

On completion of this chapter, you should be able to:

1 Discuss the nature of entrepreneurship in the family business.

2 Identify six major advantages of family firms.

3 Discuss at least four relationship problems in managing family firms.

4 Differentiate between values and policies that reduce conflict between family members.

5 Discuss four techniques for developing a successor to a family business.

6 Outline three types of planning for retirement.

7 Compare three options for transferring a business to the next generation.

8 Outline four common problems as a next-generation leader of a family business.

9 Prepare the components of the business plan related to taking over a family business.

Ask yourself: Is a second-generation owner of a family business a true entrepreneur? If you think back to the definition of entrepreneurship found at the beginning of Chapter 1, you will remember that it involved risking money to make a profit. So let's say you inherit a family business worth $100 000. You are now faced with a choice:

- You can sell the business and spend the $100 000, or maybe just put it in the bank for safekeeping. In this case, you will definitely not be an entrepreneur.

  Or,

- You can keep the business running—in which case, every day that you remain in business, your $100 000 is at risk. That makes you 100 percent entrepreneur. After all, someone who buys an existing business from a stranger is still an entrepreneur. It doesn't matter that you didn't start the business. It doesn't mean that you can't innovate and change the business as much as you want.

If there is any difference in the nature of the entrepreneurship between starting a new business and taking over the family firm, it is probably that it requires more personal courage to take over the family firm. That's because the long-term success rates for family businesses when they have been taken over by the second generation are not much different than the success rates for brand-new start-ups. However, in the family business the cost of failure is higher—not just because of the greater value of assets usually at risk, but because of the personal cost. Comparisons to a more successful founding parent (at least one who is seen that way[1]) or getting the blame for diminishing the family reputation or financial status can be painful. So, the second-generation entrepreneur is, at the very least, worthy of the respect accorded to a start-up entrepreneur.

WHAT IS THE FAMILY BUSINESS?
Definitions

Ask yourself: What is the definition of a family business? It may be easier to recognize a family business than it is to define the term.[2] Which of the following could be considered family businesses?

1. A woman is the sole owner of a dental supply company in which her four adult sons are the senior managers.

2. Three brothers are equal partners in a house-building firm, which does not employ any other members of any of their families.

3. A childless couple jointly owns a catering business, which has no other employees.

4. A woman from a big family, but with no spouse or children of her own, owns a printing business. Every year she gives summer jobs to three or four of her nieces and nephews, who work loading and unloading trucks.

5. A man has inherited full ownership of a bakery that was handed down from his grandfather and father. The owner's own children express no interest in the bakery and no other family members are involved with the company.

6. A man owns 49 percent of the shares in a furniture business where his son works as a cabinetmaker. The man's partner owns 51 percent and has no family members involved with the company.

☑ **Memory Check 8.1**
True or False? Someone who takes over ownership of a family business is not a true entrepreneur.

The definition for a **family business** is usually along the lines of "a business where controlling interest is held by one or more (collectively) members of a family and where at least two members of that family are involved with the company." By this definition, scenarios 5 and 6 above do not qualify as family businesses. But it wouldn't take much for either of them to qualify: Scenario 5 would qualify if one of the kids were to get involved, and scenario 6 would qualify with the transfer of 2-percent ownership. By some definitions, all of these scenarios would easily qualify as family businesses.

A less formal but widely held understanding of family business is that ownership or management of the business will, to some extent, be by family relationship rather than merit. In principle, this idea does not offend most people's sense of justice because one of the main reasons for starting a business is to be able to provide income and employment for family members. Nevertheless, this issue of management control by family members represents the major pitfall of family firms. A major U.S. study of family firms found that on average, the stronger the family control over a firm, the more poorly it performed financially.[3] However, understanding the problems of running a family firm may help to overcome this drawback.

family business A company where controlling interest is held within a single family and at least two members of the family work for the business.

⭐ Head Start Exercise

8.1 Briefly describe the history of your family business and explain which family members are currently involved with the firm (1/2 page maximum). Note: Students who are using the Head Start Exercises as class assignments will each have to interview an owner of a family business whose company will be used as an example for the exercise assignments in this chapter.

Still, there are many benefits to family firms, including

- the opportunity for family members to spend much more time together than would be allowed by most other types of employment
- a common purpose and sharing among family members
- a level of trust in family managers that is difficult to achieve with those outside the family
- the opportunity to provide secure employment for family members
- the chance to be involved with an organization that holds other values above the need for profit
- the ability to leave a legacy for future generations of the family

For immigrant families, there is the special benefit of being able to use the business as a way of sponsoring family members into the country. This is generally available in cases where you can demonstrate that you need a relative for a position of trust in the business and that the relative is qualified to do the job.

⭐ Head Start Exercise

8.2 Briefly describe how your family members would benefit from being in business together.

Family vs. Business Relationships

Family relationships tend to be highly emotionally charged. Business relationships also have a strong emotional component. When the same relationship has both business and family elements, the emotions become magnified. The tendency to support one another is much stronger, but so is the tendency to fight with each other. *Ask yourself: Is it better to live a life with more emotional volatility or less of it?* Your answer will depend on your personality as well as family and cultural values.

Many family businesses consist of spouses or life partners working together as business partners. When you are in business with your spouse, this has practical advantages, such as saving on transportation costs to work. Or, depending on the nature of the business, you may take shifts alternating between work and home so that one of you is always available at the business. For some pairs, the extra closeness of living and working together is the ideal shared experience.

On the negative side, at start-up or other times when income from the business is slight, there is no steady source of cash from an employed spouse to rely on—and failure of the business means you are both unemployed. Also, when you are both entrepreneurs, you may have none of the **family benefits** (dental, extended health care, insurance) that are provided by many employers, adding to your financial stress. The stress of the extended time together can also put pressure on your relationship—and a breakdown in the relationship almost certainly means that one of you must give up the business, or possibly that the business will fail. The dynamics of spouses working together are magnified when other family members are involved in the same business.

✔️ **Memory Check 8.2**
True or False? Any business that employs more than two people from the same family is a family business.

❓ **Get Help 8.1**
To find out more about sponsoring relatives to work in the family business as immigrants, check the Citizenship and Immigration Canada website at www.cic.gc.ca. Click on Canadians and then Sponsor a Family Member.

family benefits Fringe benefits paid for (at least in part) by many employers and that are extended to the spouse and dependent children of the employee. Such benefits typically include extended health care, dental care, and various types of life and disability insurance.

Another issue related to marriage and the family business is that of divorce. *Ask yourself: What happens to the business when spouses divorce?* The answer partly depends on where you live, since family law is a matter of provincial jurisdiction. It seems that family business owners tend not to consider divorce in their planning,[4] but the break-up of a marriage can in some instances force the sale or dissolution of the business. So the best advice, where business and spousal relationships are involved, is to seek legal counsel and get a pre-nuptial agreement that will help protect the business.

Ask yourself: Why is it so difficult for parents to give driving lessons to their children? The most difficult individual to delegate to is your own child, because in **delegating** you have to give up authority. This means abandoning the role of parent. And even when parents are able to delegate, the tendency is to hover over the child, endangering the very self-confidence that they are hoping to encourage.

In North America there is only about a 30 percent chance of being able to successfully transfer a business from the older generation to the children.[5, 6] This may be partly due to the freedom young people have to choose paths in life that they think will be more interesting than the family business, with which they are already familiar. But, more likely, the younger generation is trying to avoid spending their lives in what they see as the permanent dynamics of the parent–child relationship. This fear is influenced by the "sitcom view" that many young people have about their parents' personalities: that they are predictable and unchanging, like the characters in a long-running TV show. As a second-generation entrepreneur, however, you must get beyond this prejudice and realize that the current generation of family business owners is still in the process of maturing and learning new behaviours, and that they are capable of being influenced by you.

The natural rivalry between brothers and sisters ("I'm telling Mom and Dad and you'll be in trouble") tends to disappear with age and become more of a mutually supportive relationship—but not in all cases. In some instances, the vying for parental attention and approval continues well into adulthood. This is more likely to happen between children of the same gender who are close in age. When two such competitive family members both work in the family business, the real problem comes when one of them is put in charge and the other is unable to accept this authority.

Studies of birth order indicate that, on average, first-borns are greater achievers while later-born children tend to have more social skills and be better liked. *Ask yourself: Which would make the better candidate to take over the family business?* The answer will depend on a host of factors other than birth order, but it's not necessarily the eldest. The eldest male, however, is more likely to be selected as successor to the business, especially in families that have immigrated from other cultures. Today, this basis for selection is likely to produce resentment rather than acceptance in better-qualified siblings.

There are two categories of in-laws associated with family businesses: those who work in the business and those who don't but are married to family members who do. Those who work in the business can find themselves in an awkward position when non-family employees see these in-laws as part of the privileged group of family owners. Family members, however, may be unwilling to extend the same trust and authority to the in-laws that they would to blood relatives. So there is some potential for isolation and resentment in this role.

In-laws in the second category do not work in the business but are married to family members who do. The danger here is that these in-laws may take a hand in trying to manage the careers of their spouses in the firm. The "don't let them push you around" style of coaching can have a negative impact on otherwise stable family/business relationships. Understandably, those married to business family members may depend on the business for their livelihood, but have no real knowledge of or influence on the operation. Pressuring the spouse who works in the business is an attempt to achieve some sense of control.

delegating Giving subordinates responsibility and full authority for completing specific tasks.

Memory Check 8.3
True or False? A family business can be used as a means of sponsoring the immigration of a foreign relative into Canada.

Memory Check 8.4
True or False? Fewer than one-third of family businesses are successfully transferred to the second generation.

Memory Check 8.5
True or False? Siblings of the same gender who are close in age are more likely to continue rivalries into adulthood.

Managing Conflict

Not all conflict is bad for a family business, although this can become an extremely complex question. There is some evidence that when all family members participating in the business are from the same generation, there may not be enough healthy conflict of ideas for the best decision making. However, when there are wide generation gaps among the participants, the conflict tends to be about relationships and may have a negative effect on the business.[7]

There are proven techniques for dealing with most of the relationship problems associated with the complex politics of family firms. History has shown that family businesses are more successful when there is a family culture, or a set of values that include the following ideas:

■ The business is a long-term trust of the family rather than a source of cash and jobs for family members.

■ What's best for the business is best for the family in the long run.

■ The business is there ultimately for the benefit of the family, not the other way around. So it is not disloyal to the family to decide not to work in the business.

■ Any decision relating to the business is only business and not personal.

These values can be aided by a set of clear policies to be followed in the operation of the business, including

■ A single family member will have administrative control of the business.

■ Formal lines of authority will be followed and clear job descriptions will be available for all positions in the business.

■ Family members seeking jobs in the business must formally apply and clearly demonstrate that they have the requirements to perform those jobs.

■ Salaries for all positions in the business will be at competitive industry rates.

■ The business will not lend money or act as guarantor for loans.

Another tool that has proven effective in reducing family conflict is the creation of a **family council** to involve those family members who are not directly working in the business: in-laws, family members who are employed elsewhere, retired family members, and even younger members who are still in school. All of these groups may have an interest in the business—financial or personal—but have to rely on second-hand information or gossip to know what is going on in the business. Through regular meetings, the council can provide a source of information and a forum for airing concerns about the business.

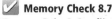 Head Start Exercise

8.3 List any informal techniques or formal company policies that are intended to reduce conflict among family members (1/4 page maximum).

HOW DO I PREPARE FOR RUNNING THE BUSINESS?

Preparation for taking over a family business cannot start too soon. Some important steps in preparing are declaring your intentions, apprenticing, studying business, getting outside experience, and building networks.

Declaration of Intentions

As soon as you see any serious possibility of a career in the family business, start to talk about this goal. Keeping your aspirations secret is a self-defeating habit. Unless you tell your

---

Memory Check 8.6
True or False? Birth order studies indicate that younger siblings tend to be higher achievers.

family council A group of family members who meet regularly to receive information about and discuss concerns relating to the family business. Council members do not generally have any active involvement in the business and have no authority over the business.

Memory Check 8.7
True or False? Conflict is reduced when an individual family member has administrative control of the business.

goals to others they cannot help you achieve them. And, when you do express your goals, help, advice, and moral support can come from many directions. It is especially important that you tell your intentions to other stakeholders in the business, for a variety of reasons:

- *Founder/parents.* Business owners will often have secret hopes that someday one of their children will be interested in taking over the family business, without ever actually having a serious two-way conversation about this possibility. This unspoken expectation may be even more common in immigrant entrepreneurs.[8] Your declaration of interest can start the conversation that will eventually lead to a plan for takeover. On the other hand, you may have an unspoken expectation of inheriting the business that is not part of the senior generation's plan. If taking over the business is not a serious possibility, it's better that you find out early and make alternative career plans.

- *Siblings.* Stating your hope of running the business can open negotiations with siblings who may have similar aspirations. If there is going to be competition for the role, making accommodations and getting it settled early will help prevent family feuds. In some cases, your announcement of wanting to run the business may bring a sense of relief to a brother or sister who feared getting stuck with the job.

- *Employees.* The sooner employees know about a long-term plan for a family member to take over the business, the sooner they can adjust their own career plans. It is totally demoralizing for a long-term employee who harboured hopes of promotion or buying the business to find a family member "parachuted" in when the owner retires.

⭐ Head Start Exercise

8.4 Explain why you are a suitable successor for leadership of the family business in terms of your personality, interests, and family position (1/4 page maximum). Note: Students who are using this exercise as a class assignment should identify likely successors to the example business and explain their suitability.

Apprenticeship

Starting at the bottom and working your way up is a great way to learn a business. Serving an informal **apprenticeship** in the business means actually doing as many jobs as possible in the company, to the point where you have developed some level of proficiency with each of them. The second generation of a family business will often start this process by taking summer and part-time jobs, and filling in for employees on vacation.

But if you intend to take over the business, this should not be a haphazard series of activities. Rather, there should be a clear plan of progress, perhaps working through all of the processing procedures of the company and then moving, step by step, to higher levels of responsibility.

Ask yourself: How will employees feel about my moving from job to job in the company? If employees do not have a clear understanding of the intention for you to eventually run the business, you will be perceived as the boss's kid dabbling in jobs that others must toil at for long periods—in some cases, whole careers. This opens the door for resentment and a lack of co-operation. But when people know that switching jobs is part of your training program, they are more likely to take a hand in helping you learn the job and understand its importance to the company.

Your own attitude during this process will make all the difference: Arrogance will get you nowhere. Many business families instill in the younger generation a belief that, because of their privileged position, family members in the business must always work harder than employees doing the same jobs. Your struggles with learning new tasks will be a humbling experience, but one that will form a bond with employees rather than make you an object of derision.

☑ **Memory Check 8.8**
True or False? The family business should be the place family members rely on for borrowing money.

☑ **Memory Check 8.9**
True or False? A family council carries the same authority as a board of directors.

☑ **Memory Check 8.10**
True or False? Any intentions you have of taking over the family business should be kept confidential for as long as possible.

apprenticeship A skill training program where the trainee performs increasingly more complex and responsible jobs over a long period of time.

❓ **Get Help 8.2**
There are a huge variety of full- and part-time business programs available right across Canada. Contact a business program coordinator at your local college or university or use www.schoolfinder.com to find programs.

? **Get Help 8.3**

Northeastern University links more than 100 universities that have family business centres. Access their online magazine at www.fambiz.com. This site has a good search engine for family business articles.

? **Get Help 8.4**

Management of the family business is becoming an area of specialization at more business schools. For example, the BBA program at Schulich School of Business (www.schulich.yorku.ca) offers a specialization in entrepreneurial and family business studies.

empathy The ability to experience the feelings and motives of others.

☑ Memory Check 8.11

True or False? Formal education helps business owners to understand why their businesses are successful.

? **Get Help 8.5**

Current events magazines such as *Maclean's* (www.macleans.ca) and *Time* (www.time.com) give good summaries of what's going on in the world at large.

networking The process of making contact and building relationships with people for purposes of mutual support.

☑ Memory Check 8.12

True or False? Family business is a field of study available at various business schools.

Study

Keep in mind that there are no formal educational requirements for taking over the family firm. But a business diploma or degree will give you a broad understanding of all the functional areas of business. In addition, some form of specialization in marketing, accounting, production, human resources, or information technology can be of great benefit, even though as a business owner you will not be working in just one narrow area. Having an in-depth understanding of one area of business gives you a greater appreciation for the complexity and depth of all of the areas.

Ask yourself: Why study business if I can learn it on the job? The big advantage of formally studying business is that it teaches you the system for classifying business information. Thus, when a problem arises in your business, you immediately recognize it as a marketing problem, or a production or accounting problem, and you are one step closer to a permanent solution through modifying your methods. The untrained business manager would tend to recognize the same problem as a problem with an individual employee or with a particular customer order and be more likely to seek a temporary fix. Understanding this system for classifying business information also allows you to analyze the good things about your business. It's amazing how many successful small business owners do not know why their businesses are successful. If you are trained to analyze your competitive advantages, you can capitalize on them to become even more successful. And when there is a threat to your business from changes in the market or the competition, you will be more likely to recognize it and take appropriate action.

Outside Experience

Working in someone else's business is an experience that is sometimes missed out on by those who have grown up with a family business. It can be humbling to be just another employee, not related to the boss. This can help you build **empathy** with your own future employees. Outside experience is another way to increase your credibility as the boss in your own business. And seeing the methods, problems, and management styles of another company can give you a new objectivity about your own family firm. Your outside employment doesn't even have to be in the same industry as your family business to teach you valuable lessons that you can bring home. And if you're not really sure about a career in the family business, working outside is one of the best ways to help you make up your mind.

⭐ **Head Start Exercise**

8.5 Briefly list relevant education and work experiences that make you a suitable successor for leading this business. Note: Students who are using this exercise as a class assignment should list the education and experience of likely successors to the example business (1/3 page maximum).

Networks

Networking is the process of making contacts and building relationships with people for mutual support. In preparing to take over a family business, part of your networking task is to make contacts with the various associates of your family's retiring generation. These include customers, suppliers, bankers, and professional advisers. Accompanying the current family owners to meetings can be used for initial contact, but often the real links are made in social situations. Intergenerational socializing can be difficult, but made easier if you are up to date on current events in politics, sports, movies, and music. Developing some level of skill in activities like golf, skiing, dancing (yes, dancing), and public speaking are all ways of increasing your ability to network.

You must also build your own network of contacts. Membership in associations is an excellent way to do this. Chambers of commerce, industrial associations, service clubs, and family business associations are all networking vehicles. The Canadian Association of Family Enterprise brings together people associated with family businesses to identify common problems and to lobby the federal government on behalf of family enterprise. The association also performs informational and educational activities. A similar Quebec-based organization is the Family Business Network (Réseau des Entreprises Familiales). Although many of their documents have not been translated into English, this is still a valuable resource, as Quebec has long been a leader in entrepreneurship research and support. The Family Business Network also has a special interest in the role of women in family firms.

HOW DO I HELP PREPARE RETIRING FAMILY MEMBERS?

When you own your own business, there is no official retirement age. But, as part of the baby boom generation, a large proportion of family business leaders in Canada expect to retire over the next decade.[9] The majority of these do not have any formal plans for what they will do when they retire, nor for passing on the business to family members.[10] This older generation of business owners may need a great deal of assistance, encouragement, and advice to prepare for handing over the reins of the business. A good starting point is to help them get lots of information and to find independent advisers.

Information and Advisers

If you are the successor to the family business, you should not be in the role of chief adviser to the retiring generation. First, you are too close to the situation and have too much personal financial interest to give objective advice. Second, your retiring relatives deserve the benefit of good professional advice for such major decisions. And third, bringing in outside advisers prevents other interested family members from complaining of undue influence or favouritism in the estate planning process, and helps avoid future family conflict.

The key advisers needed are:

- *Accountant.* The accountant's main role is to advise on the tax implications of anything the retiring business owner may decide to do with the business or other assets, and to recommend ways of accomplishing the desired goals that will reduce or defer taxes.
- *Financial planner.* A qualified financial planner can help identify the kind of financial instruments that will produce the balance of income and security needed for a particular planned retirement lifestyle.
- *Lawyer.* The lawyer's role is to advise on wills, powers of attorney, trusts, shareholder agreements, and any other documents involved in transferring authority. In addition, lawyers are often knowledgeable about options in insurance coverage.
- *Personal adviser.* A wise and experienced friend or mentor who is not part of the immediate family can be an excellent source of advice in planning retirement and the **succession** of business ownership.

⭐ Head Start Exercise

8.6 Name the specific formal advisers who could help the current business owner(s) in planning for retirement and ownership succession of the business (1/4 page maximum).

❓ Get Help 8.6
The Canadian Association of Family Enterprise has a website at cafecanada.ca

❓ Get Help 8.7
The website for the Family Business Network is at www.fbn-i.org.

❓ Get Help 8.8
The Canadian Association of Retired Persons is a non-profit group that lobbies governments on behalf of seniors' interests. It publishes its own magazine covering a huge variety of retirement issues. Check out the website at www.carp.ca.

✅ Memory Check 8.13
True or False? The Canadian Association of Family Enterprise lobbies the federal government on family business issues.

✅ Memory Check 8.14
True or False? Only a tiny portion of family business leaders in Canada expect to retire within the next few years.

succession The taking over of control by the next in line to do so.

Need/Want Identification

? Get Help 8.9
The Yellow Pages offers a category of Retirement Planning Consultants, which tends to be a combination of investment dealers, insurance brokers, and firms that make arrangements for chronic medical care. Nevertheless, there are some reliable specialists in the retirement field.

Retirement from the business should not be seen as giving up a major source of satisfaction in one's life. Rather, it should be seen as the chance to intensely pursue those activities that will provide the greatest life satisfaction. For the average middle-aged business owner, when asked "What do you want to do when you retire?", the honest answer is "I don't know." One way of getting to an answer is to start with a "wildest dreams" type of question. *Ask yourself: If you could do or be anything in the world, limited only by your own fantasies, what would it be?* Extreme answers such as write a great novel, win the Canadian Open, become a famous movie star, travel around the world, discover a cure for heart disease, or coach in the NHL should be encouraged, regardless of how unrealistic they may seem. That's because this kind of exercise points in the direction of interest and satisfaction for the future retiree. Later, when the constraints of reality (such as health, skills, finances, agreement of spouses) are applied, achievable but fulfilling ambitions can be identified. So, writing a novel can become completing a college journalism diploma, movie stardom can become active membership in an amateur theatre group, world travel can become overseas work on foreign-aid projects. None of these more realistic ambitions means settling for less than one's dream. Instead, they are achievable steps in the direction that will provide individual fulfillment.

A retiring owner—especially a founder—may have a strong need for continuing involvement in the business in some capacity, and this should be incorporated into the succession plan. For example, the owner may go from being president of the company to chair of the board of directors, or chair of the advisory board.

⭐ Head Start Exercise

8.7   Briefly list the retirement goals of the current owner(s) (1/4 page maximum).

Future retirees must know what they want to do before they can figure out what it's going to cost. But aside from money to be spent on "want" satisfaction, retirees must plan for regular living expenses including food, shelter, gifts, transportation, and all the other items in the normal household budget. In addition, contingency planning for medical emergencies and possible disability becomes more important as one gets older.

✓ Memory Check 8.15
True or False? As successor to the family business, you should be the primary adviser to the senior generation on retirement and estate planning.

Open and frank discussion should be held with all interested parties including spouses, children, other family members, and non-family managers in the business. One study indicates that the majority of family businesses have no clear plan in case of the death or disability of the controlling owner.[11] But for many business owners, "succession" is a difficult subject. The deep emotional attachment entrepreneurs can have to their businesses must be recognized and discussed, along with how they will cope with giving up authority.[12] A worst-case scenario is when the older-generation owner agrees that you will take over the business, but then has a change of mind during the transition phase before you have assumed any legal ownership.

Preparing a Plan

estate All the assets owned by a person.

living will A statement of how a person wishes to be cared for in case of incapacitating or terminal illness.

trust An arrangement where a person transfers ownership of assets to a responsible party (the trustee), who may use the assets only for the benefit of certain parties (the beneficiaries) as instructed.

The owner of a family business who is planning to retire should really make three separate but interrelated plans:

- A *retirement plan.* This covers retirement goals (education, travel, sports, arts, business, volunteer work, hobbies), living arrangements, health management issues, and a budget for retirement.

- An *estate plan.* The **estate** plan covers sources of retirement income, a will, powers of attorney (including a **living will**), and any **trusts** that are set up to manage assets.

- A *succession plan.* Decisions about who will eventually run the family business and how it will be owned are included here. It should also explain the transition role of the retiring generation.

A Growing Family, A Growing Business

In 1983, Bruno Martino's mother ran a small variety store in Toronto's middle-class Queensway-Royal York neighbourhood. Business in the store was declining because of competition from large discount chains. At that time, Bruno was managing a club in the city and even though he was a young man, he knew a great deal about the restaurant business. He had been working in restaurants from the age of 12 or 13 years, starting as a dishwasher and moving up through jobs as bus-boy, server, cook, bartender, host, and manager. Bruno also knew that his mom was a great cook, so he suggested that his parents turn the variety store into a restaurant. And this was the beginning of a Toronto culinary legend: Mamma Martino's Pasta & Pizzeria Restaurant.

For the first 7 years, Bruno worked in the kitchen with his mom while his dad ran things out front. Bruno describes his father as "old school" which conflicted with Bruno's more modern approach, producing the usual intergenerational conflicts. But everything worked out and the restaurant was an unqualified success. Mamma's recipes were based on the cooking style of her home province in Italy, Campobasso. Mr. Martino senior is long retired and Mamma Martino passed away in 2006, but her recipes live on: generous portions of simple fare made with fresh ingredients and cooked to perfection.

Mamma Martino's has had to expand four times since start-up. Bruno attributes much of the success to sticking with a proven formula. The restaurant takes no reservations (to Bruno this would mean empty tables while reserved customers are stuck in traffic) and there is usually a lineup of eager patrons. The menu is largely unchanged from the original of 30 years ago. Throughout the life of the restaurant there have only been four increases in the meal prices. And the family decision to stay closed on Sundays has been maintained, even though the surrounding competitors are open 7 days a week.

Today, Bruno owns the restaurant and one of his sisters works with him. Over the years it has been a wonderful source of employment for family members and Bruno's children, still completing their education, all work part-time. Bruno expects that one of his kids will take over the restaurant in the future. View Mamma Martino's website at www.mammamartinos.ca.

For the steps in creating these plans, take a look at Figure 8.1, the retiring business owner checklist.

The succession is most likely to be successful if control is left in the hands of an individual family member. Remember, this does not necessarily mean majority ownership, just owning a majority of the voting shares. There are many Canadian examples of family businesses being damaged or destroyed when second-generation owners have spent their efforts in battles for control of the company rather than in managing it.

The succession plan should be written with clear timelines for transferring control of the business. Without this, as heir to the business you are left in the demoralizing position of waiting in the wings indefinitely. Clear dates for a transition period made up of steps of increasing responsibility are necessary for you to prepare yourself as an entrepreneur. A date for final transfer of power should be decided on. Interestingly, there is some research to indicate that family business owners are most likely to commit to a succession plan when they are in their fifties.[13] Prior to this, they are generally not ready to consider retirement—and after this decade, there seems to be an increasing reluctance to give up power. If the current owners of the family business are not able to commit to a timetable, this is the strongest of signs that they are not psychologically prepared to give up the business.

Memory Check 8.16
True or False? The majority of family business owners in Canada have fully discussed issues of inheritance with their children.

★ Head Start Exercise

8.8 Identify the projected date for the current owner(s) to retire from running the business and briefly explain the rationale for this time frame (1/4 page maximum).

? Get Help 8.10

Two excellent books on estate planning are *Winning the Estate Planning Game* by Tim Cestnick, published by Prentice Hall Canada, and *The Canadian Guide to Will and Estate Planning* by Douglas Gray and John Budd, published by McGraw-Hill Ryerson.

? Get Help 8.11

The non-profit Centre for Family Business (cffb.ca) offers workshops, seminars, and networking opportunities.

? Get Help 8.12

The Canada Business website (www.canadabusiness.ca) offers a section on "Exiting Your Business" that includes tips on succession planning.

Figure 8.1 Retiring Business Owner Checklist

RETIREMENT

❑ Hold discussion with spouse

❑ Attend retirement workshops

❑ Read current literature on retirement

❑ Join retirement networking group

❑ Set retirement goals

❑ Decide on living arrangements

❑ Analyze income requirements

❑ Set retirement budget

❑ Create retirement schedule

ESTATE

❑ Read current estate planning books

❑ Identify and meet with advisers

❑ Evaluate estate (including business)

❑ Hold discussions with family

❑ Decide inheritance issues

❑ Create/revise will

❑ Decide incapacity/medical issues

❑ Create power of attorney

BUSINESS SUCCESSION

❑ Hold discussions with legal and financial advisers

❑ Project outlook for business

❑ Hold discussions with family

❑ Hold discussions with senior employees

❑ Identify successor(s)

❑ Decide on control of the business

❑ Negotiate roles of successors and other family members

❑ Identify transfer mechanism

❑ Create timetable for steps in transferring responsibility

❑ Set date for final takeover

WHAT ARE THE LEGAL ISSUES?

Taking over the family business is really about two separate issues:

1. taking over management authority for the business, and
2. taking over legal ownership of the business.

As a second-generation leader of a family firm, you may find yourself in the chief executive role long before you have legal control of the company. And in some ways, you're never really the boss until you have legal ownership. There are various ways you can receive legal control of the family company, including

- inheriting ownership through a will, on the death of the business owner
- receiving ownership in the business as a family gift or a series of gifts over time
- buying the business from the retiring generation, usually with payments spread over an extended period

Some combination of these methods can be used. Depending on the method of transfer, the number of family members involved, and the time frame, the legal complications can be endless and certainly require professional help.[14] But the more you understand about the legal implications of transfer decisions, the more you can influence the process.

Taxation Issues

When you buy an asset and keep it for a while, then sell it or give it away, the increase in value of the asset while you owned it is a **capital gain**. Capital gains are taxable. So if your parent started a business 20 years ago for a $10 000 investment and today the business is worth $900 000, the capital gain is $890 000. If your parent gives you the business as a gift, or sells it to you, then the capital gains tax on the business becomes payable.

And even though capital gains taxes fluctuate from time to time, you would still be looking at a tax bill in the hundreds of thousands of dollars. Even worse would be if your parent died and left you the business: You would likely have to pay **probate** fees on the estate on top of the capital gains tax.

There are exemptions to and methods of deferring capital gains taxes that should be employed wherever possible. These techniques include:

- employing the lifetime capital gains exemption, which can allow up to $500 000 of capital gains to be exempt from tax on the sale or giving away of shares in a small-business corporation
- transferring or **bequeathing** shares of the family business to a spouse. This can be done without triggering the capital gains tax, and could be employed as a way of delaying the tax when the spouse is expected to outlive the business owner.
- giving shares in the business to children early in the life of the business, before the shares have appreciated to the value they would have at the time of the owner's retirement
- employing an **estate freeze**. This fairly complicated manoeuvre allows the business owner to create two types of shares in the business. One type, retained by the owner, stays frozen at the current assessed value of the business. The other type, given to heirs, receives all the growth in value of the business from that point on. The capital gains tax becomes payable on the frozen shares only when they are passed on to the heirs. As long as the heirs retain the new shares, they do not have to pay tax on this increased value.[15]
- using farm asset exceptions. If the family business is a farm, assets used in the business can be transferred to succeeding generations of family members free of capital gains.
- using the capital gains reserve exception. When the shares of a small business corporation are transferred to succeeding generations of a family, payment of the capital gains tax may be spread out over a period as long as 10 years.

Identifying which of these and other transfer options have the greatest advantage for your own situation will certainly require the help of a tax professional. The process usually involves projecting various financial scenarios and assessing the relative risks and benefits. The earlier a knowledgeable accountant is involved in the planning process, the better.

Memory Check 8.17
True or False? Setting a retirement budget is part of the succession plan.

Get Help 8.13
Tax rules are always changing. To find the latest information on any particular tax, check the Canada Revenue Agency website at www.cra-arc.gc.ca.

capital gain The increase in value of an asset over a period of time.

probate The legal procedure of getting a court to declare a will valid. Probate fees are charged as a percentage of the estate and vary from province to province.

bequeath Leave assets to someone in a will.

estate freeze A legal manoeuvre designed to freeze the value of the shares of a business owned by the retiring owners. All the new value from the growth of the business can then be owned by the next generation of the family.

Get Help 8.14
The accountant who acts as an adviser on business succession taxes will typically have a CA (www.cica.ca) or CGA (www.cga-online.org) designation and should have specific experience in the transfer of family business ownership.

Get Help 8.15

The website for Canada Revenue Agency has a search feature that can produce regulations and a vast number of articles on specific tax issues. Start with the main menu at www.cra-arc.gc.ca.

Legal Form Issues

If the business is not incorporated prior to succession of control, the retiring owners have the option of removing assets from the business (for example, land and buildings) so that they can keep personal title to these assets and then lease them back to the business. The assets can then become a source of income for the retired family members. At the same time, the possibility of having the succeeding generation put these assets at risk (by borrowing money against them) is minimized. At some future time, the assets could be sold to the company or willed to the successors of the business.

In order to take advantage of the $500 000 lifetime capital gains exemption, or to use the estate freeze as a way of avoiding taxes, the family business must be set up as a corporation. When more than one family member will be taking over the business, it can also be an advantage to have a corporation because it becomes easier to distribute varying percentages of ownership among the heirs. Also, by using two classes of shares (voting and non-voting), it is possible to distribute equal amounts of ownership among various children but to leave control of the company with a single member of the family or group of family members who will be directly involved with the business. With a corporation, the retiring generation can retain shares in the company for a source of income but give up control by keeping only non-voting shares.

Considering the various tax options in transferring corporate shares, this is often a more advantageous legal form for passing a business to the next generation. And, presumably, a family with a well-established business would have enough other assets that it would want to protect them by incorporating. Any corporation with more than one owner should have a shareholder agreement.

Memory Check 8.18

True or False? Transferring a business to the next generation works best when control of the business is spread among as many family members as possible.

This may be even more critical to a family business because it can reduce the potential for conflict among family members. The shareholder agreement may include company rules on:

- paying dividends versus keeping earnings in the company
- salary limits for company officers
- protection for minority shareholders, requiring unanimous shareholder consent for certain decisions
- details of a **buy/sell agreement**

The buy/sell agreement allows remaining shareholders to buy the shares of a shareholder who dies or becomes disabled. Usually, the money for this purchase will come from insurance policies carried on each of the shareholders.

The lawyer advising on succession planning should have experience in both family business matters and estate planning, or should belong to a firm with experts in each area who can be called on. Be sure to ask specific questions about experience.

buy/sell agreement A contract between owners of a company stating that in the event one of them dies, the remaining owners have the right and obligation to buy the deceased's share of the business.

⭐ Head Start Exercise

8.9   Briefly outline plans for how the business will be passed on to the successor(s) and how control will be distributed (1/3 page maximum).

Insurance Issues

Memory Check 8.19

True or False? Business owners are most likely to commit to a succession plan when they are in their fifties.

Aside from the regular kinds of insurance required by a business, special coverage may be needed for a family business—especially a firm being passed from one generation to another. Insurance can help protect the business while ownership is in the hands of the older generation, during a transition phase, and when you take over the business. For example, if the business is highly dependent on the skills, abilities, and relationships of an older-generation entrepreneur, it may be wise to have this business owner covered by key person insurance while you and/or other family members are in training for this role.

During the transition phase you may be sharing ownership of the business with older-generation family members. Or you may be taking over the business in partnership with other family members. In these situations you will need life insurance on each other as partners or shareholders, so that in the event of death, you or other remaining partners/shareholders can purchase the shares of the deceased partner (from their heirs) as per your buy/sell agreement. Naturally, if you are the beneficiary of your family partners—thus inheriting their share of the business anyway—such insurance may not be necessary.

If you and other members of the family sit as directors on the board of the family corporation, you may require **directors' and officers' insurance**. This is because directors and officers of a company can be sued for decisions they make (or fail to make) that result in some harm to another party.

Alternative Compensation Issues

A general theme among succession planners is that when it comes to estate planning, business owners should treat their children fairly, not equally. For example, let's say you are one of four siblings with a parent who owns a business that has a net value of about $1 million, representing most of the parent's wealth. Of the family children, you are the only one who has shown interest in the business, and you have worked there for seven years while your brother and sisters have pursued alternative careers. There are unlimited numbers of ways the estate could be disposed of on the death of your parent, but consider these three:

- The entire business, representing most of the estate, could be left to you as a reward for your interest and work in the business. This would likely be perceived as unfair by your siblings, who may have been equally devoted to the parent but just not interested in the business. In this case, they could have grounds for contesting the will, which would result in expensive litigation, as well as hard feelings among the family members.

- Shares of the business could be divided equally, four ways, among the siblings, giving you and each of the others about $250 000 of stock in the company. Even if the shares are classified to give you voting control of the company, you may well believe this to be unfair because the value of the company could be due, at least in part, to your hard work. And while you were working to make the company worth more, your siblings were making themselves wealthier through their own chosen fields.

- A more complex formula could be worked out to calculate the increase in value of the business during the time you worked there and award you that amount (or some portion of that amount), with the rest of the value of the estate being divided equally among you and the other heirs. This is the solution that, although not equal division, would most likely be perceived as fair by all of the parties.

If a business founder has lots of assets outside of the business, heirs not involved with the business could be fairly compensated with non-business assets. But for most Canadian business owners, the majority of their wealth is tied up in the business. In these cases, other techniques to achieve fairness in the distribution of an estate could include:

- removing assets such as land or buildings from the business and giving these (possibly through a trust) to heirs not involved with the business. This would be done on condition that the assets are rented back to the business, with the heirs who now own them receiving rent on the assets as compensation; or

- arranging for heirs not involved with the business to hold notes payable by the business over an extended period of time.

directors' and officers' insurance Insurance policies that protect members of the board of directors or the senior managers of a company if they are personally sued for decisions or actions they take on behalf of the company.

Memory Check 8.20
True or False? To use most of the tax deferral options available to family businesses, the company must be a corporation.

Memory Check 8.21
True or False? In passing on the family business to the next generation, it is best to treat all children in the family equally.

A Change in Direction For a Family Firm

West End Offset Plate Service still provides complete pre-press services to commercial printers. But that end of its business, in just the past few years, has become obsolete with the widespread use of automatic "computer-to-plate" systems. The business is more than 50 years old. Brothers Paul and John Moran started working there part-time as kids, for their father, the owner. As adults, Paul and John pursued their own interests in theatre and film and never expected to work in the family printing business. But when their father became seriously ill and died shortly after, the brothers stepped into the business as partners and started planning the long-term future of their firm.

With the rapidly changing technologies and markets in the printing industry, the Morans realized that they would need to find a more specialized niche. Capitalizing on their arts backgrounds, they started offering unique printed products for visual media. For example, a TV commercial may be set in a kitchen containing boxes and jars of household products, which are realistic looking, but not actual consumer products. These "fake" products are one of the services that West End now provides. Books, posters, or any other printed product that a director or set designer might look for are also within their capability. The business now has three full-time employees and one part-timer, with good growth prospects.

After five years of working together, the brothers have specialized in their contributions to the company, with John handling sales and customer service and Paul taking care of production inside the shop. Paul's advice to others who can never picture themselves in a career with the family business is "never say never."

Visit the website for West End Offset Plate Service at www.westendoffset.com.

WHAT TAKEOVER PROBLEMS WILL I FACE?

Second-Generation Pitfalls

There are a great many factors that contribute to the poor success rates for second-generation entrepreneurs. Typical mistakes of second-generation owners can be grouped into the general categories of hasty expansion, alienation of key employees, succumbing to family politics, and lack of strategy.

Get Help 8.16
The Business Development Bank of Canada offers a variety of Transition Program consulting services. Search its website at www.bdc.ca.

Hasty Expansion As a new successor to the business, you may feel a great urgency to assert your own identity, to start implementing your many ideas, and, unfortunately, you may feel in a rush to make the business grow. This will take money. You may be tempted to borrow money for expansion capital. In an established business, especially one with lots of assets, borrowing money for expansion can be almost too easy. But when you increase the debt load of the business, you have the extra expense of servicing that debt. This means you are operating closer to your break-even point. You will have reduced the safety margin of your company—a safety margin you will need in case there is an unexpected downturn in business.

This is where many recent business successors get caught. Any investment in expansion takes a while before it starts to produce cash flow. If there is a significant drop in the market while you're waiting for the expansion to produce cash, you may find yourself losing money. When your business is operating at a loss, it's hard to borrow more money. And if the losses go on for long, creditors will start to go after the business assets. So begins the downward spiral of a failing business.

This does not mean that you should forget about expansion. The lesson here is that borrowing money to expand should not be entered into hastily. Expansion should be part of a well-planned strategy, building on the factors that have led to the success of the business so far. Expansion may be exactly what your business is ready for. But as a new leader, it is better to err on the side of caution.

Losing Key Employees When the older generation of owners retires from the business, this could be a trigger for senior employees to start thinking along the lines of retirement for themselves. And if you are taking over the business quickly (not a slow transition) it may be difficult to transfer the loyalty employees have felt for the previous generation to yourself. There may also be cases of long-term employees who held out hope of equity in the business who will see your appointment as an end to this hope. Combine all these factors with possible overzealousness on your part to get rid of a few problem employees. This will give everyone some concern about their job security—and the result could be employees looking for new jobs.

Being the new boss requires a careful balance between exercising firm authority and avoiding the alienation of key employees. When you first assume leadership of the company, it may be important to remind employees about the advantages of working for a family business: that the organization has values other than just the pursuit of profit. Assurances that you will uphold whatever values (tradition, quality, honesty, reputation) are associated with your firm can make longtime employees more comfortable. To ensure that you keep important non-family managers, you may also consider forms of profit sharing and even equity sharing while still retaining control of the company.

Succumbing to Family Politics History has shown that family business leaders can be sidetracked from the job of running the company by the energy-draining feuds, power struggles, and favour-seeking of families. As leader of the family business, you may find yourself faced with a choice between doing something that is in the best interest of the business or in the best interest of an individual family member. Or you may face choices between the interests of one family member over another. Your best way of coping with these problems is to stick to business and stay out of family politics. You must make decisions based on the long-range interests of the business, explain your reasoning, and be clear that it is only business, not personal.

Failing to Develop a Strategy The changes you eventually make in the business should be part of a long-term strategy. But some second-generation owners fail to become strategically focused after taking over the business. Reasons include:

- long-held habits of dealing with operational problems as a junior manager;
- over-conservatism, especially if the fortunes of many family members are dependent on the business; and
- indoctrination by the previous generation: This is what has always worked for our business; this is what always will work for our business.

Business training and outside experience will make you more aware that you need a strategy for responding to changing market conditions. This includes having a written business plan. Otherwise, changes you make in the business will be haphazard and maybe even unnecessary.

An active board of directors (or in some cases a board of advisers) can be an excellent source of support and advice for broad strategic issues. As the day-to-day boss of the company you can easily lose sight of a long-term strategy for the firm, but board meetings should be primarily for this purpose. The board will likely be made up of family shareholders, and may include the previous generation of owners and senior, non-family managers of the business.

Many family-business consultants recommend keeping the board small and including directors from outside the family and the business. These outside directors are chosen for their broad business knowledge and their objectivity about the business. For a small

> **Memory Check 8.22**
> True or False? Increasing the debts of the business by borrowing to expand is a common error of second-generation owners.

> **Memory Check 8.23**
> True or False? Leading the family business requires being deeply involved with the family politics.

business, directors generally get paid around $3000 a year (depending on the size of the company) and attend about one meeting a month.

⭐ Head Start Exercise

8.10 Briefly describe your long-term plans for the business (1/4 page maximum).

Managing the Transition

When you take over the family business, in all probability your intention is not to continue running things the way the previous generation did. You will want to make changes. And even though those changes may be part of a well-thought-out strategy, and even though you will be the boss, you will run into resistance.

Ask yourself: Do most people resist change? Look at people's hairstyles. Many people sport the hairstyle that they had when they left high school, keeping it the same for 30 or 40 years—or longer! Yet many of those same people update their clothing styles on a fairly regular basis. This is mostly because of style changes in the clothing available for sale. Nevertheless, this tells us that most people will not initiate change (the hair), although they are perfectly capable of accepting it (the clothes). To actively resist change, however, people need a reason. The most common reasons that people resist changes in a business are:

- *Resistance to force.* People don't like to be bossed around, even when it's their employer doing the bossing. *Ask yourself: How do I feel when my boss at work suddenly tells me to do something a different way?*

- *Fear of losing an advantage.* Asking people to change an old work habit, one that took a long time to perfect, means extra work. It may be easier to find reasons why the change won't work.

- *Personal antipathy.* Not everyone is going to like having you as a boss. You may even find some with an active dislike of you to the point where they are obstructive when you try to make changes. It's not business; it's personal.

The ways you can overcome resistance to change include:

- *Providing ongoing communication.* This process should start with sharing your vision for the future of the company; the reasoning behind changes should always be explained.

- *Empowering employees.* Employees who have an active hand in the planning process are quicker to implement changes than those who are just receiving orders.

- *Rewarding support.* When employees can see a personal benefit to themselves for participating in the change process they are more likely to support it. And employees learn quickly from seeing others rewarded.

- *Exercising authority.* Sometimes, especially during a crisis, change must come about quickly. At such times your leadership may have to become less consultative and more decisive. And if there is an employee whose personal antipathy toward you affects job performance or the performance of the organization, you may have to exercise the full extent of your authority and dismiss the employee.

The transition phase should follow the steps outlined in the succession plan. Taking over management of the business is a process that's best done patiently and in stages. A transition of steadily increasing responsibility gives you the opportunity to:

- *Make mistakes.* Your right to make mistakes is an important issue to discuss with the retiring owner(s), especially if they are your parents. Getting agreement that the mistakes you make are less important than how you go about fixing them will help build confidence in your judgment.

☑ **Memory Check 8.24**
True or False? It is usually an advantage to include outside directors on the board of directors for the family firm.

☑ **Memory Check 8.25**
True or False? The majority of people do not like to initiate change.

- *Take advantage of the retiring founder's experience.* A true desire to learn from the retiring generation will build mutual respect. By asking more questions and expressing fewer opinions you are demonstrating how you value experience.
- *Build leadership skills.* Employees will need some time to adjust and accept a new boss. Asking them for advice in their areas of expertise is an important factor in achieving mutual respect.
- *Transfer customer loyalty.* In an abrupt transition of power, customers are likely to scrutinize the takeover, wondering if there will be problems with supply or service. A gradual transition will help maintain confidence in your company.
- *Leave your options open, just in case.* As you get closer to assuming full leadership of the company you may decide it's really not for you. Or, the retiring owners may decide that they just can't give up control. While the transition of power is not complete, there is always the option of changing plans.

Answers to Memory Check Questions

8.1 F   8.2 F   8.3 T   8.4 T   8.5 T   8.6 F   8.7 T   8.8 F   8.9 F   8.10 F
8.11 T   8.12 T   8.13 T   8.14 F   8.15 F   8.16 F   8.17 F   8.18 F   8.19 T   8.20 T
8.21 F   8.22 T   8.23 F   8.24 T   8.25 T

Questions for Discussion

1. Are there differences in the problems faced by male and female entrepreneurs when taking over a family business? Discuss.
2. Some definitions of "family business" indicate that at least two members of an owning family must work in the firm. Other definitions indicate that at least two members of an owning family had to work in the business at some point. Think up some scenarios showing that the second definition would be better.
3. Discuss the advantages and disadvantages of working full-time with your spouse in a business where only the two of you are the owners and in a business where other family members also have ownership.
4. What are the major causes of intergenerational conflict? How do these manifest in a family business?
5. Discuss the idea that normal intergenerational conflicts are magnified in immigrant families.
6. What are the reasons that aging business owners tend to resist preparing for retirement? (Be careful of age prejudice in your discussion.)
7. What is the rationale behind capital gains taxes when a business is transferred? What is the rationale behind allowing significant capital gains exemptions for Canadians?
8. Do parents have an obligation to treat all of their children equally? When might this not be the case? How can this apply to issues of inheritance?
9. Is it possible to transfer employee loyalty to a new generation of business owners? How?
10. What are the concerns and problems of non-family members who work for a family business? How can these be dealt with?
11. Why is it important for everyone to have a will? Why are people reluctant to prepare their wills?

Case for Discussion

Over the years, the Vanova family has made a lot of money from their boat-cleaning business. Grandpa Stephan Vanova started the business in the 1960s, when he was working at one of the marinas at the west end of the city's lakeshore. Grandpa Stephan had been amazed that most pleasure boats in Canada spent less than half the year in the water. And the half that they were out of the water was when he could make some money. So he bought an old truck body plant (with huge roll-up doors) near the marinas and took in boats for cleaning during the winter.

Today, Vanova Boat Lifting and Detailing Inc. has contracts with four marinas to crane-lift boats out of the water at the end of the season, and to inspect and shrink-wrap them for the winter. When the boats are inspected, each owner is provided with a price for general exterior cleaning and another price for interior and exterior detailing. If an owner chooses either of the services, Vanova completes the work at some point before the end of the winter and re-wraps the boat, returning it to the marina. When the boating season starts, Vanova unwraps the boat and lifts it back into the water.

Grandpa Stephan is long gone, and today, the company is operated by Grandpa's son, Steven, the company president. Steven, himself, is nearing retirement age but resists any talk of giving up the company reins. Steven's 33-year-old son, Stevie Jr., also works in the business and is eager to take over the firm at some vague point in the future. Vanova is a corporation and all shares are held by family members who form a board of directors. Even though Steven runs the company, he only owns 45 percent of the shares. Steven's three sisters, who do not work in the business, each own 15 percent. And Stevie Jr. and his wife, Lorna, own the final 10 percent, a wedding gift from Grandpa Stephan, just before his passing.

Steven does not get along with his sisters, who have always criticized the way he runs the company. Stevie Jr. always found this amusing because, working in the business, he knew his dad's decisions were almost always the right ones. And even though Steven only has a 45 percent minority of the shares, he always carries the company decisions because Stevie Jr. has always voted his and Lorna's shares with his dad, providing a 55 percent majority.

For several years, Steven's sisters have been pushing for a major expansion of the company into boat repair, marine engine repair, or even the purchase of a marina. Steven has successfully resisted this, arguing that a better way to expand would be to increase capacity for the services the company already provides, just doing more of the same.

But now things are becoming complicated, just before an upcoming directors' meeting. Stevie Jr.'s wife has filed for divorce, claiming half of their joint ownership in the company, 5 percent of the shares. Stevie Jr.'s three aunts have told him that, at the meeting, they will propose expansion of the firm into boat repair and that Lorna has agreed to vote her 5 percent of the shares along with their 45 percent. If Stevie Jr. votes with his dad, each side will have 50 percent, producing a deadlock, and no decisions can be made. On the other hand, the aunts propose, if Stevie Jr. votes with them, they will also vote to make Stevie Jr. president of the company, replacing his dad.

If Stevie Jr. votes with his aunts, he will be betraying his father. If he votes with his father, the company will be unable to move forward with any major decisions.

1. What provisions could this company have put in its shareholder agreement to prevent a vote deadlock, such as could happen here?

2. What are the likely reasons that no clear plans have been made for Stevie Jr. to take over the firm at some point?

3. If Stevie Jr. votes with his aunts and estranged wife, what will this likely mean for the future of the company? What will it mean for future family relationships?

4. If Steven has been running the company profitably for many years, why might his sisters be constantly disagreeing with him?

5. What are some possible solutions to end the deadlock and ensure stable management for the company in the future?

The Business Plan, Alternative Module:
THE FAMILY FIRM

Family/Business Structure

1. Briefly describe the history of your family business, identifying those family members currently involved with the company. If necessary, attach a family tree as an appendix.

2. Explain the legal form and the distribution of ownership of the business.

3. Briefly explain the advantages and disadvantages for your family members of being in business together.

4. Describe any formal company policies or informal techniques used by the family that are designed to reduce conflict among family members.

The Successor(s)

5. Describe the response of family and employees to your declaration of intent to take over leadership of the family business.

6. Briefly explain your suitability to lead the business, in terms of your work experience and education.

7. Describe any personal contacts, association memberships, or other techniques that you will use to stay abreast of issues related to family businesses.

Current Leader/Owner(s)

8. Identify specific sources of information on retirement and succession, as well as the particular advisers the current business owner(s) will rely on for planning advice.

9. Briefly outline the retirement plans for the current owner(s) of the business, including retirement goals, income, living arrangements, ongoing involvement in the business, and planned dates for retirement.

10. Explain the estate planning for the current owner(s), describing major provisions of wills and powers of attorney as well as the types of insurance carried.

Business Succession

11. Describe specifically the mechanism for transferring control of the business to the successor(s) and how ownership of the business will be distributed and controlled.

12. Describe the steps in the transition of control from the current owner(s) to the successor(s), with a clear time frame for each step.

13. List the major problems you expect to face as the new leader(s) of the business and how you will deal with these issues.

14. Briefly describe your planned changes for the business and how they will avoid the typical pitfalls of second-generation owners.

Chapter 9

Managing for Growth: How Can I Expand My Business?

So far, this text has been about becoming an entrepreneur. Part 1 was about starting your own brand-new business. Part 2 was about alternative ways of becoming an entrepreneur. Now, in Part 3, we will focus on the knowledge and skills needed to keep a business running profitably. With what you know about the income statement, you should recognize that there are two basic ways to increase profits: either increase sales or decrease costs and expenses. The first option is about business growth. This is covered in Chapter 9. The second option is about managing for greater efficiency, covered in Chapter 10. Chapter 11 is about the issues an entrepreneur has to deal with in today's fast-changing business environment. And the final chapter, Chapter 12, is a detailed discussion of business plans.

This chapter will help you plan for *business growth* by answering the following questions:

- **Does My Business Need to Grow?**
- **How Will I Increase My Sales?**
- **Should I Consider Exporting?**
- **How Do I Finance Growth?**

Learning Objectives

On completion of this chapter, you should be able to:

1 Delineate five stages of the business cycle.

2 Discuss five early warning signs of decline for a small business.

3 Explain the four factors involved in SWOT analysis.

4 Outline and discuss the three basic strategies for increasing sales.

5 Compare building a chain with selling franchises.

6 Discuss at least two advantages and two disadvantages of export markets for small firms.

7 Identify three aspects of a company's finances that concern lenders or investors.

8 Calculate a *payback period*.

9 Prepare a *strategic growth plan* for an established business.

DOES MY BUSINESS NEED TO GROW?

Business Cycle

Many businesses never really get a proper start in life and die in their infancy. Of those that survive and become established, some remain for many years pretty much the same as they were at start-up. But these are a minority. More typically, small enterprises are seen as going through a life cycle with several specific stages:

- *Start-up.* Little revenue, high expenses (therefore little or no profit), and a high failure rate are the characteristics of this stage.

- *Growth.* At this stage the business experiences increasing revenue and profits, plus a declining risk of failure.
- *Maturity.* The business levels off in this stage, with stable sales and profits, plus a low risk of failure.
- *Decline.* Here is where profits fall; this stage will ultimately lead to the failure of the business. *Ask yourself: Does this mean that my business is doomed from the start?* The length of the cycle is hugely variable depending on your services or products and your markets. It may take only months for your business to go into decline or it may take many decades.

Fortunately, another stage in the cycle can counteract decline:

- *Renewal.* This stage is where the business adapts to the changing environment—changes in customer needs, in technology, in the competition, and so on. In many ways it is similar to the start-up stage, with high expenses and very slow growth (see Figure 9.1).

⭐ Head Start Exercise

9.1 Estimate where your company fits in the business cycle. Give reasons for your placement (1/4 page maximum). Note: Students who are using the Head Start Exercises as class assignments will each have to interview an entrepreneur with an existing business. Each student can use this firm as an example for the exercise assignments.

✓ Memory Check 9.1
True or False? The growth stage of the business cycle is characterized by stable sales and profits.

The business life cycle is still not well understood, but it is clear that it functions independent of the economy. Even when a whole industry is going through growth, a certain number of firms in that industry will still be in decline.[1] The sooner an entrepreneur recognizes (or better, anticipates) the start of decline, the sooner the process of **renewal** can be started so that the business may continue to grow. *Ask yourself: Does a business have to grow?* There is the old saying "grow or die," but a truer saying for business might be "change or die." When a real opportunity for growth presents itself, if you don't take it, your competitors will. And if your direct competitors are allowed to grow unchallenged, they will eventually be in a position to overwhelm your enterprise. But this doesn't mean that you must always meet your competition in a head-to-head battle. Renewal for your firm may mean a strategy of finding a new direction, a new **niche**. In fact, growth for some firms comes by selling fewer products or services to fewer types of customers—in other words, greater specialization. By becoming more of a specialist, you could be turning your direct competition into indirect competition.

renewal A part of the business cycle; the process of refocusing the business, leading to a new phase of growth.

niche A very small market segment that a business satisfies with specialized products or services.

Figure 9.1 The Business Life Cycle

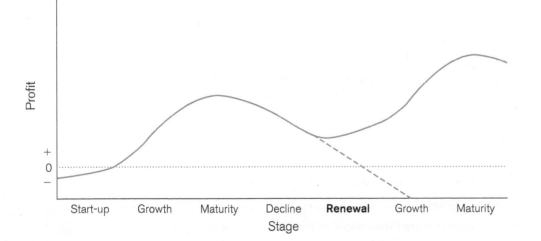

Growing in a Shrinking Market

Thirty-five years ago, Ed Guca was just an average moviegoer when his wife, Wanda, bought him an original movie poster for Ridley's Scott's sci-fi classic *Alien*. This sparked an interest that led to trading in posters at movie memorabilia shows, where customers eventually started to ask Ed where his store was located. Leasing was an option, but Ed decided to take a risk and buy a store, a risk that would pay off well, in time.

The store opened in 1980, at a time when the new technology of home video cassette players was just starting to catch on. Movies for the new machines tended to retail at around $120 a piece and not many places were renting them. So Ed decided to augment his movie poster business by renting out movie cassettes, starting with just 44 titles. It didn't take long for movie rentals to become the largest source of income for the business, with the store recently boasting over 26 000 titles. The industry went through a number of technology changes (including Beta, VHS, 12" laser disks, and others), finally settling on DVD as the prime movie medium. Ed resisted moving into Blu-ray, already anticipating the shift toward downloading movies. And it was this shift that started the movie rental business into its huge decline.

Ed blames the decline not just on the technology changes that allowed downloading but also on issues of digital piracy—the weakness of the technology. The closing of the large video rental chains, however, was what allowed Ed to stay profitably in business during that decline. As the competition disappeared, Ed, with his high-traffic, high-visibility site, was able to get a larger and larger share, albeit of a shrinking market. And even with the decline of his own rental business, Ed has been able to shift the focus of the business back to movie posters.

At the time of interviewing, Ed predicted that the future of home viewing for movies would be through systems like UltraViolet, where the viewer has no physical medium holding a copy of the film. Instead, you purchase access to the film, which remains in "the cloud," and you can stream it anytime, to any device registered to you. The UltraViolet system is a partnership of many film studios, TV companies, and internet companies. This system (and other competing models under development) gives the film studios much more control over the distribution of their products and may herald increasing prices for home use of video.

Over the past few years, the movie poster business has stayed pretty steady and even increased as Ed has turned to internet advertising. But he cautions anyone interested in the movie memorabilia industry that "the internet has changed everything. Now, this is mostly an online business and it is difficult to sell these items through a store." And even though the goodwill value of the business may have declined, the past few years have been a boon for commercial real estate. So Ed's risky investment has paid off. Although Ed and Wanda are still running the store, they no longer need the 3000 square feet of retail space for their business and are looking to bring in a coffee shop or some other complimentary business to take half the space. See the Movie Art Decor website at www.movieartdecor.com.

Indicators for Renewal

The warning signs or indicators that your business needs renewal can be either internal or external to the business and include issues relating to:

- sales and profits
- employee turnover
- available capacity
- market share/market potential
- competition
- various other cues that might be particular to your industry

Sales and Profits Sales forecasting for a business at start-up is both difficult and inaccurate. But for the established firm, sales are more predictable because the forecast is based on past sales. Past sales are then adjusted for your growth pattern, for known changes in the market or changes in the competition, and for any changes in your own products, services, and promotion. For example, if you know that 20 percent of sales are a direct result of customers seeing your ads, and you are going to increase your advertising budget by 50 percent, you may reasonably forecast a 10 percent increase in sales (50 percent of 20 percent = 10 percent). But let's say your actual sales have fallen short of the forecast for several periods in a row. This may be an early indicator that your business is going into decline. For some firms, a more immediate warning is the loss of a key customer, which could represent a substantial portion of the company's sales. In such a case, it is imperative to find out why the customer has switched suppliers in order to determine if the same cause could result in a pattern of decline.

Not reaching your expected profit, or a pattern of falling profit, should also act as a warning that strategic changes may be needed. But apart from the pure value of your profit is the issue of profitability, or relative return on investment (ROI). For example, you might have $200 000 invested in a silk weaving business. Last year, after paying yourself a reasonable salary, the business made $8000 in net profit. This would be a 4 percent return on your investment (ROI) of $200 000. Now, you may think this is an acceptable return—but if at the time the average silk weaving business in Canada is making an 8 percent ROI, your business cannot be considered particularly profitable—another warning sign. In this case, you are comparing your profitability to the average profitability of companies in your industry, usually based on information from Statistics Canada. This sort of ratio analysis (see Chapter 6, "Valuation Concepts") is not a very accurate process since the statistics you will use may be several years out of date. Nevertheless, it can serve as an indicator of your performance pattern and where you are in the business cycle.

Employee Turnover Losing employees and hiring replacements is normal for most businesses, and the rate at which this takes place can vary significantly from industry to industry, and from company to company. But for any firm with employees, there is usually some recognizable pattern of employee turnover. Any sudden increase in turnover is a warning sign, especially when lost employees can be seen going to the competition. And just as the loss of a key customer can be critical for a small firm, the loss of a key employee can be devastating when there is no one else available to fill the role.

Whenever an employee decides to leave your business, it is very important that you conduct an **exit interview** with the departing member of your staff. One objective in holding such a meeting is to make sure that the employee leaves on good terms, keeping the door open for return and ensuring that the employee will have good things to say about your firm. But the most important purpose of the exit interview is to find out why the employee is leaving. This may take some patience and careful discussion. Employees who may be leaving because they can't stand your management style, or who feel that their future is much more secure with the competition, may be reluctant to come out and say so. On the other hand, an employee who is leaving may not feel the need to be diplomatic and could end up informing you of some critical problem in the organization. There are no guarantees on the outcome, but you cannot afford to let slip an opportunity to interview any employee who quits.

Available Capacity A more subtle issue that can indicate a firm's need for a new strategy relates to the idea of operating capacity—**100 percent capacity** represents the highest amount of activity (sales revenue) that a business can handle in a year without buying more equipment, hiring new staff, opening another store, or in some other way increasing the capacity of the business. For example, if your business consists of you and a small excavating

Get Help 9.1
Financial ratios, including indicators of profitability, are listed by industry on the Industry Canada SME Benchmarking site, at www.sme.ic.gc.ca. This site has a feature that allows you to input your own financial data and receive a report comparing your firm to the industry averages. When using this site, a good hint is to select the Incorporated Businesses option for building your profile, since more financial data is available for corporations. Your accountant is an important aid in interpreting ratio analysis information.

exit interview An interview with a departing employee intended to find out any reasons for the employee's dissatisfaction as well as to have the employee leave with positive feelings about the company.

Memory Check 9.2
True or False? Sales forecasting for established firms is easier than for start-ups.

100 percent capacity The maximum amount of sales or production that a company could generate in a year as the company currently stands in terms of space, equipment, and employees.

machine (for landscaping, or digging pools and small foundations), you may hire out yourself and the machine for, let's say, $100 per hour. Considering some downtime for maintenance of the equipment and some time for inclement weather, you could still probably work as many as 45 hours a week, or (45 × 52 =) 2340 hours a year. At $100 per hour, this would mean that your business, under perfect conditions, could bring in (2,340 × $100 =) $234 000 in a year. This would be 100 percent capacity for your firm. To have sales in excess of $234 000, you would have to increase your capacity, likely by buying a second machine and hiring another operator.

The concept of 100 percent capacity can be applied to most businesses. Picture yourself owning a restaurant that seats 50 people, where the average meal price is $20 and, on average, customers spend about an hour eating. For your market, under the best possible circumstances, you could turn over each of your seats twice at lunchtime and three times in the evening. This means that all of your seats would be full between noon and 2:00 pm (50 × 2 = 100 meals) and between 6:00 and 9:00 pm (50 × 3 = 150 meals), for a total of 250 meals per day. Over a year, this would produce sales of $1 825 000 (250 meals × $20 per meal × 365 days). This represents your 100 percent capacity. Most restaurants operate at only a tiny percentage of their full capacity, while businesses like the example of the excavator often have to operate at better than 50 percent just to break even.

Like the concept of break-even, with which it can be associated, 100 percent capacity is not a very precise tool. Typical methods of estimating 100 percent capacity for a business include:

- *Machinery or equipment capacity* (the dollar income value of everything your equipment could produce in a year)

- *Facilities capacity* (e.g., the number of seats in your theatre × the number of performances a year × the average ticket price)

- *Employee capacity* (e.g., the maximum number of customers your travel agents can serve in a day × your average commission × the number of working days per year)

- *Best sales period* (e.g., using the best day of sales your business has ever had × the number of selling days per year; or your best week or month or quarter projected to the entire year)

It is usually convenient to express 100 percent capacity in dollars, but this is not always a valid measure. For example, as a freelance writer you may be capable of producing and selling 1500 words a day of quality copy. But 1500 words can represent a huge variation in revenue. You could be paid very different amounts for the same amount of work, depending on whether it is for work on a children's advice column in a small local paper or an internationally best-selling novel. You may be writing as much as you are capable of each day (working at 100 percent capacity), but not necessarily bringing in as much money as you are capable of. So, instead of dollars, some firms must represent 100 percent capacity in terms of units of output (in this case, words).

Memory Check 9.3
True or False? Sales forecasting for established firms is easier than for new firms.

Head Start Exercise

9.2   Estimate 100 percent capacity for your business, clearly explaining the method you use (1/4 page maximum).

If you know your 100 percent capacity, you can easily calculate the percentage of capacity that your business is currently operating at:

$$\frac{\text{Current sales volume}}{\text{Sales at 100\% capacity}} \times 100\% = \text{Current \% of capacity}$$

Your operating level, or current percentage of capacity, and your growth pattern expressed as a percentage of capacity are important inputs for strategic planning. For example, your business may be operating at 80 percent capacity. Last year, you were at 60 percent, and the year before at 45 percent. By projecting the annual growth rate (115 percent, 120 percent, 125 percent), you get a pattern of 45 percent, 60 percent, 80 percent, and for the next year 105 percent—5 percent more business than you can handle. If you don't move to either increase capacity, or, alternatively, change the focus of your business, you will be encountering problems before the year is out. Signs that your business is operating at close to 100 percent can include turning away new customers, turning down jobs, late deliveries, or failure to meet deadlines.

Ask yourself: Is it good to have lots of spare capacity? You may have a business that consistently operates at only a small fraction of its full capacity. Considering that capacity is usually reflected as fixed expenses, operating at a low level is not the most economical way to run—spare capacity means unrealized profits. A pattern of operating at a small percentage of capacity is a clear indicator that your renewal strategy should be to increase sales (either through better promotion or finding new markets) in order to take advantage of the spare capacity.

Market Share and Market Potential It's possible that you are in a position where your sales and profits have been increasing by, let's say, 3 percent a year for the past three years. This might lead you to believe that your enterprise is comfortably growing. But if you are in an industry where the overall market potential (see Chapter 2, "Defining Market Potential") has been growing at 10 percent per year, your share of the available business has been shrinking despite your increasing sales. You will have been losing market share. Your market share is calculated as:

$$\frac{\text{Your sales of a particular product or service}}{\text{The market potential for that product or service}} \times 100\%$$

Ask yourself: Would I be able to calculate my market share? Obviously, in order to calculate your market share you must have some estimate of the entire market potential. Many entrepreneurs will estimate market potential as part of their start-up business plans and then carry on business for years, never giving a thought to how the market might change. However, for most industries there are convenient secondary sources an entrepreneur can use to maintain some ongoing sense of what is happening to the size of a particular market. These sources include:

- *Industry publications.* Trade journals and association newsletters are often the best way to keep abreast of market trends since the publishers know that market issues are of primary interest to their readers. In fact, trade journals will often conduct their own primary research to get information about industry trends. *Ask yourself: Are you familiar with all the publications aimed specifically at your industry?*

- *Economic reports.* The federal government (mostly through Industry Canada) provides a variety of economic reports showing trends in various sectors of the economy. As well, private groups, such as the Conference Board of Canada, publish their own analyses and projections for the economy. Large banks also produce a variety of published reports based on the predictions of their own economists.

- *Business periodicals.* These days there is no shortage of daily business news, but for strategic planning it is better to look at the broader kind of analysis found in magazines such as *Canadian Business* or *Report on Business Magazine.* And because Canada so often follows American trends in business, it may be worthwhile to look at publications such as *The Economist* or *Forbes* magazine.

Get Help 9.2
Speak to a reference librarian at your public library or community college to make sure you are familiar with all the publications related to your industry.

Get Help 9.3
Start with the Canada Business Network, at www.canadabusiness.ca and click on Planning, then Market Research and Statistics, then Canadian Economy, for links to a variety of reports. For examples of bank reports, try www.bmo.com.

Get Help 9.4
Use your search engine to look for "media monitoring services" if you require clippings about your products or services, your own company, or even your competitors.

■ *Trend newsletters*. These reports provide broad analysis of current trends (growing or declining markets, changing attitudes, new technologies, etc.), often with some expert predictions for the future. These reports are prepared from analyses of items in a broad range of media. It is even possible to have your own customized reports or even just electronic clippings of the current media stories on any topic you specify.

Clearly, it is important to know how the market potential—how much business is out there—is changing over time. Is it growing? Shrinking? Remaining stable? For example, the consumer market for mobile phones grew at a very rapid pace for several years, then fell steeply to a point where it levelled off. The big drop came when pretty much everyone who was going to get a mobile phone had one. This was the market saturation point. The relatively steady business that came after the drop was from the natural growth in the population, as well as current users replacing and upgrading equipment. Markets tend to be cyclical, picking up with the introduction of new products and falling after the market is saturated. By historically tracking the market potential, you can have some idea about the future demand for your products or services. An approaching saturation point is a definite warning that you must embark on some form of renewal.

Competition—Direct

Identifying your direct and indirect competition was part of the start-up business plan. But once your business is running, you must develop ways of regularly monitoring the competition for changes. Have your competitors decided to open new locations? Where? Are they purchasing a new type of machinery? What? Are they starting new advertising campaigns? When? Are they hiring new managers? Who? Are they laying off employees? Why? You'd like to know all of this, and just about anything else of strategic value concerning changes in your competition. Techniques for keeping an eye on the direct competition include:

Memory Check 9.4
True or False? Market potential is made up of your market share plus the market share of all your competitors.

■ Bookmarking and regularly monitoring the websites of competitors, looking for changes in their marketing mix and for any special announcements.

■ Following competitors on Twitter, Facebook, and other social media.

■ Doing regular web searches for recent references to competitors.

■ Participating in trade associations where you can meet with other entrepreneurs in the same industry and where the natural lunchtime topic of conversation is business. It's surprising what your competitor may reveal in a social setting.

■ Using clipping services to let you know what the media are saying about your competitors (see above).

■ "Shopping" competitors regularly by making phone calls requesting information, or taking trips to retail sites. (Note the ethical issue of being careful not to abuse the time of commission salespeople who will think you are a prospective customer.)

■ Gathering information from your own sales prospects and new customers (who presumably are or were dealing with your competition).

■ Undertaking formal primary marketing research that surveys customer experiences with you and your competitors.

Competition—Indirect

It is a definite warning for renewal when competitors, perhaps many times larger than your company, invade your territory. Huge indirect competitors often strike terror into the hearts of small entrepreneurs, who complain that they cannot compete with the big box retailers or the giant **multinational** manufacturing and service companies. True, you usually cannot compete on price against such large buying power, but these big companies are committed to a strategy of serving the broadest possible markets. Your small-town paint store does not have to go out of business when Home Depot opens up in your area. But you may have to redefine what you are selling (perhaps specialize

multinational A very large company that typically has supply sources or facilities in several countries and markets its products internationally.

in high-end designer wallpaper) and redefine to whom you are selling (perhaps target the new downtown condo-dwellers and wealthy owners of older homes).

It is necessary to look carefully at your large competitors and identify goods and services that they do not provide or groups that they do not cater to. You are looking for things that are just not economical for them to get into, or areas where they cannot be flexible. Burger King will not make your favourite meal of a chicken salad sandwich on rye with a side order of beans. But the local diner where you regularly eat lunch will have no problem filling your order. The smaller firm has the advantage of flexibility.

> **A Note of Perspective:** Theoretically, it would be nice to think of a business as continually assessing and renewing itself, constantly anticipating and smoothly responding to changes in the environment. In reality, businesses, like most other forms of human endeavour, develop in fits and starts. Rarely are major changes to a business proactive in nature. More typically, the entrepreneur is responding to problems in the enterprise or the environment. Entrepreneurs who are true visionaries are rare, and the best that the rest of us can hope for is to recognize the warning signs when it's time for change.

⭐ Head Start Exercise

9.3 Make a list of any warning signs that might indicate your business is approaching decline (1/4 page maximum).

SWOT Analysis

Identifying the need for renewal in your business is only recognizing the problem. To address the need, you still have to develop a revised business plan. But before doing that, you should perform some form of **SWOT analysis**. This means a broad look at the internal and external advantages and disadvantages of your business: strengths, weaknesses, opportunities, and threats.

SWOT analysis is a form of marketing research that includes the kind of information described in the "Indicators for Renewal" section above. But SWOT is also much wider in focus. In your original feasibility research, you knew exactly what you were trying to calculate. In SWOT analysis, you start out not knowing as precisely what you are looking for. What you perceive as your greatest strength may, in fact, just be the industry average. You may have very little idea of where your opportunities and threats lie. Because of this, much of SWOT consists of **hypothesis testing**. For example, you may believe that low pricing is the single biggest factor that your customers use in deciding to buy from you. When this hypothesis is tested (perhaps a telephone survey conducted on a sample of your customers), it may turn out that most of them come to you simply because of your convenient location—and that they would continue to come even if your prices were higher. Your hypothesis, or assumption, was wrong.

SWOT analysis Research and drawing conclusions about the strengths and weaknesses of a particular company, as well as about the opportunities and threats that it faces.

hypothesis testing Research to see whether a particular assumption can be supported by the evidence.

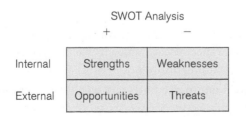

SWOT Analysis

	+	−
Internal	Strengths	Weaknesses
External	Opportunities	Threats

This research is more complicated than gathering the descriptive kind of information used in your feasibility research. In addition, it requires more careful analysis and the drawing of conclusions (the creation of new hypotheses) on which you are going to base the future strategy of your business. Presumably, the research is also taking place when the value of your business is much greater than it was at start-up. This means that you have more to lose from bad strategic decisions. As a result, the likelihood of your needing professional help in performing the SWOT analysis is greater than it was for start-up research.

Strengths and Weaknesses *Ask yourself: What could be the difficulties in identifying the strengths and weaknesses of my enterprise?* Like many entrepreneurs, you may find describing the weaknesses of your business as difficult as describing the shortcomings of your own children. It's hard to be objective. And in describing the strengths of your business, there is a tendency to list vague platitudes like saying that you have a good reputation or that you provide excellent customer service. Such comments have little meaning unless you can specifically answer the question: Compared to what? Even though strengths and weaknesses are internal factors of a business, the benchmarks for describing them are usually external: compared to specific competition, compared to industry averages, or compared to customer expectations.

Examples of internal issues that would be described as strengths or weaknesses include:

- *Site.* For example, if you have a retail store that gets considerably less traffic than your direct competitor gets, this would be a considerable weakness.
- *Image.* If your ice-fishing business is widely recognized as the cheapest place to rent a hut (and if low price is an important issue for your market), this would be a powerful strength.
- *Product/service mix.* Your business may sell industrial filters and have the exclusive rights to distribute an improved patented filter throughout Canada—for you, a huge competitive strength.
- *People and expertise.* Let's say you have an interior design firm and your partner is the only interior designer in your town who has a certificate in feng shui (the Chinese art of creating harmony in the human environment). During a time when feng shui is wildly popular, you would have a big strength.
- *Financial position.* You may have very little equity in your company and almost no cash reserves compared to your larger competitors. This weakness makes you less likely to survive tough sales periods.

Contracts, intellectual property, methods, systems, and many other aspects of your business can be seen as relative strengths or weaknesses.

⭐ Head Start Exercise

9.4 List your major assumptions or beliefs about the strengths and weaknesses of your business (1/4 page maximum).

Opportunities and Threats Opportunities and threats can arise whenever something (just about anything) in your environment changes. Just a few examples of such changes are:

- *Legislation.* A law that perhaps changes the way education is funded by giving an annual education allowance to each student would represent a great opportunity for your small aesthetics-training institute.
- *Demographics.* A rapid fall in the birth rate would be a serious threat for your baby-furniture plant.

- *Competition*. The bankruptcy of your leading direct competitor would be a wonderful opportunity for your custom bookbinding company.
- *Technology*. The invention of truly wrinkle-free, stain-free, odour-free clothing would be a serious threat to your small dry-cleaning chain.

Changes in social patterns, fashion, the economy, government foreign policy, climate, disease patterns, population, lifestyle—any of these could hold threats or opportunities for your business.

⭐ Head Start Exercises

9.5 List your major assumptions or beliefs about the opportunities and threats facing your business (1/4 page maximum).

9.6 Briefly describe research approaches you could use to test your SWOT assumptions (1/2 page maximum).

In the SWOT analysis you investigate your hypotheses, modify them as required to fit the evidence, and so identify the real strengths, weaknesses, opportunities, and threats facing your business. Then, on the basis of this analysis, you can decide how to either expand or refocus your venture for long-term profitability.

HOW WILL I INCREASE MY SALES?

In many cases, the sales of a business will change because of changes in the marketplace. For example, if the population in the area of your market grows, you will likely have an increase in sales. Conversely, if four new competitors move into your stable market area, you will likely have a decrease in sales. You cannot control changes in the marketplace, but you can control your own strategy in an attempt to increase sales.

You can choose from three basic strategies to help your company grow:

- You can sell more of what you're already selling to the customer groups you're already selling to. This is **market share expansion**, since generally you are getting your new sales by taking business away from the competition.
- You can sell new things to the customer groups you're already selling to. This is called **product/service expansion**
- You can sell what you're already selling, but to new groups of customers. In this case we are talking about **market segment expansion**.

Memory Check 9.5
True or False? Strengths and weaknesses in SWOT analysis refer to external factors of a business.

market share expansion
Growth by selling more of the same products and services that a business is already selling to the same customer groups that the business already targets; capturing a greater portion of the market potential.

product/service expansion
Growth by selling new products and/or services to the customer groups that a business already targets.

market segment expansion
Growth by selling the products and services that a business already offers to new groups of customers.

> **A Note of Perspective:** It is also possible to grow your business by buying other businesses in the same field and incorporating them into your firm. This acquisition strategy is a less common approach to growth for small firms and it involves all the complexity of buying a business (see Chapter 06, "The Purchase Alternative") as well as the many problems of integrating the ventures or attempting to run them as separate entities. As a result, business acquisitions are not dealt with in this text.

As part of a well-managed growth strategy, you should not embark on more than one of the three basic strategies at a time. If you attempt to sell totally new products or services to totally new groups of customers, you are essentially starting a new business. If you attempt one strategy at a time, you will be facing much lower risk. For example, you may own a full-service car wash that has declining sales due to the growth of mini-washes in franchise gas bars. You may decide to fight back through

- market share expansion, perhaps with an advertising and sales promotion campaign mailing discount coupons to consumers in your area; or

- market segment expansion, maybe by trying to get high-volume contracts with local used-car dealers who could use your wash facilities; or

- product/service expansion, possibly by installing your own pumps and selling gasoline.

Ask yourself: What would be the problem with attempting these three strategies simultaneously? By taking on so much change, there is a huge risk that your business—even your life—will become unmanageable. While trying to plan, execute, and measure the effectiveness of your advertising campaign, you will also be negotiating with gasoline suppliers, franchisors, construction people, auto dealers, and doubtless the bank or some other source for financing it all. With so many issues to deal with, there is the danger that you will lose your strategic focus and have your time and attention used up by the thousand small issues that will arise. Also, by employing one strategy at a time, you will be more able to measure the effectiveness of your approach.

 Get Help 9.6

The website for *Profit* magazine offers tools and links to help entrepreneurs plan business expansion: www.profitguide .com. Click on Essential Web Guide.

Market Share Expansion

An increase in market share (selling a greater percentage of the products and services purchased by your current target groups) is usually related to changes in your price and promotion strategies. A recent study of small manufacturers indicates that the fastest route to growth is by competing on the basis of price.[2] But before lowering your price in the hope of greater market penetration, consider the effect this will have on profit. A lower price means a lower per-unit profit, so the increase in volume you are expecting will have to be more than enough to make up for lost profit—enough to actually increase the profit. And it is a dangerous strategy to lower your price temporarily to get new customers, hoping that you can later raise prices and that the customers will stay with you because of some other competitive advantage (such as superior products, services, location, etc.). If you are working in a price-sensitive market, the customers will tend to leave when your prices go back up.

Ask yourself: How will I know the optimum amount to lower prices to get the market share I want? Marketing research can make predictions about your future market share using techniques like surveys and even test marketing. As well, you can make financial projections by having your projected income statements on a spreadsheet where you can change sales and cost figures to see the impact on your future profit. In some cases, however, you will have to use a system of trial and error by changing your prices in slow increments and measuring the effect on your sales volume and profit.

Memory Check 9.6

True or False? Market segment expansion means growth by selling to new groups of customers those products and services that you already provide.

⭐ **Head Start Exercise**

9.7 Estimate how low you could move your prices and still make a profit (refer to your break-even point). Speculate about how such pricing would affect your market share and how your competition would likely respond (1/2 page maximum).

Changes in promotion that you may consider for increasing your market share would include

- increased personal selling, through the hiring of more sales staff or a more aggressive sales approach that could include changing the incentives for your salespeople;

- increased sales promotion and publicity activities, although these tend to have only a short-term effect on sales activities as opposed to a more permanent capture of market share; or

- increased advertising, through either greater frequency in currently used media or an expansion to new advertising media.

As you plan any changes in your promotion, you must also plan methods for measuring the effects of those changes. And by making one change at a time, you will more easily be able to measure the effects of your changes.

With changes in either your prices or your promotion techniques, there is the constant possibility that your competition will quickly make similar changes in response. And there is even the possibility that this could trigger an advertising war (where you and your competitors are spending an uneconomical amount to vie for the attention of customers) or worse, a price war (where neither you nor the competition can make money at the prices being charged). If the competitors decided to wage such a war indefinitely, the natural outcome would be that only the richest competitor would survive to own the entire market. Even with legislation to protect businesses against **predatory pricing** practices, the costs of getting involved in such a war (lost profit, time, legal costs) can be very high.

One dangerous assumption about increasing your market share is that if you are getting more of the pie, then all of your competitors must therefore be getting less. Envision that you own a remedial tutoring business that targets high school students in your suburban area. You estimate that last year you had 20 percent of a market that you share with three other independent firms (20 percent each) and a franchise unit of a national operation (20 percent). This year, because of new advertising, your share has increased to 25 percent, and for the next year you are targeting 30 percent. What you may not know is that the franchise operation this year grew to 35 percent of the market and next year is targeting 60 percent. The growth of this competitor represents a substantial threat to your business. This is an argument for why your knowledge of your market should not be a single research event at start-up, but more of an ongoing process.

A second tricky issue about increasing market share is that you must be careful not to be a victim of your own success by gaining market share beyond 100 percent of your capacity. For example, you may decide to increase market share for your gas fireplace company, which sells to consumers in your town. So you increase the commissions paid to your salespeople and step up your advertising until the orders start to pour in. But if you don't have the capacity to supply and install the volume of business you have created, you will be facing cancelled orders, an image problem with your new customers, and likely the alienation of your own sales staff, who will probably not be paid for cancelled work. Any attempt, therefore, to increase the market share should be undertaken cautiously and with consideration for your capacity to deliver.

Product/Service Expansion

The second obvious way to increase your sales is by finding something new to sell to your existing clientele. But introducing a new product can affect other elements of the marketing mix. It is best to start by adding products/services that work with your existing promotion, distribution, and pricing strategies. If you have a high-end shoe store that is already pricey, adding the option of custom-made shoes would be well in line with your image. But if yours were a discount shoe store, adding the custom-made option would require a change in pricing strategy that won't work for your market segment.

Any products or services that you add to your mix must be perceived as logical by your customers. For example, you may have some spare floor space in your party supply store and decide to install a key-making machine. Now, you may get the odd customer who is in the store and, on seeing the machine, remembers the need to have a key duplicated. But if your customer is at home, the need to get a key made will trigger a trip to the hardware store, not your business, since long habit makes this seem the logical supplier. Giant retailers, because they generate so much traffic and have so much advertising power, are able

predatory pricing Where a company loses money on a product or service by charging prices so low as to drive competitors from the market. Then the company recoups its losses by overcharging in a market where it has no competition.

Get Help 9.7
Canada's Competition Bureau administers the Competition Act, which forbids predatory pricing as a way of eliminating competition. See the bureau's website at competitionbureau.gc.ca.

to change customer perceptions about the logical product/service mix. So Walmart can teach you pretty quickly that it's normal to get your hair styled and your oil changed at the same place you buy underwear. But with a small business you will not have this power and so must cater to the already existing perceptions of customers, making only small logical changes. For instance, your bottled water delivery service could probably add ice delivery to the mix, but adding garden supplies would make no sense to the consumer.

✓ Memory Check 9.7
True or False? Predatory pricing usually benefits a smaller competitor.

You also must be careful not to add products that will not bring new profit. For example, you may have an ice cream store that carries 10 flavours of ice cream, which you sell in either cones or sundaes. In an attempt to get more business, you may decide to go to 20 flavours of ice cream plus 5 fresh-fruit flavours of frozen yogurt. You will now have the expense of increasing your freezer space and buying the equipment to mix the yogurt and fruit. It will also cost you money for the extra time it takes to prepare the yogurt cones—and you may find a problem with customers slowing the lineup because, with more to choose from, they are taking longer to make up their minds. And it's possible that, in the long run, you have absolutely no increase in sales at all. Sure, the customers are happy to pick from your new product selection, but without this expansion you might have had the same customers who would just choose from the original 10 flavours and be satisfied.

✓ Memory Check 9.8
True or False? A business cannot supply products or services beyond 100 percent of its capacity.

This example of adding extra flavours is an increase in the depth of the product mix. Adding yogurt, cakes, doughnuts, or other confection lines would be examples of increasing the breadth of the mix. *Ask yourself: Is it best to increase the breadth or depth?* Generally, it is easier and cheaper to increase depth, but less likely to bring new profit from existing customers. Deepening the mix is more likely to be a move in response to competition or changing trends. Offering whole new product lines (more breadth) has greater potential for new profit, but also greater risk.

❓ Get Help 9.8
There are many international trade directories, which can be searched for specific product categories Search for B2B (business-to-business) trade directories or check the Business.com search engine for trade directories or even specific products: www.business.com.

Finding or Developing Products If your business involves reselling products (you're a wholesaler or retailer), then your task is to find appropriate new products for your customers. If you're a manufacturer or pure service business, you are more likely to be developing the products or services yourself. *Ask yourself: How do I know which products or services to find or develop?* Conventional business advice would be to formally research the needs and wants of your customers before seeking or developing new offerings for them. Certainly, this is the professional marketing approach and should be used whenever economically possible. But with smaller retailers and wholesalers it is more likely that the process starts with finding a product that you then realize would be ideal for your customers. The solution may present itself before you have even identified the problem. You may, then, as a small retailer or wholesaler, see your task as staying up to date on what products are available. *Ask yourself: Where could I find out about new products to resell?* This task has been made easier than ever with the growing number of online product catalogues and trade directories. There are also the more traditional sources of information such as trade associations, trade shows, industry publications, and world trade centres. Many large cities have World Trade Centers, supported by various levels of government, local chambers of commerce, and other non-profit organizations. These centres offer a variety of activities and services that promote international trade.

❓ Get Help 9.9
You can find the world trade centre closest to you from the website of the World Trade Centers Association: wtca.org.

Shopping for products that you can resell is still shopping, an activity that most of us enjoy. Keep in mind, however, that finding new products is a process of shopping for your customers' needs, not your personal tastes. So it shouldn't be a seat-of-the-pants exercise. At least some research should be carried out before any final decision on whether to carry a new product. For example, you may want to determine:

✓ Memory Check 9.9
True or False? It's always best to trust your instincts when looking for new products to resell.

- *Customer needs and benefits.* Interviews with customers and providing samples for customers to try out will show if the new product can satisfy a true need.
- *Sales potential for the product.* This can be determined by test marketing with a representative sample of your customers and extrapolating from the sales results.

- *Profit potential for the product.* This should include an estimate of your sales as well as your direct costs plus all related overhead for promoting, storing, delivering, and servicing related to the product.

- *Length of the product life cycle.* Fashion issues or leapfrogging technologies can mean that even though a product is new, it is going to become obsolete so quickly that it's not economical for you to offer it. For some products, an estimate of the length of this cycle may be the deciding factor in whether it will be added to your product mix.

Like the business cycle, individual products tend to have their own life cycle with the stages of

- *Introduction.* This is when the product requires high levels of promotion and high levels of monitoring (research) for future profitability.

- *Growth.* During this stage, successful methods for promoting the product have been refined and sales are increasing.

- *Maturity.* In this stage, the product is widely accepted by the market, providing high profits for relatively little maintenance cost. Methods to extend the life of the successful product (improvements) should be considered at this point.

- *Decline.* This is where sales of the product drop because of market saturation, product obsolescence, or high numbers of competing products. The product should be closely monitored for profitability and considered for abandonment.

Understanding, predicting, and extending the product life cycle is particularly important in industries with short cycles, such as information technology businesses. This has given rise to the specialized study of **product life-cycle management (PLM)** and even PLM software that can organize and share information about factors that can affect the cycle. Formerly a tool of large firms, PLM is becoming increasingly important to smaller companies,[3] especially those that depend on large firm suppliers and customers.

product life-cycle management (PLM) Methods and systems for organizing and sharing product-related information that can affect the length of time a product can be viable.

✓ Memory Check 9.10
True or False? Products in the maturity stage of the product life cycle require high levels of promotion.

Product/Service Development Finding products or services for resale may not be appropriate for your company. Your task may be to create new products and services or to improve existing ones. This means innovation, which is commonly associated with entrepreneurship. The belief that innovation by itself produces entrepreneurial success is found in the old saying:

> Build a better mousetrap and the world will beat a path to your door.
> —Ralph Waldo Emerson (popular American Writer, 1803–1882)

This belief, however, may be more myth than reality since the relationship among the growth of sales, profits, and innovation turns out to be rather more complex. In fact, over 80 percent of new products will fail to produce new profit.[4] True, the success of new products and (we can assume) services is closely connected to having superior quality or value of the product.[5] But factors such as timing, targeting, price, and promotion are also critical.

Ask yourself: How do you come up with the idea for a new product or service? There are many different routes that can be taken for the development of a new product or service. Here is one example of steps that can be followed:

- *Customer research.* As in finding new products, the first step is to identify unsatisfied needs of your customers through formal (surveys, focus groups) or informal (sales conversations, observation) methods.

- *Idea development.* This can involve creative idea-generating sessions with sales reps, end-users, outside experts, production engineers, etc., as well as the scanning of competitors, journals, and trade shows to produce a great many new ideas. The ideas must then be screened and ranked to come up with the few most feasible (cost-efficient, potentially profitable) approaches. This might be accomplished with a small committee discussing each idea and using a **weighted ranking** approach to evaluate and compare the ideas.

■ *Product testing.* Production of a **prototype** and/or samples of a new product can provide data about the cost and problems of producing the new item. Samples can then be tested for function, safety, durability, and so on. Testing can be done in-house, with customers, through independent laboratories, or by the **Canadian Standards Association (CSA)** for safety certification.

■ *Test marketing.* This involves promoting and providing your product or service to a limited segment of your target customers. For example, if your business is a small chain of coffee bars in the Montreal area, you may use only one of your outlets to introduce and test the new mocha-banana–flavoured iced coffee that you have developed.

Product/service development does not always mean coming up with brand-new offerings. Modifying products or services that you already produce is a way of improving the product mix economically as well as a way of showing customers that you have been listening to them. Product materials, features, size, and packaging can all be changed to make the product more appealing and increase sales. This can be accomplished by following the steps, described above, for developing a brand-new product. A modification to an existing product should be a legitimate improvement, not just a minimal change so that the product can be promoted as "new and improved." So-called changes that the customer cannot readily appreciate can damage your credibility, your firm's image. Regardless of whether you are coming up with whole new products or services, or modifying your existing offerings, there is some evidence that product development is a more powerful method of improving your profits than putting the same energy into improving your efficiency.[6]

⭐ Head Start Exercise

9.8 Briefly identify any new products or services that could logically be added to your current mix (1/4 page maximum).

Market Segment Expansion

Remember that at start-up it is safer for your business to specialize in a very narrow group of customers (a specific age range, a particular type of institution, or a defined geographic area) rather than a broad segment. Later, when expanding your range of customers, you should ideally expand one segment at a time. The selection of the appropriate segment to start your expansion should be influenced by the need to disrupt the rest of your marketing mix as little as possible.

For example, you may be a cleaning supplies distributor that targets government institutions in the greater metropolitan area of your city. You are considering several new target segments, each of which may require some changes to your product/service, price, promotion, or distribution strategies. Right now, you carry a narrow range of products in bulk containers, your prices are a little on the high side (which your customers accept because of your reliability), you promote only by personal selling, and your distribution relies on your online ordering system and same-day delivery from your warehouse. Among your targets under consideration are:

■ *Industrial cleaning services within your city.* This option would require a change in your packaging (using smaller containers since these services carry all their supplies in car trunks), and your distribution would have to include allowing the cleaners to pick up supplies at your warehouse at night.

■ *Consumers in the area of your warehouse.* This option would mean changing your packaging into much smaller containers and remodelling part of your warehouse into retail space. As well, your promotion would have to include some form of local advertising and provision for dealing with cash or retail credit cards.

- *Discount retailers across the country.* With this option you have to be able to deliver nationally, since most of the discount stores are national chains. Again, you would need a change in packaging and labelling, perhaps as the house brands of the stores you will sell to.

- *Government institutions throughout the province.* For this you would need to improve your ability to deliver throughout the province.

  Ask yourself: Which of the above options would require the fewest changes to the marketing mix?

⭐ Head Start Exercise

9.9 List various market segments that you could logically expand into, noting any changes to the marketing mix that each would require (1/2 page maximum).

✅ **Memory Check 9.13**
True or False? It is best to expand into several new market segments at one time.

Expanding to new markets may require changing distribution channels. For example, you may have a business packaging organically grown herbs, which you sell directly to health food stores across Canada. Upon expanding to the UK market, you deal through a British importer that sells to stores over there. Now you are dealing through two different distribution channels for customers in different locations. For larger firms that are already highly complex, dealing through multiple distribution channels may not be a problem. For example, Nike sells their products through their own retail outlets, as well as through department stores, large shoe chains, and even smaller specialty chains. For a small company, however, multiple channels may add a layer of complexity and cost that is too great to bear.

New markets may also require adding new ordering and delivery modes. For example, your business may be a store in Vancouver that sells high-end hiking equipment, which you advertise in sports magazines. When the business first opened, all sales were over the counter to walk-in customers. Later, you started to use the company truck to deliver items in the Vancouver area that were not in stock when customers ordered them in the store. Later still, you started to accept phone orders from regular customers, which you would deliver within the city or mail to customers outside the city. Eventually, you advertised the company number in your magazine ads and included an order form that could be mailed in with a cheque. Finally, you configured your company website for online ordering, giving customers the option of delivery by post or, at extra cost, courier. In each of these cases, distribution is still direct to the end-user but you are offering four different ordering modes (in-store, phone, mail-in, online) and four different delivery modes (pick-up, truck, post, courier). And since you have a website, of course, you are now promoting to a worldwide market, inviting all of the ordering complexity (time zones, languages, exchange rates) and delivery complexity that this involves (foreign postal services, package tracking, receipts).

Ask yourself: Is it even possible to restrict your business to a narrow market segment in the age of the internet? Not only is it possible, but it is imperative that the growing small business stick to a planned marketing strategy in a time when market forces could overwhelm the business with complexity.

✅ **Memory Check 9.14**
True or False? It is best for a small firm to deal through as many different distribution channels as possible.

Replicating the Business

Expanding to new geographic segments, especially for retail and consumer services, can mean opening new sites in new territories. This usually means copying, as closely as possible, the original successful business in increasingly distant geographic locations, thus building a network of outlets. You have a choice between two basic approaches for doing this:

1. building a chain of company-owned sites

2. selling franchises

Get Help 9.10

If you consider selling franchises, an early consultation with a lawyer who specializes in franchising is a good idea. For a referral, check the website of your provincial or territorial Law Society.

master franchise An arrangement where a master franchisee buys the right to sell franchises to others within a given territory.

Memory Check 9.15

True or False? In "the age of the internet," small firms should still try to target narrow market segments.

Get Help 9.11

A good collection of resources for helping you understand the issues involved in exporting and planning any attempts to pursue foreign customers is found on the Canada Business website at canadabusiness.ca. Click on Exporting.

If you opt for building your own chain, the money needed to open the second site—or at least part of the money—will have to come from the profits of the first. Then, the profits from two sites can eventually be used to open a third, and so on. This will produce an accelerating growth (sites will open at a faster and faster rate), but it is still a slow process compared to the option of selling franchises. With the franchise option, you can initially invest your profit from the first store in setting up a system to sell franchises. Then, each new site will be set up using the money of the franchisees, who will also pay you a fee for the privilege of using your business method. This allows the chain to grow about as fast as you can sell franchises.

Ask yourself: Is franchising the best way to expand? Not all businesses are suitable for franchising. If the potential franchisee could just look at your business and do pretty much the same thing in a different location, why bother paying you a franchise fee? Your franchising operation must be providing some value to the franchisee in terms of an established name, a proven concept, training, or something else they will not have if they start up on their own. And even if your business could be replicated as franchises, the obvious drawback of franchising is that you will be sharing the company profits with the franchisees.

With your own chain, you get all the profit and everyone working in the business is an employee that you can direct, although you will have to build a management hierarchy to do so. Franchisees are not your employees, but you still have control over them, although control is only through the complex contract that the franchisees must sign. See Figure 9.2 for a brief comparison of these two expansion techniques.

In the past decades, franchising has continued to grow at a very strong rate. This has been facilitated by the growth of free-trade areas, making foreign franchising and licensing much easier.[7] Exporting your franchise can mean selling large area or **master franchises**, which allows the master franchisee to sell individual franchises to others. Potentially a very fast way to grow, this involves a highly complex contract (and the associated legal fees) but also faster cash returns. See information on master franchises in Chapter 8.

Head Start Exercise

9.10 Briefly discuss the feasibility of opening new sites for your company (1/3 page maximum).

SHOULD I CONSIDER EXPORTING?

Moving to new, larger geographic segments ultimately leads to an export market. When we think of exporting, the tendency is to see this as something for manufactured products. True, there have been long-standing traditions among governments to encourage the

Figure 9.2 Business Replication Comparison

	Company-Owned Chain	Franchise Operation
Growth rate	Slower	Faster
Cash outlay	More	Less
Profit	Your own	Shared with franchisees
Legal complexity	Minimal	Complex
Control	Direct	Via contract
Management staff	Larger	Smaller

Business Reality 9.2 Seaflora Ltd.
Product Lines Growing Like Seaweeds

Sooke, B.C., is near the southern tip of Vancouver Island, about 35 km east of Victoria. It's from here that Diane Bernard runs her seaweed business: Seaflora Ltd. This business started out of Bernard's home in 2001, and since then the demand for the company's products has been growing steadily.

There are many hundreds of species of seaweed, a range of fast-growing ocean plants that thrive in the swift currents of the Strait of Juan de Fuca. There are many uses for seaweed, ranging from industrial chemicals to cosmetics to just plain eating it in a variety of forms. In Japan, where seaweed is practically a staple, the industry is worth billions of dollars annually. But even in Canada, it is used as a fish wrapping, in salads and soups, or as a dried snack. When harvested

properly, seaweed continues to grow, making this a totally renewable resource for which Bernard pays a licensing fee to the federal government.

Although she had some general knowledge about the product, Bernard's education (master's degree in criminology) and previous careers (local politician) were totally unrelated to this form of marine farming. In Bernard's case, she simply saw an opportunity in her own backyard, the Pacific Ocean, building her own Seaflora Seaweed Manufacturing Centre. The business has grown to thirteen full-time employees plus additional seasonal and part-time help she needs for harvesting. The two main uses for the seaweeds collected by Bernard are cosmetic products and gourmet foods. She ships fresh seaweed to upscale restaurants in Canada and the United States, and she produces a range of high-quality, seaweed skin products for sale to spas. Her business has also expanded to include overseas markets.

Bernard's current growth thrust is targeting the spa industry with her Seaflora skin care products. Her wild organic seaweed skincare line has grown to include 29 products. She has an effective website that appeals to both consumers and spa owners and stays in touch with her fans through Twitter and Facebook.

In addition, tourists to Vancouver Island can book one of several Wild Seaweed Tours, where education is combined with a fun, hands-on seaweed experience. Check the Seaflora website at www.sea-flora.com.

---

export of manufactured products, especially those made from local raw materials. And recent history indicates that Canadian manufacturing, agriculture, and natural resource-based industries are more successful exporters than retail or service industries.[8] But export markets are a possibility for all types of business—everything from stand-up comics and jazz bands to air-conditioning consultants and graphic artists. *Ask yourself: What are the problems of becoming an exporter?*

The decision to export is a major one, full of risks. Potential problems of exporting include complex foreign regulations; shipping costs and unreliable carriers; difficulties in getting payment; and, in some countries, corrupt systems and officials. There can be, however, significant advantages to moving into export markets. Obviously, moving to additional markets increases the sales potential for a product or service but it is also a kind of diversification that can reduce risk. For example, if the local market for your product dries up or you are losing customers to competitors, you might still have foreign customers to keep you afloat. As well, exporting can be a method of extending the product life cycle for some services or products.[9] For example, you may be selling training programs in Canada for the use of a particular flight simulator, which is now becoming obsolete as the aging aircraft it simulates are less frequently used here. The used aircraft, however, have likely been sold in developing nations, where there will continue to be a demand for your training programs for many years.

? Get Help 9.12
Visit the Department of Foreign Affairs and International Trade website at www.dfait-maeci .gc.ca.

? Get Help 9.13
Check the EDC website at www.edc.ca for a large variety of export information and services.

Selling Abroad

Canada is, to a great extent, a nation of immigrants, many of whom have extensive family and business connections in their countries of origin. Recognizing the competitive advantage of a Canadian product or knowing of demand in their originating country has been the impetus for many small Canadian exporters to set up businesses using family or friends as the importers. This kind of arrangement eliminates many typical exporting problems such as dealing in foreign cultures or trust issues with importing partners. It is possible, however, to find customers and navigate these problems in countries where you have no previous contacts or experience, but the key is to specialize in very few export targets in order to build expertise in those markets.[10]

All the prospecting and promotional methods that we use in Canada to find new customers can apply to looking for foreign customers. For example, you may choose to run an ad in a foreign trade journal or newspaper. Both of these would likely be accessible through websites that would tell you about their customer types and circulation numbers. When looking for foreign customers, though, a great starting place is the website of the federal ministry responsible for trade, International Trade Canada (ITC). This ministry sponsors several initiatives to help exporters find customers. One of these is the Virtual Trade Commissioner, where your company profile is matched with international business opportunities. Another ITC program is the series of Team Canada trade missions. These are visits by groups of Canadian businesspeople to countries where there are markets for Canadian products. Offshore customers can also be found using the same resources that are available for finding foreign products to import: trade fairs, world trade centres, your own listings in trade directories, and so on.

We know that selling to government, on average, carries considerably lower risk than selling to private-sector customers. This principle also holds true for export markets, and many foreign governments have been customers for Canadian goods and services. A source for finding tenders or requests for proposal from foreign governments is the website of the **Canadian Commercial Corporation (CCC)**. Small Canadian firms can register with the CCC and have their products, services, or capabilities listed in the database that CCC shares with Industry Canada. The firms are then notified of appropriate opportunities, and CCC offers a variety of support services for securing export contracts.

There are other excellent sources to assist small Canadian exporters. Canada's Department of Foreign Affairs and International Trade (DFAIT) provides travel, cultural, and market information for most areas of the world. As well, this department actively promotes the sale of Canadian technology, products, and services around the world. Export Development Canada (EDC) is a federal Crown corporation with programs to help Canadian small businesses with exporting in a variety of ways. This includes credit insurance (in the event a buyer does not pay you), bonding (to protect a buyer in case the Canadian exporter fails to perform), and even loans to foreign businesses (so they can buy from Canadian exporters).

Regulations

Ask yourself: Is it still exporting if I have a contract for my personal services in a foreign country? Exporting a service, such as consulting, training, or entertaining, is often a matter of applying for and securing a visa and or temporary work permit for the country where you will be selling your service. But the shipment of goods is usually more complicated. As a Canadian exporter, you will have both foreign and Canadian regulations to deal with. For example, you must file a Canadian export declaration with the **Canada Border Services Agency (CBSA)** before shipping anything to a foreign country. As well, you may need a permit, certificate, or licence for exporting any sort of goods that are controlled by legislation (e.g., protected species or dangerous goods).

? Get Help 9.14
Visit www.scc.ca, the website for the Standards Council of Canada, a federal Crown corporation that provides information and services related to international product requirements.

? Get Help 9.15
A handy U.S. resource to help decipher trade documents is the TradePort Reference Library for Global Trade. Go to www.tradeport.org and click on "Library" then select the "Trade Units and Terms" tab.

✔ Memory Check 9.16
True or False? Selling franchises is a faster way to expand than building a company-owned chain.

Canadian Commercial Corporation (CCC) A federal Crown corporation that works with many government departments and businesses to facilitate international trade. Its website is www.ccc.ca.

Canada Border Services Agency (CBSA) The CBSA is a federal government agency (formerly the Customs portion of Canada Customs and Revenue Agency) responsible for controlling the flow of goods, services, and money across Canadian borders (www.cbsa-asfc.gc.ca).

The import rules and documents vary for each country, but most countries have some requirements for the quality or safety of specific goods with which the exporter must comply. In recent years there has been increasing international co-operation in standardizing some of these requirements across many countries. Generally, as an exporter, you will have to investigate these requirements, including the need for any certification, before concluding any deals. A good place to start is the website of the Standards Council of Canada, which has links to several important international standards organizations.

Shipping and Payment Systems

As an exporter, your primary document is the contract between you and your foreign customers. This will cover information like

- specifications of goods to be supplied
- delivery dates
- who is responsible for shipping arrangements and from what point (**F.O.B.**)
- who (the buyer or the seller) will be designated as the official **importer of record**
- who is responsible for any export licences, customs duties, and insurance charges
- who is responsible for completing all required documentation
- how much is to be paid for the goods, when, and under what circumstances.

The complexity of moving goods to other countries is the reason that most new and small exporters will use a **freight forwarder** to act as a sort of travel agent for their goods. Freight forwarders arrange shipping and packaging of your goods to comply with regulations. As well, they will complete and forward documentation, which will likely be critical to your getting paid. Some freight forwarders also function as customs brokers, or they may arrange for any **customs broker** services you need. Customs brokers are more involved in the import side of international trade, offering services like warehousing, arranging customs inspections, duty payments, and local deliveries. (These can be your responsibility as an exporter if the contract designates you as the importer of record.)

A foreign buyer will often pay for goods through using a **letter of credit**. A letter of credit is a document from a foreign bank promising to pay a certain amount of money (on behalf of the buyer) on receiving documented proof that certain conditions have been met (such as the goods have been delivered as specified and on time). Here's an example of how this can work: After the goods have been delivered as promised, your freight forwarder will provide the necessary documents, as specified in your contract with the buyer, to your bank in Canada. Your bank will then contact the foreign bank to execute the letter of credit, and payment will be sent to your bank. It all sounds quite simple, but there is lots of room for problems or delays because of minor disputes or even the tiniest mistakes in the paperwork.

Ask yourself: What happens if the foreign bank refuses to honour the letter of credit because of some minor paperwork error, even though the goods have been delivered? Generally in business, when someone owes you money and doesn't pay up, you sue them. This recourse to the courts, which we take for granted here, may not be easily accessible or economically feasible in other countries—another argument for using the professional help of a freight forwarder to keep all the documentation correct.

You can reduce the risk of a foreign customer not paying for goods by checking on the past performance and creditworthiness of your customer. The EDC offers their EXPORT Check service through the EDC website, providing several options for obtaining financial history and credit report information about foreign companies. Always ask for credit references and make sure the wording on contracts and letters of credit does not give the buyer unreasonable options for withholding payment.

F.O.B. (free on board) The point in the shipping process to which the seller bears all of the costs and risks. For example, F.O.B. the buyer would mean that the seller is totally responsible for the merchandise right up to the point where it is delivered to the buyer's place of business.

importer of record The party (buyer or seller) specified as being responsible for paying duties and ensuring that traded goods are in compliance with customs regulations.

freight forwarder A company that acts on behalf of exporters, providing services such as regulations information, cargo pick-up, negotiation and booking with carriers, document preparation, shipment monitoring, and delivery of documents required for payment.

customs broker A company that acts on behalf of importers (remember that the exporter can be the importer of record) providing services such as document completion, tariff payments, inspections, temporary secure storage, and delivery of goods.

letter of credit A guarantee from a bank to pay, on behalf of a purchaser, a specified amount of money after receiving documented proof that certain conditions have been met.

Get Help 9.16
The Export Check service is available through the EDC website at www.edc.ca. Click on Our Services and then Customer/Credit.

U.S. Market

For most Canadian small firms, the first choice in export targets is the United States because of its proximity, cultural similarity, and large wealthy markets. There is also a lot of reliable, easily accessible market research information for the United States. Furthermore, the North American Free Trade Agreement (NAFTA; intended to reduce trade barriers between Canada, the United States, and Mexico), makes the United States an even more attractive market. The vast majority of Canadian small business owners consistently express strong support for NAFTA. For many, it has reduced the red tape on U.S. imports, and for some, the U.S. market has been a golden opportunity. But along with great successes, the history of Canadian business is filled with failed attempts to penetrate the U.S. market.

Ask yourself: What are the dangers of chasing U.S. business? The sheer size of the U.S. market (or even the size of its many segments) should raise concern about stimulating a market that your small firm may not be able to satisfy. There is also the risk of putting all your efforts and money into chasing the U.S. pot of gold and letting your attention slide from your local customer base. As well, there is an aggressive entrepreneurial culture in the United States; there are many government programs to support U.S. entrepreneurs; and there is a political system that can give great influence to protective industrial lobbies. Nevertheless, of all the nationalities exporting to the United States, Canadians have the inside track because of the systems in place to expedite the huge trade we already share (we are the biggest trading partner of the United States). As well, we have a deep knowledge of the country and its culture (most of us have grown up watching more U.S. TV than Canadian). Furthermore, there is some argument against the apparent logic of saturating local or national markets first before expanding to foreign territory.[11] For many Canadian firms, **contiguous growth**, geographically, is most naturally into the United States since our own population tends to be concentrated in a few, separated pockets along the U.S. border.

contiguous growth
Geographic expansion into immediately adjoining areas, as opposed to skipping over areas to more distant markets.

The United States is a nation of divergent viewpoints and political influences—some that support Canadian exports, and some that represent potential roadblocks. For example, many American political leaders support the expansion of NAFTA to an ultimate Free Trade of the Americas agreement that would include North, South, and Central America as well as the Caribbean. This would be the world's largest trading bloc and represent many opportunities for Canadian exporters. Recently, however, the United States has imposed various protectionist tariffs against several of its trading partners to protect U.S. industries, making trade more difficult. Over the years since the 9/11 attacks, U.S. Customs has attempted to implement a set of security guidelines for exporters—**Customs–Trade Partnership Against Terrorism (C–TPAT)**—that are widely expected to become firm regulations. Compliance with these guidelines has meant considerable cash outlay for some Canadian exporters. (At the time of publication, the EDC is offering substantial unsecured loans to Canadian exporters that will cover up to 85 percent of costs associated with C–TPAT.) Despite these sorts of hurdles, thousands of Canadian companies export successfully to the United States each year.

Customs–Trade Partnership Against Terrorism (C–TPAT)
A set of security guidelines that U.S. Customs is requesting exporters to the United States to comply with, in order to maintain expeditious clearance for entry of goods to that country.

⭐ Head Start Exercise

9.11 Make up a list of the advantages and disadvantages your company would face in deciding to export to the United States. Be as specific as possible (1/2 page maximum).

Get Help 9.17
If you plan on exporting to the United States or Mexico, see the NAFTA customs website, www.cbp.gov/nafta/nafta_new .htm, which offers forms and procedures common to the three countries.

HOW DO I FINANCE GROWTH?
Varieties of Growth Capital

All the sources of finance previously discussed (see Chapter 5, "Where Will I Get the Money?") can be considered as sources of expansion capital, but some will be considerably more available than they were at start-up.[12] Typically, at start-up the new entrepreneur must rely on personal savings or loans from family and friends. Then, as the business becomes established, larger amounts of capital will become available from bank and government lending programs. Eventually, as the business grows, it can access very large amounts of capital from venture capitalists, or (the ultimate source of growth capital) with a public share offering. Over this cycle, the shift in the available capital has been from little or no outside capital to debt capital to equity capital. Now, there is a positive relationship between the ability of a company to grow rapidly and the use of equity capital.[13] But this requires a willingness of the entrepreneur to share ownership. Ironically, the older the entrepreneur (and presumably the longer in business), the less willing the entrepreneur is to share ownership in order to finance growth.[14] While younger (newer) entrepreneurs are very willing to share ownership, no one wants to invest with them. Reasons for this change in the attitude of entrepreneurs are not clear, but the implied warning is clear: If your business is ready for growth, re-think any reluctance you might feel toward bringing in other investors.

Once your business has become established, with a proven track record of paying your bills and making a profit, both lenders and investors are more interested in participating. Remember, however, that they want to finance a logical growth of your already successful venture, not to take a high risk on some radically new direction for your firm. Keep this in mind when writing your *strategic growth plan*. Your plan must recognize that lenders and investors are now interested in three aspects of your finances: the past (financial history), the present (financial position), and the future (financial projections):

- *Financial history.* This includes looking at credit reports for a pattern of the business paying its bills on time and checking whether there are outstanding judgments against you or the company. Your financial sources will be looking for a consistent pattern of profit growth (income statements) as well as patterns of reducing debt and increasing equity (balance sheets). A history of good cash management (e.g., your collection period) will also be important. Anything that indicates a pattern of careful financial management (Did you file and pay your taxes on time?) could be helpful.

- *Financial position.* Where your company stands right now in terms of equity and unencumbered assets that can be used for collateral is important. As well, detailed ratio analysis (see Chapter 6) will indicate the financial health of your business relative to others in the industry. Break-even analysis will indicate how safe the current sales/profit position is in case of changes in the market.

- *Financial projections.* Your projected income statements, balance sheets, and cash flow must all be conservative and backed up by research evidence (see Chapter 2). Together, they must form a realistic plan showing how the new funds will be used and how the business will provide a good return to investors or consistent loan repayment to lenders. The recently published Survey on Financing of Small and Medium Enterprises[15] in Canada shows that the number one reason that lenders give for turning down loans is insufficient sales or cash flow for repaying the loan.

Increasingly, financial institutions are offering new and more creative finance options to small businesses, some which blur the line between debt and equity financing. An example of this is quasi-equity capital or **subordinate financing**, which is offered through flexible programs that can include features like

- temporary share ownership by the financing institution;
- options for permanent equity positions;
- royalties on company sales;
- deferred interest and principal payments;
- flexible repayments based on actual company cash flow; and possibly
- even more complex features that most business owners would need professional help in negotiating.

✔ **Memory Check 9.17**
True or False? Governments in Canada offer many services to assist small exporters.

✔ **Memory Check 9.18**
True or False? "F.O.B. the seller" means that the buyer will be responsible for all shipping costs.

❓ **Get Help 9.18**
If you are looking for large amounts of expansion capital, you will require significant assistance from your accountant in preparing the financial projections. As well, you will need your accountant's advice in choosing the form of funding that's best suited to your needs.

✔ **Memory Check 9.19**
True or False? Customs brokers are more involved with the export side of international trade.

subordinate financing A hybrid form of financing involving features of both debt and equity but for which the debt is usually ranked below (subordinate to) the claims of other secured creditors.

If your business is one of those rare companies that are clearly poised for massive growth, requiring massive capital, you will likely consider the option of going public. Such a move marks the transition from small- or medium-sized business into the realm of big business, at least in terms of the capital involved. Typically, though, it also means a transition from being an entrepreneur to CEO of a publicly traded company. And even though you may effectively control the company, you will still be ultimately responsible to and under the scrutiny of the other shareholders. Going public is an expensive manoeuvre involving complex negotiations for the underwriting and floating of a share issue. It is usually designed to both provide expansion capital to the company and give the entrepreneur the opportunity to become incredibly wealthy.

⭐ Head Start Exercise

9.12 Briefly explain the most likely source of growth capital available to your firm. Explain the reasons for this (1/4 page maximum).

Financial Analysis

payback period The length of time it takes to recoup the amount of a particular investment.

Lenders look at financial projections in a business plan to see that they will be repaid as per the terms of the loan. Investors are looking to see the returns they can expect on their investment. But for an entrepreneur, choices about bringing new capital into the business are analyzed from a different viewpoint. For example, in assessing the value of borrowing a particular amount of money, the business owner may use the idea of **payback period**.

Let's say you have a refrigeration supplies business where all your customers are within a two-hour drive of your site. Currently, all customers must place their orders by phone and then pick up the orders or pay for their own courier services. A recent survey has shown that your customers have a desire for both delivery by you and for the capability of ordering from you online. You decide that you can afford to invest in only one of these new services at a time and in each case you will have to borrow money. *Ask yourself: Which of these new services should be the priority?* The cost of purchasing two trucks that you will need for delivery, including the interest over the three-year loan period, will be about $70 000. You know that by charging your customers for delivery, you will be able to increase your revenues by $180 000. The drivers' salaries and benefits and operating cost of the trucks (depreciation, fuel, repairs, etc.) will come to about $160 000 per year. So, this will give you a net increase in revenue ($180 000 – $160 000) of $20 000. The payback period for this option, then, will be:

$$\frac{\$70\ 000}{\$20\ 000 \text{ per year}} = 3.5 \text{ years}$$

The cost for an online ordering system (hardware, software, installation, training, etc.), including interest over the three-year loan period, will be about $55 000. Your annual revenue will increase by the amount of money you save on an order-taker salary and benefits; about $30 000 minus the costs of maintenance and hosting for your new system, around $5000 per year. This will give you a net increase ($30 000 – $5000) of $25 000 per year. For this option, the payback period will be:

$$\frac{\$55\ 000}{\$25\ 000 \text{ per year}} = 2.2 \text{ years}$$

This is an indicator that the online ordering system is your best bet as the more immediate priority.

In assessing the value of bringing new equity capital into the business, an owner might employ return on investment (ROI) calculations. For example, you might have $100 000 owner's equity in a business that produced $10 000 net profit last year. For you, this is an ROI of 10 percent. You have estimated that by investing $50 000 in a new promotional program, you could double your sales and triple your profits to $30 000 annually. A friend offers to give you the $50 000 in exchange for one-third ownership of the business. It seems fair and if things work out, both you and the friend will have a 20 percent return on your investment for next year. Your friend, in fact, may feel that he or she is being generous because it is the friend's one-third investment that will result in two-thirds of the new profit. True, the $50 000 investment will result in new returns of $20 000 (a 40 percent ROI) but this is really just a **project ROI**. It is valuable to show that the project is worthwhile; however, your friend is investing in the whole business, not just the project. So, *Ask yourself: Is one-third ownership a fair exchange for the $50 000?* What if, in exchange for the $50 000, you gave your friend only 25 percent ownership in the business, not the asked-for one-third? In this case, your friend would expect a return of (25 percent of the $30 000 profit) $7500 on an investment of $50 000. This would be an ROI of 15 percent, still a healthy return. And the value of your friend's investment is not just based on the rate of return, but on many other factors (see "Valuation Concepts" in Chapter 7) that would become part of a negotiation process. Even though ROI is a valuable concept for assessing new equity investment, no single ROI calculation by itself can assess how good a particular deal to share ownership is for you.

project ROI The additional annual profit expected from a new investment, divided by the total cost of that particular investment (expressed as a percentage).

⭐ Head Start Exercise

9.13 Describe how you will assess the value of any new debt or equity capital that your firm pursues (1/2 page maximum).

Answers to Memory Check Questions

9.1 F	9.2 T	9.3 T	9.4 T	9.5 F	9.6 T	9.7 F	9.8 T
9.9 F	9.10 F	9.11 T	9.12 F	9.13 F	9.14 F	9.15 T	9.16 T
9.17 T	9.18 T	9.19 F	9.20 T	9.21 F			

Questions for Discussion

1. "Grow or die." Discuss the merits of this statement as a philosophy for running a small business.
2. Why might some entrepreneurs not recognize the warning signs that their businesses are in decline? Why might some choose to ignore the warning signs?
3. Entrepreneurs must estimate the *market potential* for their products or services on a regular basis. Why is this so important? What does it have to do with *market share?*
4. Picture yourself as a graduate of your current program looking for a job in the marketplace. Prepare a brief SWOT analysis of yourself.
5. Some small business owners follow a *one-change-at-a-time* policy. How could this apply to *market expansion*? To *product expansion*? To *advertising*? How does this approach affect a business owner's ability to measure the effects of change?
6. How are the *business cycle* and the *product cycle* similar? How are they different?
7. The fastest way for most businesses to increase sales is to compete on the basis of price. Discuss why this might be true. What are the dangers of a penetration pricing strategy?
8. Discuss the benefits and drawbacks of NAFTA for Canadian small firms.
9. In recent times, the United States has passed protectionist legislation while simultaneously trying to negotiate a Free Trade of the Americas agreement. What are the forces involved in this apparent contradiction?
10. Canadian companies trying to export to developing nations may encounter corruption at many government levels. For example, the paying of certain bribes might be

expected and commonplace. When dealing in foreign countries, should these companies participate in behaviour that would not be acceptable in Canada? What are the dangers of doing so?

11. On average, entrepreneurs become more reluctant to share ownership in their firms as they become older, even though bringing in new investors could lead to faster growth. Explain this reluctance of older entrepreneurs.

Case for Discussion

Stacy's grandmother from Nepal had taught her to create henna tattoos (or *Mehndi*, as her grandmother called them) when she was a young teenager. By the time she was in college, she was making a good part-time income by selling her henna services to South Asian immigrants for weddings and festivals. While in college, Stacy experimented with other forms of temporary tattoos, including ballpoint pens and transfers. She found that by using airbrush equipment and a variety of dies and stencils, she could create temporary tattoos that looked like the real thing and would last a couple of weeks or more. By the time she graduated, Stacy had regular clients who would come to her home to get "temp-tats."

One day, while getting her hair done at her favourite salon, Stacy noticed that the salon had a spa section at the back for waxing, threading, and massages, but that this area was rarely busy. She realized it would be perfect for applying her temporary tattoos.

Stacy negotiated a deal with the salon owner where she would come to the salon one day a week and provide her air-brush tattoos to clients. The salon would display pictures of Stacy's work along with a price list and would make the appointments. Stacy and the salon would split evenly whatever the tattooing brought in and Stacy would keep her own tips. The idea was a success and the salon was able to pretty much fill Stacy's schedule for the one day a week. Within a few months, Stacy was able to find five other salons that would work with her on the same 50-50 basis, one day a week, so she ended up with a full six-day week. The salons were all in upscale areas and the clients were predominantly women aged 30 to 60.

After 18 months, Stacy's business seemed to be doing well. She was fully booked most days. The salons were happy because Stacy, on a daily basis, was providing them with more profit than most of the stylists or estheticians. More was being written about temporary tattoos in fashion magazines. The "ink" displayed by movie stars was increasingly of a temporary variety and dermatologists were giving more warnings about the permanent varieties of body art. So the market was expected to keep growing.

But Stacy was starting to have some concerns.

Stacy's own profit was declining because she had started to use new, more elaborate, but more expensive stencils. As well, there were some new dyes that Stacy wanted to try because they provided brighter colours and were longer lasting. But they also were more expensive. And Stacy felt that she could not raise her prices because even though she was busy, none of her salons were refusing appointments. On a personal level, she felt she was no longer making use of her henna skills. And to top things off, one of her salon owners had been asking Stacy where her niece could get training as a temporary tattoo artist.

1. Where is Stacy's company in the business life cycle? What are the indicators of this?

2. At roughly what percentage of her capacity is Stacy operating? Explain your answer. How could she increase her capacity?

3. If Stacy uses longer-lasting dyes, what is the implication for her profit? Argue both how it could increase and how it could decrease her profit.

4. Could Stacy use *market share expansion* to increase her sales? How? Be specific.

5. Could Stacy use *product/service expansion* to increase her sales? How? Be specific.

6. Could Stacy use *market segment expansion* to increase her sales? How? Be specific.

7. Which expansion strategy should Stacy use first? Justify your answer.

THE STRATEGIC GROWTH PLAN

The Need for Growth

1. Briefly outline the history of the business.

2. Identify any obvious internal indicators of the need for renewal in your business such as changes in sales, profits, employee turnover, operating capacity level, etc.

Market Analysis

3. Estimate the current market potential for each of your major product/target groups and explain your sources. (See Chapter 2 for assistance.) Discuss any changes in your market share.

4. Identify any significant activity or changes in your direct and indirect competition.

5. Summarize the above findings and any other relevant information about your business under the SWOT headings of strengths, weaknesses, opportunities, and threats.

Growth Strategy

6. Briefly discuss the strategy that you will use to make best use of your strengths and opportunities while at the same time attempting to overcome your weaknesses and protect against threats.

Small Business Management for the Long Term

7. If your strategy involves increasing your market share, outline the specific tactics you will use for this and list the costs involved. State your new sales forecast and explain the basis for it.

    or

    If your strategy involves selling new products or services, outline the specific tactics you will use for this and list all additional costs involved. Explain how you will test any new products or services. State your new sales forecast and explain the basis for it.

    or

    If your strategy involves selling to new market segments, outline the specific tactics you will use for this and list the costs involved. State your new sales forecast and explain the basis for it.

8. If you are pursuing new market segments, briefly discuss the option of opening new sites for your business (for new market segments) and whether this would be by building your own chain or by franchising. Briefly identify and estimate the costs involved.

9. If you are pursuing new market segments abroad, explain the details of your target market and the export distribution system you will use. Describe the shipping and payment systems you will use and provide a sales forecast and the basis for it.

Financing Growth

10. Explain in detail the sources of finance you will use for your expansion program. Discuss why this is a suitable method of finance, using any appropriate comparisons of payback period or ROI.

Chapter 10

Managing for Efficiency: How Will I Reduce Costs and Expenses?

Chapter 9 looked at making the business more profitable by increasing sales. But this is only half the puzzle of profit. This chapter is concerned with the other broad approach to improving profits: reducing costs and expenses.

This chapter will help you plan to control your business costs and expenses by answering the questions:

- **How Can I Refocus the Business for Efficiency?**
- **How Do I Retain Customers?**
- **How Do I Make Employees More Efficient?**
- **How Can I Control Costs?**

Learning Objectives

On completion of this chapter, you should be able to:

1. Identify and calculate five key ratio indicators of efficiency.
2. Describe the expansion and contraction cycles of business strategy.
3. Distinguish between systemization and automation processes.
4. Argue the importance of customer retention.
5. Summarize five recruiting sources and screening steps for hiring employees.
6. Explain at least five techniques for on-the-job training.
7. Argue the value of a leadership program in a small business.
8. Discuss the necessity of a costing system in a small business.
9. Prepare an operational efficiency plan for a small firm.

HOW CAN I REFOCUS THE BUSINESS FOR EFFICIENCY?

In a new business, you often begin with a clear focus on what you're selling and to whom you're selling it. But typically, over time, you start expanding into new products or services and new markets. Later again, financial analysis and marketing research (formal or informal) will indicate which elements of your business are most profitable and you will decide to refocus on these aspects of your venture. Refocusing is often the trigger for the renewal part of the business cycle discussed in Chapter 10. Refocusing the business is about becoming more profitable by managing for greater efficiency (reducing costs and expenses). It is possible, however, that your business is already highly efficient. *Ask yourself: How can I tell if my business is running efficiently?*

Measuring Efficiency

Ratio analysis was discussed in Chapter 7 as a method for assessing the value of a business. This involves calculating certain key ratios (using values from your financial statements), then comparing those ratios to industry averages. Some of these ratios are indicators of how efficiently your company is operating, relative to other businesses in the same industry. Statistics Canada provides average key ratios for small businesses, classified by specific industry. For example, if you own a convenience store, you can see how efficiently your store operates compared to the industry averages for convenience stores in just your province, or for all of Canada. The broadest indicator of efficiency is the **return on sales** ratio.

$$\text{Return on sales} = \frac{\text{Net profit}}{\text{Sales}}$$

Think of two firms in the heating and air-conditioning repair business that each have sales of $500 000. One of the companies has a net profit of $20 000, while the other has a net profit of $40 000. This second company would be considered twice as efficient. This ratio does not indicate where specific inefficiencies lie within the company, just that they are there. Another important efficiency indicator is **return on assets**.

$$\text{Return on assets} = \frac{\text{Net profit}}{\text{Total assets}}$$

If two small businesses in the same field have roughly the same value of assets, but one has a higher net profit, the more profitable one is using those assets more efficiently. Again, this doesn't tell you exactly where the problem lies but it does indicate the direction of the problem. For example, if your business is one where you have mostly fixed assets (machinery, equipment, buildings, tools, furniture, vehicles, etc.), the problem could lie with inefficient promotional techniques, or the fact that you have money tied up in equipment you don't need. If the assets are mostly current (inventory, cash, supplies, etc.) the problem could be inappropriate inventory or the fact that you have paid too much for it. To further narrow the source of your inefficiency might mean looking at other indicators, or other ratios, such as **inventory turnover**.

$$\text{Inventory turnover} = \frac{\text{Cost of goods sold}}{\text{Average inventory}}$$

Generally, the higher the inventory turnover, the more profitable it is for your company. For example, two companies might have the same sales, but one has an inventory turnover of three (meaning that on average inventory is replaced three times a year) and the other has an inventory turnover of four. The company with the higher turnover will likely be more profitable. Because it is replacing its inventory more often, it can keep less inventory in stock. (It only needs 75 percent of the inventory carried by the first company.) This means that it has less money tied up in inventory and will save money on the associated expenses (interest, insurance, storage, display).

Another area where your business might have money unnecessarily tied up is in your accounts receivable. There are considerable costs associated with having customers owe you money, especially for bills that are past due (lost interest, re-billing, reminders, and other collection costs). It can be important to know if you are taking longer than the industry average to collect from your customers. This ratio is the average **collection period**.

$$\text{Collection period} = \frac{\text{Accounts receivable}}{\text{Average sales per day}}$$

return on sales The ratio of net profit to sales, usually expressed as a percentage.

return on assets The ratio of net profit to total assets, usually expressed as a percentage.

inventory turnover The ratio of cost of goods sold to the average inventory.

Get Help 10.1
Small business key ratio data is most easily accessed from Industry Canada's SME Benchmarking tool at sme.ic.gc.ca. See your accountant if you need advice on this topic.

collection period The ratio of accounts receivable to the average sales per day.

One of the most obvious ways to save money, of course, is to pay less for the inventory that you will be reselling. You can check your relative cost of goods sold compared to the industry average with the **gross margin** ratio.

$$\text{Gross margin} = \frac{\text{Gross profit}}{\text{Sales}}$$

Key ratios by themselves do not tell you where you are wasting money, but they are indicators that point you in the right direction of making your business operate more efficiently.

⭐ Head Start Exercises

10.1 Using the Industry Canada SME Benchmarking tool, or some other source, calculate for your industry the key ratios for return on sales, return on assets, inventory turnover, collection period, and gross margin (2/3 page maximum).

10.2 Using your most recent financial statements, calculate your firm's ratios for return on sales, return on assets, inventory turnover, collection period, and gross margin. Briefly discuss the relative efficiency of your business (1 page maximum).

Specialization

✔ **Memory Check 10.1**
True or False? Sales/equity is a key ratio indicator of efficiency.

core business The combination of products and services and the market segments that produce most of a particular company's profit.

If you follow the business news, you will eventually notice that major announcements coming from the big public companies tend to fall into two categories: expansion (when the company has bought another firm or moved into new markets or new products) and contraction (when the company has sold part of its holdings or relinquished products or markets). When companies are announcing contractions, they will often say that this is in favour of refocusing on their **core business**. The history of business can be seen as a cycle or pendulum swing between expansion (less specialization) and contraction (greater specialization). It is during the contraction phase that the business is becoming more specialized. Naturally, there are many factors that will affect the decisions of whether to concentrate on expanding or specializing, including industry and market conditions at any given time.[1] Nevertheless, most businesses over the years will be subject to some cycle of expansion and contraction.

Ask yourself: In what way should I become more specialized? This decision is usually a case of identifying and concentrating on those particular market segments and/or product or service lines that have proven most profitable or show future promise of high profits. Greater specialization doesn't necessarily mean abandoning all products or services except the most profitable, or refusing to deal with any but the most profitable groups of customers. Better that it should be a prioritization of where your marketing resources will be allocated.[2] (See the example in Table 10.1.)

Refocusing or redefining the business can also mean a change of image, presenting yourself as more specialized. For example, if your business depends on supplying a high-quality product or service, you may have to get involved with ISO 9000 certification. The purpose of the International Standards Organization (ISO) is to set and measure quality control standards through its member organizations in 140 countries. The certification process can be long (over a year) and expensive, but many companies now demand that their suppliers be ISO 9000 registered as a way of ensuring their own quality. There are lots of consultants available who specialize in helping small firms receive ISO certification.

Table 10.1 Example Refocusing Strategy

Priority	Product and or Market Segment	Marketing Tactics
Highest	Fast-growing market potential Growing sales	High levels of promotion Intensive research Penetration pricing Innovation in distribution methods and service levels
Medium	High stable sales Stable market share Stable market potential	Maintenance of inventories and promotional levels Competitive pricing Minimal research
Low	Low sales Unknown prospects for growth of market potential or market share (possibly new product or poorly defined segment)	Minimal promotional effort Monitoring for changes in market or product innovation
Abandon	Declining market potential Low sales	Discontinue product lines or discontinue promotion to segment Provide product or service only as a customer retention issue for customers that also purchase in other more profitable categories

⭐ Head Start Exercises

10.3 Identify any products or services that you offer that provide little or no profit. List the merits of or problems with abandoning these (1/2 page maximum).

10.4 Identify any unprofitable or low profitability market segments that your business promotes to. Discuss the rationale for promoting to these segments (1/2 page maximum).

Systemization

When you order a Big Mac combo at McDonald's, the person serving you will always key in your selection, then get the drink, then get the sandwich. And the french fries will be last. It's always done in this same order, because the restaurant has figured out that this is the most efficient way. French fries cool quickly, and if they were to serve them first and there were some delay with your drink or sandwich, the fries would get cold and have to be replaced. This inefficiency would cost the restaurant time and money. Any task that you perform over and over in your business is an opportunity for maximizing efficiency. This means ensuring that the task involves the least possible time and effort, by using the best tools, methods, and even the best paperwork for the job.

Forms and Templates Let's say your business is working as a bodyguard for celebrities. This doesn't sound like a business where you would have to worry very much about paperwork. But you will have to use a contract for each job. And even though each job is different, it would be extremely time-consuming and expensive to sit down and create an original, customized contract for each new client. Instead you will develop a contract

✅ **Memory Check 10.2**
True or False? Most of a company's profit will come from the core business.

❓ **Get Help 10.3**
Many printing firms will help you design forms, often by customizing their own computerized templates to your requirements. Search online for "Printers" or check the Yellow Pages.

Looking for Efficiency in the Music Business

James Anthony is a musician from Burlington, Ontario. In fact, he's one of the most accomplished musicians in Canada as a versatile guitar player, composer, and singer. Skilled in every form of popular music, he has played with many of the greatest entertainers in the world, everywhere from New Orleans to Budapest. Turning professional at age 17, James played in a variety of bands but really honed his skill as a guitarist with the house band at the legendary Lulu's. This was the Kitchener, Ontario, landmark that for several years was billed as The World's Biggest Nightclub. At Lulu's he played with over 150 of rock and roll's biggest stars, performing for thousands of fans every weekend. For the past decade, James has been celebrated for his outstanding blues compositions and guitar technique. He is recognized in the Encyclopedia of the Blues for this work.

These days, James divides his time among live performances, studio session work, and working in his own fully digital studio in Burlington. It's here that he writes, arranges, produces, and records his own music as well as recording, producing, and tutoring other musicians.

James Anthony recognizes that he makes his money not by simply being a musician, but rather by running a music business: a technologically sophisticated, partly automated and complex business at that. For a start, James identifies a variety of distinct products that he has for sale:

- The James Anthony Band
- James Anthony solo act
- over 200 songs with copyright on words and music
- four CD albums and a fifth in production
- digital sound engineering and remixing
- digital studio recording and arranging
- TV and commercial soundtrack and jingle composition and recording
- musical instrument promotion
- musical coaching and tutoring

He also understands the complex chain of distribution for his services and products and who the customer is at various levels: music distributors, advertising agencies, music retailers, entertainment venue owners, broadcasters, film and TV producers, booking agents, other musicians, and—the ultimate consumers—the fans.

At the time of writing, James Anthony is preparing to release a new CD, and he is in the process of revising his overall marketing strategy; something he does on a regular basis. He is currently evaluating which of his main products he will concentrate on, to use his time most efficiently and profitably. He is refocusing his business. James's main promotional tool is his website (www.jamesanthony.ca), which is aimed mostly at fans, who can sample CDs for sale, check James's schedule of performances, or get information about the artist and his band.

template where you can just fill in the blanks to specify things like the number of operatives to cover the celebrity, the hours and places of coverage, fees, and so on.

Common document templates include proposals, contracts, and letter templates, including email. Typical forms used by businesses include invoices, purchase orders, bills of lading, estimates, work orders, receipts, and various forms of checklists. One critical issue in designing forms and templates is that the design should cover most eventualities—but not all. The more possibilities covered by a form or letter, the longer and more difficult it becomes to use. You have to try to strike a balance between simplicity and comprehensiveness that will give you maximum efficiency. Another issue is that forms and templates should be periodically checked and updated, not just continually reordered with the same old mistakes that reduce their efficiency.

Employee Handbooks and Operations Manuals If you have a business that is growing rapidly, or if you depend on part-time or contract employees with a high turnover, you may be spending lots of time telling new employees the same information over and

❓ Get Help 10.4
You can buy books, CDs, or downloads of business legal forms and letter templates that are easy to customize for your business. Visit your local office supply store.

over. Employee handbooks and operations manuals can serve as training tools as well as part of the contract between you and the people working for you. Normally, employee handbooks cover topics like:

- company history and mission
- employee benefits
- behaviour and dress codes
- probation periods and policies
- termination policies
- work and vacation scheduling
- pay schedules

Operations manuals (often called procedure manuals) tend to be larger and more detailed than employee handbooks. Although the two may overlap on topics such as company policies and work schedules, the operations manual is filled with the specific procedures and processes that a firm uses.

The operations manual covers much the same issues as are found in Section 4 of the business plan. While the business plan is aimed at owners, outside investors, or lenders, the operations manual is written for those who are actually performing the duties of the business. Policies and procedures for major functional areas of the business are covered, including details on topics like:

- organizational structure and job descriptions
- accounting systems and procedures
- purchasing and inventory control
- production methods and procedures
- customer service procedures and policies
- promotion methods and policies
- engineering or design process
- whatever else is a significant activity for the particular business

The need for an operations manual is related to both the size of your company and the complexity of the activities you perform. A skydiving school consisting of yourself and four employees would be quite likely to use an operations manual, but it would be unusual in a window-cleaning company of the same size. However, as the window-cleaning company grew to 50 or more employees, the likelihood of having such a manual would increase. *Ask yourself: Is an operations manual necessary for my field?*

Work Design Developing the most efficient procedures to use in a job is called **work design**. In manufacturing and some service industries, this can involve **time and motion studies** (where videos of someone performing a job are analyzed) as well as the setting of **job standards** (where a reasonable expectation of time to perform a job is calculated). Modern work design does not involve the dictatorial or exploitive approaches of the past. Today, we realize that the highest productivity comes when people can take satisfaction in their work and where employees are safe and comfortable. If your business uses processes involving highly repetitive activities, it may be worthwhile to hire an industrial engineer to analyze the process and find new efficiencies.

If this option is too expensive for you, the most obvious source of help in redesigning a job is the employee actually performing the work. You are more likely to get a significant productivity improvement if you approach the employee in a co-operative manner, explaining that you would like the employee to find ways to make the job safer, more comfortable, and less boring as well as faster. The first step is for you and the employee to measure a baseline of productivity so that you can be sure that whatever changes you try are actually improving the work rate.

Memory Check 10.3
True or False? Templates should be designed to cover all possible eventualities.

Get Help 10.5
Templates and software for writing employee handbooks and operations manuals can be purchased on CD or via the internet.

work design The process of finding the most efficient methods and procedures for doing particular jobs.

time and motion studies Research to determine the most efficient way to perform particular jobs.

job standard A statement of the quality and quantity of work that can reasonably be expected from an employee performing a particular job.

Automation

The wealth produced by the Industrial Revolution came from the ability to use machines in a systematic way to produce products more cheaply than could be done by human labour alone. The second great wave of **automation**, the one we are experiencing now, has been the application of ever-faster computers to improving productivity. And increasingly, automation is being applied not just to the manufacture of products, but rather to the delivery of services, especially those related to information. For example, when you are on vacation and determined not to answer your email, your system can be programmed to provide an automatic response with no ongoing labour from you. The jobs of telephone receptionists and information operators have largely been taken over by automatic prompts and customer searches. None of these service delivery mechanisms is without problems, controversy, and questions of cost-benefit. But the same inadequacies, concerns, and complaints were true of the telephone and automobile in 1900. Modern phones and cars are very reliable, and these developing technologies will continue to improve. Only a few years ago, microcomputers were expected to "crash" pretty much on a daily basis. *Ask yourself: At what point is it economical or efficient to adopt a new technology?* Adopting a new technology can certainly be risky. But there is evidence that those small firms that are more willing to adopt new technologies (especially in the manufacturing sector) are those with the greatest success.[3]

Automation for the small firm becomes increasingly important as the cost of labour rises and the cost of new technologies falls. Small retailers increasingly use UPC scanning at the cash register and electronic security tags. Online ordering and electronic inventory control for wholesalers and online booking for service firms are increasingly common. All provide huge efficiencies in the saving of labour costs. And small manufacturers are increasingly turning to **robotics**.

Robotics and automation are terms that are pretty close in meaning and often used interchangeably, but there are some small differences in how they apply. Robots are tools of automation. Until recently, the extensive use of robots has been the domain of large manufacturers; however, robots have now become cheaper and more flexible in that they can perform a greater number of tasks and more complex tasks. At the same time, there has been improvement in robotics software, making them easier to program, and, with learning software, to some extent even self-programming.[4] This allows the smaller manufacturer, generally producing smaller lots of a product, to reprogram the same robot for different products. And robots are not just for manufacturers, but have uses in everything from medicine to the arts, with new applications turning up constantly.

E-business Tools **E-business** tools include everything from the use of text messaging to computer-assisted manufacturing processes. Many e-business tools that have been evolving over the past few decades are now necessary to run an efficient, competitive business. Increasingly small firms are adopting sophisticated operations software, and using the internet for conducting business. In many ways, the internet itself is a sophisticated form of automation. And as the younger, net-savvy generation turns to entrepreneurship, more and more web applications are emerging. Already it can be highly efficient in all the following categories:

- *Marketing research.* Government statistics, competitor promotions, industry journals, and university research are all secondary forms of research accessible from the internet. But the internet can also be used for primary research, such as customer questionnaires, customer tracking, and specific email queries. Website statistics programs such as Google Analytics can provide information about website traffic and conversion rates.

- *Promotion.* Direct email campaigns and website advertising are widely used applications. Low-cost social media techniques are becoming more common for small firms. Sales promotion applications and publicity techniques (such as interviews on sites like YouTube) are increasingly easy to create.

automation The redesign and integration of repetitive tasks so that they can be carried out by mechanical and computerized equipment.

? Get Help 10.6
To perform job analysis and design you will likely need the help of an industrial engineer. Do a web search for industrial engineers in your area.

✓ Memory Check 10.4
True or False? Operations manuals tend to be larger and more detailed than employee handbooks.

robotics The use of automatic computerized mechanisms to carry out tasks previously performed by human labour.

✓ Memory Check 10.5
True or False? A job standard identifies a reasonable amount and quality of work to expect for a particular job.

e-business (e-biz) The use of any computerized and web-based technologies to assist the functioning of a business.

✓ Memory Check 10.6
True or False? Employees should participate in redesigning their own jobs.

? Get Help 10.7
An interesting book on e-business techniques is *Social Media 101: Tactics and Tips to Develop Your Business Online*, by Chris Brogan. It is available through most large bookstores.

- *Distribution.* For some industries, the internet serves as a means of delivering the product or service, or at least a part of it. Certainly when the product is information or a form of intellectual property, it can be delivered electronically. And the development of 3D printers hints at a future where even physical products could be delivered electronically.

- *Finance.* Everything is available online, from online banking to loan rate shopping to customer billing and credit checks.

At the time of writing, the majority of Canadian small enterprises have their own websites, and over 60 percent do at least some form of online marketing.[5, 6] Most of the firms that do not have websites or do not sell online have considered these options and concluded that these e-business tools are unsuitable for their products or services.[7]

⭐ Head Start Exercise

10.5 Make a brief list of the major repetitive tasks that are carried out in your business. Identify any systems, tools, or methods you do not currently use that would automate this work (2/3 page maximum).

HOW DO I RETAIN CUSTOMERS?

Two axioms of business that almost always hold true are:

1. Most of the profit made by most businesses comes from repeat customer purchases.
2. It is cheaper to keep an existing customer than it is to get a new one.

If you accept these two ideas, then it is not difficult to accept the notion that **customer retention** might be the most important form of efficiency that a business can practise. It often seems, however, that small businesses are more engaged in chasing new customers than managing existing ones.[8]

Let's say your business consists of supplying and installing inventory software for small- and medium-sized companies. When a company buys from you they have access to your customer service phone line, where they can call in to get help with their computer problems. You may find that a lot of your service person's time is spent patiently listening to customers talk about business and computer issues irrelevant to the problem that needs fixing. And, in most cases, when the problem is identified, you find that the customer could have fixed it just by spending a couple of minutes with the instruction manual. Therefore, you may find that it is much more cost-efficient to have the phone line go directly to voice mail, where the customer must clearly explain what the problem is and then wait for your service rep to call back. It could well be the case that if you wait half an hour before calling back, 90 percent of the customers will have already fixed their own problems—and those who haven't fixed them are no longer in a mood for time-consuming conversation. This may be a very efficient tactic, but *Ask yourself: What is the problem here?*

Be careful that your idea for efficiency is not just a way of downloading work to your own customers, unless that is what the customers want. At one time, virtually every gas station in Canada provided gas-filling service. Now the norm is self-service, because the majority of people are willing to perform this function if it's going to save them a couple of cents a litre. On the other hand, just about everyone is infuriated by telephone answering systems that make you listen to a list of options, none of which cover the reason you are calling. Beware of risking your customer relationships in the name of efficiency.

⭐ Head Start Exercise

10.6 Briefly estimate the percentage of your sales that comes from repeat customers. Explain your method. If this information is not readily available, describe a method you could use for estimating repeat sales (1/2 page maximum).

☑ **Memory Check 10.7**
True or False? Having a series of employees each performing a specialized task on a product is a form of automation.

❓ **Get Help 10.8**
The Business Development Bank of Canada offers help on using e-business tools to benefit your business. Go to www.bdc.ca and click on "Advice Centre" then select "Expand Your Sales" then click on "E-business."

customer retention
Maintaining the loyalty of existing customers for repeat sales.

☑ **Memory Check 10.8**
True or False? Robotics is a tool of automation.

☑ **Memory Check 10.9**
True or False? For most businesses, it's cheaper to get a new customer than it is to keep an existing one.

Managing Customer Relations

Businesses are increasingly taking a highly integrated approach to **customer relationship management (CRM)**. The idea behind CRM systems is to have higher retention of the most profitable customers by providing them with the highest service levels. Over the past decade, the software for CRM systems has fallen in price to the point where it is affordable by many small businesses. For example, you may own a small hotel that uses a CRM system to calculate the value of each of your repeat customers. Your system may award points based on customer behaviours that are more profitable (provide higher revenue or reduce costs) for your business. Points, or in this case stars, would be awarded based on the actual profitability of each behaviour. For instance, your system may award

- one star for each five bookings in the past six months;
- one star for every three reservations in your dining room in the past year;
- one star for each five bookings at off-peak times in the past year;
- one star for every three times that room service was ordered in the past six months;
- one star for using automatic check-out three or more times in the past two months;
- one star for using online booking three or more times in the past two months; or
- one star for every $250 of laundry service in the past six months.

Each time that someone on your staff (switchboard, front desk, kitchen) deals with a customer, that customer's file is retrieved on the employee's computer screen, indicating a customer code (the number of stars.) The employee can see the rank or importance of that customer and provide the appropriate level of service. For example, the room service order of a five-star customer would receive priority over the orders of all other customer ranks. Table 10.2 shows the kind of service levels and perks that might be received by customers at different levels.

CRM systems can be developed using existing database, spreadsheet, and communication software. Dedicated sales management and customer tracking software has been available for a long time. And, more recently, software providers such as SAGE (makers of ACCPAC), which target smaller firms, are offering sophisticated integrated CRM software at prices in line with small-firm budgets. Problems with CRM systems include the fact that

Table 10.2 Example CRM: Customer Service Levels

Included Service	New	Customer Rank				
		*	**	***	****	*****
Complimentary newspaper	✓	✓	✓	✓	✓	✓
Discount coupon via email		✓	✓	✓		
Automatic check-in			✓	✓	✓	✓
Bed turn-down service			✓	✓	✓	✓
Complimentary internet access				✓	✓	✓
Complimentary fruit and nut basket				✓	✓	✓
Telephone response priority					✓	✓
Preferred room assignment					✓	✓
Preferred room rate					✓	✓
Room service order priority						✓
Hotel car pick-up and delivery						✓
Free valet parking						✓
Live operator wake-up reminder						✓

customer behaviour is often erratic. *Ask yourself: What happens when some customers change behaviour and drop to a lower classification, receiving service that is below what they have come to expect?*

Ask yourself: What happens when a new customer, who has the potential to be a five-star customer, is not impressed with the one-star service levels on his or her first stay?

Someone might earn a five-star rating in a two-month period and then make purchases at a one-star level for the next year. Accounting for contingencies like this can make CRM systems increasingly complex.

Services Marketing

Many businesses offer their customers no physical product: hairdressers, consulting firms, delivery services, music schools, even babysitters. All these are **pure services**, and they differ in a number of ways from product-based businesses. In pure services:

- *Price differentiation is difficult to justify.* At different hair salons, you can pay anywhere from $20 to $100 or more for pretty much the same haircut. *Ask yourself: Why might you be willing to pay more?*

- *The customer may participate in the creation of the "product."* The quality of massage you get may depend on how clearly you tell the therapist where it hurts and how hard to massage. *Ask yourself: Then, how can a business control the service quality?*

- *Evaluation of the service quality may be difficult.* After a concert, a band gets feedback from one customer who thought the performance was brilliant, but for another it was weak. *Ask yourself: How can the band assess the quality of their work?*

It is by studying questions like these that the field of **services marketing** has been able to shed light on important issues of customer satisfaction and retention. These findings have implications for product-based business as well, since a firm can be judged on the quality of customer service as much as the quality of the product.

Much of the understanding of customer satisfaction comes from the examination of customer dissatisfaction. Studies of dissatisfied customers provide evidence that

- the vast majority of dissatisfied customers do not complain to the service provider;

- the average dissatisfied customer tells around 10 people of the problem; and

- the majority of dissatisfied customers who do complain are likely to be retained as customers if their complaint is resolved.[9]

This implies that customer retention depends on actively eliciting feedback from customers about whether or not they are satisfied (most won't volunteer the information) and correcting deficiencies for unsatisfied customers as quickly as possible, so the story they will be spreading is a positive one and so you will keep them as customers.

One of the biggest areas of customer dissatisfaction is wait times. Research into customer perceptions about wait times shows that how long customers feel that they have been waiting can depend on a number of factors, most of which can be influenced by the service provider.[10]

The wait feels longer when it is

- *Of unknown duration.* Keep customers informed about how long they can expect to wait.

- *Unoccupied.* Make sure there are activities or reading materials available or that customers are not left alone.

- *Pre-process, compared to waits during the process.* For long waits, move customers to a second area or have them fill out a questionnaire so that they will feel the service process has begun.

pure services Businesses offering no, or insignificant, physical product.

✅ **Memory Check 10.10**
True or False? Customer relationship management, CRM, usually refers to a retail job title.

services marketing An area of business study that examines the non-product elements of keeping customers satisfied.

✅ **Memory Check 10.11**
True or False? Pure services generally have no physical product.

❓ **Get Help 10.10**
For a series of articles on CRM, go to the Canada Business Network website (canadabusiness.ca) and select "Managing," then "Marketing and Sales," then "Sales and Customer Relationship Marketing."

- *Unexplained.* Provide reasons to a customer for any delay.
- *Unfair.* Customers are willing to wait longer when the delay was their fault, but when it's your fault, be sure to apologize.

Clearly, if a business is to be efficient, customer satisfaction cannot be handled by default, or only when the customer complains. Rather it must be a proactive process of anticipating customer perceptions and asking for feedback.

✔ **Memory Check 10.12**
True or False? The wait seems longer for a waiting customer who knows how long he or she is going to have to wait.

Satisfying the Difficult Customer

Some customers, even when treated fairly, courteously, and promptly, will remain unsatisfied for reasons that often have more to do with the customer's personal issues and history than with the service that your business provides. These customers, however, can pose a threat by disrupting your operations and/or attacking your reputation. In Figure 10.1, different types of problem customers are identified along with appropriate methods for dealing with them.

Figure 10.1 Problem Customer Types and Responses

TYPE	CHARACTERISTICS	APPROACH
Genuine	Customer is emotional, upset over a legitimate complaint of poor service or product. Perhaps this is a subsequent attempt to resolve the problem.	Apologize. Resolve the complaint as fast as possible. Explain the steps you are taking to prevent repeats of the problem. Compensate the customer for any inconvenience. Thank the customer for complaining and giving you the chance to set things right.
Bullying	Customer demands unreasonable or preferential treatment, often intimidating staff and using the threat of withdrawing business unless the demanded concessions are received immediately.	Firmly remind customer that the service you provide is directly related to the prices that you charge. Inform customer that their business is highly valued and (if possible) you are willing to negotiate additional services at prices that would be profitable for you.
Abusive	Customer is likely to create a scene, shouting and using crude language, verbally attacking staff, and deriding the company and its service.	First, isolate the customer from vulnerable staff and other customers. Let the customer vent, then ask for assurance that they have finished and are willing to let you respond. Inform the customer that you will immediately resolve any legitimate complaint, but now there is a second problem to deal with: the problem of the customer's behaviour, which puts you in an embarrassing position where you may have to use legal remedies to protect your staff and your company's reputation. Allow the customer the opportunity for apologies or assurances of no-repeats. Document the occurrence.
Fraudulent	Customer insists on unfair or even unlawful consideration from the company such as return of customer-damaged goods or false receipts for tax purposes.	Remind customer that they deal with you because they receive fair, ethical, treatment from your company and that's the only way you operate. Take the moral high ground and "red flag" this customer for careful monitoring of all interactions.
Needy	Customer uses exceptional amounts of staff time for social "chatting," repeated explanations, reassurances, "double-checking" of information, or just plain hanging out at your place of business. Often motivated by reasons of loneliness or poor interpersonal skills, this customer is seeking social interaction.	If this customer's social need was not being met, the behaviour would change. So, remain meticulously polite with the needy customer but encourage staff to treat the customer as abruptly and efficiently as possible, within the bounds of good manners. If this fails, a frank discussion with the customer and a request to engage less of the staff's time may be required.

10.7 Identify specific methods you currently use, or methods that you could use, to measure customer satisfaction in your business (1/2 page maximum).

HOW DO I MAKE EMPLOYEES MORE EFFICIENT?

Hiring the Right Staff

When starting out as an entrepreneur, you are pretty much solely responsible for the profit that your business makes. But as your business grows, you increasingly become dependent on employees to make profit for you. That, of course, is how you become rich: by having lots of people making money for you. But some people are more willing and able to make money for you than others. The trick is to hire the ones that are willing and then train them properly to be able.

The hiring process is really two separate activities: getting people to apply for a job (**recruiting**) and then choosing the best applicant (**selection**). When very small businesses are looking for new employees, a common practice among owners is to ask existing employees if they know anyone looking for a job. This is often followed by a selection process of offering the first candidate who shows up a try-out—hiring him or her for a short probation period. If the try-out is successful, the candidate is considered hired. If the try-out is not successful, the owner dismisses the candidate and starts the process over again. This hit-and-miss approach to hiring is unlikely to get you the best candidate for the job.

recruiting The process of informing qualified candidates that a job opening is available and encouraging them to apply.

selection The process of choosing a new employee, usually conducted by putting all the applicants through a series of screening steps until the best candidate remains.

Recruiting The objective in choosing a recruiting source is to try to use one that will pre-screen or attract candidates who have the kind of qualifications you need. Common recruiting sources include:

- *Walk-ins.* This refers to people who send in a résumé or who just show up and ask to apply for a job, sometimes in response to an ad in your window or sometimes on their own initiative. If the candidate is just someone looking for a job, you have no pre-screening advantage.

- *Employee referral.* One of the problems of staffing based on employee referral is that you may end up hiring people all from the same family or group of friends, in which case your employees may feel a greater sense of loyalty to their referral group than to your business. On the other hand, if you're looking for someone who can get a reliable ride to work, this type of pre-screening is an advantage.

- *Job match.* This online service from Services Canada allows employers to submit their recruiting requirements and allows job seekers to submit their qualifications and job preferences. The database then electronically matches employers with candidates, who can submit an application. Candidates are, therefore, pre-screened by qualifications, but only as far as by the information they provide themselves.

- *Employment agencies.* These companies commonly specialize in a particular type of employee (office help, legal assistants, engineers, etc.). Some pre-screening and sometimes even testing will have been conducted by the agency.

- *Professional recruiters.* Sometimes referred to as "head-hunters," these consultants do not have waiting candidates. Instead they go out and find people fitting your requirements and encourage them to apply, usually getting paid only when and if you hire one of their finds.

- *Educational institutions.* Among other things, college graduates have proven that they have the ability to learn. This is a major plus if you are hiring for a position that requires you to quickly train the new hire. Post-secondary institutions have student and graduate databases and staff that can help screen for the kind of expertise you need.

❓ **Get Help 10.11**
Service Canada has put together a website that helps entrepreneurs with hiring, training, compensating, and even terminating employees. Go to jobsetc.gc.ca and select "Human resources management."

❓ **Get Help 10.12**
When recruiting, it is worthwhile to look at Services Canada's website for job matching, at jobbank.gc.ca. The process takes only a few minutes and you may find some good candidates.

Selection The selection process is usually a series of steps where you start out with a large number of applicants. The applicants go through a series of screening steps that have the purpose of eliminating candidates, so that the final selection step involves choosing the best candidate from a very small number of qualified applicants. Screening steps can include:

- *Screening from the application.* This means carefully reading résumé letters, and application forms to eliminate all who do not have the minimum requirements you are looking for.

- *Initial interview.* Here, obviously unsuitable candidates (inadequate communication skills, poor social skills, inadequate knowledge of the field) can be eliminated.

- *Testing.* This can cover a large variety of activities including work samples, performance tests, or even aptitude testing, eliminating all but a small number of the best performers.

- *In-depth interview.* At this interview, candidates are assessed for personality and fit with the organization as well as for their expectations about the job.

- *Reference/background check.* Candidates who lied on their résumé or whose reputation is doubtful can be eliminated at this step.

- *Final selection.* This step should be relatively easy since only a very small number of candidates (and perhaps only one) will remain.

⭐ Head Start Exercise

10.8 Identify specific methods that you currently use or that you could use to measure employee productivity (1/2 page maximum).

Obviously, for high-turnover, minor jobs within your business, it would not be economical to use all of the above screening steps. But the more critical the job is to your organization, the more steps you are likely to employ in the selection process.

Staff Training

The larger and more sophisticated your business becomes, the more likely you are to send employees out for training or to bring in specialized trainers from outside the company. But the majority of training that takes place in small firms is on the job. This usually involves partnering the trainee with someone who knows the task to be learned and who will supervise the learning process. **On-the-job training** is not a passive system where trainees just hang around until they absorb the information and skills to do the job. It works best when it is well planned and the trainer provides active teaching. Techniques to use for conducting any type of on-the-job training are:

- *Incentive.* Explain to trainees why they need to learn the particular skill or task and indicate how they will personally benefit from accomplishing this (pay raise, the chance to work unsupervised, a step toward permanent employment).

- *Small portions.* Plan the training by breaking whatever has to be learned into small manageable portions, allowing trainees to progress in clear steps.

- *Demonstration.* Slowly and clearly show trainees how to perform tasks, resisting the temptation to show off your own proficiency or speed, as this will just discourage the novice.

- *Performance.* Allow the trainee to practise the task in safe circumstances (both physically, where the trainee or others cannot be injured, and psychologically, where the trainee's errors will not produce embarrassment).

☑ **Memory Check 10.13**
True or False? Professional recruiters maintain lists of candidates looking for particular kinds of jobs.

on-the-job training Where employees learn by observation and by trial and error, usually working with someone who is already competent in the particular job.

☑ **Memory Check 10.14**
True or False? The in-depth interview is where candidates are assessed to see if they fit into the firm in terms of their personality.

- *Feedback.* Carefully observe trainees so that you can correct their errors, and use plenty of positive reinforcement whenever they do something right.

- *Reward.* When the trainee has completed training, provide some reward (it does not have to be monetary) as a form of recognition. Certificates, names on plaques, new job titles—all these can be powerful motivators.

Training largely comes under provincial jurisdiction, and some provinces provide assortments of skills training and management training materials and courses to their business communities. Especially popular are train-the-trainer programs that can provide you with skills to be a more effective on-the-job trainer.

? **Get Help 10.13**
Check the web for your provincial Ministry of Education or Training for available courses, materials, and programs.

Many business owners are reluctant to get involved with any significant amount of training because they believe it is cheaper to find people who have been trained by another company and then lure those employees away from their current jobs by paying slightly above the going rate. Some entrepreneurs also feel that if they spend the money to train employees, they will not be able to afford competitive pay rates and so will lose their own employees to the competition. *Ask yourself: Is it better to spend money on training for the skills you need or better to spend money on higher salaries so you can hire from outside?* The truth is that it's not an either–or situation. The most successful companies tend to do more training than average, as well as pay competitively.

Organizational Development

The discussion of leadership in Chapter 4 is very much about how you as an entrepreneur can personally motivate those working for you to higher levels of productivity. As your business grows, however, you will have less time to spend with individual employees, possibly because you will have more of them and possibly because you will have to spend more time dealing with strategic issues rather than day-to-day operations. Because of this, employee **morale** and efficiency may slip. One option is to try to systemize the principles of good management throughout your organization by establishing a **leadership program**. Over the years many such systems have evolved, going by names like

morale The feeling of relative enthusiasm for the business collectively held by the employees.

leadership program A formal, organization-wide system to improve morale and involve employees in the decision-making process.

- Management by Objectives
- Participative Management
- Management Teams
- Total Quality Management
- The Learning Organization
- The Strategy-Focused Organization

At the time of writing, The Learning Organization is a widely popular leadership program based on the series of Fifth Discipline books written by Peter Senge. The program is adaptable to organizations of all sizes, and reports excellent improvements in organizational effectiveness. Also gaining in popularity is the leadership approach developed by Robert S. Kaplan and David P. Norton, The Strategy-Focused Organization. This approach involves the use of key performance indicators and strategy maps, which show the links across the various stakeholders and various objectives of an organization.

The main advantages of such programs are that they give a common focus to all employees and formally involve everyone in decision making. In the start-up phase of a company, such systems are not required since everyone is focused on survival of the firm and everyone feels a sense of importance while there are only a few people in the organization. As the organization grows, however, individual employees may have less and less contact with the entrepreneur and may come to feel uninvolved. A formal leadership program can often help these employees become reconnected with the company.

? **Get Help 10.14**
Before starting any kind of leadership program, check the library for recent management and organizational development texts. You will likely need outside help to start such a program. Use the Yellow Pages to start your hunt for management consultants.

Another advantage of these programs is that they emphasize both the strategic and operational aspects of the business as equally important and bring the two into alignment. A study of Scottish and Italian SMEs showed this to be a key factor in the success of organizations.[11]

It seems that pretty much any kind of organization-wide leadership program will produce a significant improvement in productivity for a period of time (roughly a couple of years) and then productivity will start to fall back to the baseline level (from before the introduction of the program). The implication of this trend for the business owner is that a new program or organizational focus should be planned for when the current one starts to fade.

⭐ Head Start Exercise

10.9 Identify two leadership approaches to organizational development and briefly outline the theories behind each (1 page maximum).

> **✅ Memory Check 10.15**
> True or False? Leadership programs tend to produce a permanent increase in an organization's productivity.

An important motivator for employees within a growing business is the opportunity to grow personally—which means getting promotions. But before you can promote from within your company, your employees must be prepared to assume new and larger responsibilities. And they must have others ready to take over the responsibilities that they leave.

Business Reality 10.2 Revue Cinema
Profit or Non-Profit, It Still Has to Run Like a Business

The 244-seat Revue Cinema has been showing movies, almost continuously, for close to 100 years. Built before the First World War, it has many of the architectural and decor touches of that era. Over the years, the movie house underwent name changes and updates in technology but eventually closed in 2006, like most other neighbourhood theatres, as a result of declining business. This was no surprise in an era of HD televisions, digital media, downloading, and giant multi-screen entertainment complexes. Local residents Danny and Letty Mullin wanted to preserve the cinema, so they bought the building and leased it to the non-profit Film Revue Society to run as an art-house cinema.

The Film Revue Society is a community-based group of volunteers that was specifically set up to keep the Revue Cinema operating. Their intention is to show a wide range of vintage, foreign, rare, and important films. The Society is funded by memberships, donations, grants, and ticket sales, and it has contracted two film theatre entrepreneurs to manage the operations of the theatre.

Daniel Demois and Andy Willick own and operate a single-screen movie theatre, similar to the Revue Cinema in size and age, but they don't see the two as being in competition. Their own theatre is a long distance from the Revue and targets a younger audience, offering a program of mainstream, independent, and cult movies.

When asked about the differences between operating a for-profit and a non-profit theatre, Daniel indicated that were some. As entrepreneurs, the pair report to no one but themselves; however, at the Revue, they report to a board of directors. This has both advantages and disadvantages. With a board, Daniel notes, "It is great to have so many more ideas." On the other hand, he says, "You can sometimes get too many cooks in the kitchen," which slows down decision making. He likes working with volunteers since they are so motivated to contribute. "People enjoy doing something that's community based—giving back to the community," he says. With volunteers, however, Daniel points out that "there is a greater need to explain why they are expected to do something."

Daniel feels that non-profits have some advantages, such as being able to get government grants and things like temporary liquor permits for special events. But for the most part, the activities of running a non-profit are pretty much the same as a regular business: planning, promoting the program, controlling expenses, directing employees/volunteers, listening to the patrons—it's all business.

Find out more about the Revue Cinema at revuecinema.ca.

For example, imagine that you are a distributor of industrial generators, ready to expand into a neighbouring province. You will need a sales manager for the new region; although several of your salespeople have indicated an interest, none of them have had any management training or experience. Besides, if you promote one of your top salespeople you will have to backfill that job. And even though one of your telephone order-takers has asked to go on the road as a salesperson, you cannot risk sending your customers someone with no experience. *Ask yourself: What will happen to morale if you do not promote from within? If you hire someone new from outside the company?* The issue is that specific staff should have been developed for future promotion before any promotions were available. This is called **succession planning**.

Good succession planning does not necessarily identify one specific understudy for each job in the organization, but it does identify certain individuals as likely candidates for promotion in certain directions. These candidates are developed by various means, such as **mentoring** (forming an association with a senior manager who will act as an adviser), **job shadowing** (spending time observing or assisting managers in their jobs), and even formal classroom training (often through continuing education courses). Succession planning not only ensures the preparedness of employees for promotion, but also acts as a great motivator for those who can see the likelihood of their efforts being rewarded.

HOW CAN I CONTROL COSTS?

Careful management of costs and expenses might be a better investment of your effort than using that same effort to increase sales. For example, you could have a business that runs with a net profit of about 3 percent of sales. By spending a little time shopping around, you may find that you could save $100 on the cost of your supplies. That savings ends up as $100 more net profit for you to keep. At the 3 percent rate, you would have to increase your sales by $3333 in order to make the same $100 net profit. Clearly, there is a point of diminishing returns when trying to reduce costs. *Ask yourself: For your business, which would be the easiest way to make $100 more net profit?*

Costing Systems

The best approach is to develop a systematic way of reviewing your costs and expenses. This could mean something like annual or even quarterly meetings with your accountant where you compare all of your costs and expenses to the industry averages (again by using key ratios). Your system could mean setting aside a regular day to shop the prices of all of your suppliers, including things like insurance and any professional services that you use (such as your accountant). The system might also include a method of checking the costs on every contract or job that you undertake, to make sure that you are covering all of your costs and expenses and therefore making a profit on every job. This is often accomplished by using some sort of costing work sheet, like the one in Figure 10.2.

Direct Materials In the direct materials section of the costing sheet, the purpose is to make sure you are listing and accounting for the costs of materials that will be used for the job. This doesn't mean small incidental supplies like paper or cleaning liquids or computer disks (these will be taken into consideration as part of overhead). Instead, it means the major predictable materials you will need along with any predictable wastage. For example, a ceramic tile installer may know from experience that a certain percentage of tiles will crack when being cut to fit around the edges. This wastage is part of the job material costs.

Direct Labour The cost of direct labour is the amount you pay to people (usually calculated at an hourly rate) for the time they will actually be working on the particular project.

mentoring An employee development technique that matches the employee with a senior manager (not necessarily in the same department) who functions as an adviser for the employee.

job shadowing An employee development technique that allows employees to observe or assist managers in their jobs

✔ **Memory Check 10.16**
True or False? Succession planning should identify one specific understudy for each senior job in the business.

❓ **Get Help 10.15**
Specific costs and expenses are listed by industry as a percentage of sales on Industry Canada's SME Benchmarking site, at sme.ic.gc.ca.

Figure 10.2 Path and Patio Cost Worksheet

Customer: Skinner, 98 Brown St., Saint John 555-5987

Project Description: Curved interlocking patio around pool (600 sq. ft.: $8^14''\times7^14''$ paver stones)

Direct Materials

Description	# Units	$\times$	Cost/unit	=	Material Cost
1440 pavers (+10% waste)	1584	$\times$	$ 1.10	=	$1,742.00
Portland cement (40-kg bag)	20 bags	$\times$	$11.50	=	$ 230.00
Sand	2 tons	$\times$	$14.00	=	$ 28.00
Edging	100 ft.	$\times$	$ 1.00	=	$ 100.00

Total Direct Materials Cost $2,100.00 $2,100.00

Direct Labour

Employee	# Hours	$\times$	Hourly Rate	=	Labour Cost
Designer	4	$\times$	$38.00	=	$ 152.00
Installer	36	$\times$	$26.00	=	$ 936.00
Assistant	36	$\times$	$15.00	=	$ 540.00

Total Direct Labour Cost $1,628.00 $1,628.00

Overhead

OH% of Direct Labour	$\times$	Direct Labour Cost	=	Overhead Charge
290%	$\times$	$1,628.00	=	$4,721.00 $4721.00

Pricing

Total Costs (Direct Materials + Direct Labour + Overhead) $8,449.00

Total Costs	$\times$	% Net Profit	=	Job Profit	+	Total Costs	=	Job Price
$8,449.00	$\times$	4%	=	$338.00	+	$8,449.00	=	$8,787.00

It doesn't include things like the hours of sales time it took to get the contract. Neither does it include things like time spent with customers while they finalize details of a job nor the time for incidental phone calls or paperwork related to the job. (Again, these are part of the overhead calculation.)

Overhead An accurate measure of your overhead (operating expenses of the company) can really only come from the income statement, after the company has been operating for a while. Attempting this before start-up, working just with your experience and financial projections, will be much less accurate. Nevertheless, in some industries—for example, a machine shop or a cabinet-making business—a costing system like this should be necessary right from the beginning.

The worksheet uses an overhead percentage of direct labour to estimate the amount of overhead that should be charged for every dollar of labour that is charged. The overhead percentage of direct labour is calculated by dividing all the annual operating expenses of the business by the amount of direct labour that would have been billed to customers during that year. This is expressed as a percentage:

$$\text{OH\% of Direct Labor} = \frac{\text{Annual Operating Expenses}}{\text{Annual Direct Labour Billings}} \times 100\%$$

Let's say that the example shown in Figure 10.2 has an overhead percentage of direct labour of 290 percent. This means that for every dollar of direct labour that this company charges, it must charge $2.90 for overhead. (This figure would normally be calculated from past customer invoices and your income statement.)

Cost-Based Pricing The overall pricing strategy for your business should always be more of a marketing issue than a costing issue, and it should be related to your company image and market conditions. But you still have to make sure that you are making a profit on each transaction. You may need a costing worksheet to ensure that you cover all of your costs and expenses as well as make a profit on every job. And, for some businesses, this tool is the most efficient way of calculating a job price—simply applying a predetermined mark-up to your costs and expenses.

Clearly, the information shown in Figure 10.2 is not something that you would want to show to a customer. The problem is that if you are showing a 4 percent net profit, the customer will wonder why you can't get by with 2 percent, or 1 percent. Your profit is none of the customer's business. The customer should be concerned only with your final price compared to the prices of competitors. If you plan on showing your costing sheet to anyone (as in the case where you are using the same form to provide price quotations to customers), you may wish to build your profit directly into your materials and labour costs.

No job costing work sheet is perfect. The assumption that the labour cost is directly proportional to the overhead does not always hold. For example, in Figure 10.2, if the designer were able to do the work in one hour, the labour cost would be reduced by $96 and the overhead would go down by $278 (290 percent × $96), which is just about equal to the job profit. For this job, however, very little of the overhead is related to the work of the designer working at a computer in the office. Most of the overhead would come from transportation and machinery expense at the job site, which would remain the same regardless of how many hours the designer puts in. For some businesses, where there is a huge variation in the overhead from job to job, a more complex costing method may be required, actually calculating an amount of overhead for each job activity. This is called **activity-based costing.**

activity-based costing A method of apportioning overhead to a job by breaking the job down into detailed activities, each of which has a specific overhead cost.

Make or Buy Decisions The "make or buy" decision refers to the individual products that your business is selling and whether you are producing those items yourself or buying

Memory Check 10.17

True or False? The pricing strategy of a business is primarily a marketing issue rather than a costing issue.

outsourcing The buying of products or services from outside a company, instead of producing them in-house, especially when producing them yourself is a feasible option or past practice.

Memory Check 10.18

True or False? The make-or-buy decision only applies to manufacturing firms.

them from some other supplier for resale to your customers. For example, you might be a manufacturer of small industrial vacuum cleaners, but about half of your company income is from selling replacement filter bags for your machines. One of your options is to invest in paper and cardboard cutters as well as industrial sewing machines, purchase pre-printed filter paper and board, and then produce your own bags in your plant. Alternatively, you could go to a firm that produces paper-filtering products and give them the contract to produce all of your bags, custom-made to your specifications. *Ask yourself: Which is the better option?*

Each of the options has its own advantages:

Make	Buy
Direct control of quality	No investment in equipment
Direct control of delivery	Greater specialization in business
Guaranteed source of supply	Easier to redesign product (not limited by own equipment)

Generally, the fewer activities your company specializes in, the more efficiently you will operate, favouring the buy option. *Ask yourself: Could the question of "make or buy" apply to service firms that have no physical product?* Yes, although the question becomes slightly different: Do it yourself or subcontract? A garage may send out its transmission work to a specialist in this area and still make a small profit on transmission work orders, without having to invest in special tools and expertise. A generalized computer-consulting firm can subcontract web design work because so many small firms that specialize in web design can do this specialty work more efficiently. **Outsourcing** is a term often used to describe the buying of a product you could choose to make, or to describe the subcontracting of a service or process instead of providing it with your own staff.

Like the issue of pricing, make or buy is sometimes a marketing issue as opposed to a cost issue. For instance, you could have a restaurant that specializes in gourmet breakfasts. It may be cheaper, faster, and a lot less work to buy pre-made scrambled eggs in 30-portion boil-and-serve bags. The eggs wouldn't taste that much different, but how would customers react if they found out? *Ask yourself: What would it do to their perception of your restaurant—your image?*

Budgeting for Efficiency Increasing the efficiency of your business can be costly. In other words: You have to spend money to save money. And in just about any business, there will be many alternatives on which you could spend money for greater efficiency. But small business owners would never have the time or money to implement all possible efficiency measures at the same time. So the logical way to manage for efficiency is to look at several of the most likely ways of saving money and then prioritize whichever would be the most profitable. The first thing you have to do is figure out the costs for any particular efficiency project being considered.

Project Budgeting Identifying the costs for any efficiency project means listing any capital outlay for new equipment, machinery, software, consulting fees, subcontract work, and so on. It also means identifying the soft or hidden costs associated with a particular project. These could include putting a value on the entrepreneur's own time that would be used by the project, along with the time of involved employees (including time for training on new systems) plus any travel costs and incidentals. This process can be difficult, will involve imaginative thinking, and may not be particularly accurate (with the tendency being to underestimate costs). The next step, perhaps even less accurate but still necessary, requires estimating the annual savings that would result from the particular efficiency measures. See the sales forecasting techniques described in Chapter 2 for ideas on methods. *Ask* yourself: How much training time would be saved in a year if new employees had a comprehensive operations manual to refer to? What would be the dollar value of that time? How much would customer retention increase with a new online ordering system? What would be the dollar value of the profit from those retained customers? Certainly, the answers to these questions would involve some speculation. But the more that numbers can be attached to decisions about efficiency, the more that the risk associated with those decisions is reduced.

⭐ Head Start Exercise

10.10 Briefly identify any costing methods that your business uses. Identify the average gross margin of your business. Using the return on sales figure from Head Start Exercise 10.1, calculate how many dollars of sales you must make for each dollar of net profit (1/2 page maximum).

Return on Investment (ROI) Analysis The cost of implementing an efficiency project is an investment that should yield savings (additional profit) for the company. But profit only has real meaning in the context of the investment needed to produce it. So, for each proposed efficiency program, it should be possible to calculate an estimated ROI where:

$$\text{Project ROI} = \frac{\text{Estimated annual savings}}{\text{Estimated implementation costs}}$$

With this calculation it will be easy to compare the relative estimated profitability of different proposed efficiency programs and prioritize them accordingly. *Ask yourself: How accurate is this comparison?* It's certainly not precise. So other considerations (changing market conditions, changing technologies, competition changes, etc.) may well be part of any decision on an approach to efficiency.

Like most decisions that an entrepreneur has to make, the choice of approaches to better efficiency (reduced costs and expenses) is one that has to be made with imperfect information and some degree of risk.

> ✅ **Memory Check 10.19**
> True or False? It is easier to have a product redesigned when you outsource it than when you make it yourself.

> ✅ **Memory Check 10.20**
> True or False? The ROI for the cost of an efficiency program can be estimated with a high degree of accuracy.

Answers to Memory Check Questions

10.1 F	10.2 T	10.3 F	10.4 T	10.5 T	10.6 T	10.7 F	10.8 T
10.9 F	10.10 F	10.11 T	10.12 F	10.13 F	10.14 T	10.15 F	10.16 F
10.17 T	10.18 F	10.19 T	10.20 F				

Questions for Discussion

1. Identify some automated services that you dislike and explain the reasons for your feelings. Could the automated service be corrected in a way to address your complaints? Discuss.
2. Imagine that you own a shoe store and your accountant, who has just performed a ratio analysis of your financial statements, tells you that your ratio of profit/sales is far below the industry average. What problems do you think might be causing this? How would you investigate your suspicions?
3. Try and identify some companies that have cut back on some products or services to get back to their core business. Why have they taken this strategy?
4. Find some commonly used forms at your work or educational institution. What generally unnecessary information does the form ask for? In what rare circumstances could that information be important? Should that information be dropped from the form?

5. "Canadian robots should be able to manufacture products of better quality and more cheaply than skilled labour in developing countries." Discuss this proposition.
6. Most small, independent clothing store owners do not have a website and tend to use the internet for little more than email. Come up with as many internet applications as possible for a small store like this.
7. Think of some large organization where you have been a repeat customer—perhaps a bank or a college or university. How do you feel when you think of yourself calling in to this organization, knowing that the person answering the phone may have significant information about you on the computer screen? What are some of the implications of this for CRM systems?
8. Customer satisfaction does not necessarily equal customer retention. Discuss some of the reasons why this might be true.
9. For a small business that needs skilled staff, discuss the advantages of training vs. hiring.
10. "Pricing should be a marketing decision rather than a costing decision." Discuss.

Case for Discussion

A History of Toys is the name of the store that has been in Hermione's family for over 50 years. She is the third-generation owner. The store is located in an area of heavy pedestrian traffic close to downtown. Hermione's grandfather bought the building back when he started the business and it has since undergone several renovations. Now it has a brightly lit 900 square foot store that is packed with toys and a basement storage area of 700 square feet that is also packed with older inventory.

The customers tend to be the parents and grandparents of children aged five to twelve, drawing from a large metropolitan area. The store sells traditional, high-quality toys and games. It has large displays showing the most popular toys over the past 50 years. In fact, Hermione keeps many of these older discontinued toys and games in her inventory, still brand-new and in the box. The store generates traffic because people love to bring their children or grandchildren and are thrilled to show the toys they themselves owned and loved as a children.

Unfortunately, many of these regular "customers" are spending less and less when they visit the store. Over the past five years, while sales have remained steady, profit has steadily declined.

This has made Hermione reconsider her strategy of concentrating on traditional toys. She has thought of bringing in some of the newer electronic game platforms. But she has found that this would require a substantial investment in the software used by these units, and the store does not have the amount of cash she would need. So Hermione has scheduled a meeting with her accountant to review her situation. The conversation went like this:

Accountant: The first problem I noticed is that your return on assets is well below the average for your industry. This indicates that you are not running efficiently.

Hermione: Yes, but we have a lot of money tied up in the building, while most stores rent.

Accountant: Ah, but the problem is not your fixed assets, it is your inventory. The average inventory turnover for your industry is about four times your own.

Hermione: That's because we have so many discontinued, vintage items. We're the only place that carries most of them and they will just keep going up in value.

Accountant: But that's not helping your profit. Your return on sales is also far below the industry average. Again, it shows you're inefficient.

Hermione: Other than inventory, where else could we be inefficient? Accountant: Your cost of salaries and benefits is way too high for your amount of sales.

Hermione: Yes, but I need a trained staff who know the history of the old toys. This is what customers are interested in.

Accountant: You don't have to use staff to answer emails and phone calls about the toys all day. There are other ways to inform customers.

Hermione: Yes, but I need to keep knowledgeable people on staff in the slow times so that I'll have them when we're busy.

Accountant: More than 50 percent of your annual sales occur between the start of November and Christmas. That's only seven weeks. I've been here at that time and seen a big long line-up at the cash register, which has got to be discouraging customers, especially those with small kids.

Hermione: Each of our customers has different needs and we take the time to treat them as individuals. This isn't a supermarket. Besides, what I really want to know is where I will get the money to invest in gaming consoles and software.

Accountant: That's what I've been trying to tell you.

1. How is it that individual customers are spending less, but sales remain steady?

2. How could Hermione modernize the image of her business? How could she become more specialized?

3. How could Hermione keep her "history of toys" theme for the store and still increase her turnover?

4. How could Hermione inform customers about toy histories without using up the time of sales staff? Indicate at least three methods.

5. How could Hermione reduce the sales staff year round, but still have knowledgeable people during the Christmas rush?

6. How could Hermione reduce wait times at the check-out? Come up with at least three methods.

7. Where will Hermione get the money for new gaming consoles and software?

OPERATIONAL EFFICIENCY PLAN

Measuring Efficiency

1. Briefly identify any general indications of a need for efficiency improvement in the business.

2. From the financial statements of the business, calculate key ratio indicators of efficiency and provide data comparing these to industry averages.

3. Discuss any conclusions about the relative efficiency of your firm and identify any serious examples of waste.

Refocusing

4. Identify any elements of the core business that you will concentrate on for greater profits.

5. Identify any products or segments that you will marginally maintain or abandon.

Systems and Automation

6. Identify any new systems, tools, or methods improvements that you will introduce for greater productivity.

7. Estimate the costs involved for all of the changes identified in question 6.

8. Estimate the productivity gain in terms of additional profit over the next three years for all the changes identified in question 6. Give a clear rationale.

Customer Retention

9. Identify any new systems or methods you will introduce to improve customer satisfaction/retention.

10. Estimate the costs involved for all of the changes identified in question 9.

11. Estimate any additional profit over the next three years expected from all the changes identified in question 9. Give a clear rationale.

Employee Productivity

12. Identify any new systems or methods you will introduce to improve employee productivity.

13. Estimate the costs involved for all of the changes identified in question 12.

14. Estimate any additional profit over the next three years expected from all the changes identified in question 12. Give a clear rationale.

Cost Control

15. Identify any new systems or methods you will introduce to control direct costs of your business.

16. Estimate the costs for all changes identified in question 15.

17. Estimate any additional profit over the next three years expected from all the changes identified in question 15. Give a clear rationale.

Chapter 11

Emerging Trends and Issues in Entrepreneurship:
How Will I Prepare for the Future?

The topics discussed in this chapter do not relate directly to a particular element of a formal business plan. Instead, this chapter is about the broad forces that are currently shaping our understanding and practice of entrepreneurship:

- What Are the Recent Challenges for Small Business?
- What Are Some Current Trends In Research?
- What Is Social Entrepreneurship?
- What Are the Emerging Trends In Entrepreneurship Education?
- What Are the Management Issues for Small Business?

Learning Objectives

On completion of this chapter, you should be able to:

1 Discuss the rate of change in e-business technologies.

2 Explain how entrepreneurs respond to economic cycles.

3 Distinguish between *ethics* and *morality*, applying these terms to business behaviours.

4 Explain the purpose and benefits of small business research.

5 Identify three major problems faced by minority and female entrepreneurs.

6 Define "social entrepreneurship" and explain some of its forms.

7 Compare at least five methods for teaching entrepreneurship.

8 Discuss the importance of management skills to entrepreneurs.

9 Explain how an entrepreneur can prepare for an unexpected crisis.

WHAT ARE THE RECENT CHALLENGES FOR SMALL BUSINESS?

Entrepreneurs, like everyone else, must deal with the challenges in a world of unprecedented change, a world where knowledge is growing at such an accelerating rate. But new knowledge itself does not mean economic growth. It takes an entrepreneur to turn new knowledge into new goods and services and ultimately into profit. And so the challenges of the changing world are also the opportunities for the entrepreneur.

Changing Technologies for Small Firms

In the time between the third edition of this text and this current edition, huge changes have taken place in electronic tools available for business. (Applying these tools is broadly referred to as **e-business**.) The rate of development in this area is so great that some of the information in this book will be obsolete by the time you are reading it. Currently, there are widely used e-business tools to help small firms manage:

> **e-business (e-biz)** The use of any of the many computerized and web-based technologies to assist the functioning of a business.

Customers CRM (customer relationship management) software keeps track of customer contacts, purchases, data on the value of individual customers, and lots more. (CRM is discussed in detail in Chapter 10.) Examples include Terasoft CRM and Maximizer CRM.

Finances It is commonplace in small firms to use software that keeps track of all financial transactions (payables, receivables, payroll, etc.), and produces financial statements. Among the most widely used packages are QuickBooks and Simply Accounting.

Projects Software used for costing and pricing contracts as well as for keeping track of project scheduling is available on its own, or sometimes as part of broader financial packages. Examples are Goldenseal from Turtle Creek Software and Microsoft Project.

Inventory Critical for retailers and wholesalers, the widespread use of barcodes has made the measuring, tracking, and ordering of inventory much easier and more accurate. Again, this may be available as stand-alone software such as SIMMS Inventory Management Software from KCSI or as part of an integrated package such as SAP Business One.

☑ **Memory Check 11.1**
True or False? Customer relationship management is about dealing with difficult customers.

Employees Human resource management systems (HRIS) can manage information on payroll and benefits for employees as well as performance, training, succession planning, job postings, and a host of other employee-related issues. Generally, this software is not economical until the small business has reached a significant size; say 50–100 employees or more. However, it is possible to subcontract this work to a third-party HR firm hosting the software. Examples of HRIS programs are HR.net from Vizual Business Tools and HRA Personal Assistant from Vantage Point Software Strategies.

As small firms have become more reliant on information technology, spyware, viruses, and hackers have become much more sophisticated. So, small companies continuously need better computer security. Firewalls, spam blockers, and anti-virus software have been used routinely for years. But now, new technologies such as **intrusion prevention systems (IPS)** are becoming more necessary. These systems take various forms and installation typically requires the assistance of information technology specialists. For example, if you run a small cosmetic surgery clinic, protecting your electronic patient files would be a major expense, but failure to do so could leave you open to even more expensive law suits. New forms of insurance against cyber risks are recently available.[1]

Currency is another technology issue. Constantly updating e-business tools to keep up with changing technologies can be a costly challenge. Often, it includes the price of re-training employees. The decision of when to update is usually made with one eye on the technology and another on the competition. And there is always the danger of your competitor **leapfrogging**, or jumping a generation of technology. For example, you might have a small film production company making commercials and industrial videos. A year and a half ago, you upgraded all your equipment to new "2K" video cameras and editing equipment at a cost of $200 000. You financed the equipment over three years, so you still owe over $100 000 on it. Just recently there have been significant advances in video equipment and the prices have fallen. Your closest competitor did not upgrade to "2K" equipment when you did, but instead has recently bought new "4K" equipment, far superior to yours, but at a cost of only $75 000. This would put you at a huge competitive disadvantage. *Ask yourself: When is the right time to upgrade?*

Research and relying on experts are often the only tools to help with a "best guess" decision.

Small Business and the Economy

Scholars generally divide the study of the economy into two categories: **microeconomics** and **macroeconomics**. Microeconomics looks at how people and companies make decisions about buying, selling, and producing things at a local level. Macroeconomics looks at

intrusion prevention systems (IPS) Real-time network security systems that can detect and disconnect from sources attempting to invade a system while the malicious activity is in progress.

leapfrogging When an individual or organization gains an advantage over competitors by skipping a generation of technology.

microeconomics The study of the relationships among supply, demand, price, and profits within closed market systems.

macroeconomics The study of the relationships among national production, consumption, prices, capital, employment, and other indicators of a country's financial health.

the bigger picture of how the whole country operates in terms of investment, production, consumption, trade, and so on. Traditionally, those teaching and studying entrepreneurship have concentrated on microeconomics as being most relevant to small business owners. But *Ask yourself: Is that approach still valid?*

Imagine that you're a small furniture manufacturer in a small Canadian city and you specialize in making dining room sets. Decades ago, all of your product would have been sold in your own city and almost all of the competing product available would have come from you and the other local manufacturers. Here, the concepts of microeconomics would have helped you determine the prices you could charge and your production levels. Today, however, the profits of your business are just as likely to be affected by things like a strike in the Indonesian forestry industry interrupting the supply of wood to Asian furniture factories, which supply Swedish furniture retailers that sell a large portion of the dining room sets in your city. In today's global economy, everything affects everything.

The Small Business Administration in the United States, in 2001, started to produce annual reports on what they called "The Small Business Economy." Over the years, it has become increasingly clear that the small business economy is the backbone of the national economy and produces all of the country's economic growth.[2]

And the single biggest influence on the small business economy of Canada is the economy of the United States. This was demonstrated in the global recession of 2008–2009 when the failure of some large U.S. banks (which had granted inappropriate mortgages based on bad policies of the US Federal Reserve Bank) triggered a near economic collapse. Despite this, most economists believe that the normal economic cycle of recession and expansion is a healthy pattern. The occasional recession is good for economic health by triggering the failure of weak and inefficient businesses that cannot survive under tough circumstances. So increasingly the small entrepreneur must be aware of what is happening in the economy and be prepared to react quickly. In the most general terms, that means looking for growth opportunities during times of economic expansion. In economic downturns it means adopting the kinds of efficiencies discussed in Chapter 11: factors such as cost control, automation, and systemization. (See an overview of this in Table 11.1.)

In business, as in many other aspects of life, timing is everything. If you could predict the beginning of the next economic downturn, the smart thing would be to start belt-tightening just before it happens. It is better to be proactive than reactive. But accurately predicting the start of the next recession or the next growth period is almost impossible, even for the best economists. So the alternative for the entrepreneur is to watch the economy (read the financial papers and websites) and be prepared to react quickly.

> **Get Help 11.1**
> Find out what's happening in the economy from Statistics Canada at www.statcan.gc.ca. Click on "Economic Accounts" and pick "Leading Indicators."

Small Business and the Environment

Any discussion of the environment these days involves the world "sustainability."

Ask yourself: What does **environmental sustainability** *really mean?* There is broad agreement among the vast majority of environmental scientists that the world is approaching a

environmental sustainability
Practices that involve consuming or polluting at a rate no greater than the rate at which Earth can clean, heal, and replenish itself.

Table 11.1 **Responding to Economic Change**

During Expansion	During Recession
Look for new markets/customers	Focus on customer retention
Develop new products/services	Develop systems and quality control
Seek financing for growth	Minimize debt
Hire new employees	Minimize staff and automate
Concentrate on sales	Concentrate on costs
Ensure high inventories	Ensure minimal inventories

A Green Business, But Is It Art?

The Junction area of Toronto is one of those exciting neighbourhoods that blend old and new, rich and poor, practical and creative. Homes and commercial buildings date back over a hundred years and include those that have been superbly renovated alongside many that have had a bare minimum of updating. First-generation, working-class, immigrant families live next to young professionals. Junk shops are next door to high-end furniture stores. But it has been this way for the past quarter century in the Junction. Here, the gentrification process has been moving slowly. So the area is a magnet for the arts community. Stores and space in renovated lofts can still be rented at reasonable rates and there is enough well-heeled traffic willing to invest in art and craft works.

This is where Phil Freire and partner Maggie Gattesco have located Metropolis Living, a gallery of what Phil calls "vintage industrial decor." This includes a huge range of items that Phil has salvaged and reconditioned, ranging from antique dressmaker's dummies to 50-year-old pickup truck doors. Old soft drink posters, apothecary bottles, ancient lightbulbs, vintage photography, Second World War first-aid kits, animal skulls...and numerous other items that would not traditionally be thought of as art or decor pieces. Most of the pieces are sold to upscale loft dwellers and homeowners in the area, but at least 25 percent of sales are to the film and TV industry for decorating period sets.

Phil acquires most of his inventory during buying trips through the U.S. rustbelt. Here, he combs an ideal combination of rural areas and high density industrial cities, estate sales, auctions, and junkyards to find the treasures he seeks. Phil's keen ability to see the artistic merit in what others might see as junk comes from his father, who was a lifelong collector of unusual items that had beauty. But even though he inherited "the eye" for art, when it comes to buying these treasures, Phil admits that he is not a good negotiator. "I'm too much of a pushover," he says. For the haggling process, he often has to rely on his girlfriend's help. For Phil, "it's more about passion than good business."

As a collector, himself, one of Phil's biggest problems is inventory control. "This is the tricky part of the business," says Phil, "controlling spending." He finds it hard to resist something of great esthetic value, so the shop has a tendency to become over-full. Currently, he deals with this by shipping excess inventory to another, larger store.

Phil explains that this is a green business because everything is being "upcycled," or re-used in a way that gives it more value than it originally had. Some of the items have to be refinished or modified to some new purpose. For example, a giant industrial cable spool might be turned into a unique coffee table. But wherever he can, Phil likes to "keep it as original as possible." Take a look at Metropolis Living's website at metropolis-living.com.

crisis. The rates at which we take fish from the oceans, cut forests, add carbon dioxide to the atmosphere, and pollute our lakes and rivers are greater than the rate at which Earth can produce new fish and trees, or clean the atmosphere and water. Earth cannot sustain the current rate of damage. The only thing the scientists quibble over now is how long we have before Earth will be unable to sustain human life.

The first step in reversing these tragic circumstances is to slow our consuming and polluting to a rate that doesn't make things worse than they are now—a rate that Earth can sustain. Otherwise, we will continue to pile up an environmental debt that future generations will have to pay. Most young Canadians are aware of and concerned about environmental threats but fail to realize that Canada is still among the worst polluters in the world, with a very poor record on protecting the environment.[3]

Nevertheless, there is room for optimism. Environment Canada (www.ec.gc.ca) is taking a lead in providing information and training on environmental sustainability. It also provides an annual report with major indicators on how the country is doing on air quality, water quality, and greenhouse gas emissions.

At the same time, the green movement is growing at all levels in our society. Educational, scientific, student, parent, and business groups are all lobbying for changes in how we use our resources. There is even a national political party, The Green Party of Canada, which, though not likely to form a government anytime soon, has clearly placed the spotlight on the environment and influenced the policies of the other political parties. Every school-age child in our nation knows the environmental mantra of "reduce, reuse, and recycle." This growing consumer and government concern over the environment means that it is in the interest of the small firm to become a **green business**, one that has environmentally sound services and products and practices. There are many informal things that a small firm can do to become more green (see Table 11.2). Or, a company can earn a formal green accreditation or certification from a variety of sources, including:

green business A company that takes a responsible approach toward protecting the environment and ensuring its sustainability through its products, services, and operating methods.

- *ISO 14000* (*www.iso.org*). The International Organization for Standardization offers various certifications relating to environmental practices.
- *Green Seal* (*www.greenseal.org*). This American non-profit organization certifies products and services for environmental responsibility.

The growing preoccupation with the environment means more than conforming to environmentally conscious practices. It also means the opportunity to make money—new gaps in the market are emerging. The list of businesses meeting the demand for green products and services is long and growing fast. Just a few examples are:

- manufacturing or distributing green packaging materials
- providing energy-saving construction or retrofitting
- selling and installing of renewable energy equipment such as solar panels and wind turbines
- installing and servicing of high-efficiency heating and cooling equipment
- running an online barter or exchange service

Get Help 11.2
Environment Canada offers lots of information on pollution and waste reduction for business. Visit Environment Canada's website at ec.gc.ca and select "Explore the Topics."

Table 11.2 Green Practices for Small Businesses

3R's	Examples
Reduce	Set printers to print on both sides of the paper and make hard copies only when necessary.
	Install low-flush toilets.
	Invest in good insulation, low heat-transmission windows, and high-efficiency heaters.
	Buy from local suppliers to reduce transportation.
	Use automatic lighting timers and set-back thermostats.
Reuse	Buy used office furniture or repair existing, rather than replacing with new products.
	Return packaging to suppliers for reuse.
	Provide china mugs instead of paper or Styrofoam cups at the coffee machine.
	Encourage employees to use reusable lunch containers.
Recycle	Buy recycled paper products.
	Provide compartmentalized recycling bins at work.
	Return printer and copier cartridges for refilling.
	Sell or donate used equipment instead of discarding.
	Provide recyclable containers for your own products.

Memory Check 11.2
True or False? Earth cannot sustain the current rates of human consumption and pollution.

- recycling and remanufacturing obsolete computer equipment
- growing or distributing organic products
- training city dwellers in micro-farming techniques
- recycling building products
- retailing and repairing bicycles or electric scooters
- setting up car pooling systems
- writing guidebooks and articles on sustainable practices
- providing energy audits of homes and businesses

And over the next few years the start-up opportunities in green areas can only be expected to multiply.

Entrepreneurship and Ethics

✔ **Memory Check 11.3**
True or False? The market for green products and services is growing rapidly.

A number of high-profile Canadian entrepreneurs have been prosecuted in recent years for serious breaches of trust. Among them are Conrad Black (media baron convicted in the United States of mail fraud and obstruction of justice), Garth Drabinsky (co-founder of Cineplex and Livent Inc., convicted of defrauding investors), and Earl Jones (Montreal financial advisor accused of swindling investors out of millions). Whatever perverted sense of entitlement motivates this kind of behaviour, it is not indicative of the behaviour of most Canadian entrepreneurs.

As entrepreneurs become more successful, their power to affect others—for better or for worse—becomes greater. With this influence also comes greater responsibility for leadership in ethical issues. *Ask yourself: What will happen when I am faced with a choice between making more profit and doing the morally right thing?*

Everyone has some sense of right and wrong. And, not surprisingly, your beliefs about right and wrong, on most issues, are pretty similar to the beliefs held by your parents, friends, and teachers. Your values don't stand in isolation from each other. Instead, they tend to be part of a system of beliefs that you share with those closest to you. This is what is meant by **morality**.

morality A system of beliefs about right and wrong.

Ask yourself: Is it morally wrong to kill another human being? Is it morally wrong to lie? For most of us, after we give it some thought, the answer to these questions is that it depends on the situation. Killing to save your own life may be a moral necessity. Lying when your aging aunt asks how you like her new outfit may be a simple kindness. So morality is situational. It can also change over time. *Ask yourself: Is it morally wrong to operate a business?* For much of the past century in Eastern Europe, not only would it have been morally wrong, but it also would have been illegal to practise entrepreneurship. Today, throughout this area, entrepreneurship is legal and even admired. Morality can change over time.

Ask yourself: Do the words ethics *and* morality *mean the same thing?* Most dictionaries will tell you that **ethics** means the branch of philosophy that studies morality. But most dictionaries tend to be pretty conservative. And, just as morality changes over time, the meanings of words tend to change. These days, the word *ethics* is widely used to mean professional rules of conduct. In this sense, we commonly talk about things like legal ethics, medical ethics, academic ethics, and, of course, business ethics. So, even though they are closely connected, morality and ethics do have different meanings. It's possible, even, to have a conflict between the two. For example, a doctor may consider it morally acceptable to end the life of a suffering terminal patient. In many jurisdictions, however, the medical society would brand this as unethical (as well as illegal). A lawyer might find it morally repugnant to help a murderer escape justice, while at the same time being ethically bound to give the best possible defence to a guilty client.

ethics Professional rules of conduct (common usage).

Business ethics are rules to protect those whom you, as an entrepreneur, have the power to harm, including:

- customers, who could be harmed by misleading information or outright lies to get them to buy; by unfulfilled contracts; or by damaged goods
- suppliers, who could be victim to late payments or cancellation of orders
- employees, who could suffer from false promises of future opportunity, harassment, or deficient pay
- competitors, who could be harmed by lies or unfair pricing practices. (Note: Any harm to your competitors from your superior services, products, or prices is certainly not unethical.)
- the community, as a whole, which could be harmed by unpaid taxes, lax environmental practices, or failure to follow safety regulations

When rules of conduct for a particular group are written into a document, this is known as a code of ethics. Many professional organizations and business associations have codes of ethics, which their members promise to abide by. Violation of the code can result in expulsion from the organization or other sanctions. Most of Canada's larger cities have Better Business Bureaus (BBBs), which keep lists of complaints made against businesses in the community. Businesses that are members of the bureau agree to abide by the Bureau's code of ethics and are permitted to advertise themselves as BBB members.

Fair Trade/Ethical Trade Many small firms buy, sell, or use products from abroad, and entrepreneurs are increasingly making supplier choices based on factors that go beyond issues of price, quality, and reliability.

The **fair trade** movement evolved in response to the exploitation of agricultural labourers and small producers in developing countries. There are many commodities grown in poor countries that are sold in Canada and provide excellent profits for foreign exporters as well as Canadian importers, processors, distributors, and retailers. But all too often the small coffee farmer or tea plantation worker is surviving at a subsistence level, sometimes in near slave-labour conditions. Canadian practitioners of fair trade try to ensure that producers of agricultural products get some fair return for the costs of producing their crops.

Over the years, the fair trade movement has set off concerns about broader ethical issues in international trade. This has coincided with the movement of agricultural workers in developing nations from the countryside, where they can no longer produce competitively, into urban areas, where they become a source of cheap labour for manufacturers. Many developing nations, including some with clear labour legislation, have such high levels of corruption that existing standards are poorly enforced and easy to circumvent. *Ask yourself: Were any of the clothes I'm wearing today made by underpaid, abused, or child labourers?* Chances are you don't know, but if you did, it might well make a difference in your choice of products. Helping you to know is one of the goals of the **ethical trade** movement. These organizations are interested in a wide range of human rights, health, and labour conditions for foreign workers. The idea behind the movement is for Western businesses to ensure that foreign suppliers, partners, and contractors adhere to some set of minimum labour standards for their employees. Someday, labelling and certification will be able to assure Western consumers that their product choices have been made by people working under reasonable conditions.

☑ **Memory Check 11.4**
True or False? The word *ethics* is commonly used to mean "professional rules of conduct."

❓ **Get Help 11.3**
For links to your local branch of the Better Business Bureau, go through the Canadian Council of Better Business Bureaus website at www.ccbbb.ca.

fair trade A movement of Western commodity processors and distributors to ensure that small producers in the developing world are adequately paid for their products.

❓ **Get Help 11.4**
For more information about fair trade, start with the website of the U.S.-based Fair Trade Federation. (www.fairtradefederation.org). The Ethical Trading Initiative offers an excellent U.K. site on ethical trade (www.ethicaltrade.org).

ethical trade A movement of Western retail and consumer groups to ensure that manufacturing labourers in developing countries have healthy and safe working conditions.

⭐ Head Start Exercise

11.1 Identify two or more unethical practices your company could likely get away with. Identify who would be hurt by these practices (1/3 page maximum).

A Hot Business in a Cold Climate

Bean North is a successful, very small coffee roasting company located in the Yukon's beautiful, forested Takhini Valley. Michael King started this "fair trade" business in 1997, buying organically grown and certified coffee beans from farmer co-operatives all over the world. The business was started to help ensure the ethical treatment of small coffee growers in developing countries. Bean North holds membership in Cooperative Coffees Inc., an organization whose 21 members across North America establish direct relationships with the small coffee producers they buy from.

This growing business sells about half of its product to upscale cafés throughout North America and Europe, and the rest to individuals via the internet. King's website (www.beannorth.com) devotes more space to promoting fair trade than it does to promoting his own coffee. As well, the site has links related to environmental issues and offers Bean North's own online newsletter: *Coffee & You*. This entertaining and informative publication educates the reader about coffee and its production. It also journals trips taken by Michael and his family to the coffee-producing areas that he buys from, and it includes descriptions of the lives, concerns, and opinions of the producers.

But fair trade is not the only agenda for Bean North. The company must make a profit. It does so by providing extremely high-quality products to carefully targeted consumers who tend to be socially, environmentally, and health conscious. Even though it is on a small scale, research, product development, and quality control are critical to this business.

So what could possibly be the advantage of roasting coffee in the Yukon? According to Michael, the secret in roasting coffee beans is that once they are roasted to the desired degree, they must be cooled as quickly as possible. For some roasters, that can mean expensive cooling and ventilation equipment. "In the Yukon," he says, "it usually means just opening the window." A significant advantage.

WHAT ARE SOME CURRENT TRENDS IN RESEARCH?

☑ **Memory Check 11.5**
True or False? The fair trade movement is broader in scope than the ethical trade movement.

Small business/entrepreneurship is relatively new as a focus of scientific inquiry. Nevertheless, a significant body of data has developed over the past three decades. Unfortunately, many of the studies use problematic or outmoded research methods, bringing their findings into question. More recently, however, there has been a definite improvement in the methods and technologies used for research into small business and entrepreneurship.[4] At the same time, there has been a virtual explosion of studies in this area so that currently there are 44 scientific journals devoted to the study of entrepreneurship.[5]

Research patterns in every field of study do not follow straight lines, where all of the scientists study one aspect of the topic and then they all logically move on to the next question to be answered. In practice, it's a lot messier than that. As in other areas of research, multiple lines of inquiry into entrepreneurship take place simultaneously and independently of each other. So in the same volume of a research journal it wouldn't be unusual to find a study on "Tribal Relationships as Barriers to Entrepreneurship in Sub-Saharan Africa" as well as a study on "Determinants of Distribution Channel Selection for European Metal Cutting Firms," and maybe another on "Venture Capitalist Preferences in Choosing High-Tech Investments." Now, let's say you are a coffee shop owner in Winnipeg, looking to improve your profits by applying the latest small business research findings. *Ask yourself: What help would you get from these three studies?* Probably none. In fact, like most people, you would probably have a hard time even understanding most of the scientific journal articles. And that's as it should be, because research studies are not intended for you, the entrepreneur, or even the undergraduate student. These works are intended to be read by

Other Researchers Scientists usually see their role as contributing to the overall body of knowledge, not necessarily looking for specific solutions to practical problems. And they use precise, complex technical language intended for their colleagues working on related problems.

Policy Makers These are the bureaucrats who advise politicians on the programs governments should use to support the economy. They study the latest research findings, looking for evidence to support particular courses of action.

Practitioners These are the various private and government consultants that provide advice, counselling, business books, magazine articles, and other services to entrepreneurs. Reading scientific journals and attending conferences are their main methods of professional development and staying current in the subject area.

Educators This group includes teachers and administrators in our educational institutions as well as those who write textbooks. It is the job of the educators to try and extract from the research broad reliable principles for entrepreneurship that are supported by substantial evidence, and to provide these principles to students and would-be entrepreneurs in an understandable manner.

At the time of writing, there is an exploding interest in e-business usage in small firms. But this fast-changing area of investigation has not yet formed into reliable patterns of data. There are, however, other recent research themes that stand out, including:

- investigation into different types of entrepreneurs;
- examinations of the factors that produce growth, and
- studies on minority and female entrepreneurs.

⭐ Head Start Exercise

11.2 Find and describe at least one research study from the journals that has implications for you or your business. Explain in (1/3 page maximum).

Classifications of Entrepreneurs

In order to understand entrepreneurs better, many researchers have been classifying entrepreneurs into three different categories for their studies:

- *Novice.* **Novice entrepreneurs** are people who have started, bought, or inherited a single business of which they are still owner or part-owner. These entrepreneurs are classified as "novice," regardless of how long they have owned the business or their years of experience in the industry.

- *Serial.* **Serial entrepreneurs** are currently owners (or part-owners) of a single business and in the past have been owners or part-owners of at least one previous business (now sold or closed).

- *Portfolio.* **Portfolio entrepreneurs** currently own all or part of at least two and maybe more independent businesses. The firms may or may not be part of the same industry cluster or supply chain.

These categories can be seen as different entrepreneurial career paths, generally associated with different skills and aspirations of the entrepreneur. Serial and portfolio firms are often referred to together as **multiple entrepreneurship**. These firms tend to be characterized by higher growth, clearer goals, broader research, and more complex distribution chains.[6] Portfolio entrepreneurs tend to start out with more resources and produce the highest growth.[7] In some ways, these categories can be seen as levels or degrees of entrepreneurship, with portfolio as the highest degree. So, *ask yourself: What category of entrepreneurship do I aspire to?*

☑ **Memory Check 11.6**
True or False: Small business research is primarily aimed at helping the small entrepreneur make better decisions.

☑ **Memory Check 11.7**
True or False: The quality of small business research has been steadily declining over the past few years.

novice entrepreneurs Own all or part of a single business, which is the only firm they have ever had ownership in.

serial entrepreneurs Own all or part of a single business, but have been an owner of at least one other business in the past.

portfolio entrepreneurs Currently own all or part of at least two independent firms.

multiple entrepreneurship A broad category of entrepreneurs including both those who have owned previous businesses and those who own two or more firms.

If you envision yourself in a specific role in a very specific company (e.g., owning a particular antique store in your hometown or becoming a potter in your ceramics studio), chances are the single-business approach of the novice will satisfy your aspirations. If it is important to you to be in business for yourself (perhaps within a particular industry or area of expertise), and if one business fails you would happily try another, then you may find your career following the serial track. And finally, if you are the type who is fascinated by the concepts and processes of entrepreneurship, regardless of the industry, you may be a candidate for portfolio entrepreneurship, applying your knowledge to a number of firms simultaneously.

Small Business Performance Drivers

A number of small-business researchers are concerned with identifying those factors that make small companies able to grow rapidly into larger firms. The underlying assumption here is that high-growth companies, sometimes called **gazelles**, are the most successful in that they contribute the most to economic and employment growth.[8] There is considerable debate about the validity of this assumption in that small businesses may be considered successful in ways other than contributing to growth. Nevertheless, it would be important to identify the factors that produce high-growth firms. So *ask yourself: What are the fast-growing gazelles like?* Surprisingly, U.S. research indicates that high-growth firms tend to be smaller and older than might be expected and not primarily in high-tech areas. Generally, these firms

> **gazelle** Rapidly growing small business. (Sometimes, this refers just to relatively new high-growth firms.)

- have fewer than 20 employees;
- are more than four years old (with an average age of 25 years);
- exist in all industries;
- exist in all regions of the country; and
- continue growing after their rapid-growth gazelle phase.

Ask yourself: Is high growth strictly the result of luck—being in the right place at the right time? Or are there specific drivers that produce these high-growth firms? There is evidence that a group of factors contribute to rapid growth.[9] These factors can be categorized under three broad headings:

The Entrepreneur The founders of high-growth firms tend to have higher levels of education and greater experience than the majority of entrepreneurs. This is significant considering that the majority of new Canadian entrepreneurs are college or university graduates.[10] They tend to have a strong entrepreneurial orientation, often being serial entrepreneurs.

The Business The firms tend to be well-established before entering the high-growth period and a high percentage of these firms own intellectual property such as trademarks. These companies are also more likely to be involved in strategic alliances with other firms.

The Environment High-growth companies tend to spring up in areas of high concentration of businesses, and venture capital (including angels) tends to be available for these firms.

⭐ Head Start Exercise

11.3 Assess the potential for your business to become a gazelle (3/4 page maximum).

Minority and Female Entrepreneurs

The studies of minority and female entrepreneurs have produced many results that could be of equal benefit to all business owners. Much of the focus on minority entrepreneurs is driven by the U.S. government attempting to redress the economic inequity suffered by African-American and Hispanic minorities, but this does not accurately mirror the situation in Canada. Disadvantaged minority entrepreneurs in Canada have traditionally included Aboriginals, new immigrants, and other non-Anglo-Saxon or non-French Canadian ethnic groups. Historically, these groups along with women entrepreneurs have encountered the same barriers to entrepreneurship faced by the minorities in other developed countries:

- discrimination on the part of the community and officials
- lack of access to start-up finance
- lack of networking opportunities

These days in Canada, however, minority and female entrepreneurship is flourishing. Immigrants are at least 1.5 times more likely to start a business than someone born in Canada. Women are opening new businesses at a much higher rate than their male counterparts. And generally, access to finance is not influenced by gender or ethnicity of the applicant.[11]

The most glaring exception to this has been the inequality of access to finance for Aboriginal entrepreneurs. Historically, Native Canadians living on reserves could not borrow money against their homes in order to start businesses. This was because banks would not have the right to foreclose on mortgages for property on reserves. Recently, however, alternative government finance programs have been developed for First Nations, Métis, and Inuit entrepreneurs including grants from Aboriginal Business Canada and business growth loans through the Federal Business Development Bank. As well, there are now numerous networking, support, and educational groups for Native Canadian business owners. For example, the Canadian Aboriginal and Minority Supplier Council (www.camsc.ca) works to assist Aboriginal and other minority groups in finding opportunities to supply goods and services to government. Future research will be on measuring the efficacy of these programs.

A strong recurring research theme of the past couple of decades has been the cultural barriers faced by women entrepreneurs. The evidence shows a disproportionate load of family responsibilities that women carry in both developing and Western societies. Many conclude, therefore, that women entrepreneurs must pay greater attention to the need for balance. That is to say, women entrepreneurs must balance time for managing the business against time for managing personal relationships and personal well-being. The Hot Mommas Project surveyed women entrepreneurs in 2005 and 2007 to identify techniques that would help women be successful in both their business and personal lives. It produced a series of cases that provide role models and tips for women entrepreneurs (www.hotmommasproject.org/home.aspx).

One study of female entrepreneurs in Illinois and California found a strong relationship between business success and satisfaction with home life and, conversely, trouble in one area likely meant dissatisfaction in the other.[12] The study does not compare results for male entrepreneurs, which may well be similar; nor does it offer solutions for striking a balance between home and business demands. Nevertheless, it is valuable for entrepreneurs to be conscious of the interaction between home and business relationships. One interesting Australian study offers evidence that those with the greatest life satisfaction are people in long-term formal marriages[13] (not just cohabitation). The reasons for this are not known, although the issues of commitment and a sense of security are likely involved.

The added stress faced by women entrepreneurs demands a greater attention to health and fitness. **Health** and **fitness** are not the same thing. Health is about coping with disease processes. Fitness is about the body's strength, endurance flexibility, and fat content. Health and fitness are closely connected but it is possible to have one without the other. For example, you could be totally healthy (no diseases, no injuries, not even a hint of a cold) and, at the same time, totally unfit (40 kilograms overweight and not able to do a

Get Help 11.5
For information on Aboriginal business and government programs, go to the site for Aboriginal Affairs and Northern Development Canada at aandc.gc.ca.

health The absence of or control over disease processes.

fitness The body's ability to cope with stress; often indicated by strength, flexibility, endurance, heart rate, and proportion of fat.

single push-up or sit-up). Or, conversely, you could be physically fit (trim and able to run a kilometre in four minutes) but taking daily medication to control a potentially fatal heart disorder: fit, but not healthy.

Memory Check 11.8
True or False? Research shows a positive relationship between life satisfaction and marriage.

In many countries, unlike Canada, personal health care decisions are largely economic in nature. With our medicare system, however, many decisions, such as whether to consult your doctor, are mere personal preferences. So the entrepreneur has few excuses for not taking advantage of every option for preventive health care. *Ask yourself: Is "too busy running a business" a valid reason for avoiding a check-up?* It's a poor excuse when you realize that an investment in your own health and the health of your employees can pay off on your bottom line.

Physically fit entrepreneurs of either gender are more likely to achieve their business and personal goals.[14] In fact, small business owners with higher cardiovascular fitness (runners) on average have higher sales.[15] Now, it is possible that having higher sales gives you more time to get physically fit. But in all likelihood it is the fitness that allows you to function better as an entrepreneur. *Ask yourself: How can you know for sure if fitness will improve your business performance?* Go and get in shape then see how you feel and how you perform in all aspects of your life. Even though the research focus on balance, health, and fitness has been for women entrepreneurs, the potential benefit for male entrepreneurs is obvious.

⭐ Head Start Exercise

11.4 Briefly explain how, in your life, you will be able to balance the pressures of work, family, and your own health (3/4 page maximum).

WHAT IS SOCIAL ENTREPRENEURSHIP?

A social enterprise, unlike a traditional business, must have a purpose other than making profit. Usually, this is a goal of providing some sort of public benefit. Nevertheless, social enterprises function in many ways like regular businesses and some of these organizations are extremely entrepreneurial. They can clearly be in competition with other organizations and can have elaborate strategies for producing and marketing their services. They can grow to have many employees (as well as volunteer workers) and have revenues in the many millions of dollars. A myriad of organizations could be called social enterprises, but most will fall into one of three broad classifications:

- non-profit corporations
- co-operative enterprises
- mutual benefit societies

Non-Profit Corporations

Memory Check 11.9
True or False? Making a profit is the main purpose of a social enterprise.

If we define entrepreneurship as risking money to make profit, then non-profit entrepreneurship is an oxymoron, a contradiction in terms. Nevertheless, it can be an appealing route for some committed entrepreneurs. The non-profit organization can be a means of providing the entrepreneur with a personal income as long as the individual is not an investor or owner of the organization. For example, let's say that the overriding interest of your life is antique motorcycles. You may be able to convince some of your like-minded friends to join with you in starting the Canadian Historical Motorcycle Society, whose mission is to educate the public about the history of the motorcycle. You get some members, form a board of directors, register as a non-profit corporation, and have the board appoint you as the chief executive officer (CEO) of the organization. You approach various foundations and arts councils to provide you with grants and you might even become a registered charity so that donations from interested individuals become tax deductible for those supporters.

And you, as CEO, could receive a salary paid out of the revenues of the organization. A word of caution is appropriate here because the rules on operating a charity registered under the Income Tax Act strictly prohibit using an organization such as this for back-door profit-making. So the salary and any expenses paid to the CEO would have to be reasonable, fixed by the board, and not a form of profit from selling something to others.

Ask yourself: What are the problems with being CEO of a non-profit organization? Some of the biggest troubles of non-profit CEOs involve

Loss of Control You can own a small business and, as long as you are operating within the law, have total control of the company. You can even bring in other investors and still maintain control of the company. But you cannot have direct, legal control of a non-profit. In the case of the Canadian Historical Motorcycle Society, for example, you might have been the one to conceive of the idea, you might have done the work of setting it up, you might have nurtured the growth in membership and revenue, but your decisions can still be overruled by your board. In fact, the board might even decide to replace you with someone else to run the organization.

Memory Check 11.10
True or False? It is not possible to be the owner of a non-profit company.

Managing the Board Because ultimate power in a non-profit rests with the board of directors, a CEO can spend more effort in trying to persuade the board to accept the CEO's vision of the organization than in actually running the operation. Furthermore, volunteer boards are likely made up of individuals with divergent views on how the organization should be run. The irony for the entrepreneurial type who starts a non-profit is that a true entrepreneur has no boss, whereas the CEO of a non-profit can find him- or herself with several bosses who disagree with each other.

Get Help 11.6
For more information about the rules for non-profits and charities, look at the not-for-profit and charity law pages (www.law-nonprofit.org) of *LawNow* magazine.

Managing Volunteers The contract between a boss and paid employee is that the employee performs the duties stipulated by the boss in return for pay. Ask yourself: What can the boss of a non-profit organization provide to compensate the volunteer worker? Individuals can certainly be motivated by things other than cash (attention, challenge, praise, opportunity, recognition). But the job of managing volunteers requires much more work to find the different buttons for each individual.

There are a number of organizations and websites to assist the CEOs of non-profits. Imagine Canada (www.imaginecanada.ca) is an umbrella group for many of Canada's non-profit organizations. It provides research, advocacy, and government lobbying on behalf of its members. Imagine Canada is itself a non-profit organization and is registered as a charity.

Co-operative Enterprises

The term **co-operative enterprise** is most commonly used to describe a company whose primary purpose is to provide employment for the worker/owners of the firm: a worker co-op. In Canada, as discussed in Chapter 1, we have a special form of corporation that can be used to organize a firm like this. For example, the owner of the box factory where you and nine other employees work decides to sell the business. One option would be for the 10 employees to pool their money and buy the company as a co-operative. In this case, each employee would own a different percentage of the shares based on his or her contribution to the purchase. Regardless of the percentage ownership, however, each would have one equal vote in setting policy and selecting a CEO to run the company.

Co-operative enterprises, although still rare in Canada, seem to be particularly effective for artist and artisan group ownership. For example, you might be a struggling painter who is having trouble getting your work into galleries. You get together with five other visual artists and form a co-operative that rents a small storefront gallery on which you all work on the renovations. As part of your co-ownership agreement each of you will receive two months of gallery time annually to display your own work. You agree that 50 percent of

co-operative enterprise
A company whose primary purpose is to provide work and incomes for the employee/owners.

the proceeds from each sale will go to the artist and 50 percent will go to the co-operative to pay the rent and other expenses and to help support the less successful members of your co-op.

Ask yourself: Can a non-profit be a co-operative enterprise? There are organizations called **sheltered workshops**, which produce and sell products and where the employees are typically disabled or otherwise disadvantaged individuals. These companies are run by non-profit organizations and are primarily intended to provide employment for particular groups. But they are not examples of co-operative enterprises, since the employees do not own the enterprises. Usually, the sheltered workshops are subsidized by the non-profit organizations so they do not have to compete under normal market conditions.

In developing nations, the term *co-operative enterprise* can also refer to the cultural elements of entrepreneurship involving family, village, or tribal affiliations, and even concepts of ownership. For example, you might be successful at selling cosmetics in a village market in rural Bangladesh and your cousin decides to copy your idea and set up a booth identical to yours, selling identical products, right next to you in the market. Naturally, this will split the sales, likely making you unprofitable. Culturally, suing or even chastising your cousin is not an option. Nor can you enter into aggressive competition trying to put your cousin out of business. Rather, you must assist your cousin in business and find a way to negotiate a business arrangement that will benefit you both. Here, like other forms of social entrepreneurship, the primary purpose is not personal profit for the individual entrepreneur.

sheltered workshop An enterprise operated and subsidized by a non-profit organization to provide work for disadvantaged individuals.

Business Reality 11.3 MUCCoBS Co-operative Entrepreneurship and Innovation Centre

MUCCoBS Co-operative Entrepreneurship and Innovation Centre

This is not a profile of a small business. It is, however, an excellent example of social entrepreneurship. Furthermore, it is not a Canadian example. But the development of this centre would not have happened without Canadian help, so it is also an excellent example of international development in entrepreneurship.

Moshi University College of Co-operative and Business Studies (widely known as MUCCoBS) is nestled at the foot of Mount Kilimanjaro in Tanzania.

Tanzania, in Eastern Africa on the Indian Ocean, is among the 10 percent poorest nations in the world. The economy is still based primarily on agriculture. This formerly socialist country with a centrally planned economy has been, over the past few years, attempting an orderly transition to a free-market, capitalist economy. At the same time, the country's leaders would like to retain the co-operative nature of their society and its existing structures. For example, the primary source of financial services for most Tanzanians is the Savings and Credit Co-operative Societies (SACCOS), a network of hundreds of small credit-union–like organizations that offer loans for the country's small entrepreneurs. Recently, much of the aid provided to developing countries has been for the facilitation of microfinance structures as a way of alleviating poverty. For example, the Canadian International Development Agency (CIDA) funded a project to assist MUCCoBS faculty in building programs to improve the management of Tanzania's SACCOS.

Professor Suleman Adam Chambo, principal of MUCCoBS, came to the conclusion that "microfinance loans are of little value unless they are accompanied by training in the skills of entrepreneurship and support for the new entrepreneur." And so the idea for the Co-operative Entrepreneurship and Innovation Centre was born: a non-profit centre that would sell training and marketing services to local entrepreneurs. And as a business venture itself, of course, the centre required its own detailed business plan. The template for this business plan was very similar to the non-profit plan outlined in Chapter 6.

For more information about MUCCoBS, visit its website at www.muccobs.ac.tz.

Mutual Benefit Societies

Mutual benefit societies are similar to co-operative enterprises in that they are not intended to benefit individuals. Rather, they benefit groups of people who may otherwise be in competition with each other. Sometimes this is called **co-opetition**. There is a long tradition of co-opetition in Canada among farming communities. Historically, Canadian farms have been individual small businesses, ostensibly competing with each other, but nevertheless working co-operatively for the good of all. Examples of this are in the many buying co-ops, marketing boards, and shared equipment agreements used by farmers. Even the traditional barn raising is a form of co-operation among farmers, with the church or farming community as an informal mutual benefit society.

co-opetition When competing businesses collaborate for their mutual benefit.

Most industries do not have the co-operative traditions of farming. *Ask yourself: Could you imagine a group of drugstore owners getting together to build a new store for one of their competitors?* Probably not. But if you owned a drugstore in Regina, chances are you'd join the Pharmacists' Association of Saskatchewan, as would your chief competitor, the drugstore down the street. The membership fees you pay would help you both to make your businesses more profitable by providing you with economical training updates, helping you buy insurance more cheaply, and making financial advice available. Other types of mutual benefit societies include

✔️ **Memory Check 11.11**
True or False? Non-profit organizations cannot be classified as co-operative enterprises.

Purchasing Co-ops This type of co-op allows groups of small businesses to pool their buying power and benefit from the lower price of larger orders.

Credit Unions These are financial services organizations where the customers are also the owners of the business.

Housing Co-ops Although there are many different models of housing co-ops, most of them are essentially non-profit companies in the rental housing business—landlord companies that rent out residences on a non-profit basis. The tenants, in this case, are members of the co-op (owners) who benefit by receiving affordable housing rather than direct profits.

Child-Care Co-ops Sometimes organized by employers, these co-ops are run by the parents who use their services. Special provisions allow these co-ops to incorporate in some provinces.

Business Associations Professional and industry associations bring a host of benefits to their often competing members. (See Chapter 4 for a more detailed discussion of these groups.)

Strategic Alliances Governments are interested in encouraging and facilitating strategic alliances among firms as a way of developing particular industries and expertise. It seems that co-opetition is particularly important for small technology-based companies.[16]

Like other forms of social enterprise, profit is not the direct goal of mutual benefit societies. Otherwise, they perform all of the functions of for-profit businesses and need the same skills and tools (business plans) to operate.

Knowledge Entrepreneurship

Knowledge entrepreneurship is partly a philosophy of education and partly about the practices of creating, storing, and distributing knowledge. It is an attempt to apply many of the approaches and tools used by entrepreneurs to the processes of research, teaching, and providing library services in our colleges and universities. Unlike traditional entrepreneurship (risking money to make profit), knowledge entrepreneurship is risking money to make knowledge. It is also an effort to instill entrepreneurial attitudes in higher education. The two key ideas that knowledge entrepreneurship imports from business are *innovation* and *vision*.

As for innovation, knowledge entrepreneurs are trying to apply new electronic tools to the design and practice of research as well as to how we store knowledge (library functions) and how we disseminate knowledge (teach). The emphasis on vision is a rebellion against the traditional way of doing things. This means not relying on patterns that have worked in the past. Rather, it is an attempt to make decisions based on envisioning or imagining what future circumstances will be like. Some outcomes of knowledge entrepreneurship include:

- the increased use of contracted specialist faculty rather than tenured professors in colleges and universities
- the use of wikis (such as wikipedia) in place of traditional hard-copy books as sources of information
- the availability of online secondary research tools such as search engines for scientific publications and access to full-text journal articles
- universities partnering with private enterprise for research and the commercialization of new technologies
- the availability of post-secondary courses (even full programs) online
- the adoption of course management and distance education systems
- using Prior Learning Assessment and Recognition (PLAR) for awarding post-secondary credits

Memory Check 11.12
True or False? Knowledge entrepreneurship is the attempt to make money by selling information.

WHAT ARE THE EMERGING TRENDS IN ENTREPRENEURSHIP EDUCATION?

Today, federal, provincial, and municipal government leaders in Canada have a clear understanding that economic growth takes place in small firms.[17] For this reason, a web search of just about any political jurisdiction in Canada will find some sort of initiative to help with the training of entrepreneurs. Post-secondary institutions have also responded to our need for entrepreneurs with new curricula and research initiatives. There are even many secondary schools fostering entrepreneurial attitudes with new courses and extracurricular programs. And the teaching of entrepreneurship has become a much more specialized field.

There is good empirical evidence that students can be taught the skills necessary for success as business owners.[18] But first they must have a belief that entrepreneurship is a valid career option. So the dual functions of most entrepreneurship educators are to both teach the skills of entrepreneurship and to promote its benefits. There are a number of groups whose purpose is to support the development of entrepreneurship by helping researchers, educators, and practitioners in the field to exchange information. Some examples of these organizations are:

- Canadian Council for Small Business and Entrepreneurship (www.ccsbe.org)
- International Council for Small Business (www.icsb.org)
- Institute for Small Business and Entrepreneurship (www.isbe.org.uk)
- Enactus Canada (www.enactus.ca)
- National Association for Community College Entrepreneurship (www.nacce.com)

Business School Approaches

Typically, post-secondary students in business programs are trying to learn all the basic business skills that will make them employable. They tend to see their courses in entrepreneurship as add-ons, rather than the primary focus of their career choice. This is changing with more schools offering dedicated programs in entrepreneurship and small business. At the same time, business schools are getting better at applying good educational principles to the teaching of entrepreneurship and recognizing that young entrepreneurs (under 35) have their own specific set of needs.[19, 20] The approaches to teaching this subject are many, each with its advantages and disadvantages as outlined in Table 11.3.

Table 11.3 Comparison of Approaches to Teaching Entrepreneurship

Approach	Description	Advantages	Disadvantages
Traditional Courses	This usually means some combination of readings, lectures, written assignments, and testing.	Students are familiar with this type of course and it is an economical way to provide instruction using large classes.	There is limited faculty–student and student–student interaction. This can build academic skills, but not entrepreneurial skills.
Business Plan Courses	Normally, this is a type of workshop course. Students individually or in groups develop the idea and write a complete feasible business plan for a new non-existing business.	Students work through every element of starting a business. The business plan template is an excellent overview of all the functional areas of business.	For individual plans, the student workload and faculty marking load may be too high. For group projects there are all the typical problems of internal group management.
Student-Run Businesses and Incubators	Typically, students or graduates operate a business on-campus or in a temporary rent-subsidized facility.	Students experience the unpredictable problems in running a business. It is often an opportunity to build customer service skills.	It is difficult to assess individual student performance and assign grades. It is difficult to wean marginal businesses from subsidized rents.
Student Consulting Projects	Senior students, under the supervision of a faculty member, undertake to solve problems being faced by small business owners for course credit and/or a small salary.	The student gets hands-on experience and the chance to network with entrepreneurs. This also provides community outreach and partnerships for the school.	A high level of faculty supervision is required and there is potential for liability on the part of the school. There is reluctance to pay for student advice and constraints of the academic calendar.
Competitive Game Courses	Teams of students (companies) compete against each other in the same market. Teams submit operational and marketing decisions and the game computer returns financial statements and market data.	Students are able to see how their own strategic decisions and external conditions affect the financial performance of a small business.	Zero sum games apportion the same pool of marks to each class. (A class of all "A" students would be penalized in this case.)
Interview Project Courses	The student meets with a small business owner and conducts a series of interviews (which become project reports) on the particular business.	The student is dealing with a live case. The practising entrepreneur can act as a mentor for the student. The project can largely comprise the business plan of the existing firm.	Variability in the communications skills and availability of the participating entrepreneurs.
Student Placements/ Internships	The student works (either paid or unpaid, part-time or full-time) in a single small business for an extended period. This is for course credit, and usually requires written reports from students.	The student receives practical experience that can be used on a résumé and can make business contacts.	Finding suitable placements can be difficult and it is costly to perform site visits. There is no guarantee that the student will be trained or employed other than as cheap labour.

So far, there is no clear evidence that any particular approach to teaching entrepreneurship produces graduates who are more likely to start and be successful in their own businesses.[21] Yet the literature abounds with anecdotal cases of innovate techniques that purport to be highly successful. These successes, however, are more likely to be the result of the strong enthusiasm generated by teachers who have faith in the strength of their own specific methods and innovations.

Post-secondary institutions also graduate many "non-business" students whose programs lead to some form of entrepreneurial lifestyle (short-term contract work, small -business ownership, or home-based self-employment). These new entrepreneurs come from a broad range of programs in the areas of Media Studies, Technology, Hospitality, and even areas like Health Sciences. Generally, these graduates have excellent program-specific skills but are poorly prepared as entrepreneurs.[22] As a result, stakeholders (advisory committees, ministries of education, faculty) frequently recommend increased business/entrepreneurial training for these groups.

The traditional solution to this problem has been to provide non-business students with a small business course, typically adapted from a course used in Business programs and typically using a textbook intended only for Business students. By and large, this approach has not been successful. Newer methods, however, are including industry-specific cases to demonstrate small-business principles. For example, the short case studies accompanying this text have been adapted for a variety of fields ranging from professional golf to internet management to paralegal studies.

E-tools for Teaching

For all types of teaching, electronic aids have been evolving rapidly over the past decade. Specifically, in the teaching of entrepreneurship, the largest changes have been in the growth of

Video/Podcasts Many video supplements are available for small business courses, including packaged broadcast TV shows such as *Dragon's Den*. Short video clips are also accessible to students through social networking sites such as YouTube, and **podcasts** can be downloaded. A great example is the audio series available from the US Small Business Administration.

podcast A series of audio or video files that can be downloaded sequentially.

Online Courses Course management systems such as Blackboard allow readings, lectures, and assignments to be delivered online. As well, they permit student–teacher communication and student–student communication, including study groups and co-operative project work such as the creation of business plans by student teams.

Websites Sites providing tools and information for entrepreneurs are available by the hundreds. Many of them are cited in this text. Luckily, among the best in Canada are those provided by government departments and agencies from both federal and provincial sources. For links, the recommended starting point is the Canada Business Network site: www.canadabusiness.ic.gc.ca.

Simulations The most common form of simulations involves competition between teams of students, each team representing one firm competing against other teams (firms) in the same industry. Typically, students submit inventory, promotion, pricing, and other decisions and receive quarterly financial statements based on how their company performed given changes in the economy, the market, and the decisions of the competition. Widely used simulations ranging from the simple to the highly complex include BizSim, Entrepreneur, GoVenture, and SimVenture.

avatar The virtual world representation or character used by a participant in an interactive game or simulation.

Adapted Games Second Life is an online 3D simulation that allows participants to communicate and interact with other players. An **avatar** is the virtual world representation of a participant. Players can set up virtual companies and engage in all of the usual competitive business activities through their avatars.

⭐ Head Start Exercise

11.5 Identify the method of teaching entrepreneurship that would best suit you personally as a learner. Explain why (1/2 page maximum).

Entrepreneurship and International Development

Ask yourself: How can you teach someone to prepare a business plan if they cannot read? The answer: with pictures. In fact, it's done every day in parts of Africa and Asia using cleverly prepared series of drawings that can be explained in any of hundreds of indigenous languages.

An interesting and growing segment of entrepreneurship teaching and consulting is in the area of international development. The problems of the world's poorest countries are many and the solutions are difficult. However, over the past few years, economists and others working in this field have come to see small-scale entrepreneurship and improved micro-credit as parts of the solution. The poorest of the poor often have valuable technical and manual skills but lack entrepreneurial approaches to use these skills profitably. In some areas, this is because of complex historical and cultural paradigms that make the competitive nature of entrepreneurship difficult to accept. Developing approaches to teaching entrepreneurship in these areas can be challenging, but the outcomes can be profound and far-reaching. Most of the Canadian-based projects trying to foster entrepreneurship in developing countries are sponsored by the Foreign Affairs, Trade and Development Canada, which typically partners with private and public-sector organizations for the delivery of the programs.

Another increasingly important issue for economic development in poor countries is that of **microfinance**. Entrepreneurs the world over complain about lack of access to capital. In developing countries, however, this problem is immeasurably greater than in Canada, even though the loans sought by entrepreneurs are tiny by comparison to ours. There are many reasons for this situation, but three of the most important are:

1. *Lack of collateral infrastructure.* Entrepreneurs in developing countries often have collateral—for example, they may own land or machinery but cannot borrow against it for business purposes because there are none of the systems required to secure this collateral. For example, there may be no proper land-titles system to secure a mortgage, or no legislation that allows for putting a lien against a truck.

2. *Loan size.* On average, these entrepreneurs are borrowing tiny amounts, but the lenders' administrative costs are proportionately high. (For example, some micro-loans require weekly travel to the borrower for collection of loan payment.) As a result, it is impossible to lend at reasonable interest rates.

3. *Mismanagement and corruption* within the micro-lenders. A high proportion of microfinance institutes lack their own business plan, have untrained managers, and are subject to embezzlement.

Understanding these issues is critical to the teaching of entrepreneurship as part of international development projects.

Entrepreneurship education is a rapidly growing field that produces high levels of career satisfaction for its practitioners. Those teaching entrepreneurship are not confined to the narrow areas of, say, accounting or human resources, but rather get to work in all of the functional areas of business and often in a global context. Furthermore, there is the huge satisfaction of seeing former students create successful enterprises.

❓ Get Help 11.7
The Canadian International Development Agency website (www.cida.gc.ca) provides details on many of the programs your foreign aid tax dollars support.

microfinance The lending, borrowing, and management of small amounts of money in small enterprises.

❓ Get Help 11.8
To learn about microfinance in the developing world, read Joanna Ledgerwood's *Sustainable Banking with the Poor, Microfinance Handbook, an Institutional and Financial Perspective.*

❓ Get Help 11.9
Next Billion Development Through Enterprise (www.nextbillion.net) is a website for those interested and involved in fostering entrepreneurship in developing countries.

WHAT ARE THE MANAGEMENT ISSUES FOR SMALL BUSINESS?

CEOs of large public corporations can often negotiate huge salaries from their boards of directors. One of the reasons for this is the evidence linking quality of management with financial performance.[23]

But *ask yourself: What about small firms? Are management skills critical to their success?* It is well established that lack of management skill is the single largest cause of small business failure in Canada and other developed countries. Yet small businesses are the least likely to spend time and money on management training.[24]

As small companies grow, there is a definite shift in the management concerns of the entrepreneur from an operational focus to a strategic focus.[25] *Ask yourself: Do the entrepreneur's concerns change because of the company growth, or is it the change in the approach of the entrepreneur that leads to the growth?* It's a bit of a chicken-and-egg question. Many business professors would argue that "strategic focus produces growth," although there is, so far, little data to support this conclusion. Nevertheless, as the business grows, the common pattern is for the entrepreneur to become more focused on long-term planning and more concerned about external influences on the business. This shift is outlined in Figure 11.1.

In Chapter 4, we looked at management in terms of its broad functional areas or activities. But here, we examine management as a set of skills. For convenience, these skills are grouped into four categories (although there is considerable overlap among them):

- leadership skills
- communication skills
- organizational skills
- crisis management skills

Leadership Skills

leadership The motivational aspects of management that encourage greater productivity from employees.

We have seen in previous chapters that **leadership** is about getting people to work harder. Traditionally, small business owners have leaned toward a highly directive, even dictatorial management style that can be an impediment to company growth. There is nothing wrong with a tough directive management style per se. In fact, this is a skill that many entrepreneurs develop. The problem occurs when this is the only style in the entrepreneur's leadership repertoire. These days, we tend to believe that the most productive managers are those who are skilled in a variety of **leadership** approaches and can switch among them, depending on what the situation calls for.[26] This requires striking a balance among discipline, coaching, delegating, and team-building leadership styles. It also means developing skills in all of these areas.

Figure 11.1 Changing Concerns of the Entrepreneur

Business Growth

Smaller	Larger

Focus of Entrepreneur

Operational	Strategic
- short-term	- long-term
- internal	- external
- process	- policy
- objectives	- goals
- reactive	- proactive

Discipline A disciplinary leadership style means tight control of each individual subordinate, giving specific directions (orders) and close supervision to make sure that the orders are followed. It usually involves seeking little employee input, with the entrepreneur acting in a militaristic manner, as the commanding officer. Feedback to employees is frequently in the form of criticism of performance. The term *discipline* is often used interchangeably with punishment, and the ultimate form of employee punishment is termination. *Ask yourself: Can I see myself as a disciplinarian? Could I fire someone?*

Naturally, this style of leadership is considered old-fashioned in most settings today. Nevertheless, there are times when an entrepreneur is facing a crisis or dealing with a problem employee and disciplinary tactics must be used. But the disciplinarian boss should be considered tough but fair as opposed to tyrannical. Most employees are willing to accept the tough-but-fair boss. However, working for a tyrant usually means looking for a new job.

Memory Check 11.13
True or False? The terms *leadership* and *management* are totally interchangeable.

Coaching As a leadership style, coaching implies working with subordinates, often in groups, in a supporting and encouraging manner, but with the coach or entrepreneur still very much in control of the process. The coach sets the objectives and then tries to shape the behaviour of the subordinates, largely with **positive reinforcement** or rewarding employee improvement. Behaviour can also be shaped by **negative reinforcement**, which is much the disciplinarian, or punishment, approach. But when applied correctly, positive reinforcement is a faster, more powerful way to change employee behaviours. The idea is to catch an employee behaving in a desired way or even just an improved way and then reward the employee. Rewarding improvement produces more improvement at an accelerating rate.

positive reinforcement Any action that makes an employee behaviour more likely to re-occur.

negative reinforcement Any action that makes an employee behaviour less likely to re-occur.

Delegating For many entrepreneurs, failure to acquire the skill of **delegating** is a roadblock to the growth of their companies. Business owners commonly have no problem giving orders to subordinates. But giving orders is not delegating. Proper delegation means assigning responsibilities to individuals and giving them the authority to fulfill those responsibilities however they see fit, without interference from you. Delegating has many benefits, including

delegating Giving subordinates responsibility and full authority for completing specific tasks.

- freeing up the entrepreneur's time for more strategic work;
- helping to develop the skills of employees; and
- building self-confidence in employees by showing trust in their judgment.

Failure to delegate properly is usually manifested as **micro-management** on the part of the entrepreneur. This is the tendency of some managers to involve themselves in extremely minor decisions, often second-guessing or overruling the decisions of subordinates. *Ask yourself: How do you feel when the boss is "breathing down your neck" or "looking over your shoulder"?* Micro-management is the fastest way to undermine the self-confidence of employees in whom you are trying to develop that very characteristic.

micro-management Getting involved in extremely minor decisions of subordinates, often second-guessing or overruling the subordinates' decisions.

Team Building Team building is like delegating to a group. In fact, the most highly developed (and most theoretical) sorts of teams are self-managed, using goals and levels of support that have been negotiated with the entrepreneur. Leadership is shared within the team and the team is held accountable for its performance as a single unit. Most practical teamwork within small enterprises, however, falls far short of this ideal.

A team-building leadership style is most appropriate when dealing with experienced competent specialists in a non-critical environment. For example, imagine you owned a forms-design software company with a secure niche. You have acquired the rights to Canadian distribution for a new product that must be translated for use in French. To accomplish this, you might assemble a team consisting of a software engineer, a translator, a forms designer, and a salesperson. Your intention is to negotiate what the finished product will look like and a deadline for completion. Then your job is to let them go to it, with just the occasional progress report. But first, you will likely have to set up some sort of process to ensure that the group will function as a team. This may involve:

- *Self-assessment tools.* There are various tests that classify personalities and then show how individuals are likely to interact with other personality types.

- *Relationship exercises.* The better people know each other, the more likely they are to build trust in one another. These exercises often involve some sort of group challenge.

- *Process definition.* The group will have to come to an agreement on who will do what, using which procedures, as well as issues of how decisions will be made and conflicts resolved.

The ultimate management skill is knowing when to use which leadership style. This choice is influenced by factors in two broad categories:

- *The development level of the employees.* This addresses whether you have mature, trained, experienced, willing employees who can be left alone; or, are they marginally competent, lazy novices who have to be directed for each step of the job and checked on after each activity? Naturally, employee development is not an either–or proposition, but rather a continuum.

- *The nature of the risk.* There are two kinds of risk involved: the risk related to the actual job the employee performs and the external risks to the business. If you have employees assembling heart pacemakers, on which lives will depend, high risk is involved, so it is expected that the control and supervision of those employees will be tight. On the other hand, if you have an employee stuffing envelopes with flyers, the job-related risk is low, requiring maybe the occasional spot-check, but not a lot of direction or control. Similarly, the risks of the business environment might be high when new competitors have entered the market or a change in the economy has killed demand and put the business into a financial crisis. The entrepreneur's assessment of risk is the combination of both the internal and external factors.

Theoretically, the most effective leadership style is the one that fits the circumstances. Figure 11.2 represents this model of leadership styles, drawing on the widely recognized theories of Hersey and Blanchard,[27] but presented here in a more entrepreneurial context.

✔ **Memory Check 11.14**
True or False? A good manager should develop a single personal leadership style and stick with it.

✔ **Memory Check 11.15**
True or False? Delegating means assigning both responsibility and authority.

Figure 11.2 Situation and Leadership Style

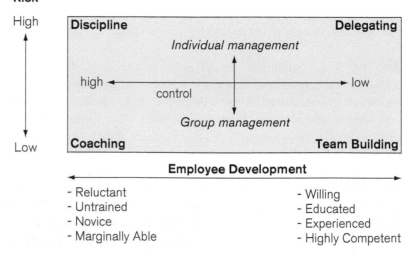

Head Start Exercise

11.6 Describe the management style that you feel you are most likely to use most of the time. Ask several subordinates, colleagues, or even friends to describe the way you typically manage people, then reassess your own description of your primary leadership style (2/3 page maximum).

Communication Skills

Think of a busy entrepreneur and *ask yourself: How much of an entrepreneur's time is spent talking on the phone, handling emails, corresponding with customers, or talking to employees?* All of these activities are some form of communication, and as a business grows, the entrepreneur spends more and more time on this activity.

Writing Unlike verbal communication, in written communication, there is no ongoing opportunity to test whether a message is being understood and to modify the communication accordingly. Writing is a one-way process. It is definitely too late for the author of this text to change the parts that you are not understanding. That's why writers must work to make things as clear as possible. Whether you are writing an offer of employment to an applicant, a sales flyer for prospects, or a complaint email to a supplier, the need for clarity is paramount.

Presenting Entrepreneurs are frequently called upon to make presentations ranging from the extremely casual (a short demonstration for employees on using the new printer) to the fully formal (the main speech at an awards dinner). And most of them get nervous about it. Everyone has some level of apprehension about public speaking. Just look at some of the world's leading entertainers at the Academy Awards: shaking hands, voice tremors, and forgotten lines. Part of the skill of public speaking is accepting your own nervousness and then moving forward. Tips for good business presentations include:

- Present from point-form notes so you do not end up reading a speech.
- Make eye contact with and speak directly to members of the audience. This keeps you in a conversational mode.
- Use visual enhancements (photos, charts, outlines, animation) but beware of Death by PowerPoint. Presentation software can be beneficial for organizing a presentation and as a visual assist. But reading something to an audience that they can read for themselves is insulting and boring.
- Anticipate likely questions and prepare answers.
- Practise. Rehearsing in front of live volunteers is best and using video is also valuable. Using the mirror is cheap and handy, and at the very least you should practise in your own head.

No matter how bad your current public speaking abilities, recognize that this is just a skill that you can learn and eventually enjoy. Some of the world's greatest presenters were absolutely awful when they first started out.

Listening When an employee, customer, child, or anyone else, for that matter, comes to tell you something, your first job is to listen. It would be rare to hear an entrepreneur admit: "I'm not a good listener. I interrupt, I jump to conclusions, I misunderstand, I offer quick advice, and I don't really care all that much." But we all know people who listen exactly like that. Now *ask yourself: How critical am I of my own listening skills?* Chances are, like most people, you think you're already a good

✓ Memory Check 11.16
True or False? Generally, the less risk involved, the less control needs to be exercised over employees.

? Get Help 11.10
Most community colleges offer short or part-time business writing courses that can be highly effective.

? Get Help 11.11
Toastmasters International is a non-profit organization that has helped many thousands of people develop public speaking skills cheaply and effectively. Through local clubs, business-like meetings are held where skills are practised in a non-threatening environment. Check the website (www.toastmasters.org) to find a local club.

✓ Memory Check 11.17
True or False? Writing is a two-way communication process.

listener, so you don't pay much attention to the issue. However, the really good listeners understand that listening, like the other elements of communication, is a skill, and, as a skill, it must be practised. To develop your skills as an active listener, practise the following:

- *Attending to the speaker*. This means facing the speaker, not interrupting, and not doing something else like checking your email at the same time.

- *Asking for clarification*. This must be done by asking open-ended questions (Can you explain?) rather than giving choices to the speaker that fit your preconceptions.

- *Summarizing*. Here you must paraphrase what the speaker has said, reflecting both the facts as you understand them and how the speaker feels about the situation.

- It's surprising what you learn when you actually listen.

Organizational Skills

Memory Check 11.18
True or False? The majority of people have apprehension about public speaking.

The term *organizational skills* is one of those overused expressions that are applied in so many different ways that they risk losing all meaning. *Ask yourself: How often have I seen a job posting requiring strong organizational skills?* What does it mean? Here, we are simply using it to group together the management skills of decision making, documenting, and planning.

administrative decisions
Routine, frequent, often minor decisions about the day-to-day operations of a business.

strategic decisions Broad, often one-time decisions that affect the long-term positioning of a business.

Decision Making An entrepreneur can make hundreds of decisions in a day: which phone call to return next, whom to choose as a supplier, how much to charge for a new product, whether to ask for better credit terms, when to hire more help, which questions to ask in the interviews, what to have for lunch. Part of the decision-making skill is differentiating between administrative (routine or minor) decisions and strategic (unique or major) decisions. **Administrative decisions** must be made efficiently. Incorrect administrative decisions carry only minor consequences and can always be changed. **Strategic decisions**, on the other hand, carry high levels of risk and potentially permanent consequences. Nevertheless, they must be made.

Such important decisions are worthy of a more formal decision-making process using the following steps:

- defining the issue
- gathering and analyzing relevant information
- listing and evaluating the possible alternatives
- selecting the best alternative based on the available evidence

evidence-based decision making Choices based on logic and measured, documented information, as opposed to choices based on intuition.

This sort of **evidence-based decision making** (as opposed to gut instinct) certainly has the advantage of making better decisions, on average. But it also provides a logical explanation for decisions that can be given to customers, employees, suppliers, partners, or other involved parties. When you explain the logic for your decisions, it makes them more acceptable to others. It also gives other parties the opportunity to point out flaws in your logic or information, and it provides a chance to correct bad decisions. If you make decisions on instinct, or gut feeling, you cannot explain them. Those you work with will come to feel that your decisions are simply because you're the boss and that's the way you want it. Such an arrogant approach is unlikely to generate support.

Memory Check 11.19
True or False? An entrepreneur never has to explain or justify his or her decisions.

Documenting Documenting is the process and skill of creating written records, either on paper or electronically. The busier an entrepreneur becomes, the more important it is to stay organized and the more difficult it is to keep everything in your head—things like appointments, scheduling promises, quoted prices, new contact names, passwords, order specifications, and thousands of other bits of essential information. Recording all of these things in a precise, logical way is vital for two reasons:

1. It provides a retrievable text that can be referred to, copied to others, or even offered as evidence in a dispute.

2. The process of making and filing the document is what rehearses and strengthens the human memory. Ironically, this can make the document itself less necessary but not the process of making it.

Planning Most of this textbook is about planning: planning a business. The start of this section on *management issues* outlines the changing focus of the entrepreneur from operational to strategic concerns. Similarly, as the business grows, the entrepreneur spends less time on operational planning and more on strategic. Regardless of the type of planning, the steps remain the same:

- Set goals or objectives.
- Assess the resources available (internal).
- Assess the environment (external).
- Set out the steps needed to reach the goals or objectives.

Developing better planning skills as an entrepreneur can mean better habits for staying informed. Strategic planning requires information about things that could affect the future of a business. *Ask yourself: How can a busy entrepreneur stay informed about the business environment?* Some methods are:

- using bookmarks on your web browser and regularly checking sites of organizations and publications relevant to your industry and location
- signing up for email newsletter and bulletin services for your industry
- meeting regularly with key advisers such as your accountant
- joining industry associations and attending occasional conferences
- reading general news magazines such as *Maclean's* or *Time* for trend information

Get Help 11.12
Business and management associations frequently sponsor two- and three-day intensive seminars in specific skills such as business writing or delegating. Also, check with the continuing education department of your local community college for short courses or seminars on management skills.

⭐ Head Start Exercise

11.7 Rank your communication skills of writing, presenting, and listening from strongest to weakest. Identify specific problems that you would like to improve. Do the same for your skills delegating, planning, and decision making (2/3 page maximum).

Crisis Management Skills

The recession of 2009 came as a shock to many young entrepreneurs who had never seen a major economic downturn throughout their careers. This was the crisis that put many small firms into failure. But an economic slowdown is not the only type of crisis that a small firm can face. Imagine

- your three most valuable employees all quit on the same day to go to your direct competitor
- your sprinkler system failed during an electrical fire in your offices. Everything is burned to the ground.
- rampaging political protesters trashed your store after police tried to break up a violent demonstration. Your insurance company refuses to pay, saying that this was an act of insurrection and not covered by your policy.

Memory Check 11.20
True or False? Minor administrative decisions should not involve a formal decision-making process.

Memory Check 11.21
True or False? As a business grows, the entrepreneur spends an increasing amount of time dealing with operational issues.

Each of these is a crisis that could mean the end of your business. Entrepreneurs will face many crises throughout their careers (not necessarily as serious as these) and must develop some skill in dealing with them. Crisis management is essentially about three things: planning, response, and recovery.

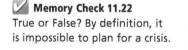
Get Help 11.13
There are several recent, interesting books on how to handle a business crisis, including one from the Harvard Business Essentials Series: *Crisis Management—Master the Skills to Prevent Disasters.*

Crisis Planning *Ask yourself: If I don't know what the crisis will be, how can I prepare for it?* For a start, you can outline in writing the general approach you and your company will take during any crisis. This could include the values and priorities that will guide how you and your employees conduct yourselves. You can also identify a crisis team, deciding who will provide legal advice, who will contact employees, and who will handle any media releases or interviews. A crisis contingency fund can be created and employees can be trained in first aid, CPR, and fire response. Finally, you can plan for a crisis by studying how others have handled crises: the sorts of mistakes they have made and the things they have done well.

Crisis Response Responding to a crisis usually means making a lot of important decisions (like the strategic decisions above) but making them quickly (like the routine decisions above). So you can still follow an evidence-based decision-making process, but recognize that there will be little time to analyze information or evaluate alternatives. It will be a best-guess situation, based on available information, predetermined principles, and the hope of buying time for making better long-term decisions. History has shown that during a crisis, best practices include

- honesty and openness in providing information to employees, customers, the public, or any other stakeholders in the situation;
- documenting decisions to show that they are best guesses based on available information;
- asking for help from appropriate sources; and
- always putting human health and security at the top of your priority list.

Crisis Recovery The effectiveness of the recovery from a crisis depends largely on the planning and response phases. But a well-handled crisis can be seen as an opportunity for growth. Returning to the earlier examples, the ship-jumping employees could be giving you an opening to replace them with better workers who are not part of a clique. The electrical fire will get you out of your lease and could present the chance to move to better premises. The political protest and vandalized store might have won you media exposure that you could never afford to buy, and the publicity could well embarrass the insurance company into waiving the insurrection clause. These sorts of outcomes result from approaching the crises as an opportunity for change.

Memory Check 11.22
True or False? By definition, it is impossible to plan for a crisis.

When it comes to developing management skills, there are countless books, blogs, and courses available to help the entrepreneur, but a recent review of the literature in this area suggests that experience is still the best teacher.[28, 29]

⭐ **Head Start Exercise**

11.8 Describe the most significant business or personal crisis you have faced and identify any ways that you could have handled it better (1/2 page maximum).

Answers to Memory Check Questions

11.1 F	11.2 T	11.3 T	11.4 T	11.5 F	11.6 F	11.7 F	11.8 T
11.9 F	11.10 T	11.11 T	11.12 F	11.13 F	11.14 F	11.15 T	11.16 T
11.17 F	11.18 T	11.19 F	11.20 T	11.21 F	11.22 F		

Questions for Discussion

1. Identify some of the reasons that small firms are slow to adopt newer technologies. Is this wisdom or folly?
2. The occasional recession is good for business. Discuss why this might be true.
3. Discuss whether the decision for a business to "go green" should be a purely ethical one or one of self-interest.
4. Argue that the funding for research into small business should be restricted to projects that would be likely to directly help entrepreneurs.
5. Discuss whether Statistics Canada should even be gathering data on the gender, race, and ethnic backgrounds of Canada's entrepreneurs.
6. Discuss ways that the CEO of a non-profit organization could unethically and illegally use the organization for personal gain. Who does this harm? How?
7. In addition to entrepreneurial skills (outlined in Chapter 1), what skills might the CEO of a non-profit organization require?
8. High-growth companies might be the result of some particular attribute or approach on the part of the entrepreneur, or they might just be a question of being in the right place at the right time (luck). Pick one side of this question or the other and, using real-life examples of companies that have gone through rapid growth, present your case.
9. Discuss how a small business that shows little or no growth can be considered "successful," not just for the individual entrepreneur but for the economy as a whole. What are the dangers for a business that is not growing?
10. Discuss the advantages and dangers of co-opetition—collaborating with your competitors. What legal issues might this raise? Think of examples.
11. Discuss the best approaches for convincing students to pursue entrepreneurial careers.
12. "Businesses only become green when they are forced to." Discuss the validity of this statement. Identify the pressures that make small businesses more protective of the environment.
13. From recent news reports, identify a major crisis that a business has suffered. Discuss how the crisis could have been avoided and the pros and cons of the way the media has been handled in this event.

Case for Discussion

In college, Julian's favourite course was Business Law. After a couple of surprise mobile telephone bills (for data that he did not know his phone was using) Julian became interested in laws intended to protect consumers. When his new TV, toaster, and electric kettle all broke down just weeks after the warranties ran out, Julian started to research the laws covering these products. He was surprised and upset to learn that so many transactions relied on the principle of *caveat emptor:* Let the buyer beware.

To Julian, this meant an open invitation for false advertising and opportunities to mislead consumers. And the more he read about consumer protection, the more offended he became by unscrupulous promotion of unsatisfactory products and services. The final straw came when Julian's doctor told him that the expensive cough syrup he had been using would have no effect whatsoever on his cough, despite the many television ads to the contrary. Eventually, he decided to build a career where he could expose and fight advertising lies and misleading business practices.

Julian felt that the best way to go about this would to set up a non-profit organization of which he could be the executive director. The organization would build a website where consumer rip-offs could be exposed: www.CaveatEmptor.org. The site would also contain advice on how consumers could protect themselves and provide links to government information about consumer laws. Julian envisioned the eventual creation of a smartphone app to read a bar code or QR code for a product and then provide consumer reviews on that product.

For a first step, Julian assembled a group of acquaintances, including a lawyer, an accountant, and three business people who agreed to join the volunteer board of directors for CaveatEmptor.org. Julian then registered a non-profit organization and applied for charitable status with the Canada Revenue Agency. He knew the next step would be to write a business plan for the organization and have it approved by his board of directors. One of the directors advised Julian to read *Business Plan, Business Reality*, and on the accompanying website he found a template for a non-profit business plan. Julian was able to complete the first item of the introduction in a few moments:

> 1. *Briefly describe the overall mission of the organization. Explain the services supplied by the organization and identify the client groups that it services.*

Julian wrote: "The mission of CaveatEmptor.org is to help protect Canadian consumers (the client group) by exposing false or misleading advertising and refuting false product claims. Through web-based media, the organization will help to educate consumers about products and services as well as the rights and responsibilities of consumers." Julian found it equally easy to complete the second part:

> 2. *Briefly explain any philosophies, approaches, or beliefs that the organization is based on and identify any other organizations with which it is affiliated. Explain the nature of the relationships with affiliates.*

Julian wrote: "The idea behind CaveatEmptor.org is that consumer laws, or lack of consumer laws, favour unethical sellers and advertisers and unfairly put the responsibility for the quality of products and services on consumers. CaveatEmptor.org is a totally independent non-profit organization that tries to make the world more fair for consumers." But when it came to the third part of the introduction, Julian was stuck:

> 3. *Identify the sources of revenue upon which the organization relies as well as alternative financial sources that it will pursue.*

This part, Julian knew, was going to take some research.

1. Explain how CaveatEmptor.org is a form of Social Enterprise. Is it ethical for Julian to pay himself a salary from this organization? Explain your answer.

2. Get your instructor to provide the Non-profit Business Plan Template. Find three ways in which this plan outline is different from the basic plan for a new business.

3. Discuss the philosophy Julian expresses in part two of his introduction. Is this valid? Will it resonate with consumers?

4. Identify three specific sources of funding that CaveatEmptor.org could pursue. Make sure you pick sources that will be sustainable for the long term.

5. Why did Julian apply for charitable status? What restrictions does this put on his organization? Can CaveatEmptor.org take funding from government sources and then try to lobby the government to change consumer laws? Is this legal? Is it ethical?

6. Identify several organizations that provide services similar to what Julian proposes. Are these competitors to Julian's organization? Explain how.

7. What competitive edge could Julian offer to consumers of his service? What competitive edge could Julian offer to potential funders?

Chapter 12

Business Plans: How Are They Important?

This final chapter brings us back to the prevailing topic of the text: business plans. It answers the questions:

- What Are the Uses of Business Plans?
- What Are the Different Types of Business Plans?
- What Does a Finished Business Plan Look Like?

Learning Objectives

On completion of this chapter, you should be able to:

1. Outline the requirements for the business plan as a document.
2. Discuss how a business plan can be an ongoing process of revision.
3. Explain how the business plan can function as a consulting tool.
4. Explain how the business plan can be an effective teaching tool.
5. Compare at least four varieties of business plans.
6. Discuss the strategic growth plan as a supplement to the basic business plan.
7. Discuss the operational efficiency plan as a supplement to the basic business plan.
8. Critically assess a detailed business plan for a start-up company.

WHAT ARE THE USES OF BUSINESS PLANS?

The Business Plan as a Document

Formal business lenders and investors require a written business plan. However, the reasons for having a written plan go far beyond this simple necessity. They include:

- *Compiling a business checklist.* By writing the plan down, you are more likely to plan all the elements of a business, rather than just those that most easily come to mind. Writing it down keeps the process of starting a business organized.

- *Communicating the plan.* Something as complex as a business cannot be explained orally. It would be like trying to explain the wiring in a car without using a diagram. For lenders, investors, partners, advisers, and other stakeholders, the only way to really understand the workings of a new business is to see them on paper.[1]

- *Making the idea real.* Writing down the idea is the first step in actually starting a business. This makes the idea tangible: There is an actual, physical document that represents the business. This work stands as evidence that you have already accomplished something in the process of starting a business—it is a motivator.

Length *Ask yourself: How long should a business plan be?* There is no standard prescribed length for a business plan. A traditional, start-up business plan that might be presented to a bank or investors can easily run in excess of 25 pages.[2] This is the kind of plan included at the end of this chapter. Alternatively, a summary business plan of the sort used to apply for some government-sponsored micro-loans might be under 10 pages in length. And the long-term plan for renewing and refinancing an established firm could run to 100 pages with appendices. However, these days, business plans are generally a little shorter, more concise than they have been in the past.

To the passionate entrepreneur, nothing could be more fascinating than the plan for his or her own new business. But business plans that are not about your own company can be among the most boring documents to read—ask any business teacher. So it is a good idea to cut out unnecessary repetition of information and vague bragging about the quality of your service—among the most common errors in first-draft business plans.

Formats There is no standard format for a business plan. The format used in this text and for the example business plan is one of the most simple and logical. Most business plan templates start with an executive summary, containing information that is repeated in the introduction and often again in the body of the plan. The format used here combines the executive summary and the overview of the business model into a single section, The Summary and Concept, to minimize repetition. Our format for the basic start-up business plan is divided into five sections. Some business plan templates use 10 or 18 or more sections. This doesn't mean that they necessarily contain more information; it's more likely that the same information is organized in a different way.

business plan template An outline providing the specific topics and pattern for a business plan.

interactive plan writers Programs that are question- or menu-driven and that do much of the calculating and reformatting needed to create a business plan.

Libraries and bookstores abound with **business plan templates**, and most banks offer free CDs, downloads, or booklets, each with its own outline for a business plan. Keep in mind when using a business plan template that the amount of space indicated for any one topic is only a guideline. Each plan is unique.

There are also a variety of **interactive plan writers** available. These packages go beyond the simple outline of a template. Instead they may be driven by menus or require the entrepreneur to answer a series of questions that the program will automatically reformat as parts of the plan. These programs can have a great many links throughout the document for automatic updating. For example, if you were to change the price of an item in the marketing part of the business plan, the software could automatically update the sales forecast, the income statement, and the cash flow statement to match. This would clearly save time and effort. For some of these packages, however, there is a great deal of time spent learning to use the software and most still require a considerable amount rechecking and proofreading.

Memory Check 12.1
True or False? A written business plan is a tangible motivator for the entrepreneur.

Memory Check 12.2
True or False? There is no single standard format for the business plan.

Style If the business plan is intended for your eyes only, the writing style is not important. If it is to be submitted to someone else, it must be written in a manner that will ensure a precise understanding of the plan. Bankers, investors, people judging business plan competitions—all of them will rate your plan not just on the content, but also on how it is written. Generally, this means using

- *Third person.* For example, if you were Maria writing the plan for your new coffee shop, it would typically read "Maria's Coffee Shop expects to have sales in the first year in excess of …" as opposed to: "My coffee shop will have …"

- *Complete grammatically correct sentences.* Formal language with proper punctuation is expected. You must pay attention to grammar even for things like lists of points, which must all be in a parallel structure, not a random point-form.

- *Clearly labelled tables and figures.* From floor plans to financial statements, all must be titled and referred to in the body of the plan. Make sure to check for correct dates and calculations where appropriate.

The keys to achieving a professional style and tone are lots of proofreading (not just by yourself but by "fresh eyes"—someone who has not read the plan) and lots of revising. For entrepreneurs with poor language skills, there are many freelance writers, proofreaders, and editors for hire. Reasonably priced proofreading services are easy to find via your search engine. It may be a good idea to use a Canadian service since the proofreaders will be more familiar with Canadian business idiom.

⭐ Head Start Exercise

12.1 Search the web looking for the shortest sample business plan you can find. Identify any important features that you feel might be missing from this plan (1/3 page maximum).

The Business Plan as Process

Most commonly, the business plan is thought of as a document that explains the structure and functioning of a business. But the business plan can also be thought of as an ordered series of logical decisions that an entrepreneur makes in the process of starting a business. For example, it is more logical to figure out exactly to whom you're going to sell, before deciding how you are going to go about your advertising. This may seem obvious but human nature is not always logical. *Ask yourself: Am I likely to think up a great idea for a product and then get carried away dreaming up some creative commercials for this product without ever defining who the customers will be?* Following a good business plan model keeps you making decisions in a logical series of steps. So, with the business plan model we are using, we could say that step one is to *define the business*, then step two is to *assess the feasibility*, and so on …

Unfortunately, the process of setting up a business is rarely a simple series of linear steps. More typically, as you make decisions for your business, you run into problems that force you to go back and reevaluate earlier decisions. For example, you might be planning to open a vertical and horizontal blind cleaning service in your hometown of Parkview. But when you *assess the feasibility* of your concept you find that there just aren't enough customers in Parkview to make the business worthwhile. So you go back to the previous step and pick a new (larger) target market for your business and then take another look at the feasibility. As shown along the top of Figure 12.1, each step in the process can force the entrepreneur to loop back and change the decisions in the previous step. For example, you could be starting a business producing custom-made silk shirts, which you are going to have hand-stitched. When you are making your decisions about *marketing strategy*, you decide to emphasize that your shirts are "Canadian-made and hand-stitched." Later, when you are deciding how to *organize the business*, it could turn out that skilled labour for the stitching is difficult to find in Canada. So now, you must loop back to the previous step and change your *marketing strategy*: Either alter the product so that hand-stitching is abandoned, or change the Canadian-made element by buying from abroad.

The last step in the planning process, *arranging the finances*, can affect all of the previous steps. Let's say you plan on opening a small leather-goods manufacturing operation. When attempting to plan the start-up capital, you may find that you have to bring in a partner. This means going back to step one and changing the ownership structure. Or by analyzing your projected financial statements you find that you would be paying too high a percentage of your sales in rent. This could mean going back to step two and finding a new site. The types of wallets you will make, your pricing strategy, your promotion techniques, your choice of employees or machinery could all have to be changed after completing the financial portion of the planning process. Again, look at this in Figure 12.1.

Finally, the business plan can be seen as part of the *renewal* process for a firm that has been up and running for a while. As discussed in Chapters 9 and 10, businesses go through cycles where the entrepreneur must focus on growing with new offerings and new customers

Memory Check 12.3
True or False? The maximum reasonable length for a business plan is 35 pages.

Memory Check 12.4
True or False? Most banks provide free business plan templates.

Memory Check 12.5
True or False? A reasonable business plan should be a minimum of 50 pages in length.

Figure 12.1 The Business Plan as Process

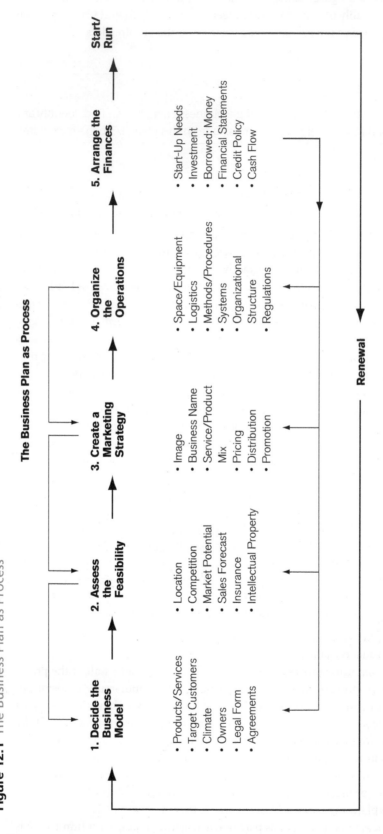

The Business Plan as Process

1. Decide the Business Model
- Products/Services
- Target Customers
- Climate
- Owners
- Legal Form
- Agreements

2. Assess the Feasibility
- Location
- Competition
- Market Potential
- Sales Forecast
- Insurance
- Intellectual Property

3. Create a Marketing Strategy
- Image
- Business Name
- Service/Product Mix
- Pricing
- Distribution
- Promotion

4. Organize the Operations
- Space/Equipment
- Logistics
- Methods/Procedures
- Systems
- Organizational Structure
- Regulations

5. Arrange the Finances
- Start-Up Needs
- Investment
- Borrowed; Money
- Financial Statements
- Credit Policy
- Cash Flow

Start/Run

Renewal

or focus on reducing costs and becoming more efficient. In either case, the process of renewal requires reiterating the entire business planning process, as indicated by the heavy line along the bottom of Figure 12.1.

⭐ Head Start Exercise

12.2 Look at Figure 12.1, The Business Plan as Process. Can you think of a better way to describe the process of revising business planning decisions? Try creating your own diagram to describe this process. Hint: Consider PERT charts or Gantt charts (2/3 page maximum).

The Business Plan as a Consulting Tool

What if you were a consultant who was asked to meet with a small business owner to help solve a major business problem? You must first interview the entrepreneur to find out what the problem is. Perhaps the conversation would go like this:

> Consultant: So what is the problem with your business?
> Entrepreneur: Well, we're not doing very well.
> Consultant: In what way?
> Entrepreneur: We aren't making as much as we should.
> Consultant: You aren't making as much product as you should?
> Entrepreneur: We don't make any products.
> Consultant: So, you aren't making as much sales as you should?
> Entrepreneur: Sales are about the same as last year.
> Consultant: So, you aren't making as much profit as you should?
> Entrepreneur: Right, and it isn't the market that's the problem.
> Consultant: So your competitors are doing well?
> Entrepreneur: I have no idea.
> Consultant: But you think your market is strong?
> Entrepreneur: It should be, with everybody buying.

Ask yourself: After seven questions, what have I learned so far? Certainly nothing that's going to help you solve the problem. And if you continue on this way, whatever information you do get will be incoherent and disorganized. Instead, as a consultant, you need a logical series of questions that will let you learn about the structure and functioning of this business. In fact, the fastest way to learn about this firm would be to read a clear, concise, up-to-date business plan. But, like most small firms, it's not likely to have one available. So instead, you can use the business plan outline as a series of logical questions to ask:

> Consultant: So what do you sell?
> Entrepreneur: Accounting software.
> Consultant: Do you just sell the software?
> Entrepreneur: No, we install it, update it, and repair it.
> Consultant: Who are your customers?
> Entrepreneur: Law firms.
> Consultant: Law firms where?
> Entrepreneur: Right across Canada.
> Consultant: And is this a good time to be in this business?
> Entrepreneur: Should be. New tax rules, so everyone needs new software.
> Consultant: Who owns your business?
> Entrepreneur: Me. And I brought in three new partners a year ago.
> Consultant: And the partners all work in the business?
> Entrepreneur: Well, they're supposed to.

✅ **Memory Check 12.6**
True or False? As a process, the steps in the business plan can be followed in any order.

✅ **Memory Check 12.7**
True or False? The business plan as a process involves looping back and revising previous decisions.

✅ **Memory Check 12.8**
True or False? Organizing the operations comes before creating a marketing strategy in the business plan process.

✅ **Memory Check 12.9**
True or False? The last major step in the business plan process is arranging the finances.

Note that the questions the consultant is asking are following our template for Section 1 of the business plan. Certainly, the problem here is far from being identified but by continuing with this list of questions, a clear picture of this company and its problems will emerge.

The Business Plan as a Teaching Tool

✓ **Memory Check 12.10**
True or False? It is better for a business consultant just to let the entrepreneur explain problems than it is to ask questions.

Ask yourself: Does writing a business plan seem like a good way to learn about entrepreneurship? There has been a long-standing debate among entrepreneurship educators about the value of having students write business plans. Some believe that this task can act as a discouragement for students to pursue careers as entrepreneurs, taking the fun out of making money. Business plan competitions are one way to put some fun back into what many see as a dry difficult task. Competitions are becoming more widely used[3] and can offer considerable cash prizes or even investment in the new business. Regardless of whether students must create an entire business plan as a course requirement, studying the organization of a business plan has its own benefits.

Business Reality 12.1 PetPod
The Evolution of a Business Plan

In 2009, Mathew Worman, along with his wife, Melanie, opened PetPod, selling middle- to high- quality pet food, treats, and accessories. Before this, Mathew, a culinary arts graduate, was becoming frustrated working 100 hours a week as a chef in the hospitality industry. Melanie had some experience in the veterinary industry but neither had a retail background.

Originally the business concept had been to open an aquarium store selling fish, tanks, and related supplies. This was largely because of Mathew's hobby interest in tropical fish. But as they developed their plan, they found that this idea would require a great amount of capital, involve many permits and regulations, and have a relatively small sales potential. Through research and a constant refining and rewriting of their business plan, the couple concluded that a pet food and accessories store, focusing on green products and local suppliers, could be successful in their high-density urban area.

Mathew's plans for the growth of the company are centred on the fact that three large condominium apartment buildings are currently under construction, all within two blocks of the store. This was a major consideration during the selection of the site. When these buildings fill with residents (and their pets), the market potential will automatically increase and presumably so will the sales of PetPod. Mathew has plans for hiring a part-time employee at that point. His secondary strategy for increasing sales is to add new products for existing customers. Based on customer feedback, he has already doubled the number of product lines he carries and he carefully monitors the inventory turnover of each new product. His third approach is to try and bring in customers from adjoining market areas by offering unique and environmentally friendly products not available from suppliers in their areas.

Promotion for PetPod emphasizes the *green* nature of the business (healthy foods and treats, natural fibre products, local suppliers) wherever possible. The company relies on low-cost social media for promotion, such as Facebook contacts for pet groups. As well, the point-of-sale software used by PetPod captures customer and purchase information in a database that has customer relations management capabilities. This same package manages inventory and financial records, and Mathew describes it as easy to use.

Mathew feels it is too early to commit to a long-term growth strategy for PetPod since the business concept is still being refined. Nevertheless, he has been considering growth through a new store (opened with an additional partner) or even a franchising arrangement. But those options are still far in the future. His advice to those thinking of entrepreneurship is: "research, research, research, plus overestimate your expenses and underestimate your revenue when preparing your business plan."

An important benefit of post-secondary education, generally, is to provide the student with a system of classifying information. It's like knowing how a library works, with all the books on medicine in one classification, all the books on child-rearing in another, and all the books on business in another. The business books themselves are divided into sub-classifications with all the books on human resources together, all the accounting books in their own grouping, and logistics books in theirs. And there are even sub-sub-classifications that an educated entrepreneur should know. Just like knowing the set-up of the library, the set-up of the business plan gives the student and the entrepreneur a matrix for organizing, storing, and retrieving information about business.

For example, you might own a business where two of your employees, Sharon and Julius, are constantly arguing with each other and disrupting the work. You might assume that the problem is a personality issue on the part of either Sharon or Julius. So, you take your best guess on who is at fault and you fire Julius, replacing him with Lawrence. Pretty soon Sharon and Lawrence are bickering; therefore, you conclude that Sharon was the problem all along. As a result, you replace Sharon with Angus but now there is squabbling between Angus and Lawrence—not a great way to run a business. If you have studied business plans, however, and your business knowledge is organized in a logical way, you are likely to approach the problem differently. When Sharon and Julius first started to fight, you would have recognized this as a human resources problem, not one of personality. You would have known that it was likely related to the organization structure or job descriptions— perhaps overlapping responsibility or authority. In this way, you would have been more likely to make decisions that would solve the problem. Knowing the structure of the business plan means knowing how all the different elements of business relate to each other. This is critical for making good business decisions.

⭐ Head Start Exercise

12.3 Find the syllabus for a post-secondary course on entrepreneurship or small business. What similarities can you find between the topic outline and the basic business plan template? (1/3 page maximum).

WHAT ARE THE DIFFERENT TYPES OF BUSINESS PLANS?

We have seen that there is a basic business plan (outlined in Chapters 1–5) that can be used for starting a business. Variations of this basic plan are required if we are buying an existing business (Chapter 6), buying a franchise (Chapter 7), or taking over a family firm (Chapter 8). There are also some variations of the plan required depending on the type of business being started (manufacturing, wholesale, retail, or service), and there are variations for changing the plan of an established business (renewal). There are even variations that allow the business plan to be used for non-businesses such as non-profit organizations or even departments of larger organizations.

Variations for Business Type

When we speak of business "type," we generally mean the classifications of: **manufacturing**, **wholesale**, **retail** and **service**. Some classification systems may include extractive industries (mining, forestry), farming, or construction as separate categories. None of these are hard and fast categories since many businesses will have characteristics of more than one type. For example, a *retail* bakery could be *manufacturing* some of its own products while selling products it buys from other bakeries. At the same time, this bakery

> ☑ **Memory Check 12.11**
> True or False? Studying business plans helps a student learn a system of classifying information.
>
> **manufacturing** Businesses that use machinery and tools to make products from raw materials.
>
> **wholesale** Businesses that act as intermediaries, generally between manufacturers, retailers, and other wholesalers.
>
> **retail** Businesses that buy products from manufacturers and wholesalers and sell to consumer.
>
> **service** Businesses that primarily sell labour, expertise, and other intangibles.

Figure 12.2 Summary of Emphasis for Business Plans by Type

Business Type	Business Plan Areas of Emphasis
Manufacturing	Products; Location; Insurance; Patents/Trademarks; Distribution; Space/Equipment; Methods/Procedures; Regulations; Cash Flow
Wholesale	Target Customers; Location; Product Mix; Distribution; Space; Credit Policy; Cash Flow
Retail	Site; Trademarks; Image; Product Mix; Pricing; Promotion; Systems
Service	Target Customers; Copyrights/Trademarks; Image; Pricing; Promotion; Methods/Procedures; Regulations

might cater weddings and banquets, in which case it is functioning as a *service* business. Despite this, the vast majority of Canadian firms will fit comfortably into one of the four categories. And the business plans for each of these types tend to have different areas of emphasis.

Compared to the plan for a retail business, the plan for a manufacturing business is likely to spend much more space describing in detail the nature and the quality of the products the company will sell and the reasons for these choices. That is because the implications of product choice are much greater for a manufacturer than for a retail firm. Let's say, for example, that you are setting up a business to manufacture very high-quality knives to be used by professional chefs and meat cutters. This decision commits you to investing in expensive, highly specialized machinery to temper and sharpen the kinds of blades you will be making. If you have made the wrong choice of product, there is little chance of correcting the decision because of the huge investment you are now committed to. On the other hand, as a knife retailer selling expensive blades, if your knives aren't moving, it is a much simpler matter to unload the current product (sell off) and replace it with a more popular (perhaps cheaper) item.

Wholesalers are likely to use more business plan space to discuss credit policies and cash flow than service or retail firms use. This is because wholesale firms often give extended credit terms to help retailers maintain inventory. Retail companies (and some consumer services) are likely to spend a greater amount of business plan space on issues related to *site*. To a retailer, the style, decor, and image presented by the actual place of business is much more important when compared to businesses where the customer never comes to the business site. And certain service firms may give more emphasis to intellectual property. For example, the business plan for a band would discuss copyright in great detail and the plan for a professional sports team would have a lot of information on trademarks. Figure 12.2 summarizes areas where each of the different types is likely to include a greater than average amount of detail in their particular business plans.

Variations for Business Stage

Chapters 10 and 11 of this text discuss how businesses go through different cycles, the first of which is the *start-up* stage. The goal of the start-up business plan is to get the business off the ground and in a position where it can grow. The business plan included at the end of this chapter (and outlined in Chapters 1–5) is a basic start-up business plan.

Later, in the life of a business, the firm will tend to go through periods of expansion and contraction, which make up the *renewal* cycle of the business (see Figure 12.1). Renewal means either following a strategy of growth (adding new products, services, customers, market segments) or a strategy of improving profits by specializing more or becoming more

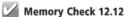
Memory Check 12.12
True or False? A manufacturing firm is likely to devote extra space to discussing "site" in its business plan.

efficient. It is usually not wise to try to do both of these things at the same time. Each of these strategies has its own specialized supplement to the business plan:

- strategic growth plan
- operational efficiency plan

The **strategic growth plan** is a process (and a document) that first analyzes any indicators showing that the company needs to grow. This includes performing a **SWOT analysis**, which is described in detail in Chapter 10. Then the strategic growth plan outlines the specific changes to be undertaken and how they are to be financed. (See the entire outline of the strategic growth plan at the end of Chapter 10.) This redefines the business, which means going back and revising Section 1 of the basic business plan and then continuing through changing the rest of the business plan steps.

Alternatively, the approach for renewal might be to focus on efficiency for greater profits. This means using an **operational efficiency plan**. This process (and document) measures the operating efficiency of the business (compared to similar firms) and outlines ways of reducing costs through:

- systemization and automation
- customer retention
- improved employee productivity
- cost control

The complete operational efficiency plan is outlined at the end of Chapter 11. Like the strategic growth plan, this supplement leads back to redefining the business and revising the rest of the basic business plan.

⭐ Head Start Exercise

12.4 Search the web looking for management consulting firms. How many of them promote themselves as experts in strategic growth or efficiency? Explain why consultants promote their expertise in these two areas (1/3 page maximum).

Non-Profit Business Plan

The goal of every business is to make profit. A non-profit organization, therefore, is not a business by its very definition. It is, however, a form of **social entrepreneurship** (as discussed in Chapter 12) and has many features in common with a true business. For example, both organizations are likely to have:

- A CEO. For a business, the CEO is often the founder and owner of the firm. Non-profit CEOs can still be the founders of their organizations, which can also be their sources of personal income. They cannot, however, be considered as owners and their role as CEO is generally at the pleasure of their boards of directors.

- *Target markets*. Unlike most businesses, the clients of a non-profit service are usually not the ones who pay for the service. For example, you may have a non-profit organization that provides language training to new immigrants (your market). Your sources of funding, however, may include government departments, charitable foundations, and private donors (a whole series of different targets).

- *Competitors*. For a business, competition means any other place that customers could get the goods or services similar to those provided by the firm. This is also true for non-profits. Using the example above, your non-profit language training organization may be in competition with religious groups, immigrant organizations, and other groups that provide free language classes. Your clients, however, also have the choice

---

strategic growth plan A supplement to the business plan that outlines how the business will add new products, services, customers, or market segments.

SWOT analysis Research into the strengths and weaknesses of a company as well as the opportunities and threats that it faces.

operational efficiency plan A supplement to the business plan that analyzes and outlines methods to reduce the expenses of the firm.

☑ **Memory Check 12.13**
True or False? The business plan for a wholesale company is likely to have extensive discussion on trademarks and patents.

☑ **Memory Check 12.14**
True or False? The business plan for a service firm is likely to provide many details on "image."

social entrepreneurship The use of business practices to achieve goals that are of public benefit.

☑ **Memory Check 12.15**
True or False? A retail business plan is likely to devote a lot of space describing the site.

☑ **Memory Check 12.16**
True or False? The strategic growth plan identifies ways to increase sales.

of getting language training from private tutors, colleges, or language schools where they will pay for the service. Furthermore, you may see your language service as being in competition with a whole variety of other non-profits (dance troupes, sports agencies, soup kitchens ...), which seek grants from the same limited resources that provide your funding.

☑ **Memory Check 12.17**
True or False? An entrepreneur may choose to own a non-profit organization.

- *Equipment and systems.* If you were running a Meals-on-Wheels organization, providing hot meals to the homes of people unable to cook for themselves, your organization might operate pretty much like a fast-food business, with kitchen equipment to be maintained, vehicles that depreciate, and employees to be trained.

- *Cash flow.* Businesses are concerned with income statements, which show revenue, costs/expenses, and profit or loss. Non-profits are similar but with budgets that typically show donations/grants, costs/expenses, and surplus or deficit. And both types of organizations must do cash flow planning to ensure that they are always able to pay the bills.

The business plan for a non-profit organization must take these similarities and differences into account.

Departmental Business Plan

strategic business unit (SBU) A division of a large organization that can be operated almost as an independent business.

Large organizations are typically divided into many departments or in some cases **strategic business units**. A strategic business unit (SBU) usually functions as an independent smaller business within a large organization and typically is responsible for its own profit. For example, a chain of grocery stores might treat each of its stores as a separate small business responsible to make a profit after paying a bill for the services provided by head office (treated as an expense). Thus, the business plan for an SBU is pretty much the same as the basic business plan.

intrapreneurship An approach to running a large organization that encourages managing each department as if it were an independent innovative, risk-taking entity.

Some organizations require all of their many departments to have separate *business plans* of a sort, even though these departments may not have any direct influence on the profit of the company. This attempt to make non-independent departments function as if they were profit-driven small businesses is often referred to as **intrapreneurship**. In this approach to business, a department's customers are seen as the internal users of the department's services and competitors are seen as other ways the company might access the same services. For example, an information technology department of a plumbing parts wholesaler might view the sales department, the shipping department, and the accounting department as separate *customers* for IT services. IT might even "bill" the other departments for the services they use. IT, however, is aware that they could lose their customers to competitors such as outside IT service providers or even see the other departments provide some of their own IT services, if that proved to be more economical.

The department business plan is likely to include the following sections:

☑ **Memory Check 12.18**
True or False? The accounting department of a large company can have its own competitors.

- *Introduction.* This will explain the mission of the overall organization and what role the department plays in fulfilling it.

- *The environment.* Here, data will show the need for the departments services and identify competitive alternatives.

☑ **Memory Check 12.19**
True or False? The term *strategic business unit* refers to the planning department of a company.

- *Goals and objectives.* This section will list the performance measures used to evaluate the department (for example: sales revenue, number of clients, number of clients served, number of units processed, number of returns/complaints, operating expense/unit, number of new services, etc.) and identify targets in terms of these measures.

- *Organization and management.* How the department's team functions. Objectives for training, hiring, and restructuring will be covered here.

- *Operations.* This section will describe the department's facilities, space, and procedures, and how they will be used to reach unit objectives.

Business Plans Are Her Business

Sandie Heirwegh is an expert in business plans. She makes her living by training and coaching new entrepreneurs as well as teaching others to train and coach new entrepreneurs. The name of her business is The Entrepreneurial Edge Inc. (www.theentrepreneurialedge.com).

Starting this company brought Heirwegh's varied career in a full circle, from entrepreneur to employee back to entrepreneur. Married at 19, she started out as a tobacco farmer and partner (with her husband) in a haulage firm. After a downturn in the tobacco industry, Sandie secured employment first as an accounting technician with a large national accounting firm, then became a director of operations for a national franchisor before moving on to a series of government and community jobs assisting new businesses. Along the way, she picked up credentials as a Certified International Trade Professional (Forum for International Trade Training) and as a Certified Business Counselor (Asia Pacific Economic Corporation).

The Entrepreneurial Edge is a one-woman company, although Heirwegh, at times, hires or subcontracts work to specialists in law, accounting, marketing, project management, and so on. Heirwegh's company has partnered with other organizations to deliver federal self-employment benefits programs to new business owners. Managing this program allowed Heirwegh to use her wide range of skills, including delivering workshops, mentoring entrepreneurs, and managing program staff.

As a business planning consultant, Sandie has designed and managed 13 programs that have supported over 3500 new businesses. For seven years, she wrote a regular column on small business issues for the *Hamilton Spectator*, and she has designed entrepreneurship curricula for numerous colleges and government programs. Sandie helped to create business support centres in Zimbabwe, China, South Africa, and Bangladesh and helped train visiting delegates from Hungary, Poland, Tanzania, Japan, Pakistan, Egypt, Barbados, and other parts of the world. Sandie is a past winner of YWCA's Women of Distinction Award for Business, Industry, and Entrepreneurship.

- *Marketing.* Any internal techniques used to choose products/services, set fee structures, or promote the department are described here.

- *Finances.* This section will include a list of all assets used by the unit and a capital budget for replacement or new asset acquisition. It will have an operating budget for the department showing the operating allocation, the projected expenses, and any projected surplus or deficit.

⭐ Head Start Exercise

12.5 Search the web looking for three recent articles on *intrapreneurship*. Try to identify a common theme in the articles (1/3 page maximum).

WHAT DOES A FINISHED BUSINESS PLAN LOOK LIKE?

Example Business Plan

Pippa's Patty 'n Pie is the start-up business plan for the first venture of brother and sister Ethel and Elliot Wilson. Ethel is 35 years old, married to a chartered accountant, and has two children. Ethel's youngest child has just started going to school full days and her part-time work teaching at a local college is not what she really wants to do. Ethel holds a

> ✅ **Memory Check 12.20**
> True or False? The departmental business plan generally includes an income statement.

bachelor of Business Administration and worked as a business analyst for a credit-reporting firm before teaching. She and her husband have been paying down the mortgage on their small home and have about $90 000 of equity plus an additional $30 000 worth of securities in their investment portfolio. They have no other debts. Ethel and her husband have agreed to cash in the portfolio and use the money to start the business, with Ethel lending $10 000 of it to Elliot so he can invest it in the business.

Elliot is 26 and has been in and out of school and various jobs (mostly part-time) for the past seven years. He has no significant assets and owes about $16 000 in student loans. This year, he graduated from a two-year Culinary Management program and intended to use his credential to work on cruise ships and in hotels around the world. Then, Ethel and Elliot's 85-year-old Jamaican-born grandmother came up with the idea for the business. The patty recipe they intend to use is a modified version of Granma's own. As well, Granma has promised to give Elliot $10 000 toward the business (repayable if it is a success). This means Elliot will have $20 000 in total for his part of the investment.

Pippa's Patty 'n Pie Business Plan—September 20XX
Confidential: Please store in a secure location
Ethel B. Wilson 905-555-5555
Elliot Wilson 519-555-5555

Summary

Pippa's Patty 'n Pie will sell inexpensive fast food to a middle-class youth market in Westdale, an upscale residential neighbourhood in Hamilton, Ontario. The fast-food market is growing and Pippa's represents an opportunity to underprice the competition and satisfy the tastes of the youth market. Pippa's will be a family business owned by a brother and sister, who together have business, finance, culinary, and fast-food experience.

Westdale has a thriving commercial core with many restaurants, but only four direct fast-food competitors. There are a huge number of students (elementary, secondary, college, and university) who frequent and traverse the area. Sales forecasts for the first three years are $206 000, $275 000, and $300 000, with costs remaining relatively stable.

Pippa's will project an image of value, speed, and cleanliness. It will be at the lowest end of the fast-food price range, producing its own beef and chicken patties and reselling some baked goods from other suppliers.

Both owners will work in the business (one in the kitchen and the other dealing with customers and administration). Initially, there will be one part-time and one full-time employee.

The business will require just over $60 000 in start-up capital with over $40 000 of that coming from the entrepreneurs, who will take a bank loan for the remaining $20 000. Most of the investment will be for the purchase of quality used restaurant equipment ($37 000), which can serve as primary collateral for the loan. Paying a reasonable salary to the owners, the business will pass the break-even point within the first four months and make a small profit ($800) in the first year and a significant one-year profit ($24 000) by the third year.

SECTION 1: THE BUSINESS MODEL

Introduction

Pippa's Patty 'n Pie, although technically classified as a "bake shop" by the municipality, will be a non-seating fast-food outlet (limited-service restaurant). The business will sell baked meat patties along with complementary food products and beverages to a local student market as well as a broader, mealtime market from the local consumer traffic. Pippa's will depend on high volume and a fast customer turnover. The menu will be limited and prices will be at the lowest end of the fast-food range. Pippa's will be located in the Westdale section of Hamilton, Ontario, a middle-class area with a high concentration of educational facilities. Some of the food products will be made at the shop and others will be bought from local suppliers.

The business model will be similar to that found in "pie shops" in the UK and developing former British colonies, or take-out delis popular in large U.S. cities. That is to say, it will offer a limited menu, low prices, and no seating. Offering "fresh" products that have been quick-cooked from frozen will follow the model of Tim Hortons (although preparation and freezing of some of the products will initially be performed on-site at Pippa's).

Products and Services

The products offered by Pippa's are intended to satisfy hungry young appetites inexpensively. This means a generally high-starch, high-fat product, although all products can be produced as "trans-fat free," since this is a growing health concern.

Most of the products sold by Pippa's will be consumable using only one hand and no utensils—ideal for on-the-go snacks or a stand-up meal (with a patty in one hand and a drink in the other). Although Pippa's will not have seating, there will be several narrow countertop areas where customers can remain inside and stand to consume their food.

The Customers

The primary customer groups for Pippa's will be students of the elementary school, secondary school, and business college, all of which are within a three-minute walk of this business. A secondary target will be the many university students from the McMaster campus and medical centre about a six-minute walk away. Many of these students frequent the Westdale retail neighbourhood where Pippa's is located. The general traffic of consumers who live and work in this area forms another segment. A specific Caribbean immigrant segment will not be targeted, although Pippa's will likely get some customers from this and other immigrant groups, since the business concept is similar to one widely used in Africa, Europe, and the Caribbean. Nevertheless, the immediate location has a relatively low immigrant population.

The Opportunity

The fast-food industry has clear leaders in the categories of hamburgers, pizza, submarine and pita sandwiches, as well as in the coffee and doughnut areas. Pastry or pie shops, common in Africa, the Caribbean, and Western Europe (all having immigrant populations in Canada), represent an unexploited approach to fast-food customers. As well, the market for fast food is still growing. According to the Canadian Restaurant and Foodservices Association, there was an 8.5 percent sales increase in the first quarter of this year for "limited service restaurants."[1] Also, as lifestyles become busier, we are eating on the go more. By 2010, 6 out of every 10 restaurant meals were eaten "off-premise."[2] These factors indicate that the timing is excellent for a new product mix entry into the fast-food market.

The Owners

The business will be owned by Ethel and Elliot Wilson, a brother and sister. Ethel Wilson is a graduate of Kwantlen University College, where she graduated with a BBA in entrepreneurship. She has several years' experience working for a large credit-reporting firm in the role of analyzing small- and medium-sized companies and preparing credit reports on them. She is currently teaching part-time, but her youngest child is now old enough to attend school full days and Ethel is ready to return to a full-time endeavour. Ethel's husband, a chartered accountant, is committed to supporting Ethel in this venture. He will not be working for Pippa's in any paid capacity, as he works full-time and wishes to devote more time to child care, especially when Ethel is busy. Elliot graduated from Niagara College's Culinary Management Co-op program. His training provided him with baking and kitchen management skills. As well, he has worked full-time and part-time in a range of restaurants from fast food to fine dining.

Neither of the partners has experience as an entrepreneur, although other family members own businesses. The partners are both goal-oriented as shown by their completion of their post-secondary programs. Because of gender and age differences (nine years) between Ethel and Elliot, sibling rivalry is not a significant issue. The partners come from a close-knit family and work well together. They have complementary skills (Ethel is more strategic and Elliot is more hands-on) and have the high levels of trust that are found in family relationships. The timing is good for them to open a business together since Ethel is looking to re-enter the workforce on a full-time basis and Elliot is looking to establish a career with more focus and long-term prospects.

The partners will each draw a salary of up to $2500 per month from the time the business seems to be in positive cash flow. Ethel, with the support of her husband, could survive indefinitely without turning to the business for money, and Elliot has the support of his parents, with whom he will be living. The parents have agreed to cover all of Elliot's basic living expenses for up to two years, or until the business becomes profitable, whichever comes first. Both partners are prepared to waive their monthly salary any time the business is facing a cash shortage. (See Résumés in Appendix 1.)

The Legal Organization

The business will be a corporation under the Canada Business Corporations Act. One hundred voting shares of the corporation will be issued: 49 shares to Elliot Wilson and 51 shares to Ethel Wilson.

The company will be organized as a corporation in order to protect the personal assets of Ethel Wilson and her husband (including the home they own) against any catastrophic liability of the company. Federal incorporation was chosen simply because of the ease of the online incorporation feature available at the time. Elliot and Ethel Wilson will be the only directors of the company, although there is already a volunteer advisory board consisting of:

- the outside accountant that Pippa's will use;
- a former food services professor of Elliot's;
- a retired vice-president of marketing of a large company (family friend); and
- the branch manager of a bank (personal friend of Ethel).

This board will meet one month before start-up and every six months after that, at Pippa's. Members will receive a $100 honorarium for each meeting and a free meal.

There is a partnership agreement between the two shareholders, attached as Appendix 2. The agreement allows Ethel to lend Elliot $10 000, half of his share of the owners' investment in the company. Elliot agrees that his share of any dividends that the company pays out will automatically be turned over to Ethel, until all the loan (plus interest at an annual rate of 5 percent) has been paid back. As well, there is a dispute settlement mechanism in the partnership agreement. Even though Ethel has voting control and can overrule Elliot on any day-to-day decisions, for important strategic decisions on which the partners disagree, they will use one of the members of their advisory board as an arbitrator. (See Partnership Agreement in Appendix 2.)

SECTION 2: FEASIBILITY

Location

Pippa's Patty 'n Pie will be located in the Westdale section of Hamilton, Ontario, right in the thriving commercial section referred to as Westdale Village. Hamilton is a city of half a million people, in the centre of the London-to-Oshawa industrial corridor. The Westdale area is a solid middle-class section of the city with owner-occupied homes and small rental apartments. Many of the residents are families with children. The entire city of Hamilton has a median family income[3] that is well above the national average and Westdale would be well above the city average. Assuming that pedestrians will use a fast-food outlet within a seven-minute walk of where they work, live, or go to school, Planning Department information indicates a residential population of about 10 000[4] within the 1.75-kilometre radius around the site. As well, the two closest schools in the neighbourhood have a combined student population of 2500.[5] In addition, a personal estimate of the number of people who work in the shops, offices, and small service businesses within the 1.75-kilometre drawing area would add about another 600 potential customers.[6] This would total about 13 100 potential customers, not counting the drive-by traffic. Hundreds of McMaster University students would pass the site on a daily basis en route to school or the Westdale Village, but most would be in cars so they have not been included. Also, numbers for the elementary students have not been included because of the lower likelihood of their making their own lunch purchases.

This location is also important because it is very close to a medium-sized commercial bakery that will be the supplier of important items on Pippa's menu. There is also easy access from the 403 highway for bringing in supplies from food wholesale operations and fresh items from the Ontario Food Terminal. If for no other reason, Hamilton is a good location because it gave birth to the greatest Canadian fast-food success story: Tim Hortons. This may be because it is in the very centre of Canada's densest population and could allow for easy contiguous expansion of the business.

Site

The site is a 1000-square-foot store in a three-unit strip plaza on Paradise Road. There is a large retail window and on-street parking as well as parking for three cars in the front. The unit on one side of the site is a denture clinic and on the other side is a tax service office. The road is the main access into West Hamilton, and the large grocery store directly across the street also generates automobile traffic. A study of automobile traffic has not been performed. Drivers are not a primary target since no drive-through capacity is possible at this site. (Note: None of the competing fast-food services have drive-throughs either.) A three-day sample of pedestrian traffic (Thursday, Friday, Saturday) showed an average of 502 people[7] walking in front of the site between the hours of 8:00 a.m. and 6:00 p.m. and many hundreds more walking on Main Street, from which the site is clearly visible.

The front door is wide enough to be considered wheelchair accessible, and there is no bump or elevation change on entry. But there is no automatic door opening mechanism.

The site is appropriate in that it is naturally divided into two large areas that will become the serving area and the kitchen, with a small office in between them. The site is also accessible to the targeted younger market physically (it is easy to see into and the window is close to the sidewalk). It is also accessible in a psychological sense in that it is an average-looking store, not intimidating or exclusive as are some of the high-end retailers in the village. See the Floor Plan diagram under Space and Equipment.

Site Expenses

A conditional offer to lease has been accepted by the landlord at the site. In return for one month's rent as security deposit, the partners have six weeks to arrange financing for the business. (If the lease is not finalized, the deposit becomes non-refundable.) When the condition is removed and the lease finalized, the security deposit will be considered paid and the partners will pre-pay the first month's rent at that point.

The lease is for five years at a flat monthly rent of $1400 plus a one-third share of the maintenance costs (garbage removal and snowplowing, etc.), which will run as high as $185 per month. Central heating and air conditioning for the building are included with the rent. The lease allows for the rent to increase each year in proportion to the annual Consumer Price Index as reported by Statistics Canada. There is no provision for the rent to go down if the CPI were to drop. The lease is renewable for an additional five years, but at that point rent can increase above the base rent if sales of the business are in excess of $400 000. The annual increase will be equal to 1 percent of sales in excess of $400 000.

Market Potential

The market potential for Pippa's would be the total fast-food expenditure of the 13 100 potential customers in the drawing area. Higher income brackets (which would apply to Westdale) spend about $3070 per person annually on food.[8] Of this, about 7 percent is spent on fast food. Therefore, the total market potential would be (7% × $3070 × 13 100) $2.8 million.

Competition

There are 18 restaurants in the Westdale Village area, but only four of them are direct fast-food competition: Basilique Gourmet Pizza, Pita Pit, Subway Subs, and Tim Hortons. All are within 400 metres of Pippa's. Three out of the four are successful national franchises. The average fast-food sales of the four is about $700 000 (1/4 of the market potential) and may be considerably higher because some percentage of the automobile traffic coming through Westdale (not included in the market potential) would stop to use well-known national franchises. Pippa's sales will come from taking local pedestrian customer sales from these establishments and by competing on price and speed of service.

Indirect competition will include the small food counter in The Barn grocery store across the street, as well as school cafeterias and vending machines. Pippa's will be superior to The Barn in price and food quality and superior to the school cafeterias in terms of food appeal and environment.

Sales Forecast

The food and beverage industry has total annual sales in Ontario of about $32 billion[9] and employs approximately 170 000 people,[10] for average sales of about $188 000 per employee. Considering that Pippa's will have three full-time employees in total, one estimate of sales could be $188 000 × 3 = $564 000. The average sales per fast food business in Ontario is $480 000. On average for Canadian limited service eating places, the ratio of revenue to equity is 34.2 : 1.[11] Despite the balance sheet, Ethel and Elliot will have about $30 000 of true equity in the business (Elliot must repay $10 000 to Ethel), so using this ratio the sales would on average be 34 × $30 000 = $1 020 000. Elliot's experience includes several months of working in a submarine sandwich shop in a location similar to Pippa's. Based on memory, he estimates that the sub business was bringing in about $1000 per day. Using only 300 days per year, this would give an estimate of $300 000 in sales. Based on limited knowledge, Elliot's former food services professor gave a best-guess estimate of "somewhere around a quarter million" as his sales forecast. In rank order, these estimates are:

- Equity to revenue ratio: $1 020 000
- Ratio of sales to employees: $564 000
- Average per fast-food business: $480 000
- Elliot's similar-business estimate: $300 000
- Expert opinion (guess): $250 000

Since Pippa's will have none of the brand recognition of its competitors, it is reasonable to use the most conservative estimates. Averaging the bottom two gives a sales rate that could be achievable by the end of the first year ($275 000). It will take time (estimate of six months) to build up to this rate, starting from a sales rate of 0 on the first day. So the first year forecast for Pippa's will be ($275 000 × 0.75). A small increase will be forecast for the third year.

- Year 1 $206 000
- Year 2 $275 000
- Year 3 $300 000

Protecting the Business

A comprehensive small business package covering liability, fire, theft, and retail window insurance has been quoted at $1900 annually, payable in quarterly pre-paid instalments of $475. The business will not carry life insurance on the partners at this time since both are currently covered by family policies and the business capital is not yet enough to be concerned about.

A coded security alarm system is already in the unit and Pippa's will only have to pay the $30 per month monitoring fee. Only one person at a time will have access to the cash register and a new cash float will be started anytime there is a switch in cashiers.

A trademark will be applied for on the name Pippa's Patty 'n Pie and the $350 fee will cover the cost, provided that the trademark is accepted without objection. Pippa's will not extend credit to customers or accept third-party credit cards. However, it will accept debit payment since teenagers find this a prestigious way to make a purchase. If it becomes too costly with too many debit transactions for small amounts, a minimum order size will be applied to these transactions.

SECTION 3: MARKETING

Image

The main elements of Pippa's image will be:

- *Value.* This is important to younger people who have relatively little disposable cash and are not prepared to pay for the frills of fine dining.

- *Speed.* Fast food should be that. When you're hungry, you shouldn't have to wait for the kitchen to prepare something and Pippa's will be the fastest.

- *Cleanliness.* This is important to the middle-class customers being targeted who (although they won't admit it) carry most of the values of their middle-class parents.

Business Name

The name "Pippa's Patty 'n Pie" projects the three mainstays of the image. Traditionally, meat pies have been heavy, filling, and high value. The name has a speedy staccato sound to it, making it natural to say it quickly. (Try saying it out loud.) The name Pippa is Scandinavian, with the appropriate reputation for cleanliness. Finally, the company has a human name, like Harvey's or Wendy's or Tim Hortons, as opposed to Burger King or Red Barn. Just looking at the most successful franchises indicates that this might have some value.

Service/Product Mix

The initial menu will consist of

Breakfast:	
Ham 'n Egg Pie	$1.55
Cheese 'n Egg Pie	1.55
Sausage Roll	2.05
Regular	
Beef Patty	$1.55
Chicken Patty	1.55
Veggie Patty	2.05
Spicy Beans	1.15
Spicy Rice	1.15
Veggie Sticks	1.75
Beverages	
Canned Soft Drinks	$1.25
Coffee	1.25/1.50
Tea	1.25/1.50
Juice	1.25
Desserts	
Apple Pie	1.15
Cherry Pie	1.15

All pies, patties, and sausage rolls will be served in an open-ended waxed paper envelope imprinted with Pippa's logo. Veggie sticks will consist of a small serving of carrot, celery, and zucchini sticks in a poly bag, which is sealable for freshness.

Spicy beans or rice will be served in a 10-ounce Styrofoam cup with a plastic lid. Plastic spoons will be provided, but enterprising youth will probably take to eating (drinking?) the beans or rice directly from the cup. Drinks will be served in the original container only. The only value-added service will be that customers will have the option of eating at the two stand-up counters in the serving area.

Pricing

According to the Canadian Restaurant and Foodservices Association, the average per-person expenditure at chain restaurants is just over $5.00.[12] The pricing strategy to appeal to the younger market will be to keep the price of a snack (patty and drink) under $3.00 and to keep the price of a meal under $4.75 (including taxes). So, for example, a customer could get a beef patty, drink, and apple pie; or a patty, spicy beans, and drink; or two patties and a drink—all for under $4.75.

No individual pricing discounts will be offered but a family value meal may be introduced (if it seems that customers are buying take-home-for-dinner quantities). The meal would contain six–eight patties, a large order of beans, rice, and veggie sticks. (Price to be determined.)

Distribution

Distribution is direct from Pippa's to the end-user, but Pippa's is acting as an intermediary for several products that come from the manufacturer (sausage rolls, fruit pies, etc.). As well, some of the products (carrots, zucchini, celery) will come from a wholesale distributor.

The site is designed for speed, with customers coming in, reading the menu, ordering and paying at the cash (close to the entrance), moving to their left to pick up orders, and moving again to their left to make room for new customers. The serving area is a narrow workspace for efficient service. The colours will be predominantly white (sterile) with purple, orange, and green highlights. All surfaces will be of easy-clean materials, and lighting and fixtures will be of simple, plain designs.

Promotion

Because Pippa's is targeting a small geographic segment, no mass media will be used. The sign will be the major form of advertising. Small ads in yearbooks will be taken, more as a community gesture than good advertising. A press release will be sent to community media one week before the official opening and press will be invited to a small opening ceremony, where free samples will be distributed. The only personal selling will be asking early customers if they have tried this or that (things on the menu that they did not order).

Around start-up, high levels of product wastage are expected because of slow sales. For this reason, patties, etc. that have been in the warming ovens near their maximum time will be removed, cut in half, and placed on a tray. Ethel or Elliot will take the tray into the street (weather and time of day permitting) and offer free samples to passersby.

Promotion Evaluation

Promotion will frequently be evaluated by engaging customers in conversation during slow periods, always asking, "What made you come in the first time?" A record of responses will be kept in a notebook by the cash register for analysis.

SECTION 4: OPERATIONS
Space and Equipment

Pippa's will need the following standard commercial kitchen equipment, which can all be purchased used and in excellent condition: 35-ft. commercial refrigerator; under-counter 14-litre refrigerator; 35 cu. ft. freezer; portable blast freezer; three commercial microwave ovens; commercial gas grill (installed); and commercial gas oven (installed). The following equipment will be needed new (more difficult to find used, in good shape) commercial pastry roller, kitchenware, and utensils. Unfortunately, the building currently has commercial carpet throughout. The kitchen and customer areas will need this replaced with commercial vinyl and seven different counter areas will need to be installed. A second two-piece washroom must be installed. Labour for paint and other decor will be provided by the partners. The partners also have a computer and office furniture that they will contribute to the business.

Floor Plan

An outside illuminated sign of stretched canvas (to conform to existing signs and as required by the lease) will be ordered at a price of $2300. An illuminated sign with menu item pictures will be ordered for behind the counter. Part of the sign will be a reader panel where individual menu items, along with prices, can be listed and easily changed. This will cost $1850.

"Floorplan."

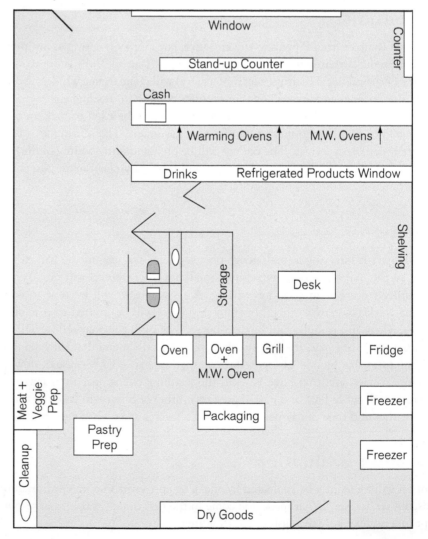

Logistics

The ordering system will be refined based on proven usage rates. But the plan at start-up is to have a minimum of three weeks' supply of all patties and pies and sausage rolls on hand, even though the lead time required at the bakery is only one week. Nevertheless, this will ensure a safety margin in case of supply interruption. All poly bags will be labelled with a date of receipt, and a first-in-first-out policy will be used for all foods, to maximize freshness. When the inventory reaches the minimum level plus a one-week supply, another week's supply will be ordered. At present, there is little cost advantage to ordering and storing really large quantities. Supplies to make the patties are easily available.

The Lindsay Commercial Bakery, located in Ancaster, just south of Hamilton, has been identified as a supplier of individual-sized quiche (cheese or ham) that will be renamed as Ham 'n Egg Pie, etc. Lindsay will also supply sausage rolls. (Only beef fat and unsaturated vegetable oils will be used to minimize trans fats, as per Pippa's specifications.) These items will be flash-frozen at Pippa's in vacuum poly bags to prevent freezer damage. As well, Lindsay will supply small individual fruit pies that will be refrigerated. Due to the high sugar content, spoilage is less of an issue. Lindsay is not yet prepared to extend credit terms, but will accept Pippa's company cheque on delivery.

A lawyer has been hired for the partnership agreement at a cost of $620. The company accountant has not yet provided any direct services but will be used for tax and financial statements and planning at an annual cost of about $1200.

Methods and Procedures

All patties, egg pies, and sausage rolls will be frozen (patties will be frozen immediately after baking and cooling, and egg pies and sausage rolls immediately after delivery from the commercial bakery). Items will be sealed in polyvinyl bags with most of the air removed and the bags labelled for baking date. Patties and pies will be microwaved to an edible temperature (about three minutes for eight pies from frozen) and transferred to the warming ovens, where they can safely remain from 3 to 12 hours, depending on the product.

Beans will be prepared from commercial canned beans with the addition of desiccated onions and spices. Rice will be cooked from parboiled on a boiler on the grill and spiced with commercial salsa. Both beans and rice can remain covered in the Crock-Pots for an entire day with minimal loss of quality.

For wastage, Pippa's can be expected to discard on average one-half tray of ham 'n egg and cheese 'n egg pies after breakfast each day (16 to a tray); one-half tray of beef and chicken pies and veggie pies, after lunch rush hour and at the end of the day; one-half tray of sausage rolls, one-half cooker of beans, one-half cooker of rice, for total wastage of about $18.00 per day at cost. Some of this may be recouped through storing and freezing waste and selling it to local pig farmers. Over the next couple of years, however, legislation might ban all animal product contents in feed because of concerns about mad cow disease. Therefore, no income is shown as coming from this source.

Quality control will depend on checking temperatures coming from the microwaved products until cooking times for all products are precise enough to maintain food at about 55 degrees Celsius. Pippa's policy will be to replace any item that a customer finds unsatisfactory with the same or an alternative of the customer's choice.

Systems

All financial and inventory records will be kept using QuickBooks, with which Ethel is already familiar. A separate journal will be kept of all batch numbers of products that are baked or received for freezing. In case a problem occurs with a particular batch, it can be traced back to the time of baking or receipt.

Organization

Ethel will handle all administrative duties and Elliot will perform all kitchen duties. The full-time employee will work the counter serving customers, assisted and replaced by either Elliot or Ethel depending on the time of day. Generally Ethel will open in the morning and prepare the first batches of food, and the full-time employee will arrive at about 7:30 a.m. and work through the breakfast and lunch rushes until 3:30 p.m. Elliot will arrive in the mid-afternoon and both he and Ethel will work the counter for the after-school rush. Then at 4:00 p.m., a part-time employee will work with Elliot, and Ethel will leave. In the evening, with the part-timer on the counter, Elliot will do the day's baking and lock up at around 10:00 p.m. as a closing time. (The area appears quiet around then, even in the summer, but the schedule can change to meet demand.) For the Saturday schedule, the part-timer will cover the 7:30 a.m. to 3:30 p.m. shift, and on Sundays the shop will close.

The employees will initially be paid just above minimum wage, which, including employer CPP contributions, will work out to about a total cost of $9.50 per hour for the part-timer and $11.00 for the full-timer. CPP contributions will be made for both Elliot and Ethel based on their salary.

Regulation

Since Pippa's is technically a bakeshop, as opposed to a restaurant, it does not have to meet local requirements for separate male and female and disabled washroom facilities. Nevertheless, a single wheelchair accessible washroom is being added to the facility for customer use. Because it is a food preparation business, the employee washroom cannot directly access the food preparation area so an additional door must be built in the kitchen area.

Pippa's will require a bakeshop licence from the City of Hamilton at a cost of $185 annually. There are no plans to join any business associations during the start-up phase.

SECTION 5: FINANCES

Start-Up Requirements

See chart: MATERIAL AND OPERATING CASH NEEDS (For Start-up), attached as Appendix 4.

See chart: EQUIPMENT NEEDS (For Start-up), attached as Appendix 5.

Owner(s)' Investment

Ethel and Elliot will be contributing $42 100 in equity ($20 000 each in cash and $2100 in equipment).

Borrowed Money

Pippa's will need to secure a loan of about $20 000 for operating expenses as the business gets off the ground. This should be at an annual interest rate of about 9.5 percent and paid off over the first three years of the business at monthly payments of $640. The $36 000 of kitchen and restaurant equipment and fixtures could be used as collateral.

Sales Income by Month

See chart: PROJECTED SALES INCOME BY MONTH, attached as Appendix 12.

Most of the variation in sales for the cash flow is the result of growth in the business. Sandwich and pizza sellers in Westdale estimated that loss of student business in the summer was offset about equally by the increase in holiday traffic. Increasingly, colleges and universities are running courses right through the summer, and the good weather makes it more likely that people will be out for lunch.

The business will operate almost entirely on a cash basis until credit can be established with Pippa's own suppliers. There are no foreseeable circumstances of Pippa's extending credit.

Sources of Data

1. Canadian Restaurant and Foodservices Association Report, "Foodservice Sales Jump." www.crfa.ca/research.
2. Canadian Restaurant and Foodservices Association, "Six in 10 Restaurant Meals Eaten Off-Premise." www.crfa.ca/research/2013.
3. Statistics Canada, "Median Total Income, By Family Type, by Census Metropolitan Area," 2009.
4. Hamilton Planning and Economic Development Department, Tax Roll information and maps.
5. Calls to Westdale Secondary and Columbia Business College.
6. Personal observation and estimate.
7. Site observation by partners during May when high schools and elementary schools were in session but college was between winter and spring terms (although some students were still about).
8. Statistics Canada, "Detailed Average Household Expenditure for Canada, Provinces/ Territories and Selected Metropolitan Areas," 2008.
9. City of Hamilton, Economic Development Department, "Hamilton Food and Beverage Industry Profile."
10. Ontario Job Futures, "Overview of Ontario Employment Patters," 2004.
11. Industry Canada, SME Benchmarking Tool, small business ratios for Limited Service Eating Places, NAICS Number 7222, 2007 data.
12. Canadian Restaurant and Foodservices Association, "Menu Trends: Chains vs. Independents." www.crfa.ca/research/2005/menu (adjusted for inflation).

Balance Sheet (Opening Day)

ASSETS

CURRENT ASSETS

Cash	$20 000	
Accounts receivable	0	
Inventory/supplies	1 750	
Prepaid expenses	3 460	
Other current assets	100	
Total current assets		$25 310

FIXED ASSETS

Land and buildings	0	
Fixtures	17 950	
Equipment	18 670	
Vehicles	750	
Other fixed assets	0	
Total fixed assets		$37 370
Total Assets		**$62 680**

LIABILITIES

CURRENT LIABILITIES

Accounts payable	0	
Short-term loans payable	0	
Taxes payable	0	
Other current liabilities	0	
Total current liabilities		

LONG-TERM LIABILITIES

Mortgage payable	0	
Long-term loans payable	$20 000	
Other long-term liabilities	0	
Total long-term liabilities		$20 000

SHAREHOLDERS' EQUITY

Capital investment	$42 680	$42 680
Total Liabilities and Equity		**$62 680**

Balance Sheet Year End (Year 1)

ASSETS

CURRENT ASSETS

Cash	$21 158	
Accounts receivable	0	
Inventory/supplies	1 750	
Prepaid expenses	3 460	
Other current assets	100	
Total current assets		$26 468

FIXED ASSETS

Land and buildings	0	
Fixtures	16 150	
Equipment	14 270	
Vehicles	750	
Other fixed assets	0	
Total fixed assets		$31 170
Total Assets		**$57 638**

LIABILITIES

CURRENT LIABILITIES

Accounts payable	0	
Short-term loans payable	0	
Taxes payable	0	
Other current liabilities	0	
Total current liabilities	0	

LONG-TERM LIABILITIES

	0	
Mortgage payable	0	
Long-term loans payable	$14 169	
Other long-term liabilities	0	
Total long-term liabilities		$14 169

SHAREHOLDERS' EQUITY

Capital investment	$42 680	
Retained earnings	789	
Total equity		$43 469
Total Liabilitles and Equity		**$57 638**

Balance Sheet Year End (Year 2)

ASSETS

CURRENT ASSETS

Cash	$21 026	
Accounts receivable	0	
Inventory/supplies	1 750	
Prepaid expenses	3 460	
Other current assets	100	
Total current assets		$26 336

FIXED ASSETS

Land and buildings	0	
Fixtures	14 650	
Equipment ($15 000 new equip.)	21 570	
Vehicles	750	
Other fixed assets	0	
Total fixed assets		$36 970
Total Assets		**$63 306**

LIABILITIES

CURRENT LIABILITIES	0	
Accounts payable	0	
Short-term loans payable	0	
Taxes payable	0	
Other current liabilities	0	
Total current liabilities		0

LONG-TERM LIABILITIES

Mortgage payable	0	
Long-term loans payable	7 835	
Other long-term liabilities	0	
Total long-term liabilities		$ 7 835

SHAREHOLDERS' EQUITY

Capital investment	$42 680	
Retained earnings	12 791	
Total equity		$55 471
Total Liabilities and Equity		**$63 306**

Balance Sheet Year End (Year 3)

ASSETS

CURRENT ASSETS

Cash	$25 954	
Accounts receivable	0	
Inventory/supplies	1 750	
Prepaid expenses	3 460	
Other current assets	100	
Total current assets		$31 264

FIXED ASSETS

Land and buildings	0	
Fixtures	13 150	
Equipment ($18 000 new equip.)	34 870	
Vehicles	750	
Other fixed assets		
Total fixed assets		$48 770
Total Assets		**$80 034**

LIABILITIES

CURRENT LIABILITIES

Accounts payable	0	
Short-term loans payable	740	
Taxes payable	0	
Other current liabilities	0	
Total current liabilities		740

LONG-TERM LIABILITIES

Mortgage payable	0	
Long-term loans payable	0	
Other long-term liabilities	0	
Total long-term liabilities		0

SHAREHOLDERS' EQUITY

Capital investment	$42 680	
Retained earnings	36 614	
Total equity		$79 294
Total Liabilities and Equity		**$80 034**

Costs and Expenses

See chart: ONGOING COSTS & EXPENSES (Worksheet), attached as Appendix.

Pippa's Patty 'n Pie Inc. | Income Statement

Income Statement (Projected) for the One-Year Period Ended: (Year 1 End)

SALES

Sales	$206 000	

COSTS

Cost of goods sold	$ 78 280	

GROSS PROFIT

Gross profit		$127 720

EXPENSES

Rent	$ 16 800	
Utilities	0	
Equipment lease	0	
Salaries/deductions	89 000	
Insurance	1 900	
Depreciation expense	6 200	
Interest	1 849	
Maintenance	2 220	
Professional fees	2 800	
Advertising	1 200	
Supplies	4 300	
Delivery	0	
Travel	500	
Total operating expenses		$126 769

NET PROFIT

Net before income tax		$951
Income tax		$162
Net Profit after Income Tax		**$789**

Income Statement (Projected) for the One-Year Period Ended: (Year 2 End)

SALES

| Sales | $275 000 | |

COSTS

| Cost of goods sold | 104 500 | |

GROSS PROFIT

| Gross profit | | $170 500 |

EXPENSES

Rent	$ 16 800	
Utilities	0	
Equipment lease	0	
Salaries/deductions	115 070	
Insurance	1 900	
Depreciation expense	9 200	
Interest	1 346	
Maintenance	2 220	
Professional fees	3 000	
Advertising	1 200	
Supplies	4 300	
Delivery	0	
Travel	500	
Total operating expenses		$155 536

NET PROFIT

Net before income tax		$ 14 964
Income tax		2 968
Net Profit after Income Tax		**$ 11 996**

Income Statement (Projected) for the One-Year Period Ended: (Year 3 End)

SALES

Sales $300 000

COSTS

Cost of goods sold $110 400

GROSS PROFIT

Gross profit $189 600

EXPENSES

Rent	$ 16 800	
Utilities	0	
Equipment lease	0	
Salaries/deductions	120 048	
Insurance	4 400	
Depreciation expense	6 200	
Interest	585	
Maintenance	2 220	
Professional fees	2 600	
Advertising	1 800	
Supplies	5 328	
Delivery	0	
Travel	996	
Total operating expenses		$160 977

NET PROFIT

Net before income tax	$28 623
Income tax	$ 4 800
Net Profit after Income Tax	**$23 823**

Pippa's Patty 'n Pie Inc.

Projected Cash Flow

						Year 1 of Operation						
Month	1	2	3	4	5	6	7	8	9	10	11	12
Sales	5 000	7 000	8 500	12 000	14 800	21 900	22 000	22 800	23 000	23 000	23 000	23 000
Cash In-Flow												
Cash Sales	5 000	7 000	8 500	12 000	14 800	21 900	22 000	22 800	23 000	23 000	23 000	23 000
Payments Received	0	0	0	0	0	0	0	0	0	0	0	0
Total Cash In-flow (a)	5 000	7 000	8 500	12 000	14 800	21 900	22 000	22 800	23 000	23 000	23 000	23 000
Opening Cash Balance (b)	20 000	11 996	7 437	3 609	1 426	38	3 152	5 403	8 975	12 471	15 962	19 356
Cash Out-Flow												
Advertising	200	0	200	0	200	0	200	0	200	0	0	200
Inventory	1 900	2 560	3 230	4 560	5 624	8 322	8 360	8 664	8 740	8 740	8 740	8 740
Rent/Maintenance	1 585	1 585	1 585	1 585	1 585	1 585	1 585	1 585	1 585	1 585	1 585	1 585
Insurance/prof. fees	1 275	0	0	725	0	0	725	0	0	475	0	1 500
Loan payments	640	640	640	640	640	640	640	640	640	640	640	640
Salaries/deductions	6 334	6 334	6 334	7 800	7 800	7 900	7 900	8 000	8 000	8 000	8 032	8 032
Supplies/equipment	1,00	300	300	300	300	300	300	300	300	300	300	300
Taxes	0	0	0	0	0	0	0	0	0	0	0	162
Other expenses	70	40	39	39	39	39	39	39	39	39	39	39
Total Cash Out-flow (c)	13 004	11 559	12 328	14 183	16 188	18 786	19 749	19 228	19 504	19 779	19 336	21 198
Closing Cash Balance (a¹ b² c)	11 996	7 437	3 609	1 426	38	3 152	5 403	8 975	12 471	15 692	19 356	21 158

Pippa's Patty 'n Pie Inc.

Projected Cash Flow

						Year 2 of Operation						
Month	1	2	3	4	5	6	7	8	9	10	11	12
Sales	23 000	24 000	24 000	24 000	24 000	24 000	20 000	20 000	23 000	23 000	23 000	23 000
Cash In-Flow												
Cash Sales	23 000	24 000	24 000	24 000	24 000	24 000	20 000	20 000	23 000	23 000	23 000	23 000
Payments Received	0	0	0	0	0	0	0	0	0	0	0	0
Total Cash In-flow (a)	**23 000**	**24 000**	**24 000**	**24 000**	**24 000**	**24 000**	**20 000**	**20 000**	**23 000**	**23 000**	**23 000**	**23 000**
Opening Cash Balance (b)	**21 158**	**7 201**	**9 869**	**11 638**	**13 532**	**16 001**	**17 970**	**17 184**	**17 373**	**18 522**	**19 796**	**21 645**
Cash Out-Flow												
Advertising	200	0	200	0	200	0	200	0	200	0	200	0
Inventory	8 740	9 120	9 120	9 120	9 120	9 120	7 600	7 600	8 740	8 740	8 740	8 740
Rent/Maintenance	1 585	1 585	1 585	1 585	1 585	1 585	1 585	1 585	1 585	1 585	1 585	1 585
Insurance/prof. fees	775	0	0	775	0	0	775	0	0	775	0	1 800
Loan payments	640	640	640	640	640	640	640	640	640	640	640	640
Salaries/deductions	9 589	9 589	9 589	9 589	9 589	9 589	9 589	9 589	9 589	9 589	9 589	9 589
Supplies/equipment	15 358	358	358	358	358	358	358	358	358	358	358	358
Taxes	0	0	700	0	0	700	0	0	700	0	0	868
Other expenses	70	40	39	39	39	39	39	39	39	39	39	39
Total Cash Out-flow (c)	**36 957**	**21 332**	**22 231**	**22 106**	**21 531**	**22 031**	**20 786**	**19 811**	**21 851**	**21 726**	**21 151**	**23 619**
Closing Cash Balance (a^1 b^2 c)	**7 201**	**9 869**	**11 638**	**13 532**	**16 001**	**19 970**	**17 184**	**17 373**	**18 522**	**19 796**	**21 645**	**21 026**

Pippa's Patty 'n Pie Inc.

Projected Cash Flow

						Year 3 of Operation						
Month	1	2	3	4	5	6	7	8	9	10	11	12
Sales	25 000	25 000	25 000	25 000	25 000	25 000	25 000	25 000	25 000	25 000	25 000	25 000
Cash In-Flow												
Cash Sales	25 000	25 000	25 000	25 000	25 000	25 000	25 000	25 000	25 000	25 000	25 000	25 000
Payments Received	0	0	0	0	0	0	0	0	0	0	0	0
Other Cash Received	0	0	0	0	0	0	0	0	0	0	0	0
Total Cash In-flow (a)	**25 000**	**25 000**	**25 000**	**25 000**	**25 000**	**25 000**	**25 000**	**25 000**	**25 000**	**25 000**	**25 000**	**25 000**
Opening Cash Balance (b)	**21 026**	**4 520**	**7 564**	**9 108**	**10 902**	**13 646**	**15 490**	**16 984**	**20 028**	**21 572**	**23 366**	**26 110**
Cash Out-Flow												
Advertising	300	0	300	0	300	0	300	0	300	0	300	0
Inventory	9 200	9 200	9 200	9 200	9 200	9 200	9 200	9 200	9 200	9 200	9 200	9 200
Rent/Maintenance	1 585	1 585	1 585	1 585	1 585	1 585	1 585	1 585	1 585	1 585	1 585	1 585
Insurance/prof. fees	1 250	0	0	1 250	0	0	1 250	0	0	1 250	0	0
Loan payments	640	640	640	640	640	640	640	640	640	640	640	640
Salaries/deductions	10 004	10 004	10 004	10 004	10 004	10 004	10 004	10 004	10 004	10 004	10 004	10 004
Supplies/equipment	18 444	444	444	444	444	444	444	444	444	444	444	444
Taxes	0	0	1 200	0	0	1 200	0	0	1 200	0	0	1 200
Other expenses	83	83	83	83	83	83	83	83	83	83	83	83
Total Cash Out-flow (c)	**41 506**	**21 956**	**23 456**	**23 206**	**22 256**	**23 156**	**23 506**	**21 956**	**23 456**	**23 206**	**22 256**	**25 156**
Closing Cash Balance (a¹ b² c)	**4 520**	**7 564**	**9 108**	**10 902**	**13 646**	**15 490**	**16 984**	**20 028**	**21 572**	**23 366**	**26 110**	**25 954**

12.6 Write a brief essay explaining why it would be a bad idea for you personally to try to start up Pippa's Patty 'n Pie Shop as a real business (1/2 page maximum).

Answers to Memory Check Questions

12.1 T   12.2 T   12.3 F   12.4 T   12.5 F   12.6 F   12.7 T   12.8 F   12.9 T
12.10 F   12.11 T   12.12 F   12.13 F   12.14 T   12.15 T   12.16 T   12.17 F   12.18 T
12.19 F   12.20 F

Questions for Discussion

1. Identify some uses of the business plan not discussed in this chapter. Could the business plan be used as a contract? Explain. Could it be used for ethical purposes? How?
2. Why are business plans often considered too long and boring? How can the business plan be kept short and interesting but still supply all the necessary information?
3. What assumptions will a business plan reader make about the entrepreneur, based on the style of writing? How can an entrepreneur use this to his or her advantage?
4. What kinds of problems would entrepreneurs typically take to management consultants? How would a written business plan aid the consultant?
5. Debate the pros and cons of having students write full original business plans. What are the problems of doing this in groups?
6. Which type of business (manufacturing, wholesale, retail, service) has the greatest need for a written business plan? Why?
7. Discuss how the business plan for a start-up company will be different from the plan for a company that has been established for several years and is looking to expand into new markets.
8. How can a non-profit organization be "entrepreneurial"? How would the business plan for a non-profit affect the relationship between the CEO and the board of directors?
9. Discuss the advantages to a large organization of fostering a climate of intrapreneurship. What disadvantages could there be for the employees?
10. Assume you are being asked to lend the $20 000 Pippa's Patty 'n Pie is looking to borrow. Based on the written business plan, find as many reasons as possible for turning down the loan.

Case for Discussion

The dean of Business at Drummond Hill College always made a great effort to keep local business leaders involved in planning and operating her college's business programs. One of the college's biggest supporters was James Alexander Ross, founder and president of a major food processing company that owned three factories close to the college. Ross, through his company, had just given a sizable research grant to the college and he volunteered as an advisor on the Business School Steering Committee. At a meeting of the committee, Ross and the dean had a difference of opinion on the curriculum that business students should be studying.

"The role of the school is to train managers and consultants for companies such as ours," Ross pointed out to the dean. "We need graduates who can understand how large organizations function and who can manage within those organizations. The curriculum should emphasize management training."

The dean did not agree. She made the point that "Today, businesses need managers who think like entrepreneurs; managers who see themselves responsible for the profit of their departments; people who can innovate and adapt. You need managers who see everything in terms of a business plan. That's what the curriculum should emphasize."

Ross considered the dean's position, then shook his head. "Business plans are for entrepreneurs and financiers, not for the managers who have to carry out those plans, and not for the operational people."

The dean pressed her issue. "You can't expect a driver to take the bus where you want to go, if she can't read a road map. Business plans are road maps for managers."

"All she needs is a GPS." Ross laughed. "Besides, I'd think that many employers might be reluctant to hire managers who would see themselves as highly entrepreneurial. Entrepreneurs see the big picture, but we need managers who are specialists in human resources, operations, finance, or marketing."

"And the best way to teach those things," the dean said, "is by using business plans. Finance managers need to see where their role fits in relation to marketing and operations. Managers have to be able to think like entrepreneurs."

Ross responded quickly, "Entrepreneurs are not created in business schools. You can teach management or marketing, but entrepreneurship is something you are born with, like creativity or musical talent."

The argument had to be curtailed so that committee business could be completed. But Ross was clearly eager to continue the discussion. "I'm not convinced," he said. "But let's meet on this next week. If you can persuade me that business students should be spending their time studying business plans, I'll give you another donation so you can run a yearly business plan competition. The top entry will win $10 000, the second place will get $5000, and there will be $2000 for third place."

The dean smiled tentatively as they shook hands, realizing that she now had the task of preparing her best arguments in favour of business plans as teaching tools.

1. Explain what you think is the single strongest argument in favour of using business plans to train people who do not intend to become entrepreneurs.

2. Support the argument that "all business students should be taught entrepreneurship."

3. Explain Ross's position that "employers may be reluctant to hire managers that see themselves as future entrepreneurs." Argue for or against.

4. Discuss how strategic growth and operational efficiency supplements to the business plan are important for training future managers.

5. If the competition goes ahead, should it accept non-profit business plans as entries? Departmental business plans? Explain your reasoning.

6. If the business plan entries are marked out of 100, how many marks should be set aside for grammar and style? Justify your answer.

7. For which of the following business plan sections should the greatest portion of the marks be allocated: Business Model, Feasibility, Marketing, Operations, or Finance? Justify your answer.

Endnotes

Chapter 1

1. United States Small Business Administration, Guide to SBA's Definition of Small Business, Washington, www.sba.gov/size/indexguide.html (April, 2010).
2. Industry Canada, *Key Small Business Statistics*, January 2009, Cat.No. Iu186–1/2009–1E-PDF, ISSN 171–3456, www.ic.gc.ca/sbstatistics.
3. Statistics Canada, *Survey on Financing of Small and Medium Enterprises*, 2001.
4. Developed for the Business School, Humber Institute of Technology and Advanced Learning. Used by permission.
5. Sjoerd Beugelsdijk and Niels Noorderhaven, "Personality Characteristics of Self-Employed: An Empirical Study," *Small Business Economics*, 24 (Tilburg, The Netherlands: Spring 2005): 159–167.
6. E. Yaniv and D. Brock, "Reluctant Entrepreneurs: Why They Do It and How They Do It," *Ivey Business Journal Online* (Nov/Dec 2012): N/A.
7. Jamal Muhammed, "Job Stress, Satisfaction and Mental Health: An Empirical Examination of Self-Employed and Non-Self-Employed Canadians," *Journal of Small Business Management*, 35, 4 (October 1997): 48–58.
8. Industry Canada, *Key Small Business Statistics*, (July 2012):, www.ic.gc.ca/eic/site/061.nsf/eng/h_02711.html, Page E061-H02711.
9. Hyungrae Jo and Jinjoo Lee, "The Relationship between an Entrepreneur's Background and Performance in a New Venture," *Technovation*, 16, 4 (Amsterdam: April 1996): 161.
10. John R. Baldwin, Lin Bian, Richard Dupuy, and Guy Gellatly, *Failure Rates for New Canadian Firms: New Perspectives on Entry and Exit* (Statistics Canada, 2000).
11. Statistics Canada, "Study: Business Dynamics in Canada," *The Daily*, Tuesday, February 15, 2005.
12. Industry Canada, *Micro-Economic Monitor*, Third Quarter (Ottawa: Micro-Economic Directorate, Industry & Science Policy Sector, 1998).
13. Conference Board of Canada, "Canada's Underground Economy," *Canadian Business Review*, 21 (Ottawa: Summer 1994): 26.
14. G. Tyge Payne, Kevin H. Kennedy, and Justin L. Davis, "Competitive Dynamics among Service SMEs," *Journal of Small Business Management*, 47, 4 (October 2009): 421–442.
15. John A. Gromala and David F. Gage, "Mediating Personality Differences behind Internal Business Disputes," *The CPA Journal*, 72, 3 (New York: March 2002): 68.
16. Robert E. Staub, "The Primacy of Courage in Partnering with Others," *The Journal for Quality and Participation*, 23, 3 (Cincinnati: May/June 2000): 16.
17. Ray A. Knight and Lee G. Knight, "Planning: The Key to Small Business Survival," *Management Accounting*, 74, 8 (February 1993): 33.

Chapter 2

1. Ho Yeon Kim, "The Locational and Functional Behavior of U.S. Autoparts Suppliers," *Small Business Economics*, 24 (Spring 2005): 79–95.
2. Peter Lindelof and Hans Lofsten, "Proximity as a Resource Base for Competitive Advantage: University–Industry Links for Technology Transfer," *Journal of Technology Transfer*, 29, 3–4 (August 2004): 311–326.
3. Saul Sands, "Improved Pedestrian Traffic Counts for Better Retail Site Location," *Journal of Small Business Management*, 10 (January 1972): 27–31.
4. Carol Kerns, "Making the Right Impression: How Fastsigns Uses Site Selection as a Marketing Tool," *Franchising World*, 24, 4 (July/August 1992): 15–17.
5. Michael D. Geurts and David B. Whitlark, "Six Ways to Make Sales Forecasts More Accurate," *Journal of Business Forecasting Methods and Systems*, 18, 4 (Winter 1999/2000): 21–23.
6. Mike Jakeman, "Small Business Coverages: Cost-Effective Delivery," *Canadian Underwriter*, 72, 4 (April 2005): 40–42.
7. J. Geesey, and C. Rocha, "Self control theory: Recognizing your company's vulnerability to employee theft," *Journal of American Academy of Business*, 17, 2 (2012): 198–203.
8. Michele Tonglet, "Consumer Misbehaviour: An Exploratory Study of Shoplifting," *Journal of Consumer Behaviour*, 1, 4 (June 2002): 336–355.
9. Alex Cameron and Alex Cameron Michelet, "Competition Policy and Canada's New Breed of 'Copyright' Law," *McGill Law Journal*, 52, 2 (Summer 2007): 291–337.
10. Christopher Heer, "Employees and Trade Secrets: How the Concept of Inevitable Disclosure May Fit Into Canadian Law," *Intellectual Property Journal*, 19, 2 (April 2006): 323–350.

Chapter 3

1. Ali Kara, John E. Spillan, and Oscar W. DeShields, Jr., "The Effect of a Market Orientation on Business Performance: A Study of Small-Sized Service Retailers Using MARKOR Scale," *Journal of Small Business Management*, 43, 2 (April 2005): 105–119.
2. Jay J. Ebben, "Product Offering, Operational Strategy, and Performance of Small Firms," *Journal of Small Business and Entrepreneurship*, 20, 3 (2007): 245–256.
3. Julia Chang, "How Service Impacts Your Brand," *Incentive*, 180, 7 (July 2006): 12.
4. John A. Wood, James S. Boles, and Barry J. Babin, "The Formation of Buyer's Trust of the Seller in an Initial Sales Encounter," *Journal of Marketing Theory & Practice*, 16, 1 (Winter 2008): 27–39.
5. F. P. Karimov, M. Brengman, and L. Van Hove, "The effect of Website Design Dimensions on Initial Trust: A synthesis of the empirical literature," *Journal of Electronic Commerce Research*, 12, 4 (2011): 272–280, 282–301.
6. T. H. Davenport, P. Barth, P, and R. Bean, R., "How big data is different," *MIT Sloan Management Review*, (2012): 54(1), 43-46.
7. C. Boutet and L. Quoniam, "Towards Active SEO (search engine optimization), *Journal of Information Systems and Technology Management: JISTEM*, 9, 3 (2012): 443–458.
8. A. J. Kumanar. "5 Strategies for Better 'Link Building' and Improving Your SEO," *Entrepreneur*, (February 28, 2013) www.entrepreneur.com/article/225964
9. Grigorios Zontanos and Alistair R. Anderson, "Relationships, Marketing and Small Business: An Exploration of Links in Theory and Practice," *Qualitative Market Research*, 17, 3 (2004): 228–239.
10. Shuba Srinivasan, Koen Pauwels, Dominique M. Hanssens, and Marnik G. Dekimpe, "Do Promotions Benefit Manufacturers, Retailers or Both?" *Management Science*, 50, 5 (May 2004): 617–630.
11. John M. Browning and Ronald J. Adams, "Trade Shows: An Effective Promotional Tool for the Small Industrial Business," *Journal of Small Business Management*, 26, 4 (October 1988): 31–36.

Chapter 4

1. Randolph P. Johnston, "High Tech for the Small Office," *Journal of Accountancy*, 200, 6 (December 2005): 41–45.
2. Eward A. Metzger, "Adjustable Seating Promotes Lab Productivity," *Laboratory Product News*, 36, 4 (June 2006): 6–7.

3. John Davies and Nicolas Tilley, "Interior Design: Using the Management Services Approach in Retail Premises," *Management Services*, 48, 7 (July 2004): 10–16.
4. Jay J. Ebben, "Product Offering, Operational Strategy, and Performance of Small Firms," *Journal of Small Business and Entrepreneurship*, 20, 3 (2007): 245–256.
5. Adil Baykasoglu, Turkay Dereli, and Ibrahim Sabuncu, "An Ant Colony Algorithm for Solving Budget Constrained and Unconstrained Dynamic Facility Layout Problems," *Omega*, 34, 4 (August 2006): 385.
6. Tony Polito and Devin Watson, "Just-in-Time Under Fire: The Five Major Constraints Upon JIT Practices," *Journal of American Academy of Business*, 9, 1 (March 2006): 8–14.
7. Réne Gélinas and Yvon Bigras, "The Characteristics and Features of SMEs: Favorable or Unfavorable to Logistics Integration?" *Journal of Small Business Management*, 42, 3 (July 2004): 263–279.
8. Stephen C. Jones, Tami L. Knotts, and Karen L. Brown, "Selected Quality Practices of Small Manufacturers," *The Quality Management Journal*, 12, 1 (2005): 41–54.
9. J. Carlton Collins, "Small Business Software Grows Up," *Journal of Accountancy*, 201, 3 (March 2006): 50–57.
10. Joris Jeijaard, Maryse J. Brand, and Marco Mosselman, "Organizational Structure and Performance in Dutch Small Firms," *Small Business Economics*, 25, 1 (August 2005): 83–93.
11. A. Silliker, "Money Not Among Top 10 Motivators for Workers," *Canadian HR Reporter*, 25, 9 (2012): 3–3,8.

Chapter 5

1. Anthony J. Berry, Robert Sweeting, and Jitsu Goto, "The Effect of Business Advisers on the Performance of SMEs," *Journal of Small Business and Enterprise Development*, 13, 1 (2006): 33–48.
2. Suzanne Gaspar, "Managing Technology Turnover," *Network World*, 19, 42 (October 21, 2002): 56–57.
3. Anuradha Basu and Eser Altinay, "The Interaction between Culture and Entrepreneurship in London's Immigration Businesses," *International Small Business Journal*, 20, 4 (November 2002): 371–382.
4. Stephen Prowse, "Angel Investors and the Market for Angel Investments," *Journal of Banking & Finance*, 22, 6–8 (August 1998): 785–793.

Chapter 6

1. Mark Bruno, "Private Equity Powers More MBOs among Larger Firms," *Pensions and Investments*, 34, 12 (June 12, 2006): 1–4.
2. Gene H. Johnson, Rudolph S. Lindbeck, and Winston N. McVea, Jr., "Traps to Avoid When Purchasing a Business," *Journal of Financial Planning*, 7, 1 (January 1994): 38–42.
3. Howard Levitt, "Competition Is Hard to Restrict, in Most Cases," *National Post* (November 30, 2005).
4. Margaret D. Nowicki, Eric E. Lewis, and Jeffrey W. Lippitt, "Preparing Your Business for Valuation," *New England Journal of Entrepreneurship*, 8, 1 (Spring 2005): 59–64.
5. George S. May International Co., "Sizing Up Small Business," *Journal of Accountancy*, 208, 5 (November 2009): 1–17.
6. Lawrence W. Tuller, *The Small Business Valuation Book, Second Edition* (Avon MA: Adams Media, 2007), 12.
7. S. Alan Aycock, "The Impact of Fairness, Reference Points, and Human Decision Processing on Negotiations," *Journal of Financial Service Professionals*, 54, 2 (March 2000): 26–82.
8. Peggy A. Lambing and Charles R. Kuehl, *Entrepreneurship*, 4th ed. (New Jersey: Pearson Education Inc., 2007), 52–54.

Chapter 7

1. Richard C. Hoffman and John F. Preble, "Convert to Compete: Competitive Advantage through Conversion Franchising," *Journal of Small Business Management*, 41, 2 (April 2003): 187–205.

2. Gregory Pang, "Multi-level Marketing," *Edmonton Journal* (February 21, 2004).
3. D. Hussain, D. and J. Windsperger, "The Choice Between Single-unit and Multi-unit Franchising: Combining Agency and Transaction Cost Perspectives," *Journal of Applied Business Research*, 28(5) (Sept./Oct. 2012): 769–776.
4. See the Competition Act on the Department of Justice website at http://laws.justice.gc.ca/en/c-34/text.html.
5. N. Ghantous and F. Jaolis, "Conceptualizing Franchisee-based Brand Equity: A framework of the sources and outcomes of the brand's added value for franchisees," *International Business Research*, (Feb. 2013): 6(2), 112–125.
6. Ram C. Rao and Shuba Srinivasan, "An Analysis of Advertising Payments in Franchise Contracts," *Journal of Marketing Channels*, 8, 3–4 (2001): 85.
7. Steven C. Michael and James G. Combs, "Entrepreneurial Failure: The Case of Franchisees," *Journal of Small Business Management*, 46, 1 (2008): 73–90.
8. Ibid.
9. Kimberley A. Morrison, "How Franchise Job Satisfaction and Personality Affects Performance, Organizational Commitment, Franchisor Relations and Intention to Remain," *Journal of Small Business Management*, 35, 3 (July 1997): 39–68.
10. Flenn Withiam, "Who's the Customer? The Franchisee," *Cornell Hotel and Restaurant Administration Quarterly*, 41, 3 (June 2000): 12–13.
11. Scott Shane, Venkatesh Shankar, and Ashwin Aravindakshan, "The Effects of New Franchisor Partnering Strategies on Franchise System Size," *Management Science*, 52, 5 (May 2006): 773–788.

Chapter 8

1. Tammi S. Feltham, Glenn Feltham, and James J. Barnett, "The Dependence of Family Business on a Single Decision-Maker," *Journal of Small Business Management*, 43, 1 (January 2005): 1–15.
2. Jess H. Chua, James J. Chrisman, and Pramodita Sharma, "Defining the Family Business by Behaviour," *Entrepreneurship Theory and Practice*, 23, 4 (Summer 1999): 19–40.
3. Sharon Oswald, Lori Muse and Matthew Rutherford, "The Influence of Large Stake Family Controls on Performance: Is It Agency or Entrenchment?" *Journal of Small Business Management*, 47, 1 (January 2009): 116–135.
4. Naomi Birdthistle, "Splitting Heirs_ Divorce Planning for Family Businesses (interm results)" *Proceedings of the 30th Institute for Small Business & Entrepreneurship Conference* (November 2007, Glasgow Scotland).
5. Michael G. Stevens, "Passing the Family Business Mantle," *The Practical Accountant*, 31, 7 (July 1998): 20–25.
6. Byrne Fergal, "Keeping the Squabbles out of Succession: Family Businesses" (Part One), *Financial Times* (October 12, 2000).
7. Kimberly A. Eddleston, Robert F. Otondo, and Franz Willi Kllermanns, "Conflict, Participative Decision-Making, and Generational Ownership Dispersion: A Multilevel Analysis," *Journal of Small Business Management*, 46, 3 (July 2008): 456–484.
8. Sarah Crosbie, "The Immigrant Succession Planning Crisis," *The Globe and Mail, Report on Business* (January 8, 2010).
9. Eileen Fisher and Rebecca Reuber, "The State of Entrepreneurship in Canada," Report Compiled for Industry Canada. www.ic.gc.ca/sbresearch, February, 2010.
10. RoDoug Bruce and Derek Picard, "Making Succession a Success: Perspectives from Canadian Small and Medium-Sized Enterprises," *Journal of Small Business Management*, 44, 2 (April 2006): 306–309.
11. Robert Napoli, "Selling Out," *CA Magazine*, 139, 4 (May 2006): 43–46.
12. Daniel H. Markstein III, "Business Succession Planning That Meets the Owner's Needs," *Estate Planning*, 33, 7 (July 2006): 20–27.

13. James P. Marshall, Ritch Sorenson, Keith Brighamm, Elizabeth Wieling, Alan Reifman and Richard S. Wampler, "The Paradox for the Family Firm CEO: Owner Age Relationship to Succession-Related Processes and Plans," *Journal of Business Venturing*, 21, 3 (May 2006): 348.
14. William S. White, Timothy D. Drinke, and David L. Geller, "Family Business Succession Planning: Devising an Overall Strategy," *Journal of Financial Service Professionals*, 58, 3 (May 2004): 67–87.
15. Glenn Feltham, Tammi S. Feltham, and Robert Mathieu, "The Use of Estate Freezes by Family-Owned Businesses," *Canadian Tax Journal*, 51, 4 (2003): 1570–1588.

Chapter 9

1. Brian Headd & Bruce Kirchhoff, "The Growth, Decline and Survival of Small Businesses: An Exploratory Study of Life Cycles," *Journal of Small Business Management*, 47, 4 (October 2009): 531–550.
2. Nicholas O'Regan, Abby Ghobadian, and David Gallear, "In Search of the Drivers of High Growth in Manufacturing SMEs," *Technovation*, 26, 1 (January 2006): 30.
3. Anonymous, "Innovations: PLM for the SME," *Strategic Direction*, 20, 11 (November/December 2004): 31–34.
4. Bruce Tait, "The Failure of Marketing 'Science'," *Brandweek*, 43, 14 (April 8, 2002): 20.
5. Peggy A. Lambing and Charles R. Kuehl, *Entrepreneurship*, 4th ed. (New Jersey: Prentice Hall Inc., 2007), p. 107.
6. James A. Wolf and Timothy L. Pett, "Small-Firm Performance: Modeling the Role of Product and Process Improvements," *Journal of Small Business Management*, 44, 2 (April 2006): 268–288.
7. Chad Rubel, "Franchising Fellowship," *Marketing Management*, 4, 2 (Fall 1995): 4.
8. Jean Bosco Sabuhoro, Bruno Larue, and Yvan Gervais, "Factors Determining the Success or Failure of Canadian Establishments on Foreign Markets: A Survival Analysis Approach," *The International Trade Journal*, 20, 1 (Spring 2006): 33.
9. G. Hilton, "Knocking Down Export Barriers to Smaller Firms," *Business and Economic Review*, 51, 4 (July–September 2005): 18.
10. Lance Brothers, George Eliot Nakos, John Hadjimarcou, D. Keith Brothers, "Key Factors for Successful Export Performance for Small Firms," *Journal of International Marketing*, 17, 3 (2009): 21–38.
11. Michael Tobin, "Debunking the Five Myths of Global Expansion," *Financial Executive*, 22, 2 (March 2006): 57–60.
12. Brian T. Gregory, Matthew W. Rutherford, Sharon Oswald, and Lorraine Gardiner, "An Empirical Investigation of the Growth Cycle Theory of Small Firm Financing," *Journal of Small Business Management*, 43, 4 (October 2005): 382.
13. Tze-Wei Fu and Mei-Chu Ke, "Capital Growth, Financing Source and Profitability of Small Business: Evidence from Taiwan Small Enterprises," *Small Business and Economics*, 18, 4 (June 2002): 257.
14. Statistics Canada, *Survey on Financing of Small and Medium Enterprises*, 2004 (February 2006), Table 31.
15. Ibid., see Table 10.

Chapter 10

1. Glenn R. Carroll, "The Specialist Strategy," *California Management Review*, 26 (Spring 1984): 126–137.
2. Carl W. Stern, *Perspectives on Strategy from the Boston Consulting Group: The Best Strategic Thinking from the Boston Consulting Group* (New York: Wiley, 1998).
3. Rosli Mohamad and Noor Azizi Ismail, "The Extent of E-business Usage and Perceived Cumulative Benefits: A Survey on Small and Medium-sized Enterprises, *Information Management and Business Review*, 5(1) (Jan. 2013): 13–19.
4. David H. Freedman, "The Rise of the Robotic Work Force," *Inc*, 34, (Oct. 2012): 76–83.
5. Industry Canada, *Key Small Business Statistics*, July 2009, Cat. No. Iu186–1/2009–2E-PDF, ISSN 1718–3456, www.ic.gc.ca/sbstatistics.
6. Statistics Canada, "Survey of Electronic Commerce and Technology, Enterprises that Have a Website on the Internet," Table 358–0008 (March 2010), http://cansim2.statcan.gc.ca/cgi-win/cnsmcgi.pgm.
7. Sumaria Mohan-Neill, "An Analysis of Factors which Influence Small Businesses: Decision to Have a Website and to Conduct Online Selling," *Journal of American Academy of Business*, 8, 2 (March 2006): 204–210. (Note: U.S. data.)
8. Robert Hale, "Customer Wise—Do Business Look After Their Customers?", *Proceedings of the 30th Institute for Small Business & Entrepreneurship Conference* (November 2007, Glasgow Scotland).
9. K. Douglas Hoffman and John Bateson, *Essentials of Services Marketing: Concepts, Strategies and Cases* (New York: Harcourt, 2002), p. 297.
10. Ibid., pp. 276–280.
11. Patrizia Garengo and Umit Bititci, "Management Development Needs in SMEs: Managerial Practices versus Theory," *Proceedings of the 30th Institute for Small Business & Entrepreneurship Conference* (November 2007, Glasgow Scotland).

Chapter 11

1. Jeremy Quittner, "Technology: Could You Survive a Cyberattack?" *Inc*, 35, (April 2013): 100–101.
2. Chad Moutray, "The Small Business Economy, A Report to the President," The Small Business Administration Office of Advocacy (2008) http://www.sba.gov/advo/research/sb_econ2008.pdf.
3. David R. Boyd, "Sustainability within A Generation," David Suzuki Foundation (2004): Appendix.
4. M.R. Mullen, D.G. Desislava, and P.M. Doney, "Research Methods in the Leading Small Business-Entrepreneurship Journals: A Critical Review with Recommendations for Future Research," *Journal of Small Business Management*, 47, 5 (2009): 287–307.
5. Donald F. Kuratko, "A Tribute to 50 Years of Excellence in Entrepreneurship and Small Business," *Journal of Small Business Management*, 44, 3 (2006): 483–492.
6. Mika Pasanen, "Multiple Entrepreneurship Among Successful SMEs I Peripheral Locations," *Journal of Small Business and Enterprise*, 10, 4 (2003): 418–426.
7. Paul Westhead, Deniz Ucbasaran, and Mike Wright, "Decisions, Actions and Performance: Do Novice, Serial, and Portfolio Entrepreneurs Differ?" *Journal of Small Business Management*, 43, 4 (October 2005): 393–418.
8. Zoltan J. Acs, William Parsons, and Spencer Tracy, "High-Impact firms: Gazelles Revisited," Report to the US Small Business Administration Office of Advocacy (June 2008).
9. Heather Dines, James Watson and Mohammed Amir Sadiq, "High Growth Firms in the UK: Lessons from an analysis of -comparative UK performance," UK Department for Business Enterprise and Regulatory Reform, BERR Economics Paper No. 3 (November 2009): 1–78.
10. Eileen Fisher and Rebecca Reuber, "The State of Entrepreneurship in Canada," Report Compiled for Industry Canada, www.ic.gc.ca/sbresearch, February, 2010.
11. Ted Heidrick and Tracey Nicol, "Financing SMEs in Canada: Barriers Faced by Women, Youth, Aboriginal and Minority Entrepreneurs in Accessing Capital. Phase 1: Literature Review," Research Paper prepared for: Small Business Policy Branch, Industry Canada (January 2002).
12. Charles R. Stoner, Richard Hartman, and Raj Arora, "Work-Home Role Conflict in Female Owners of Small Businesses: An Exploratory Study," *Journal of Small Business Management*, 28, 1 (January 1990): 303–359.
13. M.D.R. Evans and Jonathan Kelly, "Effects of Family Structure on Life Satisfaction," *Social Indicators Research*, 69 (2004): 303–349.
14. Michael G. Goldsby, Donald F. Kuratko, and James W. Bishop, "Entrepreneurship and Fitness: An Examination of Rigorous Exercise and Goal Attainment Amon Small Business Owners," *Journal of Small Business Management*, 43, 1 (January 2005): 78–92.

15. Ibid.

16. Devi R. Gnyawali and Byung-Jin (Robert) Park, "Co-opetition and Technological Innovation in Small and Medium-Sized Enterprises: A Multilevel Conceptual Model," *Journal of Small Business Management*, 47, 3 (July 2009): 308–330.

17. Chad Moutray op. cit. #3.

18. Gary Gorman, Dennis Hanlon, and Wayne King, "Some Research Perspectives on Entrepreneurship Education and Education for Small Business Management: A Ten-year Literature Review," *International Small Business Journal*, 15, 3 (April/June 1997): 56–77.

19. Ted Leach, "Instruction-Based Action Guidelines Build on Bloom's Revised Framework: Setting Objectives for Entrepreneurship Teaching," *Journal of Small Business and Entrepreneurship*, 20, 4 (2007): 351–368.

20. Jean Lorrain and Sylvie Laferté, "Support Needs of the Young Entrepreneur," *Journal of Small Business and Entrepreneurship*, 19, 1 (2006): 37–48.

21. Pi-Shen Seet and Lip-Chai Seet, "Changing Entrepreneurial Perceptions and Developing Entrepreneurial Competencies Through Experiential Learning: Evidence from Entrepreneurship Education in Singapore's Tertiary Education Institutions," *Journal of Asia Entrepreneurship and Sustainability*, 2, 2 (2006).

22. Various, "Entrepreneurship in Higher Education, Especially in Non-Business Studies," Report to European Commission, Enterprise and Industry Directorate General (March 2008).

23. Vineet Agarwal and Richard Taffler, "Is Management Quality Value Relevant?" Proceedings of the Financial Management Association International (FMA) 2007 Annual Meeting, http://69.175.2.130/∼finman/Orlando/Papers/IsManagementQualityValueRelevant.pdf (January 2007).

24. OECD Secretariat and David Storey, "Management Training in SMESs," Report from the Organization for Economic Co-operation and Development (OECD) (2007): 5–29, http://www.oecd.org/dataoecd/20/43/2492440.pdf.

25. Gary Packham, David Brooksbank, Christopher Miller, and Brychan Thomas, "Climbing the Mountain: Management Practice Adoption in Growth Oriented Firms in Wales," *Journal of Small Business and Enterprise Development*, 12, 4 (2005): 482–498.

26. O.M. Irgens, "Situational Leadership: A Modification of Hersey and Blanchard," *Leadership and Organization Development Journal*, 16, 2 (1995): 34–40.

27. Paul Hersey and Kenneth H. Blanchard, *Management of Organizational Behaviour: Utilizing Human Resources* (New Jersey: Prentice Hall, 1977).

28. David Higgins and Mohammed Mirza, M., "Considering Practice: A Contemporary Theoretical Position Towards Social Learning in the Small Firm. *Irish Journal of Management*, 31, 2 (2012): 1–17.

29. Julian Lange, Edward Marram and William Bygrave, W., "Human Assets and Entrepreneurial Performance: A Study of Companies Started by Business School Graduates," *Journal of Business and Entrepreneurship*, 24, 1 (Fall 2012): 1–24.

Chapter 12

1. Arthur A Boni, "The Pitch and Business Plan for Partners and Investors," *Journal of Commercial Biotechnology*, 18, 2 (March 2012): 38–42.

2. Jeffry A. Timmons, Andrew Zacharakis, and Stephen Spinelli, *Business Plans That Work: A Guide For Small Business* (New York, McGraw-Hill, 2004), p. 41.

3. Sharon P. Porter, Simon Fraser, Paul Freeman, Hannah Tierney, and Pauric McGowan, "Business Plan Competitions—What Impact Do they Really Have?" Proceedings of the 30th Institute for Small Business & Entrepreneurship Conference, Glasgow (November 2007): 1–15.

Index

Note: Bolded terms and page references indicate key terms and the pages on which they are defined; an italicized "f" following a page reference indicates a figure; and an italicized "t" following a page reference indicates a table.